PIAGET'S LOGIC

PIAGET'S LOGIC

A Critique of Genetic Epistemology

Muriel Seltman · Peter Seltman

London
GEORGE ALLEN & UNWIN
Boston   Sydney

George Allen & Unwin (Publishers) Ltd,
40 Museum Street, London WC1A 1LU, UK

George Allen & Unwin (Publishers) Ltd,
Park Lane, Hemel Hempstead, Herts HP2 4TE, UK

Allen & Unwin, Inc.,
Fifty Cross Street, Winchester, Mass 01890, USA

George Allen & Unwin Australia Pty Ltd,
8 Napier Street, North Sydney, NSW 2060, Australia

First published in 1985

British Library Cataloguing in Publication Data

Seltman, M.
    Piaget's logic.
1. Piaget, Jean   II. Child psychology
III. Knowledge, Theory of
I. Title   II. Seltman, P. E. J.
155.4'13   BF721
ISBN 0-04-370154-X

Library of Congress Cataloging in Publication Data

Seltman, M.
    Piaget's logic.
Bibliography: p.
Includes index.
1. Cognition.   2. Logic, Symbolic and mathematical.
I. Seltman, P. E. J.   II. Title.
BF311.S435 1984   153   84-9188
ISBN 0-04-370154-X (alk. paper)

Set in 10 on 12 point Bembo by
Ann Buchan (Typesetters), Surrey
and printed in Great Britain
by Butler & Tanner Ltd, Frome and London

Contents

Preface

The literature relating to the work of Piaget is large and still growing. Some of it is Piagetian; some of it is critical. Most of this has been directed towards his experimental methodology and the conclusions drawn from it. The justification for the present contribution lies in what we believe to be the special embodiment in Piagetian thought of a central theme of our time. This theme is that the only possibility of truth lies in measurability and that knowledge is not recognisable unless it satisfies this criterion. The form of the paradigm in the Piagetian system is the identification of human thought itself with logico-mathematical structures, particularly cognitive activities, but also subsuming the emotional and social life of the individual under the same categories. Our critique of Piagetian thought is directed specifically at his form of the paradigm but carries an implicit critique of it wherever else it exists.

Piaget's influence extends far beyond his immediate impact. The most obvious demonstration of this lies in child psychology, which is surprising in a way. Piaget is not basically either an educational or a child psychologist. His concern with children stems from the necessity, as he sees it, to study the development of cognition in order to grasp the nature of thought as a whole. His motives are primarily philosophical and not psychological.

None the less, the Piagetian system has had most impact in the sphere of child development and far beyond explicit acknowledgement of it. Piagetian principles and approaches have penetrated, often in disguised or unrecognised forms, into countless schools and homes in the sophisticated societies of the West and are now spreading rapidly in the Third World. They are also more acceptable today in the collectivist authoritarian societies of Eastern Europe, the USSR and even China.

When we began this work we saw Piaget simply as a developmental psychologist with leanings towards epistemology. As our study progressed, however, it became increasingly clear that not only did he regard cognition as primarily a matter of logic and mathematics, but that this view was extended to the realm of individual emotional life and even to social life in general. This is why we have concentrated in the first instance on Piaget's claims that mental structures are exclusively logico-mathematical in form, especially since this part of his work has received least attention.

Apart from the initial overview in Chapter 1, the following pattern has been adopted. Chapters 2, 3 and 4 contain a detailed review of the Piagetian use of Group Theory and propositional logic as the foundation of his theory of cognition. Chapter 2 presents the Group Theoretic basis for this and Chapters 3 and 4 elaborate on the analysis in respect to the concrete and formal operational stages. It is mainly in Chapters 3 and 4 that the analysis queries the manner in which Piaget tries to apply the mathematical and logical tools he has adapted to cognition.

These queries with regard to logic and mathematics are aligned with the general system in Chapters 5, 6 and 7. In Chapter 5 the notion of equilibrium is most prominent. Chapter 6 concentrates on the related tools of the apparatus of cognition, and Chapter 7 summarises and discusses the central notions and problems of genesis and stages.

Whilst the critique up to this point is self-sufficient, its full implications can emerge only through a further consideration of the foundations of logic and mathematics themselves. This is attempted in Chapter 8 and extended in Chapter 9 with particular reference to scientific thought. Chapter 10 touches on a wider consideration of the system and its implications. All these latter chapters constantly refer back to the basic problems and, especially at the end of Chapter 9, pay special attention to Piaget's use of the symbolisms of mathematics and logic including his own notational devices. Conventional mathematical and logical terms have been kept, notably 'set' and 'class' pending discussion in Chapter 8. Similarly, Piaget's term 'logical operation' has been retained for the same reason.

It should be made clear that this critique of the Piagetian system is not intended to impugn the original motives of the man himself. Piaget certainly believed at the outset of his career that a marriage of logic and biological theory (especially Darwinian) offered the best recipe for a scientific humanism capable of explaining the psychology of human knowledge and at the same time setting up the guidelines for its perfectibility. Certainly the adoption of the system by many educationists has been prompted by the same motive.

This may be the reason, at least in part, for the lack of attention to the logical and mathematical assumptions, apart from the logical studies of Beth and Parsons. But another consideration may well be the general propensity to 'wander' between logico-mathematical categories and Actuality to be found throughout logic and mathematics and also in science itself. Hence, mathematicians and logicians would be unlikely to note their own tendencies in someone else. Additionally, mathematics carries an 'authority' which tends to be forbidding of any criticism other than by mathematicians. Piagetian commentators have almost universally accepted his 'mathematisation' as at worst 'idiosyncratic' and left it alone, concentrating on his claim to have demonstrated the process of acquiring knowledge through the clinical method.

There remain only some technicalities to be considered. The order of writing has not adhered to the chronological order of Piaget's own publications. A movement back and forth for comparative purposes is in some degree unavoidable since there is evident modification and change of emphasis throughout his writing life and nowhere were any of his earlier writings repudiated in the later.

Considerable difficulty was encountered in deciding which material should remain in the text, and what should be included in Appendices. The discussion of Relations was left in the text as it is a central issue and not too difficult conceptually. An elementary description of Lattice Theory has been put into an Appendix on the grounds that the mathematical difficulties might well be daunting to non-mathematical readers. In general, reproduced material has been kept for Appendices.

The translations of *Traité de logique* and *Logique opératoire* that have been used in these chapters are basically our own with the assistance of John Jeffery and Molly Callender, neither of whom is a mathematician, so any inadequacies in this respect are ours not theirs. For these, we apologise.

The bibliography is simply a reference list of all the principal books consulted in the fairly recent past. General background reading has not been included as this would have made it too unwieldy. All references, except where specified and in the French editions, are the English edition used and the date of publication refers to this accordingly.

Specific terms have been adopted at various points. Such terms will be defined in the text wherever their first use occurs. Precision of analysis has meant that to some extent descriptions have been 'built up' and this has resulted in some repetition, for which we apologise. In some cases diagrams have been provided for clarification. These should be regarded only as explanatory schemas and should not be interpreted spatio-temporally.

Finally, we have not always referred to the influence of others which will be very evident in places. Standardisation of style has been pursued, but the authors know that they have frequently failed. The main point to stress is that authorship is completely equal.

Acknowledgements

Our very grateful and sincere thanks are due for reading and commenting on the text at various stages to: the late Ruth Buss, Jack Callender, Molly Callender, Norman Cawley, Alan Muir, Peter Scopes, Chris Sinha, the librarians Keith Davis and Chris Andrew of the Polytechnic of North London Library, and the library staff of Avery Hill College, Eltham, London. Our thanks are also due to Enid Layson for the use of her M.Ed. thesis on Introducing Lattice Theory. The care and attention of our typists, Birthe King and Clare Henville, have been a constant support to us during some of the most burdensome periods of writing this book. Last, and by no means least, we would like to acknowledge the continuing help and encouragement of the sponsoring editors, Keith Ashfield and Gordon Smith of George Allen & Unwin, and the diligent assistance of the copy-editing staff.

Acknowledgement is due to the copyright holders for their kind permission to reprint extracts from the following works by Jean Piaget: Columbia University Press for *Genetic Epistemology*; Hodder & Stoughton Limited for *Six Psychological Studies*; Basil Blackwell for *The Development of Thought: Equilibration of Cognitive Structures*, translated by A. Rosin; M. Laurent Piaget for *Traité de logique: Essai de Logistique opératoire* (translations in this volume by M. and P. E. J. Seltman); Manchester University Press for *Logic and Psychology*; Routledge & Kegan Paul PLC for *The Psychology of Intelligence*, translated by M. Piercy and D. E. Berlyne; Routledge & Kegan Paul PLC and Basic Books Inc. for *Structuralism*, translated by C. Maschler, *The Principles of Genetic Epistemology*, and *The Growth of Logical Thinking from Childhood to Adolescence* by B. Inhelder and Jean Piaget, translated by A. Parsons and S. Milgram; Editions Bordas and M. J. B. Grize for *Essai de logique opératoire*, 2nd edition of the *Traité de logique*, établie par Jean-Blaise Grize (translations in this volume by M. and P. E. J. Seltman).

Acknowledgement is also due to the copyright holders for permission to reproduce extracts from the following works: *Jean Piaget: Psychologist of the Real* by B. Rotman, Harvester Press Limited; *Mathematical Logic and the Foundations of Mathematics* by G. T. Kneebone, Wadsworth Publishing Company, CA., and *The Developmental Psychology of Jean Piaget* by J. H. Flavell.

1 The Central Problem of Genetic Epistemology

Some Preliminary Thoughts

If there is any overriding feature of Piaget's work it is the search for the connection between human knowledge and being through an inquiry into the genesis of knowledge. This objective is truly reflected in the name he has given to his philosophy – Genetic Epistemology.

Piaget died on 16 September 1980, in his mid-eighties which gave him a long life-span stretching back to the end of the nineteenth century – a period still associated with scientific certainty. By the time he had become to some degree aware of himself, the twentieth century was at least ten years old and that scientific certainty, which had only with difficulty preserved an outward stability in the last decade of the previous century, was already seriously undermined, in physics at least. In biology, on the other hand, the field in which Piaget was initiated into science, the latter-day molecular biological extension of neo-Darwinism, with its rigid and unalterable chain of descent, was beginning to emerge.[1] As Professor Darlington expresses it:

> The whole idea that personal adaptations, the peculiarities forced upon us by lucky or unlucky circumstances, or by an ameliorative purpose in the Creator, or by the power of the will, were inherited was giving way. The new notion of hard particles . . . microscopically visible and mathematically predictable, incorrigibly deterministic and resistant to the interference of any divine purpose apart from that reflected in natural selection, was taking place.[2]

It is no accident that by his later teens Piaget was much involved in pondering the character of biological evolution and was seeking a reconciliation of developmental theory and logic. If biology was an extremely early influence on him from one source, the other, and perhaps more rooted, influence may have come from his father whose absorption in local history seems to have been conjoined with a great stress on order and deduction.[3]

The mode of approach is noteworthy. The type of reconciliation sought by the young Piaget seems very much to have been along the lines of 'logicising change' – of uncovering the *logic* of development and thus capturing its *essence*. In this he was adhering strictly to the nineteenth-century scientific tradition which affirmed first the establishment of fact and then the application of rigorous logical and mathematical instruments to that fact, subsuming it into the accepted framework of knowledge. The certainty of hard fact and an unshakeable belief in the empirical process involved in establishing it seems to have remained with Piaget all his life. In *Insights and Illusions of Philosophy* (1972, pp. 11-12) he writes:

> Although speculative reflection is a fertile and even necessary heuristic introduction to all inquiry, it can only lead to the elaboration of hypotheses, as sweeping as you like, to be sure, but as long as one does not seek for verification by a group of facts established experimentally or by a deduction conforming to an exact algorithm (as in logic), the criterion of truth can only remain subjective, in the manner of an intuitive satisfaction, of 'self-evidence', etc.

In his quest to 'logicise change' Piaget's ideas certainly corresponded to the major trends in twentieth-century Western thought. While the analytical schools (positivist and linguistic) in our era reject *becoming* by affirming the philosophical exclusiveness of the *structure* of thought alone – a selected aspect of *being* in relation to both ontology and epistemology – Phenomenology and Existentialism, despite important differences between them and between both of them and the analytical schools, also reject becoming, but do so by affirming the irrelevance of any mediation between experience and thought.[4] In a sense these latter continental schools eliminate becoming principally by absorbing it into being.[5]

Within the most recent period, however, there have been signs in certain quarters of Western thought that the forms in which being has been asserted either by the rejection of, or by the absorption of, becoming in response to the uncertainty which has underlain twentieth-century science, ever since Quantum and Heisenberg's Principle of Indeterminacy have been accepted, are being seen increasingly as restrictive and unsatisfactory. Even within the strongest citadel of contemporary philosophy, logic itself, this is evident. The genesis of thought is once more emerging as worthy of attention after having lain somewhat fallow for 50–60 years. It is perhaps because of this fallowness that Piaget's thought, while exhibiting highly conventional characteristics, has nevertheless tended to remain isolated from the main schools of twentieth-century philosophy with the possible exception of French Structuralism.[6]

Broadly speaking, this new trend takes two forms. On the one hand, there is the endeavour to cope with the question of genesis within the terms of reference of logic and/or relate the origins of logic to some biological bedrock.[7] Such approaches could be described as attempts to rectify the balance between being and becoming within the 'establishment'; however, there are interesting developments involving a challenge to the very foundations of Western thought as a whole. But let us look at the former varieties first.

Professor Quine, a foremost American logician, has conceded that the applicability of human logic to reality is only explicable biologically. The very notion that logic *is* human and does not inhere in the nature of things is a major concession to genetic themes. Similarly, the relatively recent tendency to query objectivity, per se, as a universal category in the light of what is believed to be its inappropriateness in 'the realm of quanta and the realm of the fleeting galaxies'[8] has begun to undermine the view that logic, even many-valued logic, is a certain guarantee against error. In fact, more and more the notion of 'the object' – the universal, isolated and distinguishable Thing upon which the whole gamut of scientific method depends, together with the logical process associated with it – is coming to occupy a highly conditional position. And this is seen to be directly related to the uncertainty presented by science itself. Reichenbach writes: 'With the corporeal substance goes [the] two-valued character of our language, and even the fundamentals of logic are shown to be the product of an adaptation to the simplest environment into which human beings are born' or 'the realm of the middle dimensions', as he calls this environment elsewhere.

While on the one hand one reaction to the 'thought crisis' of the century has been to reject becoming or absorb it into a being, the opposite reaction, particularly linked to growing non-acceptance of the absoluteness of the logical process, has been to relate, or reduce, our 'objective' knowledge to a biologically determined matrix. Of course, there are those who do not accept this latter (defeatist?) position, but demand a 'bigger logic'. Thus the logician Hilary Putnam (Čapek, 1970, p. 454) has put forward the view that logic, after all, may be an empirical science, and David Finkelstein (loc. cit.) has suggested that the traditional conception of logic must be 'widened' or 'generalised'. In these and other cases, it is not the *limitation* on logic (or objectivity) that must be accepted, but an extension and updating of it to encompass the quantum and the 'fleeting galaxies' – to absorb indeterminacy, in other words. Such a view carries forward, basically unmodified, the fundamental assumptions of the traditional outlook which is ultimately referable to Aristotle himself. Only the mechanism is to change. There seems to be no recognition of the likely outcome of doing this, that by 'widening' or 'empiricising' logic its presumptions themselves are brought into question. Especially and particularly is this so with logic, for whatever form it takes, logic always expresses an 'either–or' situation. It is essentially concerned with the discrete, the separate and identifiable, and not with the continuous and the fluid. To 'widen' logic, therefore, in order to incorporate problems of indeterminacy means either to abandon or circumscribe the logical process in so doing, or, alternatively, force these areas of inquiry into a distorting framework.[9]

The intertwining of biological considerations with the origins of knowledge, even logic itself, combined with an attempt to extend logic to include indeterminacy has, not surprisingly, produced a renewed interest in 'biological epistemology'. As M. Čapek writes, 'The central thesis of this theory (of which there are many varieties) is the claim that the structure of our reason, instead of being ready-made and immutable, is the result of the long process by which our mind [sic] gradually adjusted itself to that sector of reality which is biologically important for us' (Čapek, 1970, p. 448). Beneath the surface of this seemingly innocent and simple statement lies a mass of problems related to being and becoming and the perennial problems of philosophy in general. If genesis is thus made the key to all knowing and understanding there is a strong directive towards regarding the ultimate point of epistemological reference as transformation and not existence. One can detect a desire to move to the position where becoming rather than being is seen as 'real' which is a reversal of the situation pertaining over the past period. This is likely to be a much more difficult position to maintain than its opposite. For in making being predominant one can with relative impunity ignore the question of the origin either of existence, or how it is known, and still produce a coherent stance.[10] By making becoming predominant, however, accounting for the stable or temporary 'permanence' of the forms or structures of existence cannot be excluded. The former may simply exclude the problem of novelty – how new things emerge, or, alternatively, the question of how new *are* new things? The latter is bedevilled with reconciliation of the 'is' with the 'is not' all the time. To attempt this and remain within a 'respectable' frame of reference, that is, the philosophical–scientific 'establishment' as it currently exists, is extraordinarily difficult since it involves a constant threat to the self-evident truths any establishment must rest on. Such difficulty has already become obvious to many scientific workers and those generally familiar with the basic problems of contemporary science. In this reaction we may see the beginnings of a 'non-establishment' approach in the new concern with becoming in relation to being.

Such an approach is rather older than contemporary literature of this type might suggest. To some degree it is found in the interest in non-European mysticism represented by such writers as Aldous Huxley, Clive

Bell and others in the 1920s and 1930s. Alan Watts, one of the best-known writers and thinkers of this genre, produced much of his work before as well as after the Second World War. Nevertheless, it is especially since 1960 that the trend has widened and deepened to include more and more from all sections and strata of society including an increasing number of practising scientists.

The movement, if it can be called such, is characterised by a reaction against standard notions of 'objectivity', especially in the form of the 'permanent' object as such. Gaining inspiration from the oriental tradition in general, and Zen Buddhism and Taoism in particular, this thought-movement tends to abolish the concept of 'boundaries' isolating objects from each other by treating such boundaries as illusory or at least pro-visional.

Most of Watts's writings are in the fields of theology, psychology and general philosophy, although he is also concerned with the nature of science. His influence and that of others in the West, plus the more direct influences of oriental teachings themselves, have helped to spread this type of thinking within physical science especially in the last decade or so. Names such as F. Capra (*The Tao of Physics*, 1975), Gary Zukav (*The Dancing Wu Li Masters*, 1979) and David Bohm, particularly in his latest book (*Wholeness and the Implicate Order*, 1980), are representative of a trend, notably in physics, which, some say, even has its parallel in the increasing use of qualitative terms in the technical heartland of sub-atomic research itself (for example, 'strange' particles and the use of the word 'charm' in relation to certain sub-atomic particles. Note also a similar feature in astrophysics: 'pulsars', 'collapsars', 'black holes', 'quarks', and so on.)

Characteristic of all these writers, scientists and non-scientists alike, is the stress on pure relationship, the rejection of 'things' in preference to processes, the predominance of the idea of totality (wholeness) and flow. All are most clearly committed to the paramountcy of becoming within which, contrary to the earlier 'establishment' philosophical tradition in the West, being must be absorbed.

Where does Piaget fit into this picture? For most of his intellectual life, until, that is, the 1960s, the objective of 'logicising change' seems to have predominated. Put another way, the *stability* of the claimed structural character of mentality appears to have held first place, and the process of arriving at this stability was judged within its context. In the latter part of his writing life, however, Piaget appears to have swung more and more towards regarding this process as central to his theory, not the structures which are the outcome. One could perhaps describe this later emphasis as 'transformational logic' in contrast to the former phase. But in both cases Piaget reflects in his own way on the wider problems of relating being to becoming typical of this period. What we shall be considering below is Piaget's own difficulties in attempting either to impose the linearity and discreteness of logic on to Actuality or to import the continuity and flow of Actuality into the non-spatio-temporal world of logico-mathematically conceived structures. For change understood as transformation in the sense of transcendence, and not mere displacement or alteration in degree, cannot be logicised by imposing linearity upon it. In fact, the main problem, as we shall find, is to free thought from linearity in order to begin to approach an understanding of its origins. For becoming is not simply to be identified with the lapse of time, or time-governed change or evolution. Rather one should see the latter as a particular mode of the absorption of becoming into being. The historical-evolutionary concept, very much the product of the nineteenth century, is wholly linear and logico-mathematically conceived. It is more to do with predictable sequence than creativity. On the other hand, becoming-in-the-context-of-being, and vice versa (Hegel's conception of it), expresses co-existent aspects of Actuality, that is, the coincidence and co-terminousness of being-and-becoming.

Thus the (biological) evolutionary and historical aspects of Piaget's thought, whether considered individually or socially, are as much reflective of the 'logicisation of change', or alternatively 'transformational logic', that is, an imposition of logico-mathematical linearity on thought, as the structural analysis itself. It is these facts that make the study of Piagetian thought at its roots particularly useful and pertinent, which is enhanced not detracted from by the fact that he is a 'loner' with a sharply individualised approach to epistemological problems.

Piaget's Antecedents and the Lamarckian-neo-Darwinian Controversy

There has been considerable discussion of the influences on Piaget, not least by himself in his 'Autobiography' (Boring, *et al.*, 1969, *passim*) and in *Insights and Illusions of Philosophy* (1972c, Eng, edn). Such influences are very numerous and sometimes it is not clear where they derive from. It is not our intention, nor is it relevant to our purposes, to investigate these in detail. Broadly speaking, one can say that they consist of two main strands, on the one hand arising from biology and biological theory, and on the other from scientific epistemology in general and logic and mathematics in particular. There is a whole galaxy of names in this last area to be found in Piaget's writings, especially in the later books. But he himself attaches particular importance to L. Brunschvicg and, to a lesser extent, Poincaré as major influences on his thought (for example Piaget, 1950, p. 112; 1971, p. 39). Perhaps Poincaré's most significant impact on Piaget is to be seen in Piaget's comment in *Insights and Illusions:* 'as is well-known, Poincaré, despite his conventionalism, made the concept of a "group" an a priori structure' (p. 73). Brunschvicg, however, appears to have had greater influence on Piaget, especially in his earliest years.

Léon Brunschvicg, a Critical Idealist philosopher, whose outlook combined Kantian constructivism with a stress on the historical approach to the study of mental activity, regarded mathematical judgement as its highest level. For him, philosophy consisted solely in the process of judgement which performs the function of uniting conceptual form and content. This is what makes philosophy, for Brunschvicg, a sort of second echelon of thought directed at the nature of the thinking process itself. Thus, knowledge may be subjected to reflection only via this 'two-tier' system which actually provides what we know as intelligibility. It is the activity of the spirit, as it were, that is, for Brunschvicg, the principal target of thought. There is an inevitable stress in such a system on historical unfolding whereby science and mathematics, especially, embody a progressive self-understanding involving more than simply knowledge. History becomes 'le progrès de la conscience' where both conscience and consciousness are intertwined. The influence on the logico-mathematical side of Piaget's thought emerges very clearly from this. We are able to detect the central role of mental activity in the interactive relationship between the subject and his environment embodied in its highest form in logico-mathematical structure. Moreover, the two-tier form of reflective thought, in which mathematical judgement is deemed to be the most sophisticated expression of the human spirit, is clearly carried through into the fundamentals of Piaget's system. This is particularly notable in Piaget's 'operations upon operations', so important in his developmental theory. Brunschvicg, however, is more of an Idealist than Piaget. For the former the emphasis is on the human spirit acting via mental activity. Piaget shifts the emphasis from the spirit in itself to the subject-in-the-environment as the source of knowledge. Despite this, however, the strong interconnection between the process of cognition and both morality and affectivity in Piaget's thought still very much reflects the Brunschvicg influence.

The second major strand in the influences on Piaget, and in some respects the more basic, consists in the biological influences. A recent and valuable commentary is Rotman's book, *Jean Piaget: Psychologist of the Real* (1977), which examines some of the philosophical foundations of Piaget's thought, particularly its biological roots. Without doubt Piaget came heavily under the influence, at least initially, of the Lamarckian-Spencerian tradition of biological evolution. Henri Bergson's *Creative Evolution* (1907) also played a part second only to this. It is from these sources that what Rotman calls Piaget's 'naturalist conception of reason' stems. It must be remembered also that there is already a well-established collection (one cannot quite call it a school) of evolutionary writers who, mainly under Darwinian but also partly under Lamarckian influences, are applying notions of evolution, at the end of the last century and the beginning of this, to man's mind as well as to his physique. The Americans Stanley Hall and G. M. Baldwin are particularly noteworthy, especially the latter who taught at Geneva and, according to Rotman, coined the term Genetic Epistemology. Others include E. Claparède, also at Geneva, Lloyd Morgan and G. J. Romanes in England. (Rotman, 1977, p. 19)

However, the Lamarckian-Spencerian tradition cannot for long be reconciled with Darwinism. The difference lies in the affirmation by the former that physical changes occurring in the lifetime of the individual can be inherited. The more an organ is used the greater its habituation and the higher the possibility of its inheritance. The implication for reason as a 'faculty' is clear, as Herbert Spencer realised, and on these implications he built virtually the whole of his philosophy of social advance. Spencer affirms the universal propensity of life to become increasingly harmonious with itself, and this harmony is expressed through increasing structural complexity and diversified function. The realisation of this propensity involves all living things in constant adjustment of their structures, or adaptation of their 'inner relations', congruently with the 'outer relations' of the universe. The whole process is seen as 'progressive' involving the idea of ever-increasing equilibrium or stability and the diminution of disequilibrium. Of necessity it includes all human society and the individual's personal development.

The influences on Piaget of this tradition are considerable, especially on his basic notion of equilibrium. But in the end he virtually rejected Spencer and Bergson on the grounds that they were pre-Darwinian and therefore non-scientific. Nevertheless, certain views appear to be retained in Piaget's system while he stresses as his main difference with the Lamarckian-Spencerian view, the Kantian factor of the mental imposition of structure on the world.[11] But even here the issue is not certain. As we shall see, Piaget's apriorism is rather unusual in this respect in so far as he seeks to retain it while dissociating it from any preformational connection. Piaget's ultimate cognitive structures have to be 'free' to grow at the same time as having their goal of completion absolutely fore-ordained. This he is forced to do by having to reconcile learning from scratch by the subject in each new generation with the fact of inheritance in some degree by that subject.

The emphasis on the connection between the growth of knowledge and biological necessity, which is possibly the most important element of influence retained from the Lamarckian-Spencerian tradition in Piaget's system, also presents problems in the social sphere emerging particularly in *The Moral Judgement of the Child* (1932). The essence of this is to demonstrate how awareness and participation are rule-governed activities (games at first, social behaviour later) emerging from infanthood to mid-adolescence. The stress here is on the social process, which directs the individual towards his or her ultimate role in society. The only way in which this can be conceived of as biologically useful is by seeing the social code as the collective end product of what is biologically most useful for the social group. Yet here we run into great difficulties in so far as, historically, it provides no possible reason why any particular society should ever have changed into any other particular society – unless, that is, we search for (and find) biologically determining factors for the earliest historical societies and for the historical process as a whole. Few seriously entertain this simplistic notion now, although through the liberal use of the isomorphic notion in individual development, the biological origins of society lie implicitly at the base of Piaget's social concepts.

As Rotman sees it, however (Rotman, 1977, p. 22), it is in Piaget's experimental claims that he is most different from Spencer and closest to the Darwinian tradition. Rotman points to the approving quotation given by Piaget on the first page of *Biology and Knowledge* (Edinburgh: Edinburgh University Press, 1972) from Darwin: 'Whoever achieves understanding of the baboon will do more for metaphysics than Locke did, which is to say he will do more for Philosophy in general, including the problem of knowledge' – a starkly contrasting view to that of Wittgenstein expressed in the *Tractatus* (4.1122): 'Darwin's theory has no more to do with philosophy than any other hypothesis in natural science'. Piaget's endorsement of Darwin's nineteenth-century conception of epistemology relates very much to his notion of 'fact' which, as we shall see, is extremely traditional, and, indeed, is traditionally empiricist.

It is appropriate and necessary here to go further into the Lamarckian-neo-Darwinian controversy, or more precisely, the argument over the inheritance of acquired characteristics. The Lamarckian proposition that the individual organism passes on characteristics acquired in its own lifetime seems able to get no further than a mere proposition. One searches in vain for any form of mechanism that can demonstrate how, for example, an environmental factor like water can be transmuted into physiological modifications such as the horny pads on the forearms of the toad, *Alytes obstetricans*, which was the claim in the famous case of Paul Kammerer, the Austrian Lamarckian biologist about whom Arthur Koestler has written an extremely persuasive and entertaining book.[12] The Lamarckian approach, in other words, completely jumps the question of qualitatively distinct domains of phenomena and cannot cope with the fact that the tree is *not* identifiable with its molecular structure and composition, nor even with a simple sum of its organic parts. Furthermore, there is a presumption of complete separation between organism and environment without which the question of 'acquisition' becomes ambiguous. If you have a simple system of two organic elements related in a unique way and then a third element intrudes, the *total* new relationship emerging leaves it extremely difficult to settle the question who (or what) has acquired whom (or what). Elements one and two can jointly have been acquired by three or vice versa. This is not a trivial point. If the blacksmith's son is supposed to be born with bigger biceps than 'normal' because of his father's trade, questions are begged all round. What is 'normal'? Why should the correspondence between father and son in this respect *only* be attributed to the work done? How about a general type of physique in the family having encouraged the father (or grandfather) to turn to blacksmithing in the first place? And, of course, all these points ignore the social and economic factors that must be brought to bear on the question of what occupation or what trade individuals ultimately adopt in society at any time. And so on. What we have here is *a system in which it is not clear what is being actually systematised* plus a presumption that a generation sequence is identifiable with a determined and closed causal sequence. The argument here is not directed against the notion that the macro-world influences the micro-world. But unless the *mode* of this influence can be identified, even provisionally, we have not moved one inch beyond a very hypothetical proposition, as we indicated before.

One might think that the field is now clear for a neo-Darwinian 'victory' and that is certainly the viewpoint taken by many contemporary biologists who regard the Lamarckian attitude as antiquated and at best quaint. But what are the presuppositions of the neo–Darwinian position? Starting with the notion of the chromosome, and developing via the gene to DNA and RNA, the responsibility for the ongoing continuity of life (what Weissmann called the 'germ-tract') is seen to rest with an organic particle which is conceived as impregnable and uninfluenced by the world of the developed organism. Change and modification in this latter world depend exclusively upon the random mutations which occur at the former level. Yet the decision regarding the survival of such mutations rests with the macro-world solely through the operation of 'natural selection'! A fundamental conflict remains in that the ultimate causal factor is an organic particle on which rests the entire process of modification; yet this particle's very randomness must be ultimately connected with the events of the macro-world.

Genetic Epistemology, its Problems and Conflicts

What, then, is the nature of Genetic Epistemology? Piaget's view of it as a science whose progress has been hampered by speculative philosophy is amply demonstrated in the opening chapter to *Insights and Illusions*, largely devoted to a critique of academic philosophy, particularly French. Piaget remarks, almost in passing: 'If I come back to psychology it is not to concern myself with it, since this work is concerned with philosophy, but in order to show how a certain conviction in the powers of general knowledge that philosophy would allow, actually resulted in systematically delaying the rise of an experimental discipline concerned with the mind, and . . . dealing with problems of which philosophers have always spoken (for a very large number of them *before* the existence of our science, and for many others who have written afterwards, neglecting it more or less deliberately)' (Piaget, 1972c, p.27).

Piaget defines Genetic Epistemology in a number of places, but surprisingly rarely, considering the amount he has written, and mostly in the later part of his intellectual life. The source used here (Piaget, 1970) is chosen principally for its unusual clarity and fullness and for the fact that it is relatively recent and therefore benefits from Piaget's later considerations. The book opens in the following way:

> Genetic epistomology attempts to explain knowledge, and in particular scientific knowledge, on the basis of its history, its sociogenesis, and especially the psychological origins of the notions and operations upon which it is based. These notions and operations are drawn in large part from common sense, so that their origins can shed light on their significance as knowledge of a somewhat higher level. But genetic epistemology also takes into account, wherever possible, formalisation – in particular, logical formalisations applied to equilibrated thought structures and in certain cases to transformations from one level to another in the development of thought. (Piaget, 1970, p. 1)

Right away one can detect certain notions which we shall often meet. Piaget emphasises the relevance of Genetic Epistemology to scientific knowledge especially; but we shall find that 'affectivity', or the emotional and intuitional side of human mentality, is equally encompassed by the theory. Furthermore, the reference to 'sociogenesis' indicates that, despite much criticism of Piaget for failing to consider the social context of individual psychological development, he nevertheless places considerable emphasis on the social origins of thought (and in particular the social *goals* of individual development). There is even a fairly strong case for regarding the social matrix as the ultimately determining one of Piaget's system. Throughout the passage the two major aspects of the system emerge clearly, the developmental and the stable – the dynamic and the static.

Piaget continues immediately by taking up the major problem of Genetic Epistemology:

> The description that I have given of the nature of genetic epistemology runs into a major problem, namely, the traditional philosophical view of epistemology. For many philosophers and epistemologists, epistemology is the study of knowledge as it exists at the present moment; it is the analysis of knowledge for its own sake and within its own

framework without regard for its development. For these persons, tracing the development of ideas or the development of operations may be of interest to historians or to psychologists but is of no direct concern to epistemologists. This is the major objection to the discipline of genetic epistemology, which I have outlined here. (ibid., pp. 1–2)

But he comes back with the following reply:

Scientific knowledge is in perpetual evolution; it finds itself changed from the one day to the next. As a result, we cannot say that on the one hand there is the history of knowledge, and on the other its current state today, as if its current state was somehow definitive or even stable. The current state of knowledge is a moment in history, changing just as rapidly as the state of knowledge in the past has ever changed, and, in many instances, more rapidly. Scientific thought, then, is not momentary; it is not static instance; it is a process. More specifically, it is a process of continual construction and reorganisation . . . we cannot say that on the one hand there is the history of scientific thinking, and on the other the body of scientific thought as it is today; there is simply a continual transformation, a continual reorganisation. (ibid., pp. 2–4)

In these passages the emphasis is clearly on the dynamic rather than on the static. The stress is on transformation rather than stability. But a little further on we come on the following:

So, in sum, genetic epistemology deals with both the formation and the meaning of knowledge. We can formulate our problem in the following terms: by what means does the human mind go from a state of less sufficient knowledge to a state of higher knowledge? The decision of what is lower or less adequate knowledge and what is higher knowledge, has of course formal and normative aspects. It is not up to psychologists to determine whether or not a certain state of knowledge is superior to another state. (ibid., pp. 12–13)

And again:

The fundamental hypothesis of genetic epistemology is that there is a parallelism between the progress made in the logical and rational organisation of knowledge and the corresponding formative psychological processes. (ibid., p. 13)

Both of these passages exemplify the 'static' aspect of Piaget's thought. Here the stress is on plateau-like states of knowledge, identified by 'formal and normative' factors and a parallelism which carry no developmental significance of one level in relation to another notwithstanding the reference to 'formative psychological processes'.

Taking all these passages together it is easy to see two main emphases which play a central role in Genetic Epistemology as a whole. The first of these is the notion of hierarchy connected with knowledge. This notion carries with it the idea that there are superior and inferior types or forms of knowledge. As to how the superiority or inferiority of knowledge is to be judged is not the responsibility of psychologists but of specialists in particular fields of knowledge. This is a rather unsatisfactory situation in so far as the judgement of the hierarchy of knowledge is dependent on the central idea of developing stabilising equilibrium in the system. But unless we have some means of judging what constitutes more stable, or 'better', forms of knowledge, it is difficult to see how equilibrium as such can be assessed. Thus while the hierarchical notion is present and very important for Piaget, there seems to be no means for actually judging it. But the question cannot be avoided, and Piaget returns to it a few pages further on. Here, in discussing how we know reality, he says:

> Knowing reality means constructing systems of transformations that correspond, more or less adequately, to reality. They are more or less isomorphic to transformations of reality. The transformational structures of which knowledge consists are not copies of the transformations in reality; they are simply possible isomorphic models among which experience can enable us to choose. Knowledge, then, is a system of transformations that become progressively adequate. (ibid., p. 15)

Certain questions are raised by this picture. First, where do the isomorphic structures themselves derive from? If they are treated simply as reflections of reality then this is an act of description and not of explanation. Then, again, given a number of isomorphic (mental) models, what decides the choice among these? The invocation of experience does not help here since this itself involves knowledge-forms, and if we are not careful we can find ourselves on a cyclical turntable of experience–structures–experience. And even if some novelty (however unspecified) is attributed to further experience, gauging this is outside the ability of the tools provided here.

Regarding the nature of isomorphism itself, further difficulties arise, for isomorphism must assume a static and not a changing situation. If potential change is admitted into the systems isomorphically aligned, then the maintenance of one-to-one correspondence between the isomorphic model and Actuality becomes at best indeterminate. Isomorphic relations can only exist between given, or completed, systems.

Bearing these questions in mind, the phrase 'more or less' seems to play the role of disguising the problems we are indicating. Its use allows for the possibility of reconciling the dynamic and static within the same parameters. But the problem of establishing a causal relation (between cognising subject and Actuality) when all that can be affirmed is correspondence, is not obviated by this device. Nor does the introduction of the notion of action help to overcome the problem. When Piaget writes later on the same page that 'Human knowledge is essentially active . . . Knowing an object does not mean copying it – it means acting upon it' (Piaget, 1970, p. 15), he is introducing another notion which itself requires explanation.

Finally, the claim in the last sentence that implies that the progressive 'adequacy' of knowledge is causally related to the reflection by transformational (mental) structures of actual transformations in the external world is not substantiated. The notions of 'action' and 'transformation' among others, and the question of whether Piaget succeeds in reconciling parallelism and causality, are considered again in Chapter 6.

If there is a major problem in the system of reconciling the hierarchy of knowledge with the process of going from one plane of that knowledge to another, it is even more the case that there is a problem in accounting for the actual origins of knowledge, or process of learning, in the first instance, both for the species in general and the individual in particular. The question of ultimate beginnings in this sense is unavoidable, and Piaget has a formulation to deal with it.

> In genetic epistemology, as in developmental psychology, too, *there is never an absolute beginning* [our emphasis]. We can never get back to the point where we can say, 'here is the very beginning of logical structures'. As soon as we start talking about the general co-ordination of actions, we are going to find ourselves, of course, going even further back into the area of biology. We immediately get into the realm of the co-ordination within the nervous system and the neurone network, as discussed by McCulloch and Pitts. And then, if we look for the roots of the logic of the nervous system as discussed by these workers, we have to go back a step further. We find more basic organic co-ordinations. If we go further still into the realm of comparative biology, we find structures of inclusion ordering correspondence everywhere. (Piaget, 1970, p. 19)

Here, in order to satisfy the notion that there is 'never an absolute beginning' of structuration, Piaget treats every level of systems organisation from psychology to the deepest biological roots as if they are equivalent. There is no suggestion of different levels of organisation operating under different laws which makes it difficult, if not impossible, to account for the specific. This 'slipping back' to the nervous system prevents any clarification of the origins of cognition, which is a *mental* and not a biological phenomenon. By pursuing such a 'levelless' path, the central task of the 'new science' of Genetic Epistemology, the 'genetic' explication of the 'epistemology', seems to be rendered impossible.

What is the purpose of such a detailed analysis of one passage out of the immense output Piaget has produced over the last half-century? As Rosemary Dinnage remarked in a recent review of *The Essential Piaget* (ed. Howard E. Gruber and J. J. Vonèche),[13] 'in his [Piaget's] books he is carrying out a "conservation experiment" with ideas . . . and he seems sometimes to be pouring identical theory from one thick book to another'. The passages we have been looking at, in other words, stand not only for themselves but for a major dominant and ongoing theme permeating the Piagetian system as a whole. This theme is the perpetual struggle to reconcile biological and logical parameters, indicated earlier. Indeed it is easy enough to relate the Lamarck-Spencer-Bergson tradition to Piaget's general notion of increasing stabilisation (equilibrium) of all species, genera, and even the basic physical structure of the universe, which is conceived of as being powered by a mechanism of increasing differentiation and integration of things (and thoughts) and manifested in an increasingly complex and reciprocal mutual assimilation. After all, the theory of the inheritance of acquired characteristics is about a learning process for the species, and is easily carried over into the idea of 'constructivism' which is the core of Piagetian theory.[14] On the other hand, this theory presupposes that each individual must 'start again' at birth, equipped only with a common biological inheritance in the form of some sort of unspecified innate characteristics (neurological?). This area of the relation of the biological 'gift' to cognitive construction is, however, one of great obscurity. In one of his most recent books, *The Development of Thought*,[15] much influenced by Ludvig von Bertalanffy and System Theory, Piaget offers a diagrammatic account of the transition from purely biological to the earliest stages of individual cognitive functioning: see Figure 1.1. The

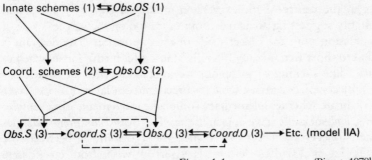

Figure 1.1   (Piaget, 1978b, p. 87)

last line here is intended to represent the (final?) interactive relation between subject and object. On the left we have 'observables relative to the subject's action' (Obs.S), leading to the 'subject's inferential co-ordinations of actions (or operations)' (Coord.S). On the right are 'observables relative to the objects' (Obs.0), and what is described as the 'inferential co-ordinations between objects' (Coord. 0) (Piaget, 1978b, p. 52).

It is important to recognise that this is not an elaborate description of a normal subject–object relationship but an attempt to interpret the relationship between the subject and the environment in which he exists in terms of how the subject relates actively to that environment. Thus the last line of this diagram is essentially to do with mental structures, and the object that is involved in the formation of such structures is only understood in terms of what the subject is able actually to observe of the object by his action upon it. There is, in other words, no suggestion here of a discussion, masked in symbolism, of the existence or otherwise of an independent object. Such is not the issue for Piaget who is concerned only with representing here the *mental* structural manifestations of the subject–object relationship. This is not an unimportant point, since when the three 'layers' of the diagram are looked at together, it can be seen that the first and to some extent the second are distinct from the third in the sense that (1) is exclusively (almost?) related to non-mental structures (or schemes).

But the arrows internal to the third layer are significant. On the left there is an arrow in only one direction, indicating in the subject the derivation of inferential co-ordinations from observables relative to the subject's actions. On the right there are two-way interactions between these inferential co-ordinations and what can be observed relative to the object. Also there is a two-way interaction between this and the inferential co-ordinations on the left-hand side deriving from it. This seems to be the distinction between object and subject. But a 'crosslink', provided by the dotted arrows, is also required. These latter links join the *susceptibility* of the object to being observed by the subject to the *susceptibility* of the subject's actions to observation, and also the subject's inferential co-ordinative action with the 'co-ordinatability' of the object. The double arrows in the centre of the expression indicate a two-way interaction presumably suggesting an actual communication on the subject's side of the expression with the object's side of the expression. The diagram is intended to show that initially (literally at just after birth), innate schemes (activities like sucking or gripping) are interacting with an undifferentiated subject–object activity which is precognive ('layer' (1)). At 'layer' (2) co-ordinate schemes (elementary composite movements, for example, gripping *and* sucking) have appeared deriving from *both* innate schemes *and* the subject–object activity (hence the cross-*arrows* between the 'layers'). 'Layer' (3) then derives, cross-arrow-wise, from co-ordinate schemes and the still undifferentiated subject–object activity. This 'layer' is intended to be descriptive of the realm of elementary cognitive growth and leads on to the earliest stages of cognitive structuration in relation to the environment, or the pre-operational stage.

This diagram is intended to demonstrate that the innate factors, whatever they are, *are incorporated while maintaining an independent existence in the constructivist process of cognitive growth*. The reader can probably see right away how similar this is to the neo-Darwinian concept embodied in modern genetic theory, whereby genetic inheritance is absorbed unmodified into the new generations, while at the same time determining the characteristics of the adult organisms which themselves engage in the process of natural selection. Equivalently, it has similar unresolved problems. But if this diagram reflects the neo-Darwinian thesis, it also reflects a Lamarckian element which persists and is embodied in the cross-arrows seemingly carrying one 'layer' of the process to another 'higher layer'. Here, as with the Lamarckian thesis, we have a description of a learning process but without any indication of the mechanism whereby one 'layer' is succeeded by another. Also, if the overall principle of increasing universal equilibrium is to be satisfied, it is unclear how that which is learned is fed back into the innate 'pool' for succeeding generations.

The question immediately arises, then, of how progressive development for the individual actually occurs in the system. Piaget expresses this most clearly on the last page of *Six Psychological Studies*:

> It is in this manner, it seems to me, that an extratemporal structure can develop from a temporal process. In temporal genesis, the stages merely obey increasing probabilities, all of which are determined by a temporal order of succession, but once the equilibrated structure is crystallized, it forces itself as necessary on the subject's mind. This necessity is the sign of the completion of the structure, which then becomes extratemporal. I am intentionally using terms which may appear contradictory. If you prefer, I shall say that we arrive *a priori* at a kind of a necessity, but it is an *a priori* which is constituted only at the end not at the point of departure, as resultant and not as a source, and hence retains only the concept of necessity and not that of preformation. (Piaget, 1968, p. 157)

Two central notions are used: (1) a sequence of increasing probabilities which turns into necessity, signalling the formation of a non-temporal structure from a temporal process; (2) this necessity is constituted by 'an *a priori*' appearing at the *end* of the process, that is, an *a priori* which is, so to speak, *a posteriori*! For it is not the *necessity* but the *a priori* which appears at the end 'as a resultant and not as a source'. This device with which Piaget tries to avoid preformation is thus questionable in the first place because the necessity is not moved to the end – only our perception of it ('forces itself . . . on the subject's mind').

Another problem is the spatio-temporal nature of the concepts involved throughout, very reminiscent of the same situation in the diagram referred to on page 15. In this diagram, the obscurity lay in how the different 'layers' derive one from the other. In the present case, there does an exist an apparent mechanism for change, that is, the hypothesis that increasing probabilities result in an a priori (seen as necessity) which involves stable structures of a non-temporal nature. Piaget does, indeed, correctly recognise the non-spatio-temporality of cognition. But having said this, his hypothesis does not survive a closer look. The 'probability' (of world-events) lies firmly in the realm of calculation with mathematical objects. 'Necessity', on the other hand, is in a different category of abstraction altogether – that of inferential logic, which may appear to be similar to calculation but only in so far as calculation itself has no room for manoeuvre and thus exhibits only a pseudo-'necessity' (see Chapter 8 below for a further discussion of this question). This is not so for the *theory* of probability whose categories participate in the same type of logical inference as 'necessity'. Piaget is not here comparing theory with theory (abstraction with abstraction) but actual practical problems (the child manipulating clay – the case study on which all of this theory is based) with the theoretical abstraction of logical necessity. It is also noticeable that he carries over a temporal relationship from the practical zone of probability into the inferential zone of logic, one following after the other without any differentiation. Lastly, even if a sequence of increasing probabilities could turn into necessity, it still remains totally unexplained how this effects the transformation of a temporal into a non-temporal structure.

Bringing all this together with the idea of the transition from innate schemes to cognitive structures shown in the diagram, we get a composite picture of biologically inborn *tendencies*, or *potentialities*, which possess a very low level of certainty (necessity) that any *particular* cognitive structure will emerge. With stage-by-stage progress out of the realm of the innate and predominantly biological and into the realm of the cognitive and rational, the level of certainty is supposed to rise as the 'probability' of a particular structure comes closer and closer to actual realisation. The process is identifiable with the other important factors in Piaget's developmental model, that is, cognitive (and affective) *differentiation* and *decentring* whereby the 'egocentric' infant, who is supposed initially to see the world revolving around himself, is said to achieve the ability to 'see the other point of view'. Piaget here seeks to reconcile the notion of the innate with the emergence of the novel. Notwithstanding inheritance, the individual and the species/society are deemed nevertheless to be able to advance upon preceding situations through such a mechanism.

The implication of Piaget's 'inversion' of the role and position of the a priori is significant when we reconsider the problem of combining the innate with the learning process. Although novelty is shown in the diagram of infant development by a 'leap' from 'layer' to 'layer', if we follow the line of thought of *Six Psychological Studies* such novelty is inevitably trapped within any given 'layer'. This is so because the unbroken linear linkage from probability to necessity (made possible only by putting the a priori/necessity at the end) shows no sign of qualitative transformation. Both appear on the same plane, as it were. The point is doubly emphasised by the fact that Piaget carries over the temporal features of probability into the non-temporal zone of logic.

There is a clue here as to why Piaget opts for his particular concept of the a priori. By regarding the a priori as an *emergent* factor, it can be interpreted as 'binding together' the internal laws of the closed 'layers' with the (universally identical) isomorphic laws of transition from one 'layer' to another. While the *existence* of the 'layer' is guaranteed by the internal character of its paradigm, the *transition* from 'layer' to 'layer' is guaranteed by a sort of convergence of probability towards certainty. Thus, biologically, it becomes more and more certain over several hundred million years that an intelligent, cognising organism will appear. This notion of certainty is close to that of equilibrium, and there is no particular reason, if the terms of reference of Piaget's system are accepted, why the mode of thought should not be transferred to the individual's own maturation. Hence the individual human subject must arrive with the same certainty at the fully matured formal operational stage (see below, Chapter 7, for Piaget's stages) matching thereby the whole of creation, every branch and sub-branch of life as well as the totality. We have seen this theme already in relation to the Lamarck-Spencer-Bergson influences on Piaget and in a curious way he almost manages to reconcile the Lamarckian tradition with the neo-Darwinian at a 'point at infinity' – the ultimate and final stage of total fully realised equilibrium.

However, a major problem, frequently admitted by Piaget, deriving from this overall perspective, is that individuals do not fully unfold, do not fully mature into the formal operational stage. And if such 'falling short' is indeed the case then we have no guarantee of the progress towards ever greater equilibrium and therefore no guaranteed reconciliation between the innateness of the biological roots of cognition and the creativity of the cognitive growth process. In fact the more closely we look at the notion of equilibrium at any stage, biological or psychological, the more we have to accept that if it exists at all it can only be conditional and relative. But recognition of this is rendered extremely difficult, if not entirely impossible, by Piaget's terms of reference. The requirement for the unfolding of necessity out of progressively more probable situations, involving (unexplained) 'leaps' from the spatio-temporal world of physical causality to the timeless (and spaceless) world of logico-mathematics, requires the adoption of closed, logico-mathematical structuration as the unique and exclusive fundamental characteristic of cognition. There is considerable reference below to the problem of harmonising the idea of a closed system (which does not by its very organisation permit of intrusion from outside) with that of novelty (continuous creation in the absolute sense of producing something, at least in part, quite new). The system must inevitably give rise to a conflict of this type since the mutual entailment of equilibrium with closure and the treatment of equilibrium as the universal goal of all processes of development (equilibration) cannot avoid subordinating novelty, with its inbuilt aspect of unpredictability, to the total control of logic.

We are brought back by these considerations to the problems enumerated previously and their relationship to the intellectual ethos of the era. The roots of Piaget's overwhelming involvement with logic and mathematics indeed lie very deep. In his extreme youth he had become consciously aware of the importance of both in relation to human thought processes, even to the extent of an early interest in Group Theory, which was to play such an important part in his later theoretical development (Boring *et al.*, 1952). In this respect Piaget, from the start, embodies the dilemma of the age represented by the struggle to reconcile the conceived stability of being with the conceived evanescence of becoming when the time-honoured certainties of the rationalist method were revealing increasing shortcomings at the most fundamental levels of research. It is not that Piaget is at all unique in this respect. But the particular form in which the dilemma manifests itself in his case, and the field of human psychology in which he actually finds himself, combine to present a particularly sharp case. Although his earliest writings clearly show Piaget to have originally been mainly interested in the non-rational and non-logic aspects of human thought processes, yet the seeds are already there (notice specially *The Moral Judgment of the Child*, 1932), of seeing development as a step-by-step ascent to ultimate complete logicality and rationality as the most basic and all-embracing characteristic of human psychological development. Long before the application of mathematical and logical processes to cognition which he was to do largely in relation to his studies of the 'concrete operational' stage (7–11 years) in the 1930s and 1940s, but which he was also later to extend to the 'formal operational' stage, his writings showed a strong predisposition to regard cognition primarily as a matter of the development of logico-mathematical abilities. The treatment of this and its significance in relation to the cognitive system is a very central part of this book – but not simply for its own sake. In examining Piaget's problems in this respect especially in relation to the overall theme of his thought, the growth of the structure of knowledge, some of the most basic issues now facing mankind's knowledge of itself and the world are met with.

Thus we can say that in Piaget's thought the struggle to maintain contradictory views of the world, those derived from biology and to some extent history, and those derived from logic and mathematics, lies at the core of all his writings over the last half-century. In effect, ideas of changing development and ideas of stability and permanence are encapsulated in this struggle in the attempt to reconcile notions of learning (acquired characteristics) with notions of inheritance (the biologically innate) and both with the notion of logico-mathematical necessity inbuilt in the universe and expressed in human thought via the structuration process.

Later Trends in Piagetian Thought

Increasingly throughout his intellectual life Piaget's drive has been towards this attempted reconciliation of the 'open' with the 'closed'. And increasingly he sought the answer by making the latter absorb and subsume the former. Logical cognition and non-logical emotion (affectivity) have more and more been portrayed as both lying exclusively within the ambit of logico-mathematical structuration (see Chapter 10 below for a further discussion of this). Yet side by side with this seeming homogeneity the problems persist, and by the 1960s Piaget was repeating the same theory in new publications without significant alteration. But in 1964 we get an indication of a possible change of direction when, in *Six Psychological Studies*, Piaget writes:

> We by no means conceive psychological equilibrium in the manner of a balance of forces in a state of rest but shall define it very broadly as the compensation resulting from the activities of the subject in response to external intrusion. It follows that equilibrium thus defined is compatible with the concept of an open system, and it would perhaps be better to speak – along with L. v. Bertalanffy (1960) – of a 'stable state in an open system'. (Piaget, 1968, p. 101)

System Theory is a particularly post-Second World War development and Bertalanffy is possibly its oldest and certainly most authoritative representative. Parallel with computer technology, System Theory (alternatively referred to as Systems theory, for example, Bertalanffy, 1971, p. 8) offers a contemporary science of organisation which in recent years has influenced all social, economic and industrial aspects of modern life. Its attraction for Piaget is obvious from the Bertalanffy reference, for it seems as if the central problem, spelt out explicitly in the Piaget quotation given here, can be solved within a System Theory context. However, there is a quite unjustifiable adaptation here of Bertalanffy's actual views on the subject of equilibrium. Far from offering a mechanism of reconciliation, Bertalanffy himself explicitly rejects the idea that equilibrium is applicable to a 'stable state in an open system'.

In fact, there are a considerable number of references to this question in

General System Theory (1968), published later than Piaget's reference, all
having a bearing on this question. For example, Bertalanffy writes:

> Concepts and models of equilibrium, homeostasis, adjustment, etc.,
> are suitable for the maintenance of systems, but inadequate for pheno-
> mena of change, differentiation, evolution, negentropy, production of
> improbable states, creativity, building up of tensions, self-realisation,
> emergence, etc.; as indeed Cannon realised when he acknowledged,
> besides homeostasis, a 'heterostasis' including phenomena of the latter
> nature. The theory of open systems applies to a wide range of pheno-
> mena in biology (and technology), but a warning is necessary against its
> incautious expansion into fields for which its concepts are not made.
> (p. 21)

Again, 'Every living organism is essentially an open system. It maintains
itself in a continuous inflow and outflow, a building up and breaking
down of components, never being, so long as it is alive, in a state of
chemical and thermo-dynamic equilibrium but maintained in a so-called
steady state which is distinct from the latter' (p. 38). And, 'The apparent
"equilibrium" found in an organism is not a true equilibrium incapable of
performing work; rather it is a dynamic psuedo-equilibrium, kept constant at a certain distance from true equilibrium; so being capable of
performing work but, on the other hand, requiring continuous import of
energy for maintaining the distance from true equilibrium' (p. 133). But
particularly relevant to Piaget's discussion of this issue, 'We are not in a
position to define such an "equilibrium state" in complicated organic
processes, but we can easily see that such a conception is, in principle,
inadequate. For apart from certain individual processes, living systems are
not closed systems in true equilibrium but open systems in a steady state'
(p. 139).[16]

The disparity between Piaget's and Bertalanffy's positions is quite clear.
How can Piaget's concept of equilibrium (even with a later stress on
equilibration as occurs in *The Development of Thought*, 1977) be reconciled
with Bertalanffy's 'open systems in a steady state'? Although the two
concepts appear to be very similar at first sight, the notion of equilibration
is tied to that of equilibrium in the sense that the fluctuations in the former
must become indefinitely close to a unique point of equilibrium. In the case
of 'steady state', no such uniqueness exists and, moreover, the fluctuations do not have to approach 'indefinitely close' to any particular 'point of
steadiness'. Interpreting this in terms of limit theory they are not required
to take on all values leading to this point. There is therefore grave doubt as
to whether Piaget's new emphasis drawn from System Theory can
resolve the problem of the interiorisation of physical causality into logico-

mathematical structures, involving both openness and closure at the same time.

A parallel development to System Theory with close affinities to it, and even more significant for Piaget, has emerged especially in France – the Structuralist movement. Structuralism is not in itself especially new. But in recent years it has assumed new forms and a new meaning in the context of the general crisis of Western thought. One hestitates to offer short or concise definitions of modern Structuralism as there is such difference of opinion among the protagonists themselves as to what it is. It is probably as useful as anything else to look at the accepted roots in modern times of the movement. These are to be found in the activities of the Prague Linguistics Circle of Slavic Philogists whose 'Thèses', published in 1929, give us some basic notion of Structuralism. The following summarises the Prague view and its extension beyond linguistics: 'the primary object of linguistic study must be the *structure of the system* rather than individual linguistic fact' (our emphasis) (Robey, 1973, p. 1). Structuralism is 'that approach – to any subject – which has as its object . . . "the laws of solidarity", "the reciprocal relations" (Thèse) of the different facts and observations rather than considering these facts in isolation' (ibid., pp. 1–2). Again, Michael Lane gives a slightly different view. 'Probably the most distinctive feature of the structuralist method is the emphasis it gives to wholes, to totality . . . The essential quality of the structuralist method, and its fundamental tenet, lies in its attempt to study not the elements of a whole, but the complex network of relationships that link and unite those elements . . . Structuralism seeks its structures not on the surface, at the level of the observed, but below or behind empirical reality' (Lane, 1970, p. 14).

Thus, Structuralism treats the *interconnections* of phenomena as the essential target of scientific investigation and understanding, not the phenomena themselves. Although Structuralism has largely expanded in the humanities, especially social anthropology and linguistics, its convergence on the same position as micro-physics is obvious. Whereas in the latter case the exigencies of observation have increasingly forced a situation where mathematical analysis of structure *without* consideration of what is the meaning of the observed is unavoidable, in language, literary criticism, anthropology, and so on, an actual policy of abandoning the 'facts' has been pursued. Essentially, Structuralism is a movement away from the identification of 'fact' altogether and towards a stress on 'holism' as the fundamental feature of scientific as well as common experience.[17] The greatest employer of structuralist methods outside the linguistics field is Levi-Strauss, whose work on the culture and language of the Nambi Kwara Indians (isolated from outside contact for about thirty years) in South America in the 1930s generated the basically structuralist notion that ritual transforms into kinship and other socio-cultural relations. In fact, Levi-Strauss's main contribution to structuralist theory is the idea of *transformation* – an idea which is *not* to be understood developmentally but much more as *displacement*.[18] One can fairly confidently argue that Structuralism, to the extent that it withdraws from the notion of 'fact', withdraws *ipso facto* from time and causality as well. What we have left is a logico-mathematical and acausal system carrying with it the features of closure typical of any such deductive axiomatic system.

The controversy and immense flood of literature generated by modern Structuralism is outside the brief of this book.[19] It is enough to say that there are numerous problems attaching to the application of structuralist method to language in general and linguistics in particular, not least the central problem of unclarity as to what level is being dealt with, with a resulting opportunity for private, unmonitored definition. Latterly, Levi-Strauss himself and other structuralists (for example, Merleau-Ponty) have introduced a note of qualification into the relativism of structuralist thought by their, often oblique, reaffirmation of the 'concreteness' of basic *emotional* thought and action which must be recognised as co-existing with the structural transformationism of 'advanced' (rational) human mental and social life. Some of the later passages from Michael Lane's Introduction usefully summarise these highly contrary situations: 'The final goal of structuralism is the realisation of the whole inventory of social relations that the unconscious reason both *makes possible and restricts*' (our emphasis) (p. 34); 'Structure should be seen essentially as a syntax of transformations' (p. 35); The structural method 'encompasses both the notions of the all-embracing, and the summation of parts. This expresses itself in a rejection of any atomistic tendency, notably in its insistence that the meaning of the individual elements which are structured arises out of *and only out of* the relations of the elements to one another and their mutual interdependence' (pp. 34–5); and completely at variance with this last: 'Structure consists in elements and in law-like relations between those elements. Any "structure" which disregards those laws, or discards any of them *or any of the elements* [our emphasis] for the purpose of comparing or generalising between sets of elements, is not, by definition, a structure at all' (p. 36). Apart from the clear internal inconsistency in Lane's own views which indicates the uncertain state of structuralist theory in general, this last reference is particularly important to bear in mind when Piaget's mathematical treatment of his own structural theory is considered below in Chapters 3 and 4.

Structuralism is very relevant to the Piagetian system, especially in its later years. In 1968 Piaget published *Structuralism* in which he openly committed himself to this viewpoint although with particular qualifications. To some extent *Structuralism* constitutes a watershed in the development of the Piagetian system. After its appearance we can detect certain differences in emphasis and even in presentation of the case, that were already evident as early as 1964 in *Six Psychological Studies*, but are chiefly represented by *Prise de conscience* (1974), *Réussir et comprendre* (1975) and especially *The Development of Thought* (1978, Eng. edn) which has already been referred to.[20] The second and third are associated with new experiments which, in view of the emphasis over the years on the standard conservation and other experiments, is noteworthy in itself. But their most important aspect is the stress on a 'lag' between action and the verbal description of such action which is said to diminish as the subject grows older. Thus, in a typical example of one of these experiments where the subject(s) is asked to throw a missile with a sling, it is claimed that verbalisation and the action itself increasingly 'interact' to produce (at the advanced age) a 'geometrised' understanding of how you carry out this action constituting full maturation of the act.[21] The object of this line of thought is, of course, to stress that with structural (mathematical) abstraction, the action itself is brought under full control. What is still more pertinent to this later period of Piaget's thought is that all these experiments are designed to show that (*a*) 'awareness' (conscience–consciousness) has a reciprocal effect on action, and (*b*) the process of going from 'unawareness' to 'awareness' is one of *self-regulating correction or compensation based on a kind of feedback*. Here, we can see not only the clear influence of System Theory but also the transformational notions embedded within Structuralism.

It is not that these notions constitute a sharp break with 'traditional' Piagetianism. It is mainly a question of emphasis. *Structuralism*[22] is sometimes treated as a lightweight piece in comparison with other publications by Piaget. However, this is very much a misconception. No one should be deceived by its brevity and relatively easy style. Without doubt this book marks an important change in emphasis in the later period of Piaget's writing life. The main point is the way in which *Structuralism* straddles the traditional Piaget and the 'new' Piaget. The role of the mathematical group is still regarded as central to the understanding of cognitive structures (Piaget, 1971, pp. 17ff.), but it is not insignificant that the group designated INRC (see Chapter 4 below), which formerly plays a key role as Piaget's goal of cognitive development, receives scarcely a mention. But the main stress is that the system which Piaget describes as 'constructivism', or alternatively 'operational structuralism', is based upon a concept of structure defined by 'wholeness', 'transformation' and 'self-regulation' (Piaget, 1971, pp. 5ff.). In this definitive view we can begin to understand the nature of the change of emphasis which has occurred and which is reinforced subsequently. For example, greatly influenced by Levi-Strauss in particular, Piaget emphatically states that 'There is no structure apart from construction' and follows this with an analysis of 'strong' and 'weak' structures in a nesting (that is, inclusion-like) relation to one another, in which the logical formalisation of one structure, because it must always be 'incomplete', provides the grounds for passage to a 'stronger' structure. The extreme abstractness of this notion, Piaget argues, provides what he calls 'the formalised inverse of "genesis"' (ibid., p. 140). Structure and genesis are, therefore, 'necessarily interdependent' and 'genesis is simply transition from one structure to another, nothing more'. Novelty, or progressive development, is accounted for by the fact that 'this transition always leads from a "weaker" to a "stronger" struc- ture . . . Structure is simply a system of transformations, but its roots are operational; it depends . . . on a prior formation of the instruments of transformation – transformation rules or laws' (ibid., p. 141).

There is vastly more involved in *Structuralism* than is referred to here. What we are mainly concerned to show is that while retaining much of the 'traditional' analysis, Piaget is already embarked on a different attempt to solve the central problem of his system, the relation of the 'open' require- ments of development with the 'closed' demands of logico-mathematical structuration. Here we can detect the attempt, as it were, to 'absorb' the former into the latter by explicitly removing the notion of structure out of the system of 'structuring' and making the latter the sole reality.[23] The affinity to conventional structuralist thought is obvious. More than this, however, Piaget is attempting to adapt a notion of phases of abstraction drawn largely from the Bourbaki school of mathematical generalisation[24] and also to utilise Gödel's theorems on incompleteness and undecidability. The most interesting point is that, while doing this, Piaget is also increas- ingly turning towards 'self-regulation', particularly as he interprets it in System Theory, and the practical structuration of anthropology and lin- guistics embodied especially in the notion of 'transformation'. Now, when we place the two 'new' ideas side by side, namely, self-regulative transformation on the one hand and a hierarchy of increasingly abstract structural systems considered totally free of the factors or elements they are structuring, we can see immediately *a restatement in updated terms of the original dichotomy*. Formerly there was a problem of discontinuity in the interiorisation of action (see Chapter 2), supposed to be the foundation of mental operations in the traditional theory. The problem is now extended to the whole relation of the subject with the external world and not just the point of transition from causality to operational structures. The problem of the *mechanism* of the passage from activity to thought is present *both* in considering self-regulative transformation *and* in considering the hier- archy of increasingly abstract structural systems. In short, in this later mode of thought Piaget has not avoided the problems of his earlier approach, but to some extent they have become more obscure or more concealed than formerly. We shall consider below (Chapters 5–7) whether the restatement can in any way be said to have bypassed or solved the original problems. Again, *because* he goes searching in contemporary thought for such a solution, Piaget's latest struggles with the problem encapsulate the latest general problems in Western thought as referred to earlier.

But perhaps the very recent *The Development of Thought* has made some progress in resolving the dilemma, for it is certain that the interim publications of *Prise de conscience* and *Réussir et comprendre* are primarily concerned with expanding the self-regulatory and compensatory views of the interaction of subject and environment and not with resolving the central problem as such. In *The Development of Thought*, however, we can detect some important culminatory results of the new trend.

The book as a whole is not one of Piaget's most difficult, especially after one grasps the underlying influence of System Theory. What makes it initially hard to follow is the intention, which emerges only slowly, of recasting the basic notions of the Piagetian system in a new context, that of a basic cycle of intrusion/disturbance, self-regulation and compensation. In effect, Piaget is attempting to retain his original basic ideas while reorienting them in this new direction. For example, on the central idea of reversibility, the following passage clearly indicates the new emphasis involved in the reorientation:

> Reversibility increases with the progress of compensation. Thus it remains legitimate, *as we have always emphasised* (our emphasis), to consider the reversibility as a result of the equilibration as a complex process which takes in the psycho-genetic variations of compensating reactions and modes of comprehension or of disturbance assimilation and not as an independent process called upon to explain the equilibrium. (Piaget, 1978b, p. 71)

And again:

> The subject's co-ordinations resulting in the logico-mathematical operations, the final operational structures, achieve a compensation in a complete form, as indicated by the fact that they are reversible, and compensation exists between all operations that show relations of inversion, reciprocity, or correlativity (duality). We have long presented this reversibility as a product of the equilibration which we have followed step by step during the formative stages; we have conceived the operation as a regulation which has become 'perfect' insofar as it anticipates all the transformations and prevents errors. Now we must justify these propositions by describing the mechanism which connects the regulation with the operation, and show why the logico-mathematical structures result in complete compensations with generalised symmetries. (ibid., p. 170)

Clearly this passage refers to the INRC group and the completed formal operational stage (see Chapter 4). Yet this is not discussed or referred to except in passing. Similarly the other key notions in the original Piagetian theory, assimilation and accommodation, are restated entirely in terms of the new disturbance–self-regulation–compensation cycle:

> The characteristic of the equilibration of the cognitive systems, as opposed to physical systems, is that they are formed of schemes whose extension and comprehension can be notably enriched by the continuous dual process of assimilation and accommodation which restricts the effect of disturbance and compensating reactions entirely to the levels considered; hence, they become available for possible assimilation: what was a disturbance on the lowest level becomes an internal variation of the system on the highest levels, and what was a compensating reaction which resulted in cancellation finally plays the role of a systematic transforming agent for the variation in play. (ibid., p. 70)

But the clearest statement of the overall intention of 'integrating' the former system into something with a new emphasis is shown in the short preface most of which we give here:

> This work constitutes a complete recast of volume II of *Etudes d'épistémologie génétique* entitled *Logique et équilibre*. The models then used clearly proved to be insufficient, and it was important therefore to restudy the problem completely, particularly as this area of investigation dominates every question on the development of knowledge. The central idea is that knowledge proceeds neither solely from the experience of objects nor from an innate programming performed in the subject but from successive constructions, the result of the constant development of new structures. With this hypothesis, we can refer only to those methods required for regulations leading not to static forms of equilibrium but to reequilibrations which improve the previous structures. That is why we will be speaking of equilibration as a process – and not only of equilibriums – and above all of 'increasing equilibrations' as the manner of correcting and completing the preceding forms of equilibriums. (ibid., pp. v–vi)

The very first paragraph of Chapter I spells this intention out still further (ibid., pp. 3–4).

Although these quotations might seem unnecessarily extensive we stress that they are provided so that the significance of the actual wording may be appreciated. It is not simply a question of what Piaget is saying but *how* he is saying it here. In all the passages referred to, as indeed the book as a whole, there is a transference of responsibility for growth from structures to *structuring* (hence the change of emphasis from equilibrium to equilibration) and an attachment of assimilation and accommodation and reversibility to the disturbance–self-regulation–compensation cycle entirely as a product of this rather than existing in their own right. The mathematical treatment of the system is also radically different in *The Development of Thought* from anything that has been undertaken before by Piaget.

Interlaced with these new developments are other writings such as *Biology and Knowledge* (1972) and *Behaviour and Evolution* (1979), both of which constitute a return to earlier stages in Piaget's thinking regarding the problem of evolution in general. None the less, these areas are not free from the contemporary attempts by Piaget finally to resolve his problem: 'It is of the essence behaviour', he writes in the latest book, 'that it is for ever attempting to transcend itself and that it thus supplies evolution with its principal motor.'[25] Once again the notion of necessity which emerges *from* the event rather than antedates it is detectable. There is also a suggestion of the disturbance–self-regulation–compensation cycle. Perhaps the most disjoint piece in his later years is the reissue of the *Traité de logique* (1949) as *Logique opératoire* in 1972. We shall be looking at both of these in some detail presently and especially their similarities and differences. The later edition gives the impression of having been updated and 'corrected' mathematically only in parts, whereas elsewhere in the book everything has been left as it was. Applications are frequently quite out of joint with definitions. In fact, the fundamental ideas of the *Traité* are out of gear with the emphasis of *Structuralism* and especially *The Development of Thought*.

In sum, then, the main objective in what follows is to consider the origins and nature of novelty in the epistemological process, seen both individually and in its social context. It is maintained that this is not to be found exclusively in either logic or mathematics per se. The intrinsically closed nature of both of these conflicts with the requirement of 'openness' which novelty demands. The problem, however, remains – the same one Piaget has addressed himself to – how to reconcile the stability of things, dependent as this is on a degree of 'closure', with the indeterminacy and randomness that goes with creativity. The resolution of this problem can only be found in the fullness of the interactions of Actuality, not in the logico-mathematical extractions from them, amongst which are included the cognising subject and its milieu.

Piaget is particularly pertinent to this problem because of the claims made for Genetic Epistemology, that is, the combination of the genesis of thought and knowledge with the absolute restriction of human mental life, emotional as well as cognitive, to logico-mathematical structures. His system also demonstrates very precisely, through its logical and mathematical method of systematising mental life, a tendency far from unique to Piaget, and which is almost universal in our age, to conflate and 'collapse' into one another zones of existence which are essentially separate, and especially those of Actuality and logico–mathematics themselves.

The study of Piaget's logical and mathematical work is hence important and central, for it shows with particular clarity that if such zones are thus conflated it becomes impossible to establish relationships *between* them that make them both comprehensible, and what purports to be analysis turns out to be, at best, description. The worst aspect of such a trend is the combination of pseudo–scientific claims with the denial to the individual of any communication other than that laid down by some depersonalised and exclusively logico–mathematical authority, and his or her consequent subjection to a seemingly unchallengeable dictatorship operating something close to thought control. The tragedy of Piaget (for indeed there *is* a tragedy) is that while believing that he was preparing for a further liberation of mankind, he was in fact forging another link, or links, in the chain of its captivity.

Piaget's work has generated hostility as well as support and an incalculable flurry of activity in relation to his claimed experimental results. All of this is good for the progress of thinking around the question of the nature of human thought. Furthermore, and this is most important, an essentially descriptive system has value in so far as it can focus attention on previously unnoticed phenomena. The term 'descriptive' is chosen advisedly, for Piaget's system *does* describe (irrespective of its inner mechanism) what happens to human beings in contemporary society, governed as it is in all respects by a deep commitment to quantification, logicality and a hierarchical power deriving from both. The question is whether the developmental picture, the end product of which is formal operations, is a natural, genuinely human situation, or a deeply socially conditioned distortion. The authors have found in Piaget's thought that, virtually by dint of 'going it alone', his system encapsulates the major problems facing contemporary society and embodies the contradictions which force themselves year by year ever more stringently on all fields of human thought, investigation and existence – the immanent expression, in short, of the perennial question of being and becoming.

2 Structures, Operations and Groups in Piaget's System: A Preliminary Survey

The notion of structure, almost in the structuralist sense, is far from recent for Piaget. Thus he writes as early as 1931,[26] 'It [structure] is a form of the organisation of experience', and in *The Psychology of Intelligence* (Fr. edn, 1947), one of the earliest general theoretical books, 'Each structure ought to be understood as a particular form of equilibrium, more or less stable in its restrained field and becoming unstable at its limits' (Piaget, 1950, p. 7). Perhaps one of the most 'structuralist' definitions is this one written just before the publication of *Structuralism*: '[Structures] do not exist because of distinct notions in the consciousness of the subject, but constitute only the tools for his behaviour.'[27]

Hence for Piaget, the notion of structure itself is longstanding. Any change in approach, such as we discussed in Chapter 1, has been intended to remove the inherent problem of 'interiorisation', or how the external experiences of the subject actually change into internal mental structures, which are regarded as logico-mathematically embodied entities. Again, this is by no means a recent characteristic of Piaget's thought. We can detect the roots, even in *The Moral Judgement of the Child* (1932) and in the series of stages through which the individual is said to pass in the growth process, which is the best-known aspect of the Piagetian system. When Piaget offers as the most important characteristic of a structure 'that of closure. A structure is a closed group',[28] he is simply stating the essence of Genetic Epistemology in a handful of words. It is the identification of structures with the mathematical group as prototypical of such structures, and thus the extension, by implication, of the characteristics of the group to *mental* structures, that possibly marks Piaget out distinctly from all other structuralists.

The Connection between Logic, Psychology and the World External to the Subject

Does Piaget regard logico-mathematical structures as only models, or are they seen by him as actually inhering in cognitive activity itself? Do they actually exist in the ontological sense? In other words, are logico-mathematical structures, with their fundamental group characteristics, actually, and in fact, *equivalent* to mental processes? To approach an answer to this one must first look at the relation between psychology and logic, action and operation, as Piaget sees it, and then relate the outcome of this examination to the mathematics of cognitive structures as he applies it.

There is a fair amount of reference below to *Traité de logique: Essai de logistique opératoire* (1949), and its second edition, *Essai de logique opératoire* (1972). Consequently the abbreviations TL and LO are used for convenience. The practice is usually adopted of indicating next to the quotation from TL the equivalent pages in LO.

Early in the introductory material in TL, Piaget writes: 'If logic is a formal theory of operations of thought, psychology and sociology, or at least certain parts of these disciplines, form a real theory of the same operations: of operations effected by the individual or exchanged through language and effected in common' (TL, p. 11; LO, pp. 10–11). It is noteworthy that the only contrast drawn here is between 'formal theory' and 'real theory', but the operations of thought are the same in both cases. The distinction between 'formal' and 'real' is difficult to establish, but one supposes that the formal is the symbolic reflection of action. The concept of one-to-one correspondence (comparable with isomorphism) is clearly implied here with its attendant problem relating to genesis, or how one phenomenon originates from another. However, the phrase 'or at least certain parts of these disciplines' introduces an important implicit qualification which, while, perhaps, providing for some genetic connection between psychology, sociology and logic, also challenges the rest of the passage because of its undefined limits.

A little further on in TL, we read: 'Logic is the axiomatic of operational structures and psychology and sociology of thought study their actual functions' (TL, p. 16; LO, p. 15). Here logic is affirmed as *part of* operational structures, and the other disciplines (psychology and sociology) are intended to study their function. In this case, logic is treated as paramount and since the axioms of a system are certainly part of that system, there is no doubt that logic and operational structures emerge as identical.

Just before these references there are statements which directly relate to Piaget's concept of operations themselves. Piaget writes:

In brief, there where logic sees in these operations formal transformations whose validity rests on axioms, psycho-sociology considers these
[operations] as interiorised actions undergone collectively or in accordance with interactions between individuals, and susceptible to equilibrated co-ordination (reversible composition) in the thought of individuals and in exchanges between individuals at one and the same time.
Considering principles, it is now clear that the formal theory of
operations, or logic, and the theory of actual experience of the same
operations, or causal and genetic analysis belonging specifically to
psychology and sociology, in no way encroach on one another but on
the contrary complement each other, in a perfectly co-ordinated
manner, without any possible conflict. (TL, pp. 12–13; LO, pp. 12–13)

Earlier Piaget refers to 'the continuity between sensory-motor co-
ordinations and effective action, then between these and interiorised
actions or symbolic acts characterising thought' (TL, p. 12; LO, p. 11).

What we have here, apparently, are three tiers of the cognitive process.
The 'lowest' appears to be virtually identical with physical action and
reaction, either carried out by the subject alone or in association with
others. The next tier, which Piaget regards as the valid field of psychological study, is that of interiorisation of such actions. The third tier,
which Piaget regards as the valid field of logic, is further removed again
and is concerned only with axioms and rigorous deduction from these
axioms in respect to the psychological structures formed as a result of the
interiorisation process. This level is formalised in logical symbolism.

At the first tier, the concept of 'action', meaning actual physical action,
constitutes the connective relationship between the subject and his environment which is both personal and social. By the second tier, the connective relationship has now become an 'operation' which is unclearly related
to the previous concept of action. The link between the second and third
tiers is relatively clear in so far as the idea of 'operation', seen psychologically and logically, does not involve a *different* operation. We seem to be
dealing with the same operation here but from two different viewpoints.
There is, of course, the point that if operations are thus 'shared' by
psychology and logic and thus constitute two different aspects of the same
thing, then some other distinction between these aspects must be sought if
they are in fact to be regarded as different features of mentality. This
becomes difficult in the Piagetian system which tends to regard operations
as virtually the means of recognising the existence of structures. In short,
we do not know whether we are dealing with psychological or logical
structures – unless these are the same. In view of the importance of the
hierarchical arrangement of external action and the processes leading to
internal operations in Piaget's system, this is a serious lack of definition.
There is also a (subsidiary?) problem of transition *from* psychological *to*

logical structures comparable to the major problem of interiorisation itself.

The crucial lacuna, the unexplained 'jump' in the system, is from the 'action' in the first instance to the 'operation' in the second. The term 'interiorisation' is intended to cover this. However, this term does not explain anything but rather obscures the issue. 'Interiorisation' says no more than that something is 'taken in' from outside. Thereafter, Piaget assumes that change has occurred in this movement from outside to inside which allows him to speak of 'operations' as distinct from 'actions'. But there is nothing to specify the actual mechanism of transmutation, for it is indeed transmutation in so far as in the external situation no cognitive structures are involved whereas in the internalised situation they are.

It might be argued that the notions of assimilation and accommodation (the two aspects of Piaget's concept of adaptation), elaborated to pinpoint the exact area of contact and interaction between the cognising subject and his environment, provide such a mechanism. But here again, as with interiorisation, we are dealing with terms which simply express the view that a phenomenon, or organism, or cognising subject, is 'related' in some way to the environment in which it exists. We are, in fact, as far if not farther from explanation of the *transition* from action to operation since we are now burdened with three concepts instead of one, namely, action, adaptation (assimilation and accommodation) and operation. What is at issue here, and is an important preliminary consideration to discussing Piaget's employment of the mathematical group in his system, is the exact order in which the world of physical causality, psychology and logic, the quintessence of the development of the thought process for Piaget, relate to each other. Consideration of the following extracts helps to illustrate further Piaget's problems in relating the external and the internal worlds of the subject where logical capacity is taken to be the undisputed pinnacle of mental growth.

In the slim volume *Logic and Psychology* (1953), described by J. S. Bruner as containing 'an excellent programmatic statement of the Geneva work' in the introductory paragraphs,[29] the Author's Introduction opens with the following comment:

> The aim of this book is not to discover how psychological theories may be formalised by means of logic, but to study the application of logical techniques to the psychological facts themselves, and especially to the thought structures found at different levels of intellectual development. (Piaget, 1953, p. xvii)

Here, it seems, it is the psychological facts that are paramount and logic assumes a 'tool' role in respect to them which is a rather different position from that in the last reference from TL (see above). But even in the short introduction to *Logic and Psychology* which follows, Piaget reverts to the earlier viewpoint: 'The algebra of logic can help us to *specify* [our emphasis] psychological structures, and to put into calculus form those operations and structures central to our actual thought processes' (ibid.). Clearly, logic is now being virtually *identified* with operations and structures special to psychology. And again: 'Logic . . . facilitates the analysis of the actual structures underlying intellectual operations' (Piaget, 1953, p. xviii). Here the identification is alleviated by the use of the word 'facilitate', and by a reference to structures 'underlying' operations. But the following passage, also from *Logic and Psychology,* probably best brings together all the issues.

> Psychologically, operations are actions which are internalisible, reversible, and co-ordinated into systems characterised by laws which apply to the system as a whole. They are actions, since they are carried out on objects before being performed on symbols. They are internalisible, since they can also be carried out in thought without losing their original character of actions. They are reversible as against simple actions which are irreversible. In this way, the operation of combining can be inverted immediately into the operation of dissociating, whereas the act of writing from left to right cannot be inverted to one of writing from right to left without a new habit being acquired differing from the first. Finally, since the operations do not exist in isolation they are connected in the form of structured wholes. (Piaget, 1953, p. 8)

Here the main point of ambiguity lies with the use of the word 'action', and the description of an operation as a specific type of action. Such actions are *characterised* by being 'internalisible', 'reversible', and so on. On the other hand, they *are* actions because they are physically carried out on objects. Whereas in the passage from TL given before, which affirmed that operations in logic do not 'encroach' on psychological-social operations, but complement them, here the *same* term is being used in two totally different senses. Obviously the intention is to solve the problem of bridging the 'gap' or 'jump' between the external and internal worlds of the subject. But in doing this the vital distinction (for Piaget's system) between the external world of objects and the internal world of cognition is simply lost. The distinction between objects and symbolisation of such objects melts away. The causality of the physical world becomes indistinguishable from the logico-mathematical, inferential relations of the internal. It is, thus, not surprising that in this passage the idea of reversibility fluctuates ambiguously between the 'back and forth' movement of the outside world and logical and mathematical reversibility which has to do with propositional choices in a non-spatio-temporal frame of reference. But if one ignores the uncertainty of movement between the external and internal worlds of the subject, and concentrates alone on the way 'internalisable' is used, the problem becomes even simpler to express. If actions are designated 'operations' because they *may* be internalised, that is, are *internalisable,* by what standards does one judge them thus except that they *have already become internalised?* This is not a trivial question since it is an early pointer to a process of 'slipping' from one usage of a term to another without changing the assumed frame of reference.

But if we may detect a certain closed circularity about the nature of 'internalisation' in this passage, there are other passages elsewhere in *Logic and Psychology,* representative of another strand in Piagetian thought, which seem to offer a possible way out of this circularity. Discussing the sensory-motor stage in the child's development, Piaget writes: '[From 0–2 years] . . . in practice even this type of intelligence shows a *certain tendency* [our emphasis] towards reversibility, which is already evidence of the construction of certain invariance' (Piaget, 1953, pp. 10–11). Immediately following this, he continues: 'These co-ordinations *presuppose* [our emphasis] that the child is able to return to his starting point [reversibility], and change the direction of his movements [associativity]' (ibid.). Again: 'Towards 1½–2 years the "symbolic function" appears . . . [as a result of which] . . . interiorisation of actions into thoughts becomes possible' (ibid.).

What is important about these three typical passages is that they indicate the possibility that there is already a tendency or presence of reversibility in the subject before anything else happens in his experience. In other words, interiorisation and co-ordination are seen as at least referable to reversibility in the first instance. What this means is that (at least when Piaget wrote these and similar passages) reversibility, and hence the logico-mathematical structural foundation of reversibility, has a much more determining influence on what the subject actually does in his environment than vice versa. Operational behaviour (innate?), in short, has possibly *more* influence on actions of the subject than action on operational behaviour.

By raising the possibility of there being some such inbuilt tendencies to structuration (always identifiable by the presence of reversibility) the hint of an *independent* assessment of internalisibility is clearly offered. Were this established as truly independent, that is, that there is an innate predisposition to establish reversible and equilibrated mental states, then Piaget would, indeed, have a sort of 'way out' from the circularity we referred to earlier. But to do this he would have to opt for the predominance of a preformationist or predestined notion of development and thereby lose the creativity that he wishes to retain albeit in a strictly logico-mathematical form. In short, should Piaget opt for such predeterminism as this, the need for his system of Genetic Epistemology would disappear. We are here touching upon some of the fundamental problems of the innate versus the acquired theories that we referred to in Chapter 1, and which haunt Piaget's system from beginning to end. It is not surprising that he does not really help us on this question, and the passages that we have just quoted are simply hinting, as so many similar passages do, at the possibility of innateness but never coming down firmly on that side of the fence. In *Logic and Psychology,* as elsewhere, the two positions – the stress on innateness and the stress on individual lifetime learning – are never worked out in respect to each other, and we are left with the same 'slipping' back and forth process we have already referred to.

Perhaps some clearer idea may now be obtained of the principal features of the system which make the mathematical treatment of cognitive structures by Piaget so important. It is part of the fabric of the Piagetian edifice that development, both of the species and of the individual without preformation beyond a limited range of basic biological inheritance, is an indispensable aspect of existence. Either this development is open-ended or it is directed to definite goals. Piaget opts for the latter, although in a very impersonal sense, and embodies this notion not in any teleological theory but in the notion of universal equilibrium characteristic of all forms of existence whatsoever. Equilibrium for Piaget is always in essence logico–mathematical, and this is the real justification for Piaget's use of the concept of isomorphism. Thus cognition and its development in the individual can be presented as identical in all respects to biological evolution, and both cognition and biological evolution are reduceable to a common logico-mathematical form of equilibrated structures. Yet while this reduction is achievable, the biological, psychological and logical can all be treated as *separate* 'levels'. If, then, the logico-mathematical form of cognitive structures can be uncovered the situation will be the same as in any other branch of science. The logico-mathematical forms will be manipulable in their own right and the results will provide 'answers' to all problems connected with cognition in particular, psychology in general and the connection between both of these and biology. Thus by combining the idea of isomorphism, or even one-to-one correspondence between two collections of phenomena, with the notion of the group as the basic form of cognitive structure, the system may obviate the problems of reconciling the external and internal worlds of the subject and, more generally, of reconciling development with stability.

The emphasis on, and centrality of, the mathematical group in Piaget's system thus becomes clear. By making the group the central feature and its properties the ultimate goal and form of cognitive development, Piaget is able to present a notion of progress, step by step, from incompleteness and imperfection associated with an *inability* to manifest, in the individual's case, logico-mathematical structures in thought (only achievable in the formal operational stage after about 11 or 12 years old) to a maturation of this ability by early adulthood. The most noteworthy feature of this process is its convergence on an exclusively logico-mathematical culmination. Mature thought can *only* be logico-mathematical, can *only* be manifest in group-like structures and to a slightly lesser extent by the lattice. Later we shall have occasion to look at Piaget's concept of the emotional and social life of the individual (see below, Chapter 10). We shall leave until then an assessment of how much these are also brought under this same aegis.

The Mathematical Group

This section is devoted to an elementary introduction to mathematical groups essential for the general reader. It is hoped that, by periodic reference to the present section, it will be possible to cope with the main line of the argument in Chapters 3 and 4 which may present some technical difficulties. Those reasonably acquainted with Group Theory will not find this section necessary.

The idea of a set is a necessary starting-point for the understanding of groups, and the orthodox mathematical definition of a set is simply a collection of 'things' (called elements by mathematicians) which have some property in common and which may be numbers, or physical objects, or non-physical phenomena, or actions, or anything you like. Examples of sets as mathematicians understand them are: the set of months in a year, the set of words on this page, the set of even numbers between two and ten (inclusive), the set of all the even numbers. This last set is infinitely large since there is no end to these numbers.

There are problems attached to this definition of a set which are discussed later (see Chapter 8). For the moment orthodox mathematical usage is followed since it is the logical foundations and not the instrumentality of Set Theory as it stands which requires further thought. It is useful to recall in this connection that the calculus was used in practice perfectly well for some 200 years before the rigorous definition of a limit.

A *group* is a special sort of set which in addition to having *elements* has a rule for combining them, the *rule of combination* with certain essential properties. Often the word 'operation' is used for the rule of combination. We shall always use the latter term to describe the group operation in order to avoid confusion. The following is an example of a group. Take two coins and put them on the table with heads uppermost and consider four possible *actions* on them. These four *actions* will be the *elements* of the group. Each action consists of simply turning over one or two coins or neither coin. These actions are:

(1)   Turn the right-hand coin over (call this R)
(2)   Turn the left-hand coin over (call this L)

(3)   Turn both coins over (call this *B*)
(4)   Turn neither coin over (call this *N*)

Now, what happens when we *combine* any one of these actions (that is, the elements of the group) with any other? What happens, for example, when we perform action *L* and then action *B,* that is, turn the *left*-hand coin over and then turn *both* coins over? It is as if the action 'turn the right-hand coin over' has been performed alone. This can be written in a sort of shorthand: $L \star B = R$. In this shorthand, '$\star$' means 'combined with' or 'followed by' or 'and then'. The results of combining different actions can be summarised in a table like the one below (Table 2.1). In this table, the effect of doing *L* and then *R* is the same as doing *B*; the effect of doing *L* and then *B* would be the same as doing *R*, and so on.

Table 2.1

$\star$	N	R	L	B
N	N	R	L	B
R	R	N	B	L
L	L	B	N	R
B	B	L	R	N

This method of recording and summarising in a table is not unlike multiplication, as is shown by Table 2.2 in which the entries in row 3 are the results of multiplying each of the numbers in the top line by 3.

Table 2.2

$\times$	1	2	3	4
1	1	2	3	4
2	2	4	6	8
3	3	6	9	12 (row 3)
4	4	8	12	16

If we examine the two tables more closely, we will see that, although they show some similarities, they also display certain differences and some of these differences are crucial in the mathematical definition of a group. Looking more closely at the first table, which has been deliberately chosen because it *does* represent a group, we can see that it consists of a set of *elements* (in this case the actions on the coins) together with a rule of combination, in this case 'combined with', 'followed by', or 'and then'. It is important to realise that the elements in this case are *not* the coins. Neither are they related to whether the coins are 'heads up' or 'tails up'. The elements are the *actions*, in this example, the 'turn' which the coins are subject to. Even more important is the fact that there has to be a rule of combination between elements in order to provide a table of combination like the one given.

We have chosen the above elements and rule of combination knowing in advance that they constitute a group. But is *any* set of elements together with any rule of combination a group? A *necessary* (but not sufficient) condition for a group is to be a set of elements with a rule (or law) of combination. In addition, a group must obey four rules – which we will see is the case for the first table above but not always with the second.

(1) THE RULE OF CLOSURE

This means that if any two elements of the set are combined, the result must be an element still in the set. In this case, whatever two actions you do to the coins, you always get a result N or R or L or B. The first table above for combining any two elements shows that the 'answer' (in the body of the table) is always N or R or L or B. Contrast this with the second (multiplication) table where several of the entries in the table are *not* the original elements 1, 2, 3 and 4.

(2) THE RULE OF ASSOCIATIVITY

This is more difficult to understand. An example with numbers might help to clarify what 'associativity' means. When ordinary whole numbers are added, it is well known that, for example, $(2 + 3) + 4 = 2 + (3 + 4) = 2 + 3 + 4$. In other words, you get the same answer to '2 + 3 + 4' whether you add 2 and 3 first and then add 4 or whether you add 2 to the result of adding 3 and 4. Here, we say that addition is *associative* for the whole numbers. What this means is that the end result is the same irrespective of the way you add up. A simple practical example may help to make this still clearer. When you make a cup of tea, you have three items to consider – tea, milk and sugar (granted you take all these). Here,

(tea + milk) + sugar = cup of tea

equally, tea + (milk + sugar) = cup of tea.

Most people do not add tea to a mixture of milk and sugar, and in fact this would make a very small difference to the taste according to the connoisseur, but the difference is small enough for the example to make the mathematics clearer. What does this mean for the Table 2.1? Remembering that '$\star$' stands for 'combined with' or 'followed by' or 'and then', it means that for the set and its rule of combination to form a group, an equality like the following must hold for all possible combinations of elements:

$$(R \star L) \star B = R \star (L \star B) = R \star L \star B$$

The reader can check for himself that the above associativity holds for the group. In fact, multiplication of the numbers 1, 2, 3 and 4 in Table 2.2 is also associative, so that both tables show this property.

(3) THE IDENTITY ELEMENT RULE

There must be an element of the set that, combined with any element of the set, has no effect on it at all. In Table 2.1 the identity element is N, meaning 'turn neither coin'. In the table, it can be seen that:

$$N \star R = R \qquad \text{Also:} \quad R \star N = R$$
$$N \star L = L \qquad\qquad\quad\ L \star N = L$$
$$N \star B = B \qquad\qquad\quad\ B \star N = B$$
$$N \star N = N \qquad\qquad\quad N \star N = N$$

Thus 'N' operating on any element leaves it unchanged. Compare this with the Table 2.2 in which the identity element is 1. Multiplying any number by 1 similarly does not change the number.

(4) THE INVERSES RULE

Corresponding to every element of the set there has to be another element such that, when they are combined by the rule of combination, the result is the identity element. Looking at the table again, and taking L as an example, it is clear that L combined with L gives N. L is the inverse of L and we say that L is its own inverse. This only happens in special cases. Very often in a group, the inverses of the elements are not themselves, but are other elements: for example, considering the infinite set of integers under addition, the identity element is 0 and, for example, the inverse of $+5$ is -5 because $(+5) + (-5) = 0$. This situation differs from that of the multiplication table shown previously, where the only elements of the set available were 1, 2, 3, 4. It can be checked that each element in the group we are considering has an inverse and that each element is its own inverse. It is clear, now, that the set of elements, N, R, L, B together with the rule of combination 'combined with', or 'followed by', or 'and then', obeys all four rules for groups, and so the set of elements together with the rule of combination is a group.

Again, the ordinary multiplication table does not include inverses because, apart from $1 \times 1 = 1$, there are no other entries that give the answer 1 (the identity element is 1). So the multiplication table shows associativity and has an identity element but it does not display closure and does not have inverses (other than 1). So it does not represent a group as the first example does.

Here are some further examples in which one or more of the above four rules does not hold. These are provided to give additional understanding of the very special character of a group.

(a)   No closure

Example: The set of chemical elements together with the rule of chemical combination is not closed since the result of combining any two elements goes outside the set.

(b)   Not associative

Example (1): Consider a piece of bread, butter and jam. It makes a great deal of difference whether you put butter on the bread and *then* add jam, or, alternatively, add the butter to the jam, and then add both to the bread! Example (2): The counting numbers 1, 2, 3, 4, . . . but not including zero, with the rule of combination being subtraction. $(5 - 2) - 1 \neq 5 - (2 - 1)$.

(c)   No identity element

Example: In the counting numbers, 1, 2, 3, 4, . . . but not including zero, if the rule of combination is addition, there is no element which can be added to other elements and make no difference to them (e.g. $2 + 3 = 5$). There is no element which can be added to 2 and give the answer 2. If, however, we included zero in the set, this number would be the identity element since 'zero plus any number equals the same number'.

(d)   No inverses

Example: If the set consists of the *actions* of eating various foods in a meal and the rule of combination is 'followed by' or 'combined with' or 'and then', no element in the set has an inverse as you cannot 'de-eat' by eating something else.

Finally, there is a special case of a group called *commutative* in which you can interchange any two elements and obtain the same result: for example, in the integers under addition, $2 + 3 = 3 + 2$. An example of a non-commutative situation from everyday life is putting on socks and putting on shoes. It makes a great deal of difference which way round you do this.

Group Theory is a relatively modern mathematical development, although some of its most important basic concepts were arrived at in the course of last century. At one stage, somewhere around the First World War and the decade following it, Group Theory acquired a considerable significance among mathematicians as it was found to be widely applicable. That view has been somewhat modified in more recent times with the emergence of many different abstract mathematical structures.

The attraction of Group Theory for Piaget is probably the fact that it deals with entirely *closed* situations in which all factors are known and are related to one another by an absolutely definitive law. The group condition cannot admit of any form of uncertainty or unpredictability. By being absolute in this way it corresponds very well to Piaget's notion of equilibrium, provided all questions of developmental change are either excluded or treated as a form of logical unfolding interior to a situation and without reference to external factors or forces. These features, of course, are true of other mathematical structures. But at the time Piaget was laying the foundations of his system these were not as well known generally. Perhaps twenty or thirty years later Piaget would have had a bigger problem in selecting a structure as a model for equilibrium. As it was, a structure known as the lattice (see below, Chapter 4) had to be incorporated.

Without doubt the group idea is connected with that aspect of life concerned with stability. It involves the most economical extraction of the purely stable aspects of real life situations to the exclusion of any disturbing or intrusive factors that may overthrow them. Thus, by adopting the group as the model for a 'unit' of cognition (a structure), Piaget gives himself a particularly sharp problem in attempting to relate the developmental process, equally essential to this system, with such an absolute concept of stability as is embodied in Group Theory.

It should now be possible to pass on and consider, in a preliminary way, Piaget's handling of the group.

Piaget's Use of the Group

In the light of Piaget's view of cognitive structures which must, by his definition, manifest wholeness and also reversibility as 'no doubt the most clearly defined characteristic of intelligence' (Piaget, 1950, p. 41), the applicability of group structure was a very feasible one. For wholeness and reversibility are easy to relate to closure and inverses as precise mathematical expressions of them. Although he was writing about this in a preliminary form from the late 1930s, the first fully developed account of his thought on the 'logic of operations' did not appear until 1949, when *Traité de logique: Essai de logistique opératoire* appeared. Soon afterwards this book was heavily criticised in a review by E. Beth ('Apropos d'un "Traité de logique"' *Methodus,* 1950, pp. 258–64), and later Piaget himself expresses disapproval of the title in *Insights and Illusions* (1972), ascribing responsibility for it to the publisher. It is possible that Piaget felt that the main title implied too exact an interpretation of his intentions regarding the precision with which mathematics should be applied to cognition.

TL appeared in a second edition in 1972, as *Essai de logique opératoire,* and this revised the earlier edition in certain ways. Other, intermediate, statements appeared over the years between, but these two books are used here as the basis for the analysis since TL is the first definitive statement regarding the 'logic of operations' and LO is the latest, and a relatively recent one.

The group is 'defined' in TL (p. 92) and an exact translation of this is given by W. Mays in *Logic and Psychology* (pp. xiv–xv):

One example of a group . . . is the system of positive and negative numbers characterised by the operation $+ n$ (addition of an integer).

It obeys the four conditions.

1. Two operations of the system have for their resultant a new operation of the system $+ 1 + 1 = 2$.
2. Every operation of the system can be annulled by an inverse operation $+ 2 - 2 = 0$.
3. There exists one, and only one, identity operator (0) which is the resultant of every operation and its inverse, and such that when applied to any operation it does not change it: $+ 1 - 1 = 0$ and $1 \pm 0 = 1$.
4. The operations are associative $(4 + 2) - 3 = 4 + (2 - 3)$.

Remembering that the word often used for 'rule of combination' is 'operation' with respect to structures such as the group, this definition presents its first surprise since the word 'operation' (and operator) is used throughout where one would have expected 'element'. However, in his cognitive structures Piaget's *elements are mental operations,* so we must keep in mind the possibility that this fact might resolve an apparent idiosyncrasy.

Condition 1 embodies the essential issue. For if the word 'operation' here refers to group element (and bearing in mind that the elements were previously referred to as 'the system of positive and negative numbers'), '$+ 1 + 1 = 2$' raises problems of notational ambiguity. For, if the elements are integers and the system is 'characterised by the operation [meaning rule of combination] $+ n$', that is, *addition* of an integer, then this is, at the very least, an oddity since the rule of combination should be simply '$+$'. It is, in fact, wrong to include the element (integer) in the operation. However, if Piaget is given the benefit of the doubt and it is assumed that the set of integers under addition is being referred to, for the integers under addition do form a group, then the above should be written either

$$1 + 1 = 2$$
$$\text{or } (+1) + (+1) = (+2)$$
$$\text{or more contemporarily } (^+1) + (^+1) = (^+2).$$

But, in this case, the elements are *numbers* and not operations as implied in Condition 1. On the other hand, if Piaget's word 'operation' is given the same meaning throughout, and thus the elements of the system are operations and not integers, such as 'the operation $+ n$', then Condition 1, '$+ 1 + 1 = 2$', lacks a rule of combination. To introduce one a *different symbol* is necessary, for example, '$\star$'. Condition 1 should then read: $(+ 1) \star (+ 1) = (+ 2)$. In this case, the elements cannot be integers but must signify 'actions' or 'operations' such as 'add 1', 'add 2' (or 'move 1', 'move 2').

This is in accord with Condition 1 which refers to 'Two *operations* of the system [which] have for their resultant a new *operation* of the system' (our emphasis). Conditions 2 and 3 can similarly be tidied up and Condition 4 reworded in accordance with this interpretation. It is clear that the source of the confusion lies in the use of the word 'operation' to mean simultaneously 'element' and 'rule of combination'. Further, from a typographical viewpoint, it is very likely that Piaget intends simple addition and subtraction by his + and − signs used without brackets and at a distance from the numerals to which they are assigned.

It might well be argued that, in considering mental operations, the rule of combination is *assumed* to be 'combined with' or 'followed by' or is, perhaps, best taken as 'and then', and that very often, following such an assumption, the symbol for such a rule is omitted in more abstract theory, just as in elementary algebra '*ab*' is written for '$a \times b$'. But the essential factor here is that the rule is quite specific and is *there* by implication. It is precisely a lack of such specificity that characterises the foregoing account. The remaining Conditions 2, 3 and 4 would also make some sense if the elements are taken to be (mental) operations, and if there is an understood (but unspecified) rule of combination, 'and then'. Thus 4 could be read as:

(Add 4 (and then) add 2) (and then) subtract 3 gives the same result as:
Add 4 (and then) (add 2 (and then) take away 3).

In all these cases, (+ 1), (− 2), etc., are elements which are actual operations such as 'add 1'. But an understood, but unspecified, rule of combination cannot be reliably extracted from Piaget's conditions as given in the passage. The ambiguity of the notation lies in the fact that it allows for (*a*) the possibility of alternative interpretations of the elements, that is, *either* integers *or* (mental) operations, and (*b*) alternative interpretations of the word 'operation', that is, as element of the group or rule of combination. The situation is further confused by the suggestion, particularly in Conditions 2, 3 and 4, of *two* rules of combination, or group operations, namely, +, −, which is certainly implied if Piaget's word 'operation' were taken in the group operational sense. The confusion arises precisely through the ambiguous (in fact contradictory) use of the word 'operation', as we have described, simultaneously with an absence of specification of the rule of combination which is the case if Piaget's word 'operation' means 'element'. One could use the word 'operation' in two senses provided one can qualify the use of the rule of combination by speaking of '*group* operation'. Thus one could have a group whose elements are *operations,* under a rule of combination called a *group operation,* but the word operation would have here two distinct meanings.

This is not simply a mathematical issue. In the discussion of action, operation and structure in the first section, we saw how the meanings of these terms *vacillated* between reference to the subject's internal, mental, world of cognition, and his external environment. Piaget's cognitive structures are internal to the subject. Their 'elements' are said to be operations and their form is meant to be related to group structure. Piaget's treatment of the group in TL manifests the same vacillation as we saw before. 'Operation' may mean (*a*) mental operation (*element* of the group) or (*b*) group operation (rule of combination), and, corresponding to this, the elements of his group are mental operations (add 1, add 2, etc.) or (*c*) external elements (here integers $+1$, -2, etc.). Fluctuations in what constitutes the element and what constitutes the rule of combination make it possible to vacillate between an internal (operational) interpretation of his structures and an external (non-operational) interpretation. We find the same type of ambiguity occurring throughout TL.

In 1972 LO appeared as the second edition of TL, and certain changes are apparent. The following is a translation of the latest definition of the group taken from LO:

> *The 'group'.* – The 'group' represents in all probability the most basic of mathematical structures. The system of whole numbers Z provides an example. Let us interpret the elements of Z as operators. Thus $+ 3$ will mean 'to add 3', $- 4$ will mean 'to subtract 4', and 0 will mean 'neither add nor remove'. Now let o be the operation which consists of composition between two elements of Z thus interpreted according to the ordinary laws of arithmetic. One will have, for example: $(- 4) \text{ o } (+ 3) = - 1$
>
> To say that Z forms a group in relation to the operation o, is to say that:
>
> 1. To each pair of elements of Z, o produces a corresponding element of Z.
> 2. The operation o is associative.
> 3. There exists in Z a neutral element 0, such that for any $x \, \varepsilon \, Z$ there is: $x \text{ o } 0 = x$.
> 4. To every element x of Z there corresponds an inverse element y, which is $-x$ and such that $x \text{ o } y = x \text{ o } (-x) = 0$. Moreover, this group is abelian, that is to say that:
> 5. For any $x, y \, \varepsilon \, Z$, we have $x \text{ o } y = y \text{ o } x$. (p. 88)

This certainly reads much more like the normal definition of a group. But some doubt stirs when one notices the use of inverted commas as in 'group'. There is a suggestion here that what is being defined is not a true group, yet it is referred to as 'the most basic of mathematical structures'. There is, however, a clear 'composition' and rule of combination and elements are distinguished from this rule.

But a major problem remains and it arises in the first paragraph. It is not now the operation which immediately is in question but the element. These are said to be 'The system of whole numbers Z'. Thus, the elements are *integers*. The next two sentences contradict this for now the elements have become 'to add 3' or 'to subtract 4', that is, actions or operations (on integers or only on positive integers?). Hence, although the rule of combination is distinctly recognised as compared with TL, the ambiguity remains by which the elements may be either numbers or operations, with the same problem of indeterminate dualism as before.

The group operation is not unimportant even in LO. First, although signified by 'o' its character is left unspecified except by the words 'composition' and 'produces'. Then, in the example given, an identification with + 'slips in' even though the first mention of 'o' refers it to the '*laws* of arithmetic' (our emphasis). Since the integers actually do form a group under addition but not under subtraction, multiplication, or division, the nature of the rule of combination must be specified if integers are actually being referred to. Thus, although signifying a rule of combination, LO still leaves the ambiguity of the element unchanged and in addition vacillates with regard to the rule of combination between generality and specificity.

We would expect that, in line with the changed definition of a group in LO, the remainder of the book would receive correspondingly new treatment. This is not, however, the case. As examples we have included in the Appendix to this chapter two passages from TL and the two corresponding passages from LO for comparison. As expected, the first has been altered in LO and now deals quite correctly with disjoint mathematical sets which form a group under symmetric difference. However, the second passage in LO remains exactly as it was in TL. And yet, it is precisely this passage which refers to logical operations and is therefore particularly applicable to Piaget's cognitive theory, and which we might above all expect to see altered. The first passage, after all, although important, is dealing with sets, purely mathematical phenomena, and not, at this point, particularly related to the cognising subject. Moreover, they have already an accepted treatment in mathematics itself. The authors have made a survey of the two books and it is clear that, apart from minor notational alterations, the overwhelming bulk of LO is identical with TL. The alteration we have given as an example is in fact exceptional. One gains a strong impression that only certain specifically mathematical definitions have been altered in LO but that the cognitive conclusions drawn from these have been left unchanged. Which makes it rather useful to look at another definition of the mathematical group taken from *Structuralism*.

This book, published in 1968, is without doubt from Piaget's own hand whereas LO certainly looks as if Professor J.-B. Grize, under whose name it is 'établi', was given the responsibility of 'correcting' the purely mathematical errors of the original leaving the interpretations by Piaget virtually untouched. Thus, the definition of a group from *Structuralism*:

> A mathematical group is a system consisting of a set of elements (e.g. the integers, positive and negative) together with an operational rule of combination (e.g. addition) and having the following properties:

1. Performed upon elements of the set, the combinatory operation yields only elements of the set;
2. The set contains a neuter or identity element (in the given case, 0) such that, when it is combined with any other element of the set, the latter is unaffected by the combinatory operation (in the given case, $n + 0 = n$ and, since addition is commutative, $n + 0 = 0 + n = n$);
3. The combinatory operation has an inverse in the system (here subtraction) such that, in combination with the former, the latter yields the neuter or identity element $(+ n - n = 0)$;
4. The combinatory operation (and its inverse) is associative $([n + m] + 1 = n + [m + 1])$. (Piaget, 1971, p. 18)

Here, the definition is unexceptionable until we reach Condition 3 when the definition suddenly goes haywire! The word 'element' is dropped and it is the 'combinatory operation' (implicitly addition) which is alleged to have an inverse, spelt out as 'subtraction'. Condition 4 repeats this. In earlier works, there was the possibility of different interpretations of the nature of the element, but here there is no such possibility. Yet the confusion between element and operation remains with a clear affirmation of a second rule of combination, subtraction.

What conclusions can be drawn from all this? It is not possible to take any complete 'block' definition and categorically state that it is all wrong. What is 'wrong' is that in any passage, according to the different assumptions made about the element and what Piaget means by operation, different parts of the passage will be 'right' or 'wrong'. It is in this variability that the nature of the error lies and which creates the possibility of 'slipping' from one interpretation to another at will.

It may well be said that such a conclusion is insufficiently precise. Are Piaget's 'groups' real groups or not? The issue here is not whether the integers under addition (or certain sets under symmetric difference, or logical propositions under exclusive disjunction) are groups (see the Appendix at the end of this chapter). This is well established mathematically. What is at issue is whether Piaget's 'groups' of (mental) operations form groups. And this is why the confusions we have been discussing are more than mere notational oddity. The main points of the argument are:

(1) In TL, if the elements are taken as integers and the rule of combination is +, then the definition can be taken as oddly expressed, but acceptable. If, however, the elements are taken as operations, then the group rule of combination is absent. This can be inserted and the definition reworded, but the issue is not settled as to which meaning is intended since Piaget vacillates from one to the other.

(2) In LO, the definition has been largely corrected, but it is still unclear whether the element is intended to be the integer or operation. Vacillation between the two interpretations remains. Moreover, the lack of specificity of the group operation here obscures the fact that the integers do not form a group under *all* operations, and thus also obscures the fact that this is the case for *any* set and will certainly be relevant when Piaget's 'groups' of cognitive operations are considered.

(3) The first passage quoted in the Appendix from TL, referring to sets, exhibits similar vacillation in meaning. If sets, as such, are the elements then, of course, they have group structure (under symmetric difference). But if the elements are operations *upon* sets, then the rule of combination is again lacking. Once more, this can be inserted but the interpretation is still an open question.

(4) The third passage in the Appendix is subject to the same argument. Of course, the set of simple logical propositions (under exclusive disjunction) exhibits group structure. But Piaget vacillates in his conception of the element from logical proposition (p) to operation (p w q) with the inevitable problem regarding the rule of combination.

(5) The second passage in the Appendix taken from LO, corresponding to the first passage in the Appendix from TL, has been completely corrected and is now an unexceptionable demonstration of the group structure of sets under symmetric difference.

(6) The fourth passage in the Appendix taken from LO, corresponding to the third passage in the Appendix from TL, remains as in TL.

Now, there is a well-known theorem in Group Theory, Cayley's Theorem, which proves that any group is isomorphic to a group of permutations (that is, a form of *operation or transformation*). Would this, in any way, solve the Piagetian problem? No, because this does not imply that any set of operations (permutations) is isomorphic to an *established* group. The group structure of any set of operations still remains to be proved in itself. And furthermore, as far as Piaget is concerned, his 'operations' are mental and it is by no means given, it is simply implied in his wording that they can be treated like mathematical operations, for example, permutations. Nowhere is it demonstrated by Piaget that cognitive-mental operations (under a rule of combination) have group structure.

This would be open to question particularly in relation to the identity element and inverses condition. First, what meaning could be attached to a cognitive operation which, when interacting with another, had no effect on it? The only possibility is 'no operation' which simply states the *non-existence* of an identity element. This particular point is relevant beyond the mathematics in itself. For it raises the issue of mathematics in a field to which it may not be applicable, or, at least, in a manner which is illegitimate. It is inconceivable that one mental operation impinging on another can do so with zero effect! Such a proposition is as unacceptable as the application of the uniqueness condition of Group Theory, which says that there can be only one result from the combination of two group elements, to the activities of human thought. In the latter case we would be left with the notion that one thought combined with another thought yields one, and one only, new thought.

Secondly, can every cognitive operation have an inverse? This would depend upon the nature of the rule of combination. This point *alone* would render the group structure of cognitive operations strictly conditional. Such conditionality shows that, even if 'inversion' or 'taking the inverse' were considered to be a second rule of combination, this would make no difference at all to the argument. For sets with this additional rule of combination would still not be groups, because if the inversion rule did not apply given one form of group definition (with one rule of combination) due to lack of inverses, then it would not apply in the other (with inversion as a second rule of combination) for exactly the same reason.

The muddle arising from the basic confusion between element and operation derives from a threefold use of the word 'operation':

(*a*)   as a rule of combination for a group;
(*b*)   for a standard operation such as + or −;
(*c*)   for a cognitive (mental) operation.

Each of these is possible in itself, but throughout his system Piaget vacillates between these three meanings and in the course of this the word 'operation' is used in such a way as to suggest that group structure has been shown to exist for mental cognitive operations when in fact it remains an initial assumption.

Despite seeming mathematical symbolisation in TL and LO we find in the end that the Piagetian system does not have sound logico-mathematical foundations, but turns out to be simply a 'symbolic' representation of notions already rooted in Piaget's original beliefs before he ever embarked upon a mathematical exposition. Piaget's systems of operations, as he deals with them, do not have group structure.

Let us suppose for a moment, though, that such mental structures do in fact exist independent of Piaget's claims for them. Let us return to a question raised in the beginning of this chapter: are the structures Piaget conceives supposed to inhere in the cognitive process or is the system intended to be a model? Of course the exactitude of the mathematical content of a scientific theory is not exemplified in Actuality. There is always a discrepancy between the model and the modelled, and this discrepancy is ultimately a source of challenge to the theory itself. So, if Piaget's system is to be taken 'only' as a model, then the foregoing discussion, although a serious criticism, would not have the same significance as if the system were intended as an actual condition of cognition, independent of the modelling process involved in uncovering and describing it. Perhaps the strongest evidence of Piaget's acceptance of the latter situation lies in his use of the notion of isomorphism. For his application of this carries with it an affirmation of identical structural characteristics to be found in *separate*, but undoubtedly *existent*, regions of biology, psychology, social organisation and logic.

Nevertheless, we are not absolutely certain whether his cognitive structures *are* inherently manifestations of groups or alternatively are thought to be organised *like* groups. The distinction is important, for in the first case the whole of mentality is pre-empted by logico-mathematics and there is no room for anything else, whereas in the second case the model may be true to itself but it is not necessarily inclusive of all mental activity precisely because, like all models, it is abstracted from its source. The following collection of references is only a sample of Piaget's uncertainty on this point. On the whole, in these references, he appears to lean more to the notion of inherence than not.

The object's permanent character results from the organisation of the spatial field, which is brought about by the co-ordination of the child's movements. These co-ordinations presuppose that the child is able to return to his starting-point (reversibility), and to change the direction of his movements (associativity), and hence they *tend to take on the form of a 'group'* [our emphasis]. The construction of this first invariant is thus a resultant of reversibility in its initial phase. *(Logic and Psychology,* 1953, p. 10)

In the problem of the conservation of motion, we encounter the simplest form of the operational schema related to group structure, for the construction of this motion by the adolescent rests directly on formal reversibility by inversion. In the equilibrium problems, of which the problem of communicating vessels gives us a first example, we come to a more complex variety of schema *resting on group structure* [our emphasis]. In every equilibrium the two possible forms of reversibility operate simultaneously: *inversion,* which corresponds to the additions or eliminations affected in the parts of the system which come into equilibrium, and *reciprocity,* which corresponds to the symmetry or compensations between these parts (thus to actions which are both equivalent as regards their respective products and orienting in opposite directions). But, inversions and reciprocities *also form a group* [our emphasis] between themselves. (*The Growth of Logical Thinking,* Inhelder and Piaget, 1958, p. 133).

Operational reversibility is the inverse of the direct (or thetic) operation. Corresponding to this form of reversibility, we have operational identity which is the product of a direct operation and its inverse (e.g. $+ 1 - 1 = 0$). Operational identity and reversibility *depend on logical 'groupings' or mathematical 'groups'* [our emphasis]. (*The Child's Conception of Geometry,* Piaget *et al.,* 1960, p. 330).

As the primary assimilation schemes become mutually co-ordinated ('reciprocally assimilated'), certain equilibrated structures, those that make for a modicum of 'reversibility', become established. Most striking among these are, first, the 'practical' group of displacements, *which corresponds* to the displacement group described in section (5) [our emphasis] (i.e. the ordinary mathematical group of displacements). (*Structuralism,* 1968 (Eng. edn, 1971), pp. 63–4)

The central problem is the confusion of physical Actuality with its logical and mathematical mappings. Examples are helpful here. There are two well-known experiments described by Piaget, the first in connection with what he calls conservation of number and the second to do with conservation of quantity. In the first case, a given number of counters are placed on a surface and the subject is questioned about the number of counters before and after rearrangement. The ability to see that the number remains the same ('conservation') is said by Piaget to depend upon the subject's grasp of 'reversibility'. In another well-known experiment, liquid is poured from a vessel into one of a different shape and the subject is similarly questioned about the conservation of the quantity of liquid. Again, understanding of conservation is said to depend upon the subject's grasp of reversibility. The situation in both these experiments is very artificial. First, neither takes account of possible circumstances which would destroy one of the counters or lose liquid in transfer from vessel to vessel. But such factors are more typical of actual life experience than not. Most people's experience of the transfer of liquid is in situations like pouring a glass of milk or a cup of tea, which is then drunk. Here, there is no 'reversibility' and 'conservation' is largely meaningless. The experience of number in everyday life is very often that it is *not* 'conserved'. If six sweets are laid out on a table, the usual rearrangement of them is to remove and eat them. This is certainly a non-reversible situation and hence cannot involve conservation in itself. If the sweet is eaten it cannot be uneaten. It is the rule of combination that links the group with conservation as it provides the conditionality for inverses. If elements are confused with operations (as above), thus removing the actual rule of combination, it is not possible to recognise the absence of inverses and, therefore, the absence of logical reversibility and, finally, the lack of conservation, in the case under consideration.

The confusion between spatio-temporal, logical and mathematical zones, referred to above, is a *conflation* of these distinct zones, and it is essential that they are separated out from each other. Actually, a sweet can be replaced after being moved only under specific circumstances. This 'circumstantiality' makes the mapping of reversal in Actuality *only* by reversibility, without qualification, in the logical zone, impossible. The map of such 'circumstantiality' in the logical zone is to be found in the axiomatic limitations of the logical system as applied to the specific case. The mathematical mapping (into the general group) is to be distinguished from this. The reversal and the circumstances of this reversal are respectively mapped into the inverse(s) and the rule of combination of the group. It is the last which maps 'circumstantiality' since the specific events in Actuality (eating or not-eating or simple rearrangement) provide the circumstances determining whether a return to the starting-point is possible. It is these circumstances which are mathematically mapped into the 'rule of combination'.

Piaget refers to Actuality and its logical mapping by the same term 'reversibility' and then identifies this with (mathematical) inverses, thus conflating the three distinct zones, or dimensions. The result is that the circumstantiality of the situation, which is the *source* of novelty, is suppressed. For Piaget, reversibility and conservation are absolute, that is, non-circumstantial.

What actually happens can be seen quite easily when the three zones of Actuality, logic, and mathematics are disentangled. If the sweets are not eaten, but are rearranged and then returned to their original positions, the notion of the circumstantiality, which is mapped logically into reversibility and mathematically into inverses, is different from the case when one or more are consumed. If, however, the sweet is eaten, it cannot be put back, and there can be no logical reversibility (or conservation), nor has the mathematical element an inverse *and there is no group*. All that may be said, as regards the logical and mathematical mapping in this case, is that there is non-reversibility and no inverses. This is not simply negative since it is a mapping of positive circumstances and an identification of the *conditions* under which a particular part of experience operates.

If, on the other hand, such real life situations are translated straight into

Group Theory terms as is done by Piaget, and if the group operation is 'followed by' or 'and then', then with non-reversed situations the element turns out to have no inverse. Additionally, since the cognitive structures as Piaget conceives them depend on this for their reversibility, these structures end up with no reversibility and, of course, no conservation! Put this way, the mathematical anomalies when fully exposed reveal the fundamental contradictoriness of the system as a whole deriving, as it does, from identifying the process of development, characterised by circumstantiality, or contingency, with logico-mathematical stability which excludes all forms of indeterminacy.

Appendix to Chapter 2

Translations of Group Identifications from *Traité de logique*
and *Logique opératoire*

(A)
The group character of the disjoint subsets of a set under the rule of
combination known as symmetric difference (TL, p. 92):

> Now, there are certain elementary groups of interest to the theory of
> sets ['ensembles']. These are the groups that B. A. Bernstein has ex-
> tracted from Boole's algebra of classes, viz., the group consisting of the
> addition of disjoint parts ['parties'] and that of equivalences. We shall
> return to this at greater length when we deal with the calculus of
> propositions (Chapter VI, Section 36), but before we do so we should
> discover whether these groups accord with the classification.
>
> In a universal [Fr. 'total'] set formed of subsets ['sous-ensembles']
> interlinking [Fr. 'interférant'] among themselves in different ways, one
> can distinguish the disjoint parts ($E\overline{F}$ and $\overline{E}F$ for the sets E and F) and the
> conjoint parts (EF and $\overline{EF}$). Now the disjoint parts form among them-
> selves an additive group of which the operation is their union. Let us
> designate by the symbol w this operation which consists in the union of
> the disjoint parts and let A_1; A_2; A_3; etc. be the disjoint parts interacting
> [Fr. 'en jeu'] in a classification. It is clear that, if the operation w
> determines the sum of two disjoint parts, the expression A_1 w A_1 will be
> equivalent to 0 since A_1 is not itself disjoint: the operation w thus
> constitutes in this case its own inverse. One can then characterise as
> follows the operations of the group:

> 1. *The direct operation* is the addition of two disjoint parts: A_1 w A_2
> 2. *The inverse operation* will be equivalent to a subtraction: A_1 w A_1 =
>   0; or $(A_1$ w $A_2)$ w $A_2 = A_1$
> 3. *The identity operation* will be 0: that is A_1 w $A_1 = 0$ and A_1 w $0 = A_1$
> 4. The operations are *associative*: $(A_1$ w $A_2)$ w $A_3 = A_1$ w $(A_2$ w $A_3)$.

(B)
The group character of the disjoint subsets of a set under the rule of
combination known as symmetric difference (LO, pp. 88–9):

> Now, there are certain elementary groups of interest to the theory of
> sets. ['ensembles']. These are the groups that B. A. Bernstein has
> extracted from Boole's algebra classes, viz., the group consisting of the

addition of disjoint parts ['parties'] and that of equivalences. We shall return to this at greater length when we deal with the calculus of propositions (Chapter VI, Section 36), but before we do so we should discover whether these groups are applicable to the classification.

Let there be a set E and $T(E)$ the set of its parts ['parties']. If A and B are any two parts of E whatever (two elements of $T(E)$), we will define the operation w in the following manner: A w B is the part of E which contains the elements of A which are not in B and the elements of B which are not in A, thus:

$$A \text{ w } B = \text{df}(A \cup B) - (A \cap B)$$

In these conditions, $T(E)$ forms an abelian group relative to the operation w:

1. To each pair of elements of $T(E)$, w produces a corresponding element of $T(E)$.
2. The operation w is associative as can easily be verified.
3. The neutral element is the empty part $\emptyset$.
4. Each subset is its own inverse element, thus A w $A = \emptyset$ (A contains no element not in A).
5. The operation w is evidently commutative.

(C)
The group of exclusive disjunctions (TL, p. 316):

1. *The group of exclusive disjunctions.* – The subsets of a set form, as we have seen in Section 10, an additive group from the point of view of the operation consisting of the union of their disjunctive parts. Such a group may thus be seen in interpropositional calculus from the viewpoint of the operation $(p \text{ w } q)$:
Definition: $(p \text{ w } q) = (p \cdot \bar{q}) \text{ w } (\bar{p} \cdot q)$

1. *Direct operation*: $(p \text{ w } q) : (q \text{ w } r)$: etc.
2. *Inverse operation*: $(p \text{ w } p) = 0$; $(q \text{ w } q) = 0$ etc. In effect:
    $(2\,4\,4)\ p \text{ w } p = (p \cdot \bar{p}) \text{ w } (\bar{p} \cdot p) = (0) \text{ w } (0) = 0$
3. *Identity operation*: 0. In effect:
    $(2\,4\,5)\ (p \text{ w } 0) = p$ and $(p \text{ w } p) = 0$
4. *Associativity*: $(2\,4\,6)\ [p \text{ w } (q \text{ w } r)] = [(p \text{ w } q) \text{ w } r)]$ [sic]

Any two operations of the set have as their product an operation within the set: it is therefore certainly a group, but a group in which the direct operation is its own inverse whenever it is applied to a common part ['partie'] $(p \text{ w } p)$.

(D)

The following is the corresponding passage from LO (p. 306):

1.   *The group of exclusive disjunctions.* – The subsets of a set form, as we have seen in Section 10, an additive group from the point of view of the operation consisting of the union of their disjunctive parts. Such a group may thus be seen in interpropositional calculus from the viewpoint of the operation $(p \text{ w } q)$:

1.   *Direct operation*: $(p \text{ w } q)$; $(q \text{ w } r)$;   etc.
2.   *Inverse operation*: $(p \text{ w } p) \longleftrightarrow 0$; $(q \text{ w } q) \longleftrightarrow 0$;   etc. In effect:
     $(2\,4\,4)\ p \text{ w } p \longleftrightarrow (p \cdot \bar{p}) \text{ w } (\bar{p} \cdot p) \longleftrightarrow (0) \text{ w } (0) \longleftrightarrow 0$.
3.   *Identity operation*: 0. In effect:
     $(2\,4\,5)\ (p \text{ w } 0) \longleftrightarrow p$ and $(p \text{ w } p) \longleftrightarrow 0$.
4. $(2\,4\,6)$ *Associativity*: $[p \text{ w } (q \text{ w } r)] \longleftrightarrow [(p \text{ w } q) \text{ w } r)]$. [sic]

Any two operations of the set have as their product an operation within the set: it is therefore certainly a group, but a group in which the direct operation is its own inverse whenever it is applied to a common part ['partie'] $(p \text{ w } p)$.

(E)

Comment

Passage (A) from TL demonstrates the confusion we have pointed out between element and operation. This passage refers to sets and the elements here are straightforward mathematical sets, not 'operations'. Under these circumstances, there is no 'inverse operation' in the Piagetian sense since an 'inverse operation' equivalent to 'subtraction' is meaningless in this context. The wording in 1. results in a similar confusion as there is here even a suggestion that $A_1 \text{ w } A_2$ might be the element. Thus, there is the now familiar confusion between the element as a set on the one hand and as a cognitive operation on the other. All this is in TL, before the tidying-up in LO. Passage (B), on the same subject, is now faultless.

Passages (C) and (D), from TL and LO respectively, are identical except for minor notational changes and repeat the element–rule of combination (operation) confusion. It is doubtful from the start here whether Piaget intends the word 'operation' to refer to 'w' or to '$p \text{ w } q$'. And does he intend the group-element to be e.g. $(p \text{ w } q)$, referred to as an 'operation', or is the element intended to be e.g. p, q or r (as in the associativity statement)? If p, q, r are elements and the operation is w, then this is simply a proof that logical propositions under w form a group – which is a well-known fact, anyway. 'Operations' of a cognitive character would not be relevant. If, on the other hand, cognitive operations are being referred to, then (p w q), etc. are elements (*called* operations) and a rule of combination (say, $\star$) is missing!

The fact that there is no clear decision constitutes what is wrong here and, as we have stated in the main body of the text, enables Piagetian theory to slither from the external to the internal world of the subject at will.

As already stated, the surprising fact is that LO did not clear up all the errors and follow on the new (and improved) definition of a group with a complete revision. Below (pages 80–3) we shall see a new version of the definition of a grouping in general, but it is clear that in the 'applicative' part of the book, no change was made in LO. One can merely speculate as to the reasons for this. At best, the appointed reviser (Professor Grise) was assigned a very limited task indeed and simply performed it, that is, he improved the general definitions of group and grouping and made some minor notational changes, which do not seriously affect the implications. The undeniable fact is, however, that had LO been revised in full, the foundations of the concrete operational stage theory would have gone and there would have been considerable repercussions with regard to formal thought, as well.

3 Mathematical Structures of the Concrete Operational Stage

The mathematics of the Piagetian cognitive structures is rarely analysed in detail.* In the following two chapters a number of cases are taken in order to examine the particular forms of these cognitive structures during the periods of 'middle childhood' and adolescence. Cognitive structure in the Piagetian sense essentially means the organisation of mental operations. It is not the thoughts themselves but the activity of thinking that is said to be organised into such structures. Putting objects and classes into order, relating them, seeing correspondences, all these are said to be forms of cognitive structuration.

The essence of Piagetian cognitive theory lies in its claim to reveal the development of a series of logico–mathematical structures identified with the individual's cognitive growth. These have their roots in the thought of the very young child which is said to be non-operational but semi-reversible. Such conditions predominate in the earlier years of childhood up to six or seven years. During these years the elementary foundations of cognitive structuration begin, principally in association with the growth of language and the ramification of symbolic functions and activity. This creates the conditions for the later much more tightly knit structural situation emerging at about the age of 7 characterised by reversibility and therefore, according to Piaget, by operational thinking.

During this latter period, the structural characteristics associated with what Piaget calls formal operations are not yet present. These begin to emerge only at the end of the period (around 11–12 years). The cognitive structures typical of what is termed the concrete operational stage are essentially related to practical activity. It is not that the subject does not

* Some of the arguments in the following two chapters may seem unnecessarily detailed and even repetitious. However, this detail has two objectives in view. First, the non-mathematician has been kept in view who may need the mathematical arguments to be continuously related to the interaction of the cognising subject with his/her world of experience. Secondly, it was thought to be very important to present the *exact manner* in which Piaget utilised groups in relation to his 'cognitive structures' without the reader having to undertake a tedious search through Piaget's writing.

think logically at this stage; but his logical thinking is said to refer only to objects and practical situations, although these need not be immediately present. It is the special type of cognitive structure belonging to this period that Piaget has called 'groupement' or 'grouping'.

We should remind ourselves that his analysis of the development of cognition is 'convergent' in the sense that the stages and the structures associated with them leading from infanthood to adulthood all culminate in the formal operational stage characterised by two structures, the group and the lattice (see Appendix A to this chapter), a principal feature of both being closure.

Such increasing closure, stability and equilibrium may be said to determine retrospectively the characteristics of the structures of the concrete operational stage. Before embarking on a detailed consideration of grouping structure it would, perhaps, be useful to provide a summary of the Piagetian view of this convergent development. The pre-operational stage, up to about 7 years old, is said to have simple semi-reversibility of the negation or cancellation type. From about 7 to about 11 true reversibility begins to be manifested. There are two forms of this inversion: cancellation, or negation, which is demonstrated in the structures associated with operations upon classes; and reciprocity, or compensation without cancellation, which is a property of the structures associated with operations upon relations. Thus, at Piaget's concrete operational stage there are two forms of reversibility which apply in different situations and which are quite different and distinct from each other. It is only at his formal operational stage that these two forms of reversibility are said to be integrated into a single closed structure – the so-called INRC group. Thus, the formal operational stage represents a mathematical-structural culmination to the system, at which closure, completeness and stability (equilibrium) have been achieved and there is, in fact, literally nowhere else to go. The intellectual and, indeed, the emotional maturation of the individual is complete.

Mathematical Structure at the Concrete Operational Stage. The Grouping

Before proceeding, a point of clarification is needed. The term 'class' is constantly used by Piaget but his usage leaves it unclear whether he means a *collection* of things/processes/transformations or whether the term signifies the logical conditions under which such collections are formed. This distinction is extremely important and the confusion between the two approaches is not restricted to Piaget. The first phase of this critique (up to the end of Chapter 7) will restrict itself to the conventional context and use of the word 'class'. Chapter 8, however, will explore the wider significance of this confusion, especially with respect to Piaget's usage.

What is a grouping? The definition of a grouping was first published in a rudimentary form in the 1930s and 1940s, first in 1937, in *Classes, relations et nombres* (1942), in *The Psychology of Intelligence* (1950), and so on. It was elaborated fully in *Traité de logique* (1949) but was treated rather differently in the second edition, *Logique opératoire* (1972). A brief summary of the *Traité de logique* approach was published in *Logic and Psychology* in 1953 which was based on three lectures given by Piaget at the University of Manchester in October 1952.

This structure is a composite, even a hybrid one. Some of its properties belong to the group and others to the lattice. Piaget uses a special case of the lattice, a set of classes in which each is included in the one above, as in Figure 3.1 below, and in which any two classes at the same level can be put together to form the one above. This is known as a semi-lattice as it does

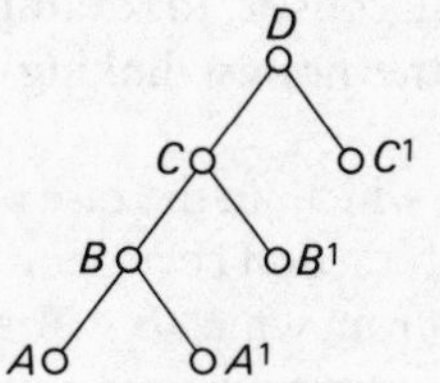

Figure 3.1

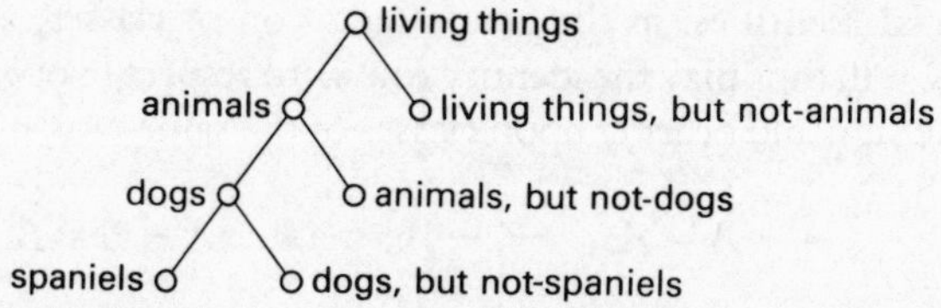

Figure 3.2

not take account of any other form of subdivision. Figure 3.1, as given by Piaget in TL, p. 95, is a semi-lattice, and this might be exemplified by Figure 3.2. This is a specific and simple case of a semi-lattice which, as an abstract logical mathematical structure, can be defined formally by specific properties in a similar way to the group. The properties are, of course, different. The particular properties of the lattice which are extracted from it as relevant to the groupings are the so-called *tautology* and *resorption*. Put simply, tautology expresses the fact that, for any class of objects, the result of 'adding' a class to itself is the same class, for example, class of dogs 'added to' class of dogs results in class of dogs. In Figure 3.1 class B 'added to' itself results in B. Resorption is similar and expresses the fact that adding a class to one which it includes, or contains, results in the original class, for example, class of dogs 'added to' class of spaniels results in the class of dogs (Figure 3.2). In Figure 3.1 B 'added' to A results in B. This so-called addition can take two forms, as can be seen from the treatment in Appendix A.

It turns out that the associativity of the group (see above, page 40) is not always satisfied if tautology and resorption are appended to group properties (see *Logic and Psychology*, p. 27). Thus, a grouping is a combination of an incomplete group together with tautology and resorption which are associated with the lattice. Three of the four group properties are said to be satisfied (composition or closure, identity element and the existence of inverses), but the fourth property, associativity, breaks down under certain conditions.

The grouping is defined in TL (p. 97):

1. A direct operation will consist, for example, of joining a class to its complement under the nearest linking class: $A + A' = B$; $B + B' = C$.
2. An inverse operation which, in the case of the additive grouping of classes, will be the subtraction corresponding to the previous addition: $-A - A' = -B$; from which $B - A = A'$; $B - A' = A$,   etc.
3. An identity operation, which, in our example, will be ± 0; that is $A - A = 0$ and $A + 0 = A$.
4. But to this general identity will be added what we will call the special identities: in the case of addition of classes, any operation + K will thus play the identity role with respect to operations of the same sign and bearing upon classes of the same rank or higher:

$$A + A = A; \quad -A - A = -A; \quad A + B = B.$$

5. The preceding operations thus constitute an associativity, subject to the application of certain rules which we shall discuss.

Chapter 2 made clear the fundamental problems arising from the confusion between element and operation (or rule of combination) in considering the group. The definition of the grouping given here brings to mind the same problems. There are four possible interpretations of 'operation' in this definition:

(1) as a complete 'equation-sentence' as in $A + A' = B$; (see Piaget's no. 1);
(2) as a 'signed term' in the equation-sentence as in $+A$ or $-A$, which means 'to set down A'' and 'to remove A'' (see Piaget's no. 2);
(3) as simply + and − as written;

(4)   as an implicit (general) rule of combination, which is not, however, referred to in the definition.

The ambiguity with respect to '−' is referred to in LO (p. 80), that is $B - A = A'$ vacillates in meaning between 'the Bs which are not $-A$s are the A's and an exclusion in the sense of a subtraction.

There is a similar confusion in what constitutes the element. There are four possibilities here:

(1)   the 'equation-sentence': $A + A' = B$;
(2)   the 'equation-sentence' with signed terms: $(+A) \text{ o } (+A') = (+B)$;
(3)   the 'signed term' taken by itself: $+A, +A'$;
(4)   the simple literal term: A, B, B'.

In fact, Piaget strongly implies that $+A, +A'$, etc., are the elements, that is, operations. If such operations are to have group structure, as Piaget affirms, then a *group* rule of combination is needed. At the same time there is, throughout Piaget's definition of the grouping, the suggestion of (4), that is, the simple literal term is the element (of the structure) and this is due to the omission of signs in front of certain terms, for example, in '$A - A = 0$'. Let us consider the four possibilities in turn.

If the equation-sentence is the element of thought, for example, '$A + A' = B$', then such elements would need a rule of combination for their composition, as in:

$$(A + A' = B) \text{ o } (B + B' = C).$$

But this could not then be manipulated as it could be if the main connecting rule of combination were '+' as in:

$$(A + A' = B) + (B + B' = C) = A + A' + B' = C.$$

Consider the second possibility. The thinking process itself might well lead us to the conclusion that simply to 'set down A' (whatever that phrase means in actuality) is insufficient as an element of thought (and such an element is certainly required if there is to be group-type structure). It could certainly be argued that such an element *should* be 'to set down A (and then) to set down A' (gives the same result as) to set down B'. This could be represented:

$$(+A) \text{ o } (+A') = (+B),$$

where 'o' represents the rule of combination which is an extended form of

Piaget's 'equation–sentence'. But composition of cognitive operations would then require a rule of combination, say '$\star$', and what Piaget calls composition of operations would then be written:

$$[(+A) \text{ o } (+A') = (+B)] \star [(+B) \text{ o } (+B') = (+C)] \Longleftrightarrow [(+X) \text{ o } (+X') = (+Y)] \ldots Z$$

in which '=' could mean 'gets the same result as' or 'is equivalent to' and '$\Longleftrightarrow$' might have the same general signification as '=' but their *meanings* might be different in different situations.

If, however, the element of the grouping were simply $+A$, $-A$, etc., as in case (3), then again, where is the rule of combination in the definition? (And why is there not a sign in front of every letter?) As before, there must be a rule of combination, not written by means of $+$ or $-$ (which have already been used), and composition would have to read, say,

$$(+A) \text{ o } (+A') = (+B).$$

Finally, if the element is simply A or B, etc., then there are two rules of combination, $+$ and $-$, logical addition and subtraction, and we are talking of classes external to the subject and not of mental operations. This, incidentally, is also suggested by the first possibility, that is, $A + A' = B$ is the element.

The four possible interpretations of the element of thought correspond to four actual situations:

(1)   If the equation–sentence is the element then the latter refers to a mental operation of the form:
      'If A and then A', then this gives the same result as B.'
(2)   If the equation–sentence with signed terms is the element then the element of thought is similar to (1) and is 'If A is set down and then A' is set down, then this gives the same result as setting down B'.
(3)   If the signed term is the element then it is referring simply to a mental operation of the form 'to set down A'.
(4)   If the unsigned term is the element, then the algebra refers to *classes* themselves, A, B and C, and has at least partially left the sphere of mentality. This confusion goes deeper and is much more significant than appears at first sight as it involves muddling classes and collections. Chapter 8 will attempt to clarify this.

This discussion has referred to the general definition of a grouping as given in TL but we will anticipate slightly by pointing out here that the vacillation in notation (and therefore in meaning) extends beyond this. In the definition of Grouping I (TL, p. 109) the equation–sentence is clearly referred to as the element of this grouping but the main definition repeats the indeterminacy in meaning. Flavell (1963) concedes Piaget's vacillation between equation and single term and accepts it as 'idiosyncratic'. But we have argued that more is involved than mere idiosyncracy of notation.

The rationale for treating signed terms rather than equation-sentences rests, in fact, upon TL (pp. 100–2) in which Piaget demonstrates that complete equations can be reduced to single terms by absorbing them on the basis of tautology and resorption and providing that certain algebraic rules are adhered to. In the definitions of Grouping I (p. 110) this is specifically referred to as the justification for assuming the operation to be $+A$, $+B$, $+A'$, etc., instead of the full equation. However, in line with the arguments in Chapter 2, three points must be made:

(1) It is operations upon classes and not classes themselves which are being defined in the grouping. What is applicable to addition and subtraction of classes is not similarly applicable to mental operations upon classes. Full equations could not be reduced (or 'collapsed') in the Piagetian way, for we are not dealing with logical addition and subtraction of classes (represented by $+$ and $-$) but with operations involving two different rules of combination, o and $\star$, which prevent manipulation of the type discussed by Piaget in TL (pp. 100–2).

(2) Even if the above argument were ignored, there is still the problem of vacillation from one meaning to another *within* the definition for the element of the grouping, the implications of which were suggested in Chapter 2.

(3) Finally, if $+A$, $+A'$, etc., are to be considered as the elements then there is still 'collapse' to '$A + A' = B$', which removes the field of discussion partially outside the subject. It arises from an 'operational' confusion, yet again. For the rule of combination between $(+A)$, $(+A')$, etc., would be *not* '$+$' but 'o', meaning 'and then'. If the rule of combination *were* '$+$' then we would obtain:

$$(+A) + (+A') = (+B)$$

and it might suggest reduction (or 'collapse') to $A + A' = B$, rather like an algebraic equation. But in $(+A) \circ (+A') = (+B)$, it is not possible to join o and $+$ (or $-$) into one symbol, $+$ or $-$ or o , as in ordinary algebra (in which, say, $x + (-y)$ can be replaced by $x - y$). The statement in our previous sentence means: 'to set down A and then to set down A' gives the same result as to set down B'. Here, 'to set down A' or to 'set down A'' (i.e. $+A$, $+A'$) are unbreakable units in themselves. To break them up makes a jump from operations to collections, involving at least in part the outer world of the subject. If 'o$(+A)$' is abbreviated to $+A$ this is merely for purposes of quick

manipulation and the correct notation must be replaced at the end
in order that the correct meaning is restored.

There are further problems. Hitherto, the '=' used in equations has
received no attention. It is all too easy when looking at the notational
layout in which familiar symbols are used to slip into an acceptance of
standard meanings. What does Piaget's '=' mean? In equation Z should
the same sign be used inside the square brackets as outside? Do these signs
mean the same thing or not? It would be all too easy to accept a simple
arithmetical interpretation. But it is not arithmetic or sets or classes which
are under discussion, but cognitive operations.

To return to equation Z, which we will repeat here:

$$[(+A) \text{ o } (+A') = (+B)] \star [(+B) \text{ o } (+B') = (+C)] \Longleftrightarrow (+X) \text{ o } (+X') = (+Y)] \ldots Z$$

X and *Y* must be left unspecified and the reason for this is to do with the
equality signs. A 'translation' of this equation might read: [to set down *A*
and then to set down *A'* gives the same result as to set down *B*] 'combined
with' or 'followed by' or 'and then' [to set down *B* and then to set down *B'*
gives the same result as to set down *C*] would be the same as, or gives the
same result as, or is equivalent to [to set down *X* and then to set down *X'*
gives the same result as to set down *Y*]. Thus the problem of the *meaning* of
the major equality sign is linked with the fact that one cannot specify *X* and
Y. For the presence of 'o' and '★' prevents reduction through tautology
and resorption as in the case of the algebra of classes, so that no conclusion
can be drawn in advance as to which *X* and *Y* we are talking about. If the
above were a valid symbolisation of the composition of what Piaget calls
mental operations, then both equality signs could mean the same thing and
this meaning could be symbolised in both cases in the same way. We
cannot assume this here, however. The 'translation', of course, raises
serious doubts as to the possibility of such an abstraction being a conceivable way of representing child thought!

This is even more the case in considering tautology and resorption.
Consider Piaget's no. 4:

$$A + B = B.$$

This must mean 'to set down *A* and then to set down *B* gives the same
result as to set down *B*'. Mental operations always take place in a living
context. If the idea 'spaniels' were set down and then 'dogs', it would not
be the same thing *mentally* as simply setting down 'dogs'. Moreover, we
have not yet questioned the curious Piagetian notion embodied in the
words 'to set down' ('poser' in French). Has this notion any meaning at all

in thought and if so what? Also, can cognition be reduced to units or elements at all?

A further problem derives from the connection of the grouping with both the group and the lattice. The group has one rule of combination (either 'combined with' or 'followed by' or 'and then') and the lattice has two such rules (taking the greatest lower bound and taking the least upper bound) which differ from the rule for the group. However, the grouping is a totally new structure and so any rules(s) of combination must refer to the grouping structure in itself. Thus, it is difficult, if not impossible, to relate the rule(s) of combination for a grouping to the rules of combination for a lattice. The idea of 'and then' may be taken over from the group to the grouping, but then the lattice rules of combination have disappeared. And if tautology and resorption remain at all under the new rule of combination, then these properties would no longer have their previous connection with the lattice. This would, of course, not occur if the '+' and '−' could be used universally and carried over, as Piaget does in fact use them.

Thus, the developmental picture of stages from less integrated and stable to more integrated, closed and equilibrated structures receives a setback. In fact, there is more to it than this. If Piaget's grouping structure does not hold at his concrete operational stage, then the formal operational stage is not a 'completion' of the concrete operational. In any event and independent of this, the formal stage exhibits less integrality than the concrete, being characterised by two structures, not one.

In the definition of a grouping in LO (1972) the treatment shows considerable changes, but as it has some rather forbidding notation it has been relegated to Appendix B together with brief mathematical comments. What is attempted here is a brief analysis of Piaget's definition of a grouping in LO based on the details laid out in this Appendix.

There are seven conditions. The element of the grouping is defined as the equation–sentence together with an inverse of this equation–sentence, an identity element, tautology and resorption. Deep problems remain, however, if we wish to relate this structure, whose definition is perfectly permissible mathematically, to Piaget's concept of a grouping as an incomplete group with lattice properties.

Having defined the element of the grouping as the equation–sentence, tautology, resorption and the identity refer to single terms only. Furthermore, there are two types of inverse, one with respect to equations and the other with respect to single terms. The form of composition is not as normally understood for group structure and there are still two sorts of identity, general and special. Associativity is still limited by tautology and resorption. Certainly, this structure is somewhat more removed from the group and lattice than was the case in *Traité de logique* in 1949.

Following the definition, Piaget gives some examples (LO, pp. 95–6, see Appendix B). Here, specifically, there is a return to the notational vacillation referred to so often already. 'In order to simplify the account ['écritures'] and prepare for reading the applications which follow, we will not put $\in G(U)$, *we will write* X *in place of* $(+X)$ *and* X $-$ Y *in place of* X o $(-Y)$' (our emphasis). Thus, despite the new definition of a grouping, there is a reaffirmation of the indeterminacy of meaning which has been discussed already:

(a)   The equation is ignored and only the single term dealt with, as if the full equation did not exist;
(b) $(+X)$ is reduced to X;
(c) X o $(-Y)$ is collapsed to $X - Y$, and we are, in fact, back to the situation discussed in reference to TL.

A comment on all this does appear as a footnote (LO, p. 97), in reference to the use of + and − in rules concerned with the correct handling of tautology and resorption. 'We also note that the definition and rules make use of signs + and −. This reminds us that the operations of groupings permit of diverse interpretations and that in the exact measure to which these structures are mid-way between the pre-operational and hypo-thetico–deductive. *(See Introduction to the second edition)*.'

There are nine groupings altogether, the first four applying to thought about classes and the remainder to thought about relations.[30] Only Group-ings I and V are discussed here since these two groupings manifest all the fundamental points in relation to Piaget's view of cognition at this stage.

Specific Examples of the Grouping

Grouping I defines the simplest operations on class hierarchies in which, say, 'animals' are considered as divisible into 'dogs' and 'animals which are not dogs' but in which no account is taken of any other possible mode of division of the class of animals nor of any further division of 'animals which are not dogs'. This grouping in TL (pp. 109–13) presents the same problems as we have already discussed with reference both to the group definition, and the definition of grouping in general.

On turning to the treatment of Grouping I in LO (pp. 103–7), we might expect a very different account from that in TL, based upon the inno-vations in the definition of the general grouping appearing in LO. How-ever, this is not so. The bulk of LO is identical with TL. The treatment of all specific groupings in LO is the same as in TL, despite the new general definition of the grouping. Since the issues arising in the treatment of Grouping I are exactly the same as those we have already discussed in connection with the general grouping, this will not be repeated. We have given a translation of Grouping I from LO in Appendix C. This is identical with TL with the exception of the omission of a small footnote and a slight change of notation, both irrelevant to our argument.

Groupings V–VIII are unlike the first four groupings in so far as they do not refer to thought about classes but to operations on *relations*. First, what is a relation? A relation exists between two or more objects, people, any elements of a set if they can be put into some sort of order: for example, 'is the brother of' or 'lives next door to' or 'is shorter than' or 'is taller than'. Grouping V is concerned with the thinking which refers to a particular sort of relation – one that is said to be asymmetric and transitive. For example, 'is shorter than' is asymmetric because if A 'is shorter than' B then it cannot be simultaneously asserted the B 'is shorter than' A. This relation is transitive because it 'carries over': that is, *whenever* A 'is shorter than' B and B 'is shorter than' C then A 'is shorter than' C. Piaget uses the example of putting rods into order of length to exemplify this grouping structure and this should be borne in mind in the following discussion.

It should also be noted that, yet again, although the general definition of a grouping is not the same in LO as it was in TL, nevertheless the treatment of Grouping V in LO is identical with TL without any of the alterations that the reader might expect due to the revision of the general definition. A full translation of the definition is given in Appendix D.

The notation here is curious. Piaget writes (LO, p. 133):

> We thus obtain a series of asymmetric relations, transitive and connected, expressing the series of differences considered:

$$0 \xrightarrow{a} A; \quad A \xrightarrow{a'} B: \quad B \xrightarrow{b'} C; \quad C \xrightarrow{c'} D; \quad \text{etc.}$$

> The arrows $\longrightarrow$ represent the asymmetric relation itself in contrast to the ordered terms 0, A, B, etc. and the direction of the arrow marks an inequality in favour of the term aimed at: '$A \xrightarrow{a'} B$' thus signifies 'B *is more (big, etc.) than* A'. The converses would be:

$$A \xleftarrow{a} 0; \quad B \xleftarrow{a'} A; \quad C \xleftarrow{b'} B; \quad \text{etc.}$$
$$['0' \text{ is alphabetic}]$$

> with the signification '0 is less (big, etc.) than A', etc.

Thus '$0 \xrightarrow{a} A$' stands for 'A is bigger than 0' and '$A \xleftarrow{a} 0$' stands for '0 is less big than A'.

Through the use of the word 'difference' relations are interpretable as differences in magnitude, although the directionality of the relation as such is still very much in evidence. Definition 24 (LO, p. 134 – see Appendix D) really emphasises *difference* as distinct from *relation* and, moreover, the operation is actually called 'serial addition'. It reads:

> We shall write $(0 \xrightarrow{a} A) + (A \xrightarrow{a'} B) = (0 \xrightarrow{b} B)$ and give the following

meaning to this operation: 'If I add the difference (a') existing between A and B to the difference (a) existing between 0 and A, I obtain the difference ($b = a + a'$) existing between 0 and B. This operation will be called serial addition.'

Thus, a, a', b are clearly treated as *differences and not relations*. Piaget is not at all consistent in interpretation, but hovers between a relational and a 'difference in magnitude' approach. The now familiar vacillation is enhanced by the use of + and − applied to relations and the constant use of the word 'difference'. But difference is measurable or calculable whereas relation as such is not. Thus, 'is longer than' cannot be calculated. 'A is longer than B', which expresses a relation between A and B, may include measurement or calculation but is, in itself, numerically indeterminate.

The starting-point of the definition of Grouping V is the 'direct operation': that is, $(0 \xrightarrow{a} A) + (A \xrightarrow{a'} B) = (0 \xrightarrow{b} B)$. The direct operation is identified with this entire 'equation-sentence' (later to be collapsed without comment to a single term) thus implying that the *element of the structure* is this equation. However, the direct operation is said to be 'addition of differences' so that it is clear from the start that the account given by Piaget has little in common with the normally accepted logical theory of relations.[31] This 'addition of differences' is a curious symbolisation of (measurable) difference *external to the subject*. In fact, there is more resemblance here to addition (and subtraction) of two-dimensional vectors than anything else. Grouping V shows the same features as did Grouping I, the definition of a grouping and, ultimately, Piaget's definition of a group itself. The indeterminacy and confusion with respect to element and rule of combination are manifested again in the context of the particularity of Grouping V. The extra step in the treatment of Grouping V for it to be isomorphic to Grouping I is the collapse of relation into difference, and the vacillation between relation and difference then enables Piaget to interpret his terms at will as either external or internal to the subject.

On the basis of Piagetian assumptions on structured cognition, the direct operation should express the asymmetric transitivity of the relation, say,

Whenever $(A < B)$ and $(B < C)$,
    then $A < C$,
i.e. $(A < B) \circ (B < C) = (A < C)$.

It might be argued that this is no different from Piaget's own direct operation, providing we replace '$\rightarrow$' by '$<$' and '+' by 'o'. This could be written as: $(A \rightarrow B) + (B \rightarrow C) = (A \rightarrow C)$ and still express transitivity. But Piaget states clearly that this is to do with 'addition of differences' and he inserts these differences (a, a', b) and expresses the connection between them:

$$a + a' = b$$
and $b - a' = a$ (Piaget, 1953, p. 14).

Once again, what is apparently merely a notational idiosyncrasy turns out to be more significant than appears at first sight, The simple symbols, $+$ and $-$, lead naturally to an acceptance of Piaget's presentation simply because people are so used to them in connection with mathematical entities. Also, the use of these symbols hides the omission of a (group) rule of combination (if the element is the whole equation–sentence). Grouping V, as an analogue of Grouping I (and thus containing all its problematic features), is constructed mainly through the use of these familiar symbols, $+$ and$-$. The isomorphism between Grouping I and Grouping V starts with the direct operation since this has the same pattern for both: ( ) $+$ ( ) $=$ ( ). But in order to achieve isomorphism between the two, relation in Grouping V has to be collapsed to some*thing* which can be added (or subtracted). The brackets, in this grouping, call for the notion of *differences* in magnitude, not relations.

Piaget is not unaware of this and refers to it obliquely in the footnote (see Appendix D, page 89). However, it is not clear how he sees the distinction between 'isomorphism' and 'simple correspondence'. Once the direct operation has been given using '$+$' and referring to 'differences' then everything else follows, and Grouping V is given the same structure as Grouping I – with the exception, of course, of reversibility, which we shall refer to shortly.

The next and very important step in the definition of Grouping V is the inverse operation (see Appendix D). This wanders even farther away from the normally accepted mathematical treatment of relations. Now, in order that Grouping V corresponds to Grouping I, the inverse operation *has* to be subtraction (of a difference), and it is defined in this way, without justification:

The *inverse operation* will be the subtraction of a difference

d:

$$(41)\,(0) \xrightarrow{-b} B) - (A \xrightarrow{-a'} B) = (0 \xrightarrow{-a} A): \text{ etc.}$$

The entire treatment of the inverse operation, leading on to the discussion of the form reversibility takes in the case of relations, depends upon this definition, that is, on the meaning of 'subtraction' in this context. The inverse operation having been defined as subtraction, it is clear that this is no more than a vector subtraction of magnitudes. This would not matter too much in itself but the problem that must be solved here is that of defining reversibility in connection with relations. There must be a form of reversibility for thinking to be operational (in Piagetian terms) and so there must be a means of defining such reversibility. Also this must be an example of the inverse operation in the case in which a 'difference' is 'subtracted' from itself: '$(A \xrightarrow{a'} B) - (A \xrightarrow{a'} B)$'. The problem now arises of the meaning to be attached to this, and Piaget argues, with a degree of plausibility, that to interpret this as modifying A or B so as to make $A = B$ would not be a relational but a class operational interpretation. There is, however, another possibility and this involves thinking of the subtraction as 'setting up a relation in the opposite direction', that is,

$$
\begin{aligned}
(A \xrightarrow{a'} B) - (A \xrightarrow{a'} B) \ &= (A \xrightarrow{a'} B) + (B \xrightarrow{-a'} A) \\
&= (A \xrightarrow{a'} B) + (B \xleftarrow{a'} A) \\
&= A \underset{o}{\overset{o}{\rightleftarrows}} A \text{ (or } A = A)
\end{aligned}
$$

(LO, p. 135). This means that to subtract a relation from itself is the same as adding its converse. This argument produces a feasible interpretation of the inverse operation and thus of the form of reversibility for a relation (reciprocity) in terms of the directionality of a relation and *not of difference*.

Of course, this is very far-fetched since it rests upon (*a*) accepting the possibility of subtracting relations as meaningful in the first place; (*b*) the existence of a form of reversibility for relations; and (*c*) a very strange piece of 'mathematics' that shows clearly that, despite all talk to the contrary, the relation is still collapsed into difference, for we have:

$$(A \xrightarrow{a'} B) - (A \xrightarrow{a'} B) = (A \xrightarrow{a'} B) + (B \xrightarrow{-a'} A).$$

What does this mean? It must be translated as 'B is greater than A (by a') minus B is greater than A (by a') is the same as B is greater than A (by a') plus A is greater than B (by $-a'$)'. It is the last that is psychologically totally implausible although in terms of Piaget's differences it is mathematically feasible. What can $(A \xrightarrow{a'} B) + (B \xrightarrow{-a'} A)$ mean psychologically?

$$
\begin{array}{l}
A\text{———————} \\
B\text{—————————————}_{a'}
\end{array}
$$

$(A \xrightarrow{a'} B)$ can only mean 'B is bigger than A (by a')'. $(B \xrightarrow{-a'} A)$ can only mean 'A is bigger than B (by $-a'$)'. The latter cannot be credibly attributed to a young child.

The implausibility in this rather contrived definition of reversibility in respect of relations lies in the fact that it means that the reciprocal of $A < B$ is $B > A$. The latter, however, is not truly a reversed form of the former, but says the same thing in a different way. What is required, especially in view of later developments at the formal operational stage, is a form of reversibility which involves compensation without cancellation. $B > A$ does not 'compensate' $A < B$. Piaget must have thought something of this sort, or he would have remained with this definition. He did not remain with it, however, and as early as 1953 in *Logic and Psychology* (p. 29) the reciprocal of $A < B$ is defined as $A > B$, that is, '$(A < B) + (A > B) = (A = B)$'. Such a definition had already been forbidden in TL, involving as it does class and not relational operations. Also, this would mean that the general identity operator would be $A = B$, which would raise considerable problems. Such conflicting definitions of reciprocity render invalid any suggestion of experimental substantiation, that is, reference to the subject's grasp of reciprocity.

The inverse operation has, moreover, already abandoned the equation as operation and reduced this to the single term which is continued in properties 3 and 4 referring to the general identity operation and tautology and resorption. This treatment is an exact replication of the TL and LO treatment of these properties in Grouping I and the TL treatment of them in the definition of the grouping. It was with reference to the last that we fully discussed this (pp. 62ff).

The implications of the definition of reciprocity in TL and LO cannot be left without our looking at it from another viewpoint. Consider the asymmetric, transitive relation 'is in authority over' on a set of people. The implication is, according to the Piagetian definition, that 'B is in authority over A' together with its reciprocal, 'A is subordinate to B', results in the neutral operation, 'B is at the same authority level as B'. We are, however, talking of personal/social relations here to which the Piagetian theory must equally apply (in fact Piaget places the origin of his mathematical structures at least partly in personal/social relations; see below, Chapter 10). But what does this notion of reciprocity mean in such a context? Is it to be assumed that this is the origin of a sense of identity in the individual?

The general conclusions to this discussion are thus very similar to those following Grouping I. Grouping VI–VIII could be analysed similarly, but not only does space forbid this but very similar conclusions follow.

To summarise, therefore, in Grouping V the Piagetian concepts are abbreviated into a notation which is uniquely and peculiarly his own, unlike Grouping I in which the notation resembles that of orthodox symbolism. This is a significant difference which makes it easier to see Grouping V as no more than a symbolic description of a preconceived conceptual framework. The basis for this is the 'collapse' of relation into difference in magnitude and a vacillation between the two interpretations. The now familiar confusion of equation-sentence and single term, based upon the fundamental element-rule of combination mix-up, and the use of '+' and '−' instead of a composition rule for relations, occurs again. So the group properties do not apply for the same reasons as in the case of Grouping I. Grouping V has been reduced to a situation exactly parallel to Grouping I and the Piagetian symmetry requirement is satisfied. But this is achieved by means of a circularity in which the preconceptions are expressed in abbreviations in order to enable them to be 'manipulated' to exhibit the grouping structure required by the system in the first place.

Before leaving this discussion of groupings we must note Piaget's diverse concepts of reciprocity. In TL and LO reciprocity is seen as the converse of a relation, that is, $A < B$ is the reciprocal of $B > A$. The notion was already established by 1949. But in *Logic and Psychology* (1953), in which reciprocity is again described as 'eliminating . . . a difference' (p. 29), Piaget writes: 'the product of an operation and its reciprocal gives us not a null class or a universal class but a relation of equivalence: $(A < B) + (A > B) = (A = B)$'. The reciprocal of $A < B$ has now become $A > B$. In short, Piaget's original converse in TL (and LO) is no longer the reciprocal. Furthermore, the right-hand side is now quite different from $A = A$. In fact, in TL inversion by negation was explicitly ruled out since it involved class operations on A and B *to equalise* them. Yet this is what we have here in 1953.

In 1958, in *The Growth of Logical Thinking* (subsequently referred to as GLT), Inhelder and Piaget wrote:

> For asymmetrical relations if $A < B$ is true, its reciprocal $B < A$ is false, but if they are both true ($A \gtrless B$) they can be reduced to $A = B$ – i.e., to an equivalence. An asymmetrical relationship such as $A < B$ expresses the existence of a difference between the terms A and B; if this difference is cancelled, or if it is expressed in the opposite direction in the form $B > A$, the equivalence $A = B$, or $A = A$, is again encountered without the terms themselves being cancelled. (p. 274)

$B < A$ is not rejected as the reciprocal of $A < B$, but what is introduced, namely, $B > A$, is the converse which was taken as the reciprocal in TL and would later be repeated in LO. This passage is a mixture of the two distinct definitions of reciprocity given respectively in the *Traité* and *Logic and Psychology*. We have seen that the passage in LO retains the treatment in TL.

In *Structuralism* (1968) this is expressed differently:

> The defining mark of order structures is that reversibility takes the form, not of inversion, as in groups, but of reciprocity: '$(A . B)$ precedes $(A + B)$' transforms into '$(A + B)$ succeeds $(A . B)$' by permutation of the '+' and '.' operators and the predecessor and successor relations. (p. 25)

This adds to the confusion as to Piaget's final conclusion on the nature of reciprocity, coming as it does four years before LO (1972) which both repeats the previous (1949) version and adds, in the *Note complémentaire* (see Appendix E), a novel definition of the grouping itself (without, however, any reference to reciprocity). The fluctuation between two different definitions of reciprocity can be explained only by Piaget's dissatisfaction with the first on the basis that it is not a true reversibility since $A < B$ and $B > A$ say the same thing. The new definition in *Structuralism* can be explained once it is seen that this definition returns to the relational one first set out in TL (as opposed to the definition involving a class operation in *Logic and Psychology*; see above, page 74). On reading it, it seems at first that it has the same disadvantage as the TL definition had but Piaget *incorporates* (double) reversibility into it by a double permutation, '+' and '.' and 'the precedessor and successor relations'.

Piaget's notion of reciprocity, one of the two forms of reversibility, is, then, mathematically deeply problematical, questionable at the psychological level and actually contradictory in various presentations. The other form of reversibility, negation or cancellation, has been shown in Chapter 2 to be highly conditional, even if it were a valid psychological concept. Yet these two notions of reversibility are central to the Piagetian theory of equilibration since thought, for Piaget, only becomes operational and formed of integrated, closed structures which are thereby equilibrated, in relation to becoming reversible. Moreover, the two forms of reversibility, separate at the concrete operational stage and applicable to classes and relations respectively, are said to become integrated into a single system at the formal operational stage as the N and R of the INRC group.

Appendices to Chapter 3

(A) Elementary Theory of the Lattice

The first section of Piaget's *Logic and Psychology* contains a brief passage on the lattice by W. Mays (p. xv).

> A lattice has certain limiting conditions – *join* and *meet*. In the case of any two classes X and Y, the *join* is the smallest of the classes in which X and Y are both included, and the *meet* is the largest class included both in X and in Y.
>
> The following classificatory system (Table (d)), given by Piaget in *Traité de logique*, p. 95, can be considered as a semi-lattice. A branch leading from one element to another means that the latter is included in it.

[Table (d)]

Each pair of classes possesses a *join*, B for A and A', C for A and B', or C for A' and B', etc., since it is the smallest class which includes both. As for the *meet*, A is the meet of A and of B, or of A and of C, etc., since it is the largest class included in both. On the other hand, the *meet* of two disjunctive classes is null, which is, of course, the definition of disjunction (i.e. they are excluded from each other), e.g. A and A', A and B', A' and B' all $= 0$.

We will go into more detail here. The most common definition of a lattice depends upon the idea of a *partially ordered set* so this must be explained. Partially ordered sets have to be understood in the context of *totally* ordered sets. The latter are exemplified on all sides. For example, the months of the year could be considered a totally ordered set as could a collection of people standing in order of their heights. Notice that in both these cases an element of arrangement exists. In the case of the months of the year the ordering is really dictated by the sequence of seasons and by the actual divisions that have been historically established, that is, the twelve months. The ordering arises here out of the necessary and unalterable sequence – January must be followed by February and February by March. They cannot be jumbled up except on paper. In the second example, a human agency has intervened to order the people, but notice that this ordering by height is not basically different from the ordering of the months of the year, in the sense that if you wish to get a number of people arranged in order of height, you *must* follow a specific procedure. It is this that is the real sense of ordering – following a specific procedure. In both the given cases and others, the procedure is entirely dependent on establishing a spcific *relation* between the elements involved.

In these examples we can see clearly the ordering function of the relation on the set. In both cases, the relation 'is next to' could do the ordering, but most important of all, without this ordering relation neither set of months nor set of people by height can make sense. A collection of months at random or a collection of people at random can be considered as sets and nothing more. It is when a relation is applied to the elements that they can be considered as *ordered* sets. In these cases we end up with totally ordered sets.

However, not all sets together with such a relation are *totally* ordered. The set of whole numbers together with the relation 'is a factor of' would give a *partially* ordered set. Choosing an arbitrary collection of these whole numbers, say, those from 2 to 12 inclusive, we can show that they will fall into subsets determined by the relation. For example, 2 'is a factor of' 4, 4 'is a factor of ' 8. Thus, 2, 4 and 8 constitute an ordered subset to which the relation applies. The same is the case for 3, 6 and 12. 3 and 9 make a subset, as do 5 and 10. Several little 'chains' can be formed in each of which the relation orders the numbers. Thus the integers between 2 and 12, under the relation 'is a factor of ', is an example of a partially ordered set. Notice, however, that the relation will not necessarily order all the numbers in quite the same way and in the particular set, 7 is not ordered in relation to another number since it is not a factor of any number between 2 and 12 except itself. Also, the numbers cannot be put into a single running sequence but only into several small sequences.

The mathematical definition of a partially ordered set is as follows:

A set S is said to be partially ordered by the relation R if the following conditions are satisfied for all elements a, b, c, belonging to S.

(i) *R is reflexive*. This means that all the elements in the set have the relation on themselves. This was the case in the previous example since every number between 2 and 12 is a factor of itself, for example, 7 is a factor of 7 since $7 = 7 \times 1$.

(ii) *R is anti-symmetric*. A relation on a set S is anti-symmetric if, whenever a R b and b R a, then $a = b$, for any a, $b \in S$. In other words, a relation is anti-symmetric if it cannot go backwards. If it is reversible between two elements, we must be talking of the same element, for example, 'is less than or equal to' on the integers. If a is less than or equal to b and, simultaneously, b is less than or equal to a, then $a = b$. This ensures that the relation does not go in two directions between two elements, and preserves the ordering directionality. In the example 3 and 6 are in a certain order since 3 is a factor of 6 and 6 is not a factor of 3.

(iii)   *R is transitive.* This means that if *a* is related to *b* and also *b* is related
to *c*, then *a* is related to *c* by the same relation. Here, for example, 2
is a factor of 4, 4 is a factor of 8 and 2 is also a factor of 8. In the little
'chain' consisting of 3 and 9 only, transitivity also holds, contrary
to first appearances. For since there are only two numbers in the
chain, there is no '*c*' different from *b*. Here, we have *a* R *b* and *b* R *b*
and *a* R *b* certainly holds too.

Two further notions have to be introduced before we can define a
lattice. These are the concepts of 'greatest lower bound' and 'least upper
bound'.   A lower bound of a subset *A*, within a set *S*, is an element of *S*
(say, *x*) such that *x* is less than or equal to every element of subset *A*. The
most important lower bound (if it exists) is the largest one, the *greatest*
lower bound. For example, in the subset (3, 6, 9) within the integers, the
greatest lower bound is 3 since it is greater than or equal to any lower
bound of the subset. Similarly, the least upper bound is defined as an upper
bound which is less than or equal to any upper bound. We can now define
a lattice. It is a partially ordered set in which any two elements have a least
upper bound and a greatest lower bound.

Returning to W. Mays's discussion from *Logic and Psychology*, the least
upper bound of any two classes *A* and *B*, where *A* is included in *B*, is *B*.
The greatest lower bound of these two classes is *A*. In the first case, if *B* is
the class of dogs and *A* that of spaniels, the least upper bound of the two
classes is the class of dogs since it is the smallest class which is greater than
or equal to the two classes, dogs and spaniels. Similarly, the greatest lower
bound of the two classes, dogs and spaniels, is the class of spaniels which is
the greatest class which is less than or equal to both the classes. In the case
of such classes, the least upper bound is called the *join* and the greatest
lower bound is called the *meet*, of the two classes concerned.

So far, we have defined the lattice in terms of set theory. However, there
is another and equivalent definition based upon algebraic structure. Two
new   ideas   are   involved   here.   The   first   of   these   is   that   of   an
'idempotent law', which does not hold in the case of ordinary numbers.
For ordinary numbers an iteration law holds whereby if you add one, the
result is always different from the number you started from. An idempotent law is one such that if an element is operated upon the result is itself.
For example, a set (or class) 'added' to itself results in the original set.
Thus, the set of all living things added to the set of all living things results
in the same set, that is, the set of all living things. There are two idempotent laws for lattices, each one applicable to a binary rule of combination
(that is, between two elements).

The second new idea involved in the definition of a lattice is that of
absorption and this is a little bit like the idempotent law. It applies in the
case of two sets (or classes) one of which is included in the other and they

are added together (by the operation 'union'). If A is the containing class and B is the one contained then $A + B = A$, for example, Animals + Dogs = Animals. We are now able to give the second definition of a lattice. This is an algebra on a set with two binary operations which satisfy for all a, b and c in the set the following:

(i)   both operations must be commutative;
(ii) both operations must be associative;
(iii) the idempotent laws are satisfied;
(iv) the operations are mutually absorptive.

The example of a lattice chosen by Piaget is that of a hierarchy of classes as shown on page 76. The two binary operations mentioned may be identified with 'greatest lower bound' and 'least upper bound' as the classes shown are such that any two have a g.l.b. and an l.u.b. The two particular lattice properties which are extracted as part of the definition of a grouping are the idempotent laws and absorption properties, called by Piaget 'tautology' and 'resorption'. It is these properties that limit the applicability of associativity in the group-part of the grouping. For, if A, A', B' are classes, as shown in the W. Mays's diagram:

$$A + (A' + B') = (A + A') + B'$$
$$\text{but} \quad A + (A - A) \neq (A + A) - A. \hspace{2cm} \text{(Piaget, 1953, p. 27)}$$

(B) General Definitions of the Grouping

(i)   From TL (pp. 97–8)

1. A direct operation will consist, for example, of joining a class to its complement under the nearest linking class:

$$A + A' = B; \quad B + B' = C.$$

2. An inverse operation which, in the case of the additive grouping of classes, will be the subtraction corresponding to the previous addition: $-A - A' = -B$; from which $B - A = A'$; $B - A' = A$, etc.

3. An identity operation, which, in our example, will be ± 0: that is $A - A = 0$ and $A + 0 = A$.

4. But to this general identity will be added what we will call the special identities: in the case of addition of classes, any operation $+ K$ will thus play the same role with operations of the same sign and bearing upon classes of the same rank or higher.

$$A + A = A; \quad -A - A = -A; \quad A + B = B.$$

5.   The preceding operations thus constitute an associativity, subject to the application of certain rules which we shall discuss.

The above definition from TL conforms in all respects to the basic definition of a group in TL and there is no need to repeat the analysis already given in detail in Chapter 3 of the typical confusions occurring relative to 'element' and 'operation'.

(ii)   From LO (pp. 93–5)

So let there be a set U.

Let us choose a finite number of subsets ['parties'] of U, here classes A, A', B, B', C, etc.

Let us call $C(U)$ the set of subsets of U thus chosen and let us assume in addition that the empty subset Ø and U are always subset(s) of $C(U)$. In these conditions, to all X belonging to $C(U)$ we shall associate two operators, the one labelled TX and which we shall call the *direct operator*, and the other labelled⊥X and which we shall call the *inverse operator*. We shall in addition posit that TØ and ⊥Ø are one and the same operator and we write this simply Ø.

If, in the example chosen, $+X$ is written instead of TX and $-X$ in place of ⊥X, we can read:

$+X$: to set down ['poser'] the elements of class X
$-X$: to remove ['se priver'] the elements of class X.

Let there be then a commutative law of composition between operators TX and ⊥X, called o, and an equivalence relation called =. In the classification of figure 4, to the expression (TX) o (TY) = TZ will correspond, for example, the equivalence

$$(+A) \text{ o } (A') = +B$$

which would signify: to set down the elements of the class A and to set down those of the class A' would be equivalent to setting down the elements of class B.

Now let us note that the entire classification may be characterised by a finite series of such equivalences:

$$(+A) \text{ o } (+A') = +B, \qquad (+B) \text{ o } (+B') = +C,$$
$$(+C) \text{ o } (+C') = +D, \quad \ldots, \quad (+T) \text{ o } (+T') = +U.$$

In a general fashion, we designate by $E(U)$ a finite series of expressions of the form:

$$(TX) \text{ o } (TY) = TZ \quad \text{where} \quad X, Y, Z \varepsilon C(U)$$

and we define a *grouping* on U, to be $G(U)$, in the following way:

(G1)   If $(TX) \text{ o } (TY) = (TZ) \varepsilon E(U)$, then
$(TX) \text{ o } (TY) = (TZ) \varepsilon G(U)$.

Each element of $E(U)$ is an element of $G(U)$.

(G2)   If $(TX) \text{ o } (TY) = (TZ) \varepsilon E(U)$, then
$(\mathcal{L}X) \text{ o } (\mathcal{L}Y) = (\mathcal{L}Z) \varepsilon G(U)$.

The equivalence obtained by replacing the direct operators by the inverse operators in an element of $E(U)$ is an element of $G(U)$.

(G3)   If $(TX) \text{ o } (TY) = (TZ) \varepsilon E(U)$, then
$(TX) \text{ o } (TZ) = (TZ) \varepsilon G(U)$ and
$(TY) \text{ o } (TZ) = (TZ) \varepsilon G(U)$.

Thus, for example, since $(+ A) \text{ o } (+A') = +B$ is an element of $E(U)$, $(+A) \text{ o } (+B) = +B$ is an element of $G(U)$. Class A resorbs class B. That is the reason why we speak of the laws of resorption to designate the elements of $G(U)$.

(G4)   If $(TX) \text{ o } (TY) = (TZ) \varepsilon E(U)$, then
$(TX) = (TZ) \text{ o } (\mathcal{L}Y) \varepsilon G(U)$ and
$(TY) = (TZ) \text{ o } (\mathcal{L}X) \varepsilon G(U)$.

If we start again with $(+A) \text{ o } (+A') = +B$ as an element of $E(U)$, we shall find for example that $+A = (+B) \text{ o } (-A')$ is an element of $G(U)$: setting down the elements of class A is equivalent to setting down those of B and removing those of A'.

(G5) $(TX) \text{ o } (TX) = (TX) \varepsilon G(U)$.

Thus, for example, we shall find $(+A) \text{ o } (+A) = +A \in G(U)$: setting down the elements of A and setting down again ['(re)poser'] the elements of A is equivalent to setting down the elements of A. We will speak of the laws of tautology to designate the elements of $G(U)$. The laws of tautology and resorption together form the special identities:

(G6) $$(TX) \text{ o } (\mathcal{L}X) = \emptyset \ \varepsilon \ G(U)$$
$$and \ (TX) \text{ o } \emptyset = (TX) \ \varepsilon \ G(U).$$

$\emptyset$ thus appears as the identity operator of the grouping. In the example, to set down the elements of a class and to set down nothing (or to remove nothing) is equivalent to setting down the elements of the class.

(G7)   If $\alpha = \beta$ and $\gamma = \delta$ are elements of $G(U)$ then
$$\alpha \text{ o } \gamma = \beta \text{ o } \delta \ \varepsilon \ G(U).$$

The composition, member for member, of the elements of $G(U)$ is an element of $G(U)$. (Rp.) Let us finally define a rule of substitution allowing us in any expression of $G(U)$ to replace any operator by an equivalent combination (composition).

Thus, a grouping structure has been defined by the stated conditions and this is a completely permissible procedure. The new form of definition has, from one point of view, altered the situation and the alterations are in line with certain of the points made in our discussion of the previous definition in TL. $(+X)$ and $(-X)$ meaning 'to set down X', 'to remove X' are identified with operators (TX) and $(\mathcal{L}X)$ and a rule of combination 'o' for (TX) and $(\mathcal{L}X)$ has been set down together with an equivalence relation '='. The seven conditions will be considered one by one.

(G1)   The element of the grouping is given here as the equation-sentence:

$$(TX) \text{ o } (TY) = (TZ).$$

This, nevertheless, raises the now tediously familiar necessity of a rule of combination (say, $\star$) for combining these sentences which is clearly absent.

(G2)   An inverse equation is defined so that each equation-sentence (element) has an inverse equation-sentence in the grouping, *by definition*.

(G3)   Resorption, too, is asserted by definition, and $(+A)$, $(+B)$ is substituted for (TX), (TZ). However, it is wrong to write 'Class A resorbs into class B' since *operations on classes* are being referred to $((+A), (+B))$ and not classes as such.

(G4)   This represents a second type of inversion, different from that in (G2), which defined the inverse equation-sentence. (G4) permits (in fact, defines) inversion with respect to single-term operators and, thus, to $+A, +B$, etc.

(G5)   defines tautology with respect to the single-term.

(G6) defines the identity operator, again with respect to the single-term.
NB (G3), (G5), (G6) all define resorption, tautology and identity
with respect to single-term operators and *not with respect to the
equation-sentence.*
Thus, despite the appearances of mathematical rigour in this new
definition, nothing new has emerged. The vacillation becomes
possible by which Piaget's dualism is manifested in the ability
to move at will from one desired interpretation to another. Where
problems crop up with one interpretation, the other may replace it.

(G7) This is a curious condition. It is not the composition normally
associated with the group, that is, if the element of the grouping is
the equation-sentence. If normal closure is a property of the structure, G7 should read:

If $\alpha = \beta$ and $\gamma = \delta$ are elements of $G(U)$ then
$(\alpha = \beta) \star (\gamma = \delta)\ \varepsilon\ G(U)$, where $\star$ is the rule of combination.

So, returning to the grouping as a combination of incomplete group and
lattice, we are no better off in LO than we were in TL. The identity
element and inverses are in serious question due to the vacillation from
single-term to equation-sentence as the interpretation of element. Similarly for tautology and resorption.

Associativity is affected more in LO than anything else. Piaget writes,
for example, in LO (p. 96):

Likewise [example 3 may be written] $(B \circ (-A)) \circ A = A' \circ A$
and we will again have:

5	$B \circ ((-A) \circ A) = A' \circ A$	4, ass
6	$B \circ (A \circ (-A)) = A' \circ A$	5, comm o
7	$(B \circ A) \circ (-A) = A' \circ A$	6, ass
8	$B \circ A = B$	1, G3
		$(1 : B = A \circ A')$
9	$B \circ (-A) = A' \circ A$	7, 8, Rp
10	$B \circ (-A) = A'$	1, G4
11	$A' = A' \circ A$	9, 10, Rp

which is additionally absurd.

He concludes that associativity must be renounced except for limited use
under special restrictive rules.

Thus, the general definition of a grouping has changed, yet the remainder of LO remains untouched as do the cognitive conclusions
regarding the logico-mathematical nature of the core of mentality and the
stage theory in its entirety. The next two appendices demonstrate the
untouched nature of the remainder of LO.

(C) Grouping I from *Logique opératoire* (pp. 103–7)

We shall now proceed to a systematic description of the four groupings of classes, beginning with that of simple (or inclusive) addition, already described in the course of the preceding remarks.

Let there be a series of classes $A \subset B \subset C \subset \ldots$ called 'primary', of which each is included in the following. These classes not being at all equivalent, but ordered according to the relation of inclusion, each can be made to correspond to its complement in relation to the one that follows:

$$A' = B - A; \quad B' = C - B; \quad C' = D - C, \quad \text{etc.}$$

Such classes, complementary in relation to the nearest including class, are called 'secondary'. Class A and the secondary classes A', B', C', . . . , together will be called the 'elementary classes' of the system. The additive grouping of classes is thus constituted by the series of dichotomous inclusions:

$$A + A' = B; \quad B + B' = C; \quad C + C' = D; \quad \text{etc.} \ldots$$

The elementary classes of the system may be singular. They are not necessarily so and the grouping will also apply to the case already described where a 'species' A is in no sense ['sans plus'] placed in relation to other species (A') in a 'genus' B, etc. However, if we keep only to the operations of this grouping I, the secondary classes cannot be considered capable of decomposition (their decomposition involves groupings II and III).

This said, any two operations of the grouping give, by their composition, a new operation of the grouping. These compositions are five in number:

1. *The direct operation* consists in a *member-by-member addition of equations* [our emphasis] of the form $A + A' = B; B + B' = C$; etc., or of identities $A = A$ and $A - A = 0$.[1] But, if one remains with these homogeneous series (definition 19) on applying the rules of calculation I–III (Section 10), *one can, by extension, call the direct operation, the addition of any class whatsoever of the system: $+A$; $+B$; $+A'$; etc.* [our emphasis].

2. *The general identity operation* is that which simultaneously satisfies the two following conditions: (*a*) combined with any other opera-

---

[1] 0 designates the empty class, which we have designated ∅ in § 10.

tion, it leaves it invariant; (*b*) it constitutes the product of the direct operation and its inverse (see 4). Thus, grouping I possesses one and only one general identity: it is the operation $0 = 0$ (or $+0 = -0$) or by extension ± 0. In effect, we have:

(19) $A + 0 = A$ [condition a]

and:

(19a) $A - A = 0$ [condition b]

3. *The special identities* (tautology and resorption) play the part (*a*) of the general identity, but distinguished from (*b*). In fact, every class added to itself and to a class of superior rank and of the same sign leaves this latter class invariant:

(20) $A + A = A$; $A + B = B$; $A + C = C$;   etc.

and:

(20a) $-A - A = -A$; $-A - B = -B$;   etc.

But $+A$ loses the identity role (*a*) with its own inverse and with classes of superior rank bearing an opposite sign:

$$A - A = 0; \quad A - B = -A'; \quad \text{etc.}$$

There are, therefore, besides the general identity, special identities (that is to say, neither general nor singular). It must be noted that these operations of tautologising ['tautification'] and resorption cannot be reduced to simplification operations, even though, in homogeneous series, the calculation seems so according to Rule 1: simplification is, in fact, an inverse operation consisting in cancelling the same term on two sides of the equation, whereas resorption is not an inversion but an operation guaranteeing inclusion and, in consequence, subject to order (A is resorbed into B and not B into A).

4. *The inverse operation* $(-A)$ is that which cancels the direct operation $(+A)$. The inverse operation is a single one despite the duality of the identities, because only the general identity determines the inverse, in virtue of its role (*b*):

(21) $A - A = 0$; $B - B = 0$; $A' - A' = 0$;   etc.

On the contrary, the special identities, which only fulfil role (*a*), do not determine any inverse.

5. *Associativity* $(x + y) + z = x + (y + z)$ is general between terms of the same sign or between terms of mixed sign not containing any special identities:

$$(22) \quad (A + A) + A' = A + (A + A')$$

because

$$(A) + A' = A + (B)$$

and:

$$(22a) \quad A + A' = B \quad \text{and} \quad A + B = B.$$

On the other hand, in series of mixed sign, there is no associativity when the same term plays alternatively the part of special identity and a different role. For example:

$$(-A - A) + B = -A + (-A + B)$$

would give $(-A + B) = (-A + A')$, that is to say $(A' = -A + A')$, which is absurd.

The elementary operation of the additive grouping of classes is thus non-disjunctive[1] addition (definition 17) in opposition to the disjunctive addition of Bernstein's group. In the case $A + A' = B$ the classes A and A' are disjoint by definition, whereas in the case $A + B = B$ the classes to be added are not. The inverse is non-disjunctive subtraction:

$$-A - A' = -B \quad \text{or} \quad -A - B = -B.$$

(D) Grouping V' from *Logique opératoire* (pp. 133–6)

Let there be a collection of terms A, B, C, etc.[2] all different from one another, but comparable from a common point of view (for example, shorter or taller objects, heavy or light, etc., darker or lighter colours,

---

[1] In the logic of propositions, this will therefore be operation v ('trilemme' = inclusive disjunction) and definitely not w ('dilemme' = exclusive disjunction). See § 39.
[2] We shall write Latin capitals here to indicate that the terms considered are not neccessarily individual.

wines (ordered) according to their bouquet or actions (ordered) according to their use or quality etc.). These terms could either consist of individual elements or classes (singular or not). Let us now order these terms according to increasing differences. We thus obtain a series of asymmetric relations, transitive and connected, expressing the series of differences considered:

$$0 \xrightarrow{a} A; \quad A \xrightarrow{a'} B; \quad B \xrightarrow{b'} C; \quad C \xrightarrow{c'} D; \quad \text{etc.}$$
['0' is alphabetic]

The arrows $\longrightarrow$ represent the asymmetric relation itself in contrast to the ordered terms 0, *A, B,* etc., and the direction of the arrow marks an inequality in favour of the term aimed at: '$A \xrightarrow{a'} B$' thus signifies '*B* is more (e.g. bigger) than *A*'. The converses will be:

$$A \longleftarrow 0; \quad B \longleftarrow A; \quad C \xleftarrow{b'} B; \quad \text{etc.}$$

with the meaning: '0 is less (big, etc.) than *A*', etc.

Definition 24: We shall write $(0 \xrightarrow{a} A) + (A \xrightarrow{a'} B) = (0 \xrightarrow{b} B)$ and give the following meaning to this operation: 'If I add the difference *(a')* existing between *A* and *B* to the difference *(a)* existing between 0 and *A*, I obtain the difference *(b = a + a')* existing between 0 and *B*'. This operation will be called serial addition.

We conclude that this serial addition *(a + a' = b)* implies *a < b* and *a' < b*, but involves no comparison between the parts *a* and *a'* (intensive quantity).

These relations set down, it is then easy to construct the following grouping:

1. The *direct operation* will be addition of differences, that is $+ \xrightarrow{x} =$

   (40)

$$(0 \xrightarrow{a} A) + (A \xrightarrow{a'} B) = (0 \xrightarrow{b} B) \text{ and } (A \xrightarrow{a'} B) + (B \xrightarrow{b'} C) = (A \xrightarrow{a'b'} C)$$
$$(0 \xrightarrow{b} B) + (B \xrightarrow{b'} C) = (0 \xrightarrow{c} C) \qquad (A \xrightarrow{a'b'} C) + (C \xrightarrow{c'} D) = (A \xrightarrow{a'b'c'} D)$$
$$(0 \xrightarrow{c} C) + (C \xrightarrow{c'} D) = (0 \xrightarrow{d} D) \qquad (A \xrightarrow{a'...c'} D) + (D \xrightarrow{d'} E) = (A \xrightarrow{a'...d'} E)$$
etc.   etc.

['0' is alphabetic]

2. The *inverse operation* will be the subtraction of a difference $- \xrightarrow{-d}$:

   (41) $(0 \xrightarrow{b} B) - (A \xrightarrow{a'} B) = (0 \xrightarrow{a} A)$:   etc.

We give a meaning to the following expression:

$$(41a) \quad -(0 \xrightarrow{a} A) - (A \xrightarrow{a'} B) = -(0 \xrightarrow{b} B)$$

which represents the composition [combination] of two subtractions of differences, hence the complete inversion of the preceding composition [combination) of positive terms (proposition 40); this combination thus symbolises a possible subtraction based on differences of higher order.

It is, on the other hand, legitimate to subtract a difference from itself, thus cancelling it: $(A \xrightarrow{a'} B) - (A \xrightarrow{a'} B)$. But this operation admits of two possible meanings, quite distinct from each other and it is necessary to choose between them: first, the cancellation of a difference between A and B could signify that one modifies A or B in such a manner as to equalise them; the product of the operation would then be $A \underset{o}{\overset{o}{\rightleftarrows}} B$, that is to say $A = B$; but secondly, the cancellation of the difference may also be conceived as establishing a relation in the direction $A \xrightarrow{a'} B$, followed by setting up a relation in the opposite direction $B \xrightarrow{-a'} A$ that is to say $B \xleftarrow{a'} A,$ the product of these two relations as set up consisting thus in joining A to A in the form $A = A$.

Now, the first of these two operations is not a relational operation but rather a class operation: it consists, in fact, of modifying the terms themselves, A or B, by addition of new elements or subtraction of given elements. Hence, it is only in the second sense that we may conceive the subtraction of a difference by reference to itself:

One has then:

$$(42) \quad (A \xrightarrow{a'} B) - (A \xrightarrow{a'} B) = (A \xrightarrow{a'} B) + (B \xrightarrow{-a'} A)$$
$$= (A \xrightarrow{a'} B) + (B \xleftarrow{a'} A).$$

Thus we come to this essential result, which is not due to a convention but expresses the mechanism appropriate for relational operations, that the subtraction of an asymmetric positive relation (= of an ordered difference) is equivalent to the addition of its converse. In other words, to add a relation consists in passing from A to B, thus setting down a difference, whereas subtraction consists in returning from B to A, that is to say traversing the same road in the opposite direction (reciprocity). Therefore, if we agree to write at the beginning and end of a series of operations the terms to be connected with each other by a final relation (by the product of transitive composition), we find:

$$(42a) \quad (A \xrightarrow{-a'} B) - (A \xrightarrow{a'} B) = (A \xrightarrow{a'} B) + (B \xleftarrow{a'} A)$$
$$= A \underset{o}{\overset{o}{\rightrightarrows}} A, \text{ let it be } (A = A).$$

One has similarly:

$$(42b) \quad (0 \xrightarrow{b} B) - (A \xrightarrow[d]{} B) = (0 \xrightarrow[b]{} B) + (B \xleftarrow{a'} A)$$
$$= (0 \xrightarrow{a} A); \quad \text{etc.}$$

3. *The general identity operation* is thus the null difference $(A\,^0A)$, or $A = A$. The null difference can, in fact, signify only the identity in this grouping, since seriated terms are, by definition, all different. We have thus:

$$(43) \quad (A \xrightarrow{a'} B) + (B \xleftarrow{a'} A) = (A \xrightarrow{0} A) \quad \text{and}$$
$$(A \xrightarrow{0} A) + (A \xrightarrow{a'} B) = (A \xrightarrow{a'} B).$$

The general identity is as always: (*a*) the product of the direct operation and its inverse; (*b*) the operation which does not modify those with which it is composed.

4. *The special identities* are tautology and resorption:

$$(44) \quad (A \xrightarrow{a'} B) + (A \xrightarrow{a'} B) = (A \xrightarrow{a'} B) \quad \text{and}$$
$$(A \xrightarrow{a'} B) + (A \xrightarrow{a'b'} C) = (A \xrightarrow{a'b'} C).$$

5. *Associativity* follows the same laws as in groupings of classes. Such a grouping, whose isomorphism[1] with the simple addition of classes (grouping I), can be established, raises a set of interesting problems with regard to the comparison of the structure of classes and the structure of relations.

(E) Complementary Note (slip included with *Logique opératoire*)

In the introduction to the new edition of our *Essay on Operational Logic*, we have taken note of the fact that three fine logicians seeking to formalise the structure of the 'grouping' have arrived either at overlarge structures or at a lattice limited by arbitrary conventions: whence the hypothesis seemingly emerges that the 'grouping' existed too close to its 'content' to provide a distinct formalisation. Now the logician H. Wermus, specialist in problems of the transfinite, has just succeeded in this axiomatisation of 'groupings', which is interesting since they

---

[1]This isomorphism supposes that we have the right to write

$$(0 \xrightarrow{a} A) + (A \xrightarrow{a'} B) = (A \xrightarrow{a'} B) + (0 \xrightarrow{a} A)$$

as we wrote $A + A' = A' + A$ in grouping I. This right to formulate it can be allowed although it does not faithfully translate the meaning of this grouping of relations. It follows that the psychological 'isomorphism' is reduced most often to a simple correspondence.

constitute without doubt one of the simplest structures used by scientific thought.

1. Extending logical language by equality (=), Wermus starts from a genuine binary predicate denoted $x \lessdot y$ and called 'immediate successor'. It is determined by two axioms:

    Ax. 1. Asymmetry of $\lessdot$: $\forall x \, \forall y \, (x \lessdot y \Longrightarrow y \not\lessdot x)$ (= not $y \lessdot x$).
    Ax. 2. Uniqueness of the successor:

    $$\forall x \, \exists y \, \forall z \, [x \lessdot y \quad \text{and} \quad x \lessdot z \Longrightarrow (y = z)].$$

    A formal theory of the immediate successor being then possible, a new symbol is introduced into his language (designated $\curlyvee$) replacing the 'U' of the lattice and expressing the 'join' increasingly appropriate to ['de proche en proche propre aux'] 'groupings'. This operation [of] 'contiguous junction' $x \curlyvee y = z$ generates the immediate successor z of two contiguous elements x and y. From which a third axiom follows:

    Ax. 3. $(x \curlyvee y = z) \Longleftrightarrow (x \lessdot z) \quad \text{and} \quad (y \lessdot z)$.

    It remains to formalise the inverse relations of $\curlyvee$ with the intention of subtracting from a class z the complement of x in order to 're-descend' to x. Thus a symbol is introduced into the language of the theory of dichotomous groupings '$\curlywedge$', for a binary operation. A fourth axiom makes the formal definition precise:

    Ax. 4. $\forall z \, \forall y \, (\exists ! \, x) \, [(z \curlywedge y = x) \Longleftrightarrow (x \curlyvee y = z)]$
    and $\forall u (u \lessdot z \text{ and } u \neq x \Longrightarrow u = y)$.

    This axiom establishes the existence and uniqueness of 'subtraction' (dichotomous) of an element from its successor.

Comment There is some improvement here regarding the General Grouping as far as simplicity is concerned. The binary predicate is virtually a relation but this is limited in meaning to 'immediate successor'. Regarding classes, the second binary operation involves inversion in the form of subtraction but it is not suggested that the condition for group inverses has to be satisfied. There seems no way of reversing the relation of 'immediate successor' to account for reciprocity (as in *Structuralism*, p. 25). Further, the perennial problem of identifying the element of the structure remains except for the reference to 'z' as a class. But this makes the structure a mathematical one and not a psychological, operational one. Piaget himself refers to it as 'one of' the most simple (not the only one) of the structures used by (but not inherent in) scientific thought.

Such a rigid structure as this could scarcely reflect the flexibility of thought to which it is attributed. Piaget himself does not treat it as a new theory, which would, in fact, entail rejecting previous work. He simply includes it with LO without relating it to his standard theory.

4 Mathematical Structures of the Formal Operational Stage

The Structures of the Formal Operational Stage

The distinction between the concrete operational and the formal operational stages is, for Piaget, structurally very marked. The stage of formal thought is not simply a culmination of the concrete (7–11-year-old) stage, as he explains (Inhelder and Piaget, *The Growth of Logical Thinking*, p. xxii–subsequently referred to as GLT), 'but involve[s] a period of new structuring leading to another level of equilibrium at about 14–15 years'. This process involves 'an entirely new set of operational structures' (loc. cit.). Whereas the concrete stage involves only operations relating to the logic of classes and relations, the new structures 'are based on propositional logic and a "formal" mode of thought' (loc. cit).

Formal thought means the appearance of new operational schemata which are based on the structures of the lattice (see Appendix A to this chapter) and a group of four transformations (I, N, R and C) known as the Klein-four group. At the same time, the cognitive structures and specific operations of the earlier period such as seriation, forming correspondences, manipulating classes, and so on, are seen as providing the basis for the structuration appearing in adolescence.

From about 11–12 years onwards, Piaget claims, the subject begins to generalise on the basis of earlier structuration. New operational schemata appear; 'these include combinatorial operations, propositions, double systems of reference, a schema of mechanical equilibrium (equality between action and reaction), multiplicative probabilities, correlations, etc.' (loc. cit.). Thus, he becomes able to think of possibilities as well as of actualities and the immediate present, of logical necessity and therefore able to reason hypothetico-deductively; he is able to generalise the empirical correspondences associated with simple two-by-two (logically) multiplicative associations into a complete combinatorial system of all possibilities. Instead of trial-and-error associations he becomes able to deal with the effects of a number of variables by the method of 'all other things being equal' and so to isolate the effect of each variable in an experimental situation. The theory explaining this change of thinking is:

(a) The incomplete combinatorial system at the concrete operational stage, associated with the semi-lattice, as discussed in Chapter 3, Appendix A, is generalised into the complete combinatorial system associated with the complete lattice of what are described as the sixteen binary operations (logical). These operations are described below in detail but an explanation is called for here of the sense in which they are a generalisation of concrete operational structures. The concrete operational subject is capable of operational thinking but only with reference to classes and relations and does not form operations upon propositions themselves. Now, let such classes be A, A', B, B', where A, A' represent 'dogs' (say) and '(animals that are) *not* dogs'. Let B, B' represent 'black things' and '(things that are) *not* black'. If it is required to consider possible combinations of these, the concrete operational subject is alleged to be capable only of taking AB, AB', $A'B$, $A'B'$ into account where juxtaposition of the terms means conjunction, working through these possibilities rather unsystematically. At the formal operational stage the subject is able to form a complete combinatorial system from A, A', B, B', taking them 1 at a time, 2 at a time, 3 at a time, 4 at a time (and none at a time). Thus, the complete combinatorial system at the formal stage formed from A, A', B, B' would be

	Number of possibilities
None of A, A', B, B'	1
A, B, A', B'	4
AA', AB, AB', $A'B$, $A'B'$, BB'	6
$AA'B$, $AA'B'$, ABB', $A'BB'$	4
$AA'BB'$	1
	16

The concrete operational subject does not consider all these possibilities but only AA', AB, AB', BB' and even these in an unsystematic way. The formal operational subject not only considers all the possible class combinations; he is able to think of all possible logical propositional combinations corresponding to the classes. (See below, page 96).

(b) The negation and reciprocity of concrete operations which were previously separate and unrelated are generalised into the inversion and reciprocity of the formal stage and are integrated into a single system, the INRC group, which is isomorphic to the coin-turning group met in Chapter 2. (See below, pages 98–101).

These structures, the lattice and the group, are closed and complete and represent, for Piaget, the apogée of cognitive development in their common property of being a 'structure d'ensemble'. The general connecting link between the two structures lies in propositional logic since the INRC group is ultimately defined in terms of binary logical propositions and the proposed lattice is itself a set of binary propositions taken in all possible combinations.

The formal operational stage is not simply another one in a general progression of stages. It constitutes the ultimate and final goal which the general structuration of cognition can reach. These formal structures are said to 'mark the completion of the operational development of intelligence' (GLT, p. xxiv). Moreover, it is intended that such structures shall apply to the affective as well as the rational. Thus, the emotional side of the subject as well as his social relations are to be subsumed under this structural concept (see below, Chapter 10). The general form of the mechanism of transition from concrete to formal thought lies in 'the end product of a series of coordinations as they attain a final level of equilibrium' (GLT, p. xxiii).

Lattice Structure

What does Piaget mean by his combinatorial system? This is most clearly exemplified in the colourless liquid experiment described in GLT (pp. 108–9).

In experiment 1, the child is given four similar flasks containing colorless, odorless liquids which are perceptually identical. We number them: (1) diluted sulphuric acid; (2) water; (3) oxygenated water; (4) thiosulphate; we add a bottle (with a dropper) which we will call g; it contains potassium iodide. It is known that oxygenated water oxidises potassium iodide in an acid medium. Thus mixture $(1 + 3 + g)$ will yield a yellow color. The water (2) is neutral, so that adding it will not change the color, whereas the thiosulphate (4) will bleach the mixture $(1 + 3 + g)$. The experimenter presents to the subject two glasses, one containing $1 + 3$, the other containing 2. In front of the subject, he pours several drops of g in each of the two glasses and notes the different reactions. Then the subject is asked simply to reproduce the color yellow, using flasks 1, 2, 3, 4, and g as he wishes.

According to Piaget's observations, the younger subjects appear not to work systematically to solve the problem and simply make trial and error correspondences. The subjects who actually solve the problem work systemically, for example, CHA, the most advanced example (GLT, p. 117):

CHA (13;0): *'You have to try with all the bottles. I'll begin with the one at the end* [*from 1 to 4 with g*]. *It doesn't work any more. Maybe you have to mix them* [he tries $1 \times 2 \times g$, then $1 \times 3 \times g$]. *It turned yellow. But are there other solutions? I'll try* [$1 \times 4 \times g$; $2 \times 3 \times g$; $2 \times 4 \times g$; $3 \times 4 \times g$; with the two preceding combinations this gives the six two-by-two combinations systematically]. *It doesn't work. It only works with'* [$1 \times 3 \times g$] –'Yes, and what about 2 and 4?'–'*2 and 4 don't make any color together. They are negative. Perhaps you could add 4 in $1 \times 3 \times g$ to see if it would cancel out the color* [he does this]. *Liquid 4 cancels it all. You'd have to see if 2 has the same influence* [he tries it]. *No, so 2 and 4 are not alike, for 4 acts on 1×3 and 2 does not.'* —'What is there in 2 and 4?'—'*In 4 certainly water. No, the opposite, in 2 certainly water since it doesn't act on the liquids; that makes things clearer.'*–'And if I were to tell you that 4 is water?'–'*If this liquid 4 is water, when you put it with 1×3 it wouldn't completely prevent the yellow from forming. It isn't water; it's something harmful.'*

The complete set of possibilities constituting the effective factors needed to solve the problem in combination with *g* are:

(1)	0	(no combination works)
(2)	flask 1 ⎤	
(3)	flask 2 ⎟	
(4)	flask 3 ⎟	(one of the flasks taken singly works)
(5)	flask 4 ⎦	
(6)	flasks 1 and 2 ⎤	
(7)	flasks 1 and 3 ⎟	
(8)	flasks 1 and 4 ⎟	
(9)	flasks 2 and 3 ⎟	(some combination of 2 flasks works)
(10)	flasks 2 and 4 ⎟	
(11)	flasks 3 and 4 ⎦	
(12)	flasks 1 and 2 and 3 ⎤	
(13)	flasks 1 and 2 and 4 ⎟	(some combination of 3 flasks works)
(14)	flasks 2 and 3 and 4 ⎟	
(15)	flasks 1 and 3 and 4 ⎦	
(16)	flasks 1 and 2 and 3 and 4	(combination of all 4 flasks works)

The subject discovers, according to Piaget, that the only combination producing the required result is ($1 \times 3 \times g$). Actually, ($1 \times 2 \times 3 \times g$) would work too, but perhaps not as well as it would be diluted with water.

The problem is solved here in a systematic way, up to a point, and demonstrates the capability by the subject (CHA) of a fair degree of systematic thinking. Trial and error is not completely absent, however, and there is some experimenter suggestion. Nor does the subject use the complete system of possible combinations. He appears to assume that only one solution is possible and does not attempt, for example, $(1 \times 2 \times 4)$ or $(2 \times 3 \times 4)$ or $(1 \times 2 \times 3 \times 4)$ or mention the sixteenth possibility. Thus, there is no evidence yet of the *complete* combinatorial system. Even more important, we are led to ask whether this step–by–step logical method of solving problems is the only method, the best method under all circumstances, or is it simply the abstracted form of a much more complex totality of insights of which logic is only a part?

So far, the sixteen combinations have been presented in terms of simple factors and not yet in terms of binary propositional logic, which is the very essence of the structures at the formal operational stage. First, the notation must be explained. The signs p and q are used by Piaget to stand for binary logical propositions, that is, sentences that have two truth-values, True or False. 'London is in England' is True. 'London is in Paris' is False. It must be emphasised that p or q in normal logical usage are completely independent of any particular sentence content. They represent *only* propositions having truth-values. However, Piaget's notation is once more ambiguous here, and he vacillates between a truth-value interpretation and a 'content-full' one, which we shall refer to presently.

Sometimes Piaget uses signs $\bar{p}$, $\bar{q}$ for the negations of propositions p and q, but they may also mean something different. For example, in the balance experiment (pages 101ff), if p stands for a proposition concerning 'increase the weight' then $\bar{p}$ stands for one concerning 'diminish the weight'. $p \cdot q$ in normal logical usage stands for a (compound) proposition which is true if p and q are both true but false if either p or q is false or if both are false. $p \lor q$ stands for a (compound) proposition which is true if either p is true or q is true, or if both p and q are true.

If two factors are being considered in terms of their causal effectiveness in a situation, then the reasoning is said to run as follows:

Either   (*a*) p and q together are effective (i.e. $p \cdot q$)

or   (*b*) p is effective, but not together with q (i.e. $p \cdot \bar{q}$)

or   (*c*) q is effective but not together with p (i.e. $\bar{p} \cdot q$)

or   (*d*) p is ineffective and (simultaneously) q is ineffective (i.e. $\bar{p} \cdot \bar{q}$).

This set of possibilities can be represented by:

$$(p \cdot q) \lor (p \cdot \bar{q}) \lor (\bar{p} \cdot q) \lor (\bar{p} \cdot \bar{q}).$$

Piaget affirms that, whereas the concrete operational subject can speculate no further than the four simple base associations applied to classes of objects (AB, AB', $A'B$, $A'B$), two principal distinguishing features of formal operational thinking are (a) the transition from thinking about classes to thinking about propositions (logical possibilities), and (b) the ability to separate effective factors out in an experimental situation by considering all the possibilities obtained by taking each of the four brackets in:

$$(p \cdot q) \vee (p \cdot \bar{q}) \vee (\bar{p} \cdot q) \vee (\bar{p} \cdot \bar{q})$$

and combining them in all possible ways, taking one at a time, two at a time, three at a time, four at a time, and 'none' at a time. Thus, the formal operational subject will not only consider whether the effective factors are p and q, i.e. $(p \cdot q)$, or p and not-q, i.e. $(p \cdot \bar{q})$, or not-p and q, i.e. $(\bar{p} \cdot q)$, or not-p and not-q, i.e. $(\bar{p} \cdot \bar{q})$, he will consider the following sixteen possibilities:

(1)	0	(9)	$(p \cdot q) \vee (\bar{p} \cdot \bar{q})$
(2)	$p \cdot q$	(10)	$(p \cdot \bar{q}) \vee (\bar{p} \cdot q)$
(3)	$p \cdot \bar{q}$	(11)	$(p \cdot \bar{q}) \vee (\bar{p} \cdot \bar{q})$
(4)	$\bar{p} \cdot q$	(12)	$(p \cdot q) \vee (p \cdot \bar{q}) \vee (\bar{p} \cdot q)$
(5)	$\bar{p} \cdot \bar{q}$	(13)	$(p \cdot q) \vee (p \cdot \bar{q}) \vee (\bar{p} \cdot \bar{q})$
(6)	$(\bar{p} \cdot q) \vee (\bar{p} \cdot \bar{q})$	(14)	$(p \cdot q) \vee (\bar{p} \cdot q) \vee (\bar{p} \cdot \bar{q})$
(7)	$(p \cdot q) \vee (p \cdot \bar{q})$	(15)	$(p \cdot \bar{q}) \vee (\bar{p} \cdot q) \vee (\bar{p} \cdot \bar{q})$
(8)	$(p \cdot q) \vee (\bar{p} \cdot q)$	(16)	$(p \cdot q) \vee (p \cdot \bar{q}) \vee (\bar{p} \cdot q) \vee (\bar{p} \cdot \bar{q})$

An important experiment in this connection is the one concerned with Invisible Magnetization (GLT, p. 94). The details will be found in Appendix A to this chapter.

This experiment is particularly interesting since the replies of one subject (GOU, aged 14 years 11 months), reported in full, are said by Piaget to be 'based on the set of sixteen binary operations in continuous transition from one to the next; their consistent integration is demonstrated with particular clarity. The following operations can be distinguished in his protocol.' Piaget lists the sixteen binary operations and attempts to relate them all to GOU's replies.

The main points of interest to us are:

(a) There is a continual shift in meaning of the symbols $p, q, \bar{p}, \bar{q}$, etc. for example, in (1) p means 'It is the distance', and in (5) p means 'A magnet is attached to the disk'.

(b) Some of the sixteen propositions cannot be found, for example,

$(\bar{p} \cdot \bar{q})$. It is admitted in the text that (13) and (14) are not stated independently but 'are found in (15)' (p. 104).

Point (*b*) is particularly important since Piaget claims the presence of all sixteen binary propositions in GOU's protocol, but here attempts to account for the absence of (13) and (14) by affirming their existence in the complete affirmation. Now, it is important to record that (15) is the *complete affirmation* of all possibilities:

$$(p \cdot q) \vee (p \cdot \bar{q}) \vee (\bar{p} \cdot q) \vee (\bar{p} \cdot \bar{q});$$
$$(13) \text{ is } (p \cdot q) \vee (\bar{p} \cdot q);$$
$$(14) \text{ is } (p \cdot \bar{q}) \vee (\bar{p} \cdot \bar{q}).$$

We can find (13) and (14) as part of (15) and thus, according to Piaget, a statement of (15) could be taken as implying (13) and (14). (In fact, in examining GOU's remarks we cannot find (15) which is shown, according to Piaget, by '[the] absence of particular links'.)

What is at issue is whether the lattice of sixteen binary propositions, which is a (partially) ordered structure based upon 'inclusion', exists as a cognitive structure. The sixteen propositions cited can easily be seen to involve 'inclusion' of some others, for example, $(p \cdot q)$ is 'included' in $(p \cdot q) \vee (p \cdot \bar{q})$, and so on. What is inadmissible is to assume the existence of unstated possibilities in the subject's mind simply because all possibilities are included in the 'complete affirmation' proposition. Furthermore, the omission of (15) is particularly significant as it is the statement of the possibility of everything co-existing simultaneously. This assumption by Piaget that a statement of (15) implies the statement of other propositions such as (13) and (14) 'collapses' the lattice and could, taken to its logical conclusion, imply the existence of the lattice in cognition merely from a statement of (15) *alone*.

Charles Parsons, in his paper 'Inhelder and Piaget's *The Growth of Logical Thinking,* II. A logician's viewpoint' (Parsons, 1960), produces a cogent analysis of the confusions and ambiguities in Piaget's logical conceptions which are hidden by his ambiguous use of notation and which are particularly relevant to this discussion. Parsons's arguments are rather technical and are not reproduced here. What he points out is that Piaget vacillates between two different meanings in his notation. First, there is the truth functional interpretation in which the formulae represent propositions whose truth or falsity depends upon the truth or falsity of the propositions represented by the individual symbols but is independent of content. At other times, explains Parsons, he uses his symbolism 'to represent propositional *functions*, e.g. what is expressed by sentences containing free variables, such as "*x* is a US Senator", which are only true or false when values of the argument variables are specified, e.g. by replacing "*x*" by "J. W. Fulbright" ' (op cit., p. 76).

There are, therefore, considerable problems arising from Piaget's logical notation similar to those we have shown regarding his mathematical notation. Parsons argues that ambiguities could be cleared up by the use of quantification theory. This might seem to solve Piaget's problems, but on the other hand would result in a very different theory since the lattice and group structure of the formal operational stage could no longer be argued. The latter depend upon the binary propositional logic which is used throughout in the Piagetian representation of cognitive development. Piaget's entire theory in which the grouping and semi-lattice of the concrete operational stage give way to the INRC (complete) group and full lattice for the adolescent would no longer apply.

What, then, of the claim made by Piaget that the lattice is a central structure of cognition? This claim must be looked at in the light of the following points. First, the Piagetian experiments are very particular and limited cases and involve problem-solving of a very circumscribed character. Not only do they represent a type of problem found only in classical physics but they are rare in formal knowledge in general. These problems are quite exceptional in living situations. Moreover, there is a hiatus between what the subject says and the logical 'modelling' of his responses by the experimenter. Not only does the subject very rarely, if ever, use all sixteen binary operations, but his thinking is actually much richer than the oversimplified, propositional representation of it in the logical model. It is not possible to tell from the subject's words whether he is thinking propositionally or in terms of classes or sets or in terms of collections. Of course, a propositional interpretation can be abstracted by the experimenter and put into propositional logical form. There is, however, no guarantee that this actually represents even the subject's propositional logical thought. The lattice is a mathematical structure corresponding to an *abstraction* of certain features of ordering, and so on, in thinking about the world and, as such, is one of many possible abstractions. It must not be treated as all-encompassing.

Group Structure

The other structure cited by Piaget as central to formal thinking, the INRC group, now needs attention. A number of different experiments are cited mainly in *The Growth of Logical Thinking* to explicate the theory of INRC group structure for cognition, but we shall refer only to the equilibrium in the balance experiment here because it presents a more familiar situation than many of the others while being completely representative. Moreover, the central connections between group structure, logic and numerical proportionality are exceptionally clearly related to one another in Piaget's discussion (GLT, pp. 178–81).

In the experiment the subject is presented with a balance and a number of weights which can be hung at different points along the crossbar. The problem is to discover the (inverse) proportionality law between weight and distance from the fulcrum (and, subsidiarily, to relate this to the heights above and below the horizontal equilibrium position). The claim is that this problem is solved by means of a certain group structure, the so–called INRC group, whose four elements, I, N, R and C, are so called because they are the first letters of the words identity, negation, reciprocity and correlative. The structure of this group of four elements is the same as that which was examined in Chapter 2 in the coin-turning experiment – the Klein-four group.

In the initial exposition of the group in Chapter 2 the group elements under the rule of combination 'combined with' or 'followed by' or 'and then' were the *transformations or actions carried out on the coins themselves,* the coins being, in one sense, partly accidental to the process. The group rule of combination was not between the coins themselves. It was between the *actions* on the coins. In the present case the cognitive group being considered consists of elements which are themselves said to be operations or transformations on logical operations (or propositions).

What is the specific nature of the group alleged to be central to the formal operational stage of cognition? Although this group (Klein-four) may be manifested in a variety of different situations, it is defined by Piaget in terms of transformations on logical propositions in GLT (p. 134).

there are more general transformations which transform particular operators into others. Thus an operator such as $p \vee q$ can be transformed by inversion or negation into $\bar{p} \cdot \bar{q}$, a transformation that we may designate by N, so that $N(p \vee q) = \bar{p} \cdot \bar{q}$. But $(p \vee q)$ can also be transformed by reciprocity R, so that $R(p \vee q) = \bar{p} \vee \bar{q} = p/q$. Again $(p \vee q)$ can be transformed, by correlativity C (*i.e.*, by permuting the $\vee$ and the .), so that $C (p \vee q) = p \cdot q$. Finally, the operator $(p \vee q)$ may be transformed into itself by identical transformation I, so that $I (p \vee q) = (p \vee q)$. Thus, one can see that I, N, R, and C form a commutative group of four transformations among themselves, for the correlative C is the inverse N [*sic*] of the reciprocal R, so that $C = NR$ (and $C = RN$ as well). Likewise, we have $R = CN$ (or NC) and $N = CR$ (or RC). Finally, we have $I = RCN$ (or CRN, etc.).

This group is of psychological importance because it actually corresponds to certain fundamental structures of thought at the formal level, for inversion N expresses negation, reciprocity R expresses symmetry (equivalent transformations oriented in opposite directions), and correlativity is symmetric with negation.[32]

What is meant here is that the subject can perform (mental) transformations upon (mental) transformations or operations upon operations – all in terms of his thinking about the possibilities in a situation, for example, the balance. For instance, with reference to the logical operation p . q the subject can perform any one of four transformations or operations upon it. If this is selected as an example (Piaget used p v q) the subject can negate it logically, that is, he can think of the negation of p . q, i.e. $N(p$. $q)$, where (logically) $N(p$. $q) = \bar{p}$ v $\bar{q}$, using Piaget's notation. Similarly, the reciprocal $R(p$. $q)$ is a possibility that the subject can think of, where $R(p$. $q) = \bar{p}$. $\bar{q}$ and the correlative $C(p$. $q)$ can be thought of, where $C(p$. $q) = p$ v q.

It would be as well to summarise Piaget's theory here:

(1)   The INRC group is a group of transformations upon logical operations, by which the subject can express the possibilities of solving particular problems (in this case the balance).

e.g.　　　　$I(p$ v $q) = p$ v q　　　Also,　　$I(p$ · $q) = p$ · q
　　　　　　$N(p$ v $q) = \bar{p}$ · $\bar{q}$　　　　　　　$N(p$ · $q) = \bar{p}$ v $\bar{q}$
　　　　　　$R(p$ v $q) = \bar{p}$ v $\bar{q}$　　　　　　　$R(p$ · $q) = \bar{p}$ · $\bar{q}$
　　　　　　$C(p$ v $q) = p$ · q　　　　　　　　$C(p$ · $q) = p$ v q.

p, $\bar{p}$, q, $\bar{q}$ etc., in the balance experiment refer to propositions about increasing or decreasing weight or the distance of the weight from the fulcrum, as possible ways of achieving equilibrium and arriving at the law of equilibrium for the balance. The subject can think of, say, p v q itself, without transforming it, he can 'leave it alone' and this is represented by $I(p$ v $q) = p$ v q, the identity transformation. The inverse of p v q is negation, in Piaget's notation $(\bar{p}$. $\bar{q})$ and this is obtained by changing p and q to $\bar{p}$ and $\bar{q}$ and changing 'v' to '.' (naturally, the negation or inverse of p . q would be obtained by changing $\bar{p}$, $\bar{q}$ to p and q and changing '.' to 'v'). The reciprocal of p v q is defined by changing $\bar{p}$, $\bar{q}$ to p, q, i.e. $\bar{p}$ v $\bar{q}$. Finally, the correlative of p v q is defined by the same propositions but with 'v' changed to '.', i.e. p . q. In this way, the I, N, R, C system of transformations is defined in terms of logical propositions. In Piaget's notation. '$N(p$ v $q) = \bar{p}$. $\bar{q}$' means 'the negation of either increase the weight or increase the distance or both' is 'decrease the weight and decrease the distance' (on one side of the balance). This works similarly for $I(p$ v $q)$, $R(p$ v $q)$ and $C(p$ v $q)$.

Two points. First, although the INRC group is defined in terms of transformations upon logical propositions, it is all too easy to slip into thinking of it in terms of transformations on the physical system of the balance, and Piaget does just this (see below, pages 101ff). This structure is the pivot upon which rests the Piagetian view that understanding numerical proportionality depends upon the possession of INRC group structure. Secondly, and apparently only a notational oddity, Piaget uses '$\bar{p}$' for negation, in other words for what is often symbolised as '$\sim p$' in normal logical usage. This means 'It is not true that p . . . ', for instance, if p represents the proposition 'London is in England' then $\bar{p}$ should represent 'It is false that London is in England' or 'London is not in England'. Now, Piaget uses $\bar{p}$ to represent not logical negation but physical cancellation. It will be seen that p represents 'the statement of a fixed increase of weight' and $\bar{p}$ represents 'the proposition(s) stating a corresponding diminution of weight' (GLT, p. 178). The proposition 'Do not increase the weight' is completely different from 'Diminish the weight', since the first may well involve keeping the weight constant. 'p' refers to propositional logic, but the use of $\bar{p}$ for negation allows Piaget to slip from logic to the physical event and, as a consequence, from transformations upon propositions to transformations upon a physical system.

(2)   Piaget's specifications for the group elements are

$$C = NR = RN; \qquad R = CN = NC;$$
$$N = CR = RC; \qquad I = RCN.$$

The table which may be constructed from this, under operation '$\star$', which stands for 'and then' is as below (Table 4.1).

Table 4.1

$\star$	I	N	R	C
I	I	N	R	C
N	N	I	C	R
R	R	C	I	N
C	C	R	N	I

It is this group that is to be central to formal thought, even more so perhaps than the sixteen combinatorial operations because N and R, the forms of reversibility which were previously separate at the concrete operational stage, are now supposedly united in this single closed structure.

The Balance Experiment

Piaget presents his definitions for the balance experiment in GLT (p. 178):

> For example, let us examine the subjects' reasoning on the changes of weight and horizontal distance (to simplify notation we shall disregard the constant weights and distances). Let p be the statement of a fixed increase of weight and q of a fixed increase of distance; let us call $\bar{p}$ and $\bar{q}$ the propositions stating a corresponding diminution of weight and distance on the same arm of the balance. Propositions p' and q' cor-

respond to p and q, and $\bar{p}'$ and $\bar{q}'$ correspond to p' and q' on the other arm. By a process isomorphic to prop. (1) of Chap. 10, the subjects understand the following relations of inversion and reciprocity (the INRC group but with $p \cdot q$ chosen as the identical operation I):

$I(p \cdot q)$ = to increase simultaneously the weight and the distance on one of the arms;

$N(\bar{p} \vee \bar{q}) = (p \cdot \bar{q}) \vee (\bar{p} \cdot q) \vee (\bar{p} \cdot \bar{q})$ = to reduce the distance while increasing the weight or diminish the weight while increasing the distance or diminish both; (8)

$R(p' \cdot q')$ compensates I by increasing both weight and distance on the other arm of the balance;

$C(\bar{p}' \vee \bar{q}') = (p' \cdot \bar{q}') \vee (\bar{p}' \cdot q') \vee (\bar{p}' \cdot \bar{q}')$ = cancels R in the same way that N cancels I.

But, since $R(p' \cdot q')$ is equivalent to compensating action $I(p \cdot q)$ with a reaction (symmetry) on the other arm of the balance, we find that it can be written $\bar{p} \cdot \bar{q}$; and since $(\bar{p}' \vee \bar{q}')$ is also equivalent to compensating the action N by symmetry, we can write it $(p \vee q)$. Therefore proposition (8) can be formulated as follows:

$$I(p \cdot q)$$
$$N(\bar{p} \vee \bar{q})$$
$$R(\bar{p} \cdot \bar{q}) \qquad (8a)$$
$$C(p \vee q).$$

p, q are propositions concerning increasing weight and distance; $\bar{p}, \bar{q}$ are propositions concerning decreasing weight and distance; $p, q, \bar{p}, \bar{q}$ refer to the original arm of the balance; $p', q', \bar{p}', \bar{q}'$ always refer to the other arm.

The first problem in this passage lies in the definitions, for example, '$N(\bar{p} \vee \bar{q})| = (p \cdot \bar{q}) \vee (\bar{p} \cdot q) \vee (\bar{p} \cdot \bar{q})$ = to reduce the distance while increasing the weight or diminish the weight while increasing the distance or diminish both'. Here, the result of transformation is muddled with what is transformed and this applies throughout. It should read:

$$N(p \cdot q) = \bar{p} \vee \bar{q} = (p \cdot \bar{q}) \vee (\bar{p} \cdot q) \vee (\bar{p} \cdot \bar{q}).$$

Notice, too, that the physical and logical are confused here. Physically $\bar{p}$ may stand for *diminishing* the weight but logically it must stand for 'it is false that the weight is increased', or 'the weight is not increased'. As we have seen, logical negation is quite different from physical cancellation.

Similarly, $R(p' \cdot q')$ is said to compensate I by increasing both weight and distance on the other arm of the balance. But if $p \cdot q$ refers to the first arm and is the operation being transformed, that is, $I(p \cdot q) = p \cdot q$, then its reciprocal (which compensates without cancellation) must be $R(p \cdot q)$ and, in the notation as given, should read:

$$R(p \cdot q) = p' \cdot q'.$$

Again, the result of the transformation is muddled with the operation transformed.

A further problem arises if Piaget is to arrive at the correct statements previously quoted from GLT, p. 134 (see above, page 99) because of the undesired presence of p', q', $\bar{p}'$, $\bar{q}'$. This is solved in the following way. Piaget writes: 'since $R(p' \cdot q')$ is equivalent to compensating action $I(p \cdot q)$ with a reaction (symmetry) on the other arm of the balance, we find that it can be written $\bar{p} \cdot \bar{q}'$. This is equivalent to saying that, because the reciprocal of $p \cdot q$ is the same as compensating $p \cdot q$ with an (equal) reaction on the *other* arm, then the reciprocal of $p \cdot q$ can be written $\bar{p} \cdot \bar{q}$, that is, in the Piagetian notation this would be decrease the weight and distance on the first arm.

Thus, what is done is this:

(a) $I(p \cdot q)$ is taken, that is, increase the weight and increase the distance on the first arm;
(b) the reciprocal on the other side of the balance is written $R(p' \cdot q')$ instead of $R(p \cdot q)$;
(c) $R(p' \cdot q')$ is then written $\bar{p} \cdot \bar{q}$ on the basis of the argument that increase on one side can be written as diminution on the other;
(d) thus, Piaget is able to write $R(p \cdot q) = \bar{p} \cdot \bar{q}$.

The last is much more like negation (cancellation). The original notational muddle contributed to this since only by writing $R(p' \cdot q')$ instead of $R(p \cdot q)$ for the reciprocal could there be a switch back to the first arm of the balance. It seems, therefore, that the original notational muddle and the unwarranted replacement of increase (of weight and distance) on one side by diminution on the other, together achieved the necessary result – and this has to be achieved if the INRC group as a key factor in cognition is to have any foundation at all. A similar procedure is followed with the negation and correlative. Hence p', q', $\bar{p}'$, $\bar{q}'$ are eliminated leaving the field free for an I, N, R, C system of transformations on two variables p and q, and involving the four transformations I, N, R, C upon them.

Let us consider N, R and C in turn (leaving out I for obvious reasons). Similarly to p. 134 (see above, page 99): $N(p \cdot q) = \bar{p} \vee \bar{q}$. Negation means cancellation so this means that cancelling increase of weight and increase of distance can be achieved by, or is the same as, decreasing weight or decreasing distance (or both) on the same side of the balance. But if only the weight or the distance were decreased this would not be annulment in the Piagetian sense. It would be more appropriate to write $N(p \cdot q) = \bar{p} \cdot \bar{q}$, that is, cancelling increase of weight and increase of distance can be achieved by, or is the same as, decreasing both weight and distance.

We have already discussed reciprocation in the context of the confusion of notation and reasoning which managed to eliminate p', q', $\bar{p}'$ and $\bar{q}'$. Certainly $R(p . q) = p' . q'$ is more suitable to represent reciprocation than $R(p . q) = \bar{p} . \bar{q}$.

With regard to correlativity, this is defined (see above, page 99) as $C = NR$, that is the negation of the reciprocal. This should be written:

$$C(p . q) = p \vee q.$$

(This is surely what is meant by $C(p \vee q)$ in 8(a): GLT, p. 178.) This means that for $p . q$, that is, increase weight and distance on the first side, the correlative would be either increase the weight or increase the distance, or increase both, on the *same* side, which makes no sense at all. It would be more suitable to write:

$$C(p . q) = \bar{p}' . \bar{q}'.$$

Thus, a more suitable set of definitions than those of Piaget would be:

$$I(p . q) = p . q;$$
$$N(p . q) = \bar{p} . \bar{q};$$
$$R(p . q) = p' . q';$$
$$C(p . q) = \bar{p}' . \bar{q}'.$$

Parsons, who arrives at the same conclusion comments: 'but here the truth-functional relations of negation, reciprocity and correlativity no longer hold' (1960, p. 81).

In fact, there are many more possibilities for adjustment in the balance experiment than are conceived of in the descriptions in GLT. If the weight is increased from W_1 to nW_1 on one side, that is, it is multiplied by n, then (as Parsons has pointed out) there are *four* possible compensations:

(1)   the weight can be decreased on the same side;
(2)   the distance can be decreased on the same side;
(3)   the weight can be increased on the other side;
(4)   the distance can be increased on the other side.

As Parsons writes, 'It seems that the four group is too simple to describe this fully, but it describes the situation where two of the variables are fixed. The advanced subjects seem to assume at the outset that if W and D are fixed, then an increase in W compensates a decrease in D' (1960, p. 80). It certainly seems that the advanced subjects make the expected, correct assumptions from the start, whereas the younger children play with possibilities in an unconstrained manner.

It appears that the INRC group, as defined by Piaget, cannot be reconciled with the balance situation as given and certainly not in its full potentialities. So, if the transformations of identity, negation, reciprocity and correlativity are performed on logical propositions in the balance experiment, then Piaget's INRC group is not obtained. Conversely, if this group is applied, then it is not applicable to Piaget's balance experiment.

It will be noted that this treatment by Piaget of the physical and logical INRC groups as synonymous and interchangeable corresponds with the treatment of groups in Chapter 2 and the groupings discussed earlier in Chapter 3, in which the treatment allowed movement at will from the internal (propositional) to the external (physical balance) world of the subject and back. Such fluidity obscures the nature of the entities being considered. We never know from instant to instant whether we are talking about objects, events, processes, propositions, logical signs, mathematical symbols, or actual quantities. It is impossible, in short, to bring the discussion or argument to any clear termination in a definite zone.

The Collapse of the INRC Group

The remainder of this chapter discusses two more outstanding problems. First, Piaget's INRC group is 'collapsed' from transformations upon transformations (operations, propositions) into logical operations themselves. (Bear in mind the identification already of the logical and physical INRC groups.) The footnote on p. 178 of GLT and the top lines of p. 179 show this:

The system of these transformations, which states only the equilibrium of weights and distances, is in itself equivalent to the proportionality:[4]

Piaget's footnote:
[4] This logical proportion signifies the following:

$$(p \cdot q) \cdot (\bar{p} \vee q) \; [\text{sic}] = (\bar{p} \cdot \bar{q}) \cdot (p \vee q) = \text{o for I} \cdot \text{N} = \text{R} \cdot \text{C} \tag{a}$$

$$(p \cdot q) \vee (\bar{p} \vee \bar{q}) = (\bar{p} \cdot \bar{q}) \vee (p \vee q) = (p \star q) \text{ for I} \vee \text{N} = \text{R} \vee \text{C} \tag{b}$$

$$(p \cdot q) \cdot (\overline{\bar{p} \cdot \bar{q}}) = (p \vee q) \cdot (\overline{\bar{p} \vee \bar{q}}) = (p \cdot q) \text{ for I} \cdot (\text{NR}) = \text{C} \cdot (\text{NN}) \tag{c}$$

$$(p \cdot q) \cdot (\overline{\bar{p} \vee \bar{q}}) = p \cdot q \cdot (\overline{\bar{p} \vee \bar{q}}) = \text{o for I} \cdot (\text{NC}) = \text{R} \cdot (\text{NN}) \tag{d}$$

$$\frac{p \cdot q}{\bar{p} \cdot \bar{q}} = \frac{p \vee q}{\bar{p} \vee \bar{q}} \quad \text{thus} \quad \frac{Ix}{Rx} = \frac{Cx}{Nx} \quad (\text{where } x = p \cdot q). \tag{9}$$

If the group of transformations I, N, R, C is being referred to, then the use of logical connectives '.' and 'v' is not permitted – in fact, it is meaningless. But it leaves the impression that what is being referred to is I o N = R o C where 'o' is the usual group rule of combination. The use of logical connectives could only have meaning if it is *not* the group of transformations which is under discussion but the logical propositions they give rise to. So, it is not right for Piaget to imply that two separate systems are being related when only one is under discussion – the logical system. Additionally,

$$\frac{Ix}{Rx} \quad \frac{Cx}{Nx} \quad \text{(where } x = p \cdot q)$$

can only be a *logical* statement since this form of proportionality is defined *only* for logical propositions (see *Essai sur les transformations des opérations logiques,* Paris, 1952).

In this way, the Klein-four group INRC and the logical compound propositions, which are the results of transformation, have been collapsed into each other, a process not to be identified with one-way reduction which seems to correspond to Piaget's ultimate perspective of a universal equilibrium (see, for example, *Structuralism*, pp. 45ff.). Instead of I, N, R, C as elements of the group with the rule of combination 'and then', the elements are, for example, $I(p \cdot q)$, $N(p \cdot q)$, $R(p \cdot q)$ and $C(p \cdot q)$ and the rule of combination is a logical connective. The above can be identified with logical propositions, thus:

$$I(p \cdot q) = p \cdot q$$
$$N(p \cdot q) = \bar{p} \vee \bar{q}$$
$$R(p \cdot q) = \bar{p} \cdot \bar{q}$$
$$C(p \cdot q) = p \vee q.$$

So the collapse has been achieved and the system enabled to vacillate between operations upon operations on the one hand and (logical) operations themselves on the other. This arises from a new form of confusion as to what constitutes the element. The vacillation is between I, N, R, C as transformations and, for example, $I(p \cdot q)$, $N(p \cdot q)$, $R(p \cdot q)$ and $C(p \cdot q)$ as logical propositions. The system is enabled to vacillate yet again between different interpretations.

The INRC group as defined on p. 134 of GLT is a Klein-four group *in itself* and under the rule of combination 'and then' (or 'combined with' or 'followed by'). In the coins experiment in Chapter 2, it was the set of actions (together with the rule of combination) that constituted the group, although the coins had to be specified. Here, it is the INRC group defined by its combinations, not the logical operations which result from its transformational operations, that show group structure. One can go farther than this, however, as we have already seen, since this is the basis for the possibility of slipping from one interpretation to another in the by now familiar manner and moving at will from the (internal) logical world to the external world of the subject's physical system. This is achieved by moving from operations upon operations to logical operations and then to numerical proportionality. In the following chapters this will be seen in its full significance. And, again, if I, N, R, C are taken in conjunction with the operations on which they act, there is no longer a group since $p \cdot q$, $\bar{p} \vee \bar{q}$, $\bar{p} \cdot \bar{q}$ and $p \vee q$ do not form a group under 'v' or '.'.

A form of summing-up might be helpful here. The system begins with logical propositions and transformations I, N, R, C on logical propositions are constructed from these. They are constructed in such a way as to form a group in themselves, whose structure is that of the Klein-four group. These transformations may be applied either to logical propositions or to certain restricted examples of physical systems of which Piaget's balance (with increase of weight and distance *fixed*) is an example. The theory vacillates between these interpretations and is enabled to do so as a result of notational and other ambiguities ($\bar{p}$ standing for negation and simultaneously for diminution, and also by the device of removing all notation such as p', q'). Additionally, with reference to the footnote on p. 178, the right-hand side statements are either about logical propositions or about transformations. If they are about logical propositions then they are simply *another way of writing* the logical statements on the left-hand side. If they refer to transformations, then the rule of combination in each case should be 'o' (and then) and they then turn out to be tautological, stating respectively no more than N = N, N = N, C = C and R = R, by definition of C as NR or RN. It is not surprising that the left-hand statements to which they then correspond also hold, and these turn out to be tautologous, too.

The second main problem in the remainder of the chapter is a further extension of the first. For, having 'collapsed' I, N, R, C into logic, this logic is now 'collapsed' into numbers themselves. The remainder of Piaget's chapter is mainly concerned with establishing a connection between the INRC group, logical proportionality and numerical proportionality.

It is on p. 179 that Piaget undertakes to establish the connection between the INRC group and logical proportions:

> Undoubtedly, this qualitative schema of logical proportions corresponds to the global intuition of proportionality with which the subject begins. And it is easy to pass on from this qualitative schema to more detailed logical proportions (involving a single proposition) and from there to numerical proportions.

In this respect, remember that, for a single proposition p, the correlative C is identical with I and the reciprocal R identical with N. From proportion (9) one can construct:

$$\frac{p}{q} = \frac{\bar{q}}{\bar{p}}, \quad \text{whence } \bar{p} = q \vee \bar{q}. \tag{10}$$

In other words, the increase of weight is to the increase of distance as the decrease of distance is to the decrease of weight.

Secondly, beyond the direct proportions of types (9) and (10) the I N R C group includes what can be called reciprocal proportions, where one of the cross-products is the reciprocal R of the other:

$$\frac{p \cdot q}{\bar{p} \cdot \bar{q}} = R\frac{\bar{p} \vee \bar{q}}{p \vee q}, \quad \text{thus}$$

$$[(p \cdot q) \cdot (p \vee q) = p \cdot q] = \tag{11}$$
$$R[(\bar{p} \cdot \bar{q}) \cdot (\bar{p} \vee \bar{q}) = \bar{p} \cdot \bar{q}].$$

Hence, by virtue of (10) and (11), the reciprocal proportion:

$$\frac{p}{q} = R\frac{\bar{p}}{\bar{q}}, \quad \text{thus} \quad (p \cdot \bar{q}) = R(\bar{p} \cdot q). \tag{12}$$

This is critically analysed by Parsons (all numbers in parentheses refer to equations in GLT, as given on the right-hand side in previous quotations):

> The proportions (10) and (11) (p. 179) which Piaget connects with the subject's attack on the problem, appear to be derived from the proportions (9), the first of which is obtained from (8a). But (10) and (11) are not derived from the first of (9) at all and not from $Ix/Rx = Cx/Nx$ where 'R' and 'C' have their truth-functional sense, but only on the assumption $q = Rp$ or $q = Cp$. These are false truth-functionally, but the latter makes empirical sense because $\bar{q}$ compensates p. The relation of (12) to (11) is the same as that of (10) to (9) and the same consideration applies. It is only by analogy that these proportions are related to the truth-functional group. We could not take them literally in that sense, for otherwise we should have logical truths (10) used to schematize empirical facts. (Parsons, 1960, p. 81)

Piaget also seems unable to decide which has priority, the I, N, R, C group or logical proportions. He writes, following (9) on p. 179:

In other words an understanding of the system of inversions and reciprocities (8) and (8a) follows directly from an understanding of this proportional relation; an increase of weight and distance on one arm of the balance is to the symmetrical increase on the other arm as an increase of weight or distance on one arm is to a reciprocal operation on the other.

Yet on p. 315 he writes: 'the logical proportions derive from both the group structures of inversions and reciprocities (INRC) and lattice structures'. This says exactly the opposite. Here, on p. 315, logical proportions derive from the understanding of INRC. The earlier passage asserts the derivation in the opposite direction.

Further, Piaget's (10) is

$$\frac{p}{q} = \frac{\bar{q}}{\bar{p}}, \quad \text{whence } \bar{p} = q \vee \bar{q}.$$

He continues: 'In other words, the increase of weight is to the increase of distance as the decrease of distance is to the decrease of weight.' This statement (apart from referring to a logical tautology) embodies the crucial unexplained *move from logic to measurable quantity*. For p, q refer to (mental) logical propositions or *sentences* about possible increase or decrease in weight and distance. It is not possible to replace propositions by measured quantities as Piaget does. The restriction of the theory to propositions concerned with an increase in weight or distance enables there to be an apparent correspondence (even 'isomorphism') between such 'logical proportions' and numerical proportionality. The use of the 'division' sign assists this, too. This underscores the dependence of the theory on particular sorts of scientific experiment and its irrelevance to cognition in general which is concerned with much more than the merely logico–mathematical.

A final problem is added when Piaget writes (p. 180):

In other words, if $p = n\text{W}$ and $q = n\text{L}$, then:

$$\frac{p}{q} = \frac{\bar{q}}{\bar{p}} \text{ corresponds to } \frac{n\text{W}}{n\text{L}} = \frac{n:\text{L}}{n:\text{W}},$$

$$\text{for example } \frac{2 \times 4}{2 \times 8} = \frac{2:8}{2:4}; \tag{13}$$

$$\text{and } \frac{p}{q} = \text{R} \frac{\bar{p}}{\bar{q}} \text{ corresponds to } \frac{n\text{W}}{n\text{L}} = \frac{\text{W}:n}{\text{L}:n},$$

$$\text{for example } \frac{2 \times 4}{2 \times 8} = \frac{4:2}{8:2}. \tag{14}$$

Now, $\dfrac{nW}{nL} = \dfrac{n{:}L}{n{:}W}$ and putting $n = 2$, $W = 4$, $L = 8$, there is inevitably an

equality $\left(\dfrac{2 \times 4}{2 \times 8} = \dfrac{2:8}{2:4}\right)$. But this is a different issue from the correspondence of this equality to the (tautological) $\dfrac{'p}{q} = \dfrac{\bar{q}'}{\bar{p}}$. Now, $\dfrac{\bar{q}}{\bar{p}}$ represents propositions about decrease of distance (divided by?) decrease of weight, so it is not reconcilable with $\dfrac{n{:}L}{n{:}W}$, although $\dfrac{p}{q}$ can be related (in Piagetian terms) to $\dfrac{nW}{nL}$, which are both associated with increase in weight and increase in distance (a fuller treatment of these notions is to be found in *Essai sur les transformations des opérations logiques* (Piaget, 1952a, Appendix).

Finally, Piaget says (GLT, p. 180) that the formulae (9)–(14) represent the actual reasoning of the subject who 'usually begins by assuming: $p \cdot \bar{q}$ $= R (\bar{p} \cdot q)$ (15)'. This is then interpreted as: 'increasing the weight and reducing the distance on one of the arms is the same as reducing the weight and increasing the distance on the other arm'. However, this depends, as Parsons points out, upon the equivalence in effects of p' and $\bar{p}$, q' and $\bar{q}$, Moreover, none of the subjects appears to begin by assuming the compensation of increased weight and reduced distance by reduced weight and increased distance (on the other side). It is clear, then, that the theory is faulty and that the subjects do not conform to it in practice. All these considerations pointed out in this chapter cast complete doubt upon Piaget's entire corpus of 'mathematics' or 'logic' of 'operations'.

The central feature of Piaget's notion of formal operations is the fact that there are actually *four* tiers to the system, the INRC group of transformations, the logical system, the physical system and the system of numerical proportions. Figure 3.3 is a diagram showing briefly how the collapses occur that enable Piaget to state that an understanding of numerical proportions depends upon the INRC group via logical proportions.

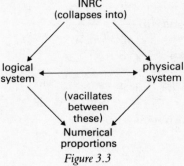

Figure 3.3

In summary then:

1 Piaget presents actions carried out on the balance in terms of, and in the 'symbolism' of, the logical propositions, $p, q, \bar{p}, \bar{q}$, etc.
2 The Klein-four group, INRC, is defined through a 'slippage' in interpretation of this symbolism, for example, $\bar{p}$ to negation of p'.
3 Through a further abuse of notation (I v N = R v C) INRC and the corresponding logical propositions are identified with each other.
4 Logical propositions are finally collapsed into measurement.
5 Thus, with 'logical symbolism' as the central link, INRC is presented as the dominant connective of the system.

The theory turns out to be, as before, a self-fulfilling prophecy.

Conclusions

It only remains to summarise the results of our investigation into the main aspects of the mathematics of Genetic Epistemology. The conclusions of Chapter 2 must influence all our considerations in this chapter, especially the confusions arising from the dual meaning of the word 'operation', the uncertainty of the element, the vacillations in interpretation resulting from this and, above all, the unproven character of the 'group' structure of Piaget's cognitive operations. This 'group' structure is so basic to the theory that its questionability must always be kept in mind when considering the remaining issues.

We may summarise this chapter and the last as follows, beginning with the grouping structure of the concrete operational stage.

Since the grouping structure is a new and different structure the lattice from which the tautology and resorption properties derive is no longer relevant. Furthermore, these properties crowd the grouping with a number of 'arbitrary conventions' as Piaget calls them himself in the *Note complémentaire* to LO. This latter sheet is a new definition of the grouping which might be said to invalidate all of Piaget's previous writings on the subject. But the sheet is inserted into LO without any denial of the previous work. The grouping, thus newly defined in this *Note*, is a perfectly valid mathematical structure, but suffers the same shortcoming as the previous system in so far as it is a mathematical entity that has not been shown to be relevant to cognitive operations as such.

As far as the grouping in general is concerned, the confusion between element and rule of combination leads to vacillation in interpretation of what is the element and what is the rule of combination. The first is interpretable either as equation–sentence, single term $(+A)$ or single term (A) of a mathematical nature. This vacillation parallels the dualism demonstrated in the discussion of action and operation (see above, pages 35ff). The indeterminacy in the nature of the element results in not knowing exactly *what* it is we are talking about. All this applies to Groupings I and V (and by implication and extension to the other groupings), as well as to the general definition of a grouping, and is still the case as late as 1972 in LO. The special factor in Grouping V is the 'collapse' of relation into difference in magnitude which leads to its symmetric correspondence in form to Grouping I – both being hybrids derived from group and lattice. These structures turn out to be merely descriptions of Piaget's own preconceptions and not 'proven' models of the cognitive process.

These considerations and more apply to the formal stage. The 'collapse' of the lattice of sixteen binary operations renders its elements (again) indeterminate with a corresponding difficulty in deciding exactly what it is we are referring to as the element. The lattice, as analysed, is not operational but mathematical and Piaget is thus enabled to vacillate from the internal to the external world of the subject in his referents. Examination of the language of both children and adolescents (see Appendix B to this chapter) in the accounts of experiments shows that this can be interpreted alternatively as concrete operational (to do with classes) or propositional (referring to propositions) and that the sixteen binary propositions are by no means implied. At best such a lattice could be construed as a logical abstraction of a very limited aspect of thought, valid in a limited sphere. Thus, the lattice structure as portrayed by Piaget is unacceptable.

Consideration of the INRC group with reference to the balance experiment shows it to be inadequate both physically and logically to represent the cognitive situation. The balance experiment itself has built-in constraints which automatically make it susceptible to INRC treatment in a self-fulfilling manner. Again, the assertion that the INRC group structure is responsible for the thinking leading to a solution of the balance problem is unconvincing. For example, certain operations are missing in the subject's remarks. There is confusion between the physical and logical, as well. This again parallels the dualism between action (external) and operation (internal). The 'collapse' from INRC transformation (upon transformation) to logical propositions themselves and then to measurable quantity, all based upon a dualistic confusion of rule of combination and element, parallels this.

The issue of the existence of concrete and formal operational stages, thus characterised mathematically, is sharply raised. Of course, people change throughout life, but the question is whether Piaget's interpretation of the behaviour of subjects is justified in part or in whole. Certainly, people become more formal-logical and less integrated with their environment as an undivided totality, and in so far as this is so, Piaget partly succeeds in *describing the outward appearance* of what happens to people as they grow up in this society. But the existence of his structures, their specifically and uniquely group or lattice character, is baseless.

It is conceivable that, early in the twentieth century when Group Theory was very much to the fore mathematically, Piaget should have attached himself to the idea of this structure as prototypical. Thinking must, indeed, reflect all aspects of the cosmos of which we as total organisms are a part, but it then follows that a great many more other characteristics than the properties of the group must necessarily characterise even the logico-mathematical aspects of cognition. At the very least, it must be asked why the Klein-four group should play a dominant and unique role when there are an unlimited number of groups (not to mention other structures) available in mathematics.

This adds up to:

(a)   Piaget's groups, lattices, groupings and the INRC structure are all invalid as an explanation of cognition.
(b)   The peculiar mathematical symbolisation allows vacillation between the three tiers referred to in Chapter 2, according to the three possible interpretations of the element of the structure. For example, for groupings:

Class (A) parallels the world *external* to the subject;
Single-term $(+A)$ parallels the *psychological* process;
Equation-sentence '$(+A) \, o \, (+A') = (+B)$' parallels the *logic* of operations.

This holds in a similar way for the INRC 'group'. There is the numerical zone; there is the physical (external) INRC zone; there is the logical zone; and there is the INRC zone itself.
(c)   The lack of element specification results at each stage in indeterminacy as to what exactly we are focusing on and what 'region' we are referring to.
(d)   One of the most important issues, about which we shall have something to say in Chapter 9, is the actual formalisation adopted by Piaget. On the face of it this appears to be mathematically and logically analytical. But we have already seen, especially in the 'collapsar' features of INRC, that the 'symbols' and 'calculations' are purely descriptive since we find ourselves at the end simply with the original presuppositions.

Certain objections may be raised here. First, since *The Development of Thought* contains, to a certain extent, a restatement of Piaget's views, why bother to go through all this investigation of his earlier writings? We have done this because it would be impossible to understand the latest position without the earlier. A study of *The Development of Thought* without knowledge of Piaget's earlier position would force one back to this anyway since the restatement in *The Development of Thought* is very partial indeed and calls upon, uses and accepts many earlier concepts (that of inverses, for example). Piaget never renounced at any time any previous positions or views.

Secondly, why does the analysis of Piaget's mathematics criticise inexactitude and vacillation when it is only too clear that there can be no precise realisation of a mathematical model in the actuality of thought? Here, it must be borne in mind that the issue with regard to a mathematical formalisation as such is faithfulness to its own axioms. Archimedes' axioms differ from twentieth century ones, but he remained true to them throughout his works and did not move from one interpretation to another. Furthermore, it is the basic paradigm that is being queried – the solely logico-mathematical nature of cognition, and this cannot be postulated without mathematical precision in the construction of the mathematical system itself.

Finally, it might be argued that Piaget is simply describing the acquisition of the tools of thinking, not its actual content. But Piaget writes in GLT (p. xxi): 'The aim of the two latter works [*Treatise on Logic* and *Essay on the Transformation of Logical Operations*] is to furnish a possible symbolic model of the actual processes of thinking.' And again (GLT, p. 180): 'Thus we are justified in considering the preceding formulae as symbolic expressions of the actual reasoning of our subjects.'

This point is linked with Piaget's conception of formal thinking as 'final' or 'complete'. He describes as his aim (GLT, p. xxiv) 'to describe the formal structures that mark the *completion of the operational development of intelligence*' (our emphasis). A similar remark appears a little earlier, though with an interesting and important qualification: 'the twofold structure found in formal thought is the end product of a series of co-ordinations as they attain a final level of equilibrium. (This is no bar to new integrations and continual growth in adult thinking)' (GLT, p. xxiii).

If formal structures mark the 'completion of the operational development of intelligence', then the 'new integrations and continual growth' of the adult are to be inevitably and for ever constrained by the logic of formal structures. There can be no escape from this prison of formal-logical determinism, whose closure prevents intrusion and absorption of any contingency or any alternative to this linear tool of intelligence. Whether the system is intended to represent content or 'tools' of thinking makes no difference. The result will be the same. And 'the successive and *hierarchical* [our emphasis] organization of thinking as it develops' (GLT, p. xxiii) treats this linear-causal limited aspect of the thinking process as the end-point of a hierarchy and, thus, implicitly *superior* to what has gone before, that is, child thinking.

The implications of Piaget's logico-mathematical treatment of intelligence is nowhere better epitomised than in *The Psychology of Intelligence* (p. 165):

Intellectual interaction between individuals is thus comparable to a vast game of chess, which is carried on unremittingly and in such a way that each action carried out with respect to a particular item involves a series of equivalent or complementary actions on the part of the opponent; laws of grouping are nothing more or less than the various rules ensuring the reciprocity of the players and the consistency of their play.

Appendices to Chapter 4

(A) Extracts from *The Growth of Logical Thinking*

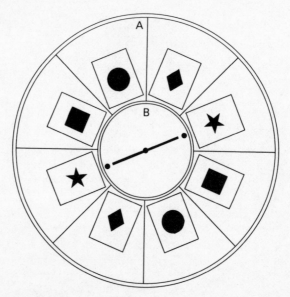

Fig. 5. One pair of boxes (the starred ones) contains concealed magnets, whereas the other pairs contain only wax. The large board (A) is divided into sectors of different colors and equal surfaces, with opposite sectors matching in color. A metal bar is attached to a non-metallic rotating disk (B); the disk always stops with the bar pointing to one pair of boxes. The boxes (which are matched pairs as to color and design) can be moved to different sectors, but they are always placed with one of a pair opposite the other. The boxes are unequal in weight, providing another variable. (p. 94)

GOU (14;11) *'Maybe it goes down and here it's heavier* (the weight might lower the plane, thus resulting in the needle's coming to rest at the lowest point) *or maybe there's a magnet'* (he puts a notebook under the board to level it and sees that the result is the same). – 'What have you proved?' – *'There is a magnet* (he weighs the boxes). *There are some that are heavier than others* (more or less heavy). *I think it's more likely to be the content'* (in substance). – 'What do you have to do to prove that it isn't the weight?' – He removes the diamond boxes which are the heaviest. *'Then I changed positions. If it stops at the same place again, the weight doesn't play any role. But I would rather remove the star boxes. We'll see whether it stops at the others which are heavier* (experiment). *It's not the weight. It's not a rigorous proof, because it does not come to rest at the perpendicular* (to the diamond boxes). *The weight could only have an effect if it made* (the plane) *tip. So I'll put two boxes, one on top of the other, and if it doesn't stop that means that the weight doesn't matter:* (negative experiment). *You see.'* – 'And the color?' – *'No, you saw when the positions of the boxes were changed. The contents of the boxes have an effect, but it's especially when the boxes are close together; the boxes are only important when they are close* (he puts half of the boxes at a greater distance). *It's either the distance or the content. To see whether it's the content I'm going to do this* (he moves the starred boxes away and brings the others closer). *It falls exactly between the round ones which are near and the stars which are far off. Both things have an effect and it's the result of two forces* (experiment in which the star is moved away by successive steps). *It's more likely to be distance* (new trial). *It seems to be confirmed, but I'm not quite sure. Unless it's the cardinal points* (he takes off the stars). *No, it's not that. The stars do have an effect. It must be the content. If it isn't a magnet, I don't see what it could be. You have to put iron on the other boxes. If the magnet is there* (disk), *it will come* (to) *these boxes. If it is in the boxes* (stars) *there is iron under the disk* (he removes the starred boxes). *I'm sure that it's the boxes.'*

We see here the great difference between substage II-B subjects, who are limited to serial correspondences of transitive equalities, and the stage III subject, who utilizes the formal combinatorial system and as a result does not experiment until he has made deductions from his preliminary hypotheses. Like the II-B subjects, GOU hypothesizes the relevance of weight, but he reasons from a set of possibilities as to ways in which it would be manifested if in fact weight had an effect (tilting the apparatus). This hypothetical reasoning not only gives him the idea of verifying whether the plane is horizontal but even the idea of placing two boxes together in order to increase the weight.

Moreover, GOU uses propositional rather than concrete operations. Most important, they are based on the set of sixteen binary combinations in continuous transition from one to the next; their consistent integration is demonstrated with particular clarity. The following operations can be distinguished in his protocol:

(1) Disjunction $(p \vee q) = (p \cdot \bar{q}) \vee (\bar{p} \cdot q) \vee (p \cdot q)$: 'It's either the distance or the content (or both)';
(2) Its inverse, conjunctive negation $(\bar{p} \cdot \bar{q})$: changing the position of the boxes verifies the hypothesis that neither weight nor colour is the determining factor;
(3) Conjunction $(p \cdot q)$: both content and distance are effective;
(4) Its inverse, incompatibility $(p \cdot q) = (p \cdot \bar{q}) \vee (\bar{p} \cdot q) \vee (\bar{p} \cdot \bar{q})$: the effect of the magnet is incompatible with moving the boxes from the center for the needle may stop without the boxes being moved and vice versa, or neither occurs;

(5)　Implication $(p \supset q) = (p \cdot q) \lor (\bar{p} \cdot q) \lor (\bar{p} \cdot \bar{q})$: if a magnet is attached to the disk, it will stop in front of the boxes containing iron;

(6)　Its inverse $(p \cdot \bar{q})$: when it does not stop, nonimplication is shown;

(7)　Converse implication $(q \supset p) = (p \cdot q) \lor (p \cdot \bar{q}) \lor (\bar{p} \cdot \bar{q})$: if there is a magnet in the box, it will stop the disk;

(8)　Its inverse $(\bar{p} \cdot q)$ operates in (1), (4), (10), etc.;

(9)　Equivalence $(p = q) = (p \cdot q) \lor (\bar{p} \cdot \bar{q})$: to assert that weight has an effect is equivalent to asserting that the needle stops because of inclination of the plane;

(10)　Its inverse, reciprocal exclusion $(p \, w \, q) = (p \cdot \bar{q}) \lor (\bar{p} \cdot q)$: the fact that the plane is horizontal excludes the weight factor, for either the plane is horizontal and weight has no effect or weight has an effect and the plane is not horizontal;

(11)　Independence of p in relation to q – i.e., $p[q] = (p \cdot q) \lor (p \cdot \bar{q})$: the stopping point may coincide either with a color or with its absence, thus color is excluded as a variable;

(12)　Its inverse (which is also its reciprocal) $\bar{p}[q] = (\bar{p} \cdot q) \lor (\bar{p} \cdot \bar{q})$: failure to stop may also coincide with the color or its absence;

(13)–(14)　Independence of q and $\bar{q}$ in relation to p – i.e. $q[p]$ and $q[\bar{p}]$: these operations are found in (15);

(15)　Complete affirmation or tautology $(p \star q) = (p \cdot q) \lor (p \cdot \bar{q}) \lor (\bar{p} \cdot q) \lor (\bar{p} \cdot \bar{q})$: all possible combinations, thus absence of particular links, for example between the box which contains the magnet and the colored sector on which it has been placed;

(16)　Its inverse, complete negation or contradiction (o): to deny that weight has an effect and to reassert it would be a contradiction.

The above examples all come from the protocol of a single substage III-B subject; thus we are not exaggerating when we claim it is possible for subjects at this level to work in turn with each of the sixteen binary combinations of propositional logic. Of course, at substage III-A the keyboard is not yet complete (for examples of this inter-mediate substage, see our previous study on the problem of magnets).[8] But when formal equilibrium has been attained the combinatorial system which characterizes the 'structured whole' pays off in full, and the subject is no longer satisfied with reasoning based on simple concrete correspondences. For example, when GOU has observed the noncorrespondence of the stopping points with weights, he does not feel that his proof is adequate ('rigorous') because he realizes that if weight acted to produce an inclination of the plane, it could be combined with other factors.

[8] *La Genèse de l'idée de hasard*, pp. 101–106.

In sum, even in a problem as simple as the present one (chosen to conclude the first section because of its very simplicity), the transition from concrete to formal operations is distinguished by the appearance of a complete combinatorial system whose various types of disjunction and exclusion are continuously linked to implications. Lacking in even the most advanced children at substage II-A and II-B, this is what gives the hypothetico-deductive new look to the responses of stage III subjects, it manifests itself even in the small details of experimentation. (GLT, pp. 102–4)

(B) Piagetian Experiments on Equilibrium in the Balance (taken from GLT, pp. 166ff.)

The following is a consideration of some Piagetian experiments on equilibrium in the balance and their interpretation, carried out on subjects ranging from 4-and-a-half to 13-and-a-half years old.

Piaget records stage I-A (pre-operational) (GLT, p. 166) as follows:

MIC (4;6), presented with two equal weights at distances of 14 and 9: 'Why is one way down and the other up high?' – He continually raises and lowers the arms of the apparatus, believing that they will maintain the forces and positions he delegates to them. – 'Can you make it straight (horizontal gesture) so it will stay there all by itself?' – Neither 'yes' or 'no'. – 'How was it before?' – *Like that'* (horizontal) – 'You can't do it with the weights?' – He shakes his head and tries to maintain the horizontal position with two unequal weights, raising and lowering the arms several times. – 'Can you do it without your hand?' – (We have him weigh the weights with his hands, then he works at a new set of trials. We suggest that he add weight to one side or the other, etc.) Conclusion: *'You can't!'* (attain the horizontal position).

MAR (4;8) suspends two weights on one side without putting anything on the other, with the aim of reaching horizontal equilibrium!

MIC at 4 years 6 months is clearly trying to find out 'what happens if –' and tries all sorts of things that interest him, and which could just as well be construed as the indispensable period of play adopted by any child (and for that matter any adult) in such an investigatory situation. It is difficult to find evidence for the experiment's interpretation (p. 167):

One can see that, in constantly interfering with the apparatus in order to correct the position of the balance arm, the subject expects the apparatus to conserve the results of his manipulations.

The fact that MIC fails to do what the experimenter asks could as well be interpreted as demonstrating that the task is beyond him because of its logical abstraction and perhaps also on account of its irrelevance to his life. (Margaret Donaldson's book *Children's Minds,* 1978, hinges precisely on this point.) This situation reveals the Piagetian model as *one only* of many possible models. If the child's responses are approached without any prior interpretation by the experimenter, such as an assumption as to what the child believes (' believing that they will maintain the forces and positions he delegates to them'), they show a child trying to find out what happens when he does certain things to the apparatus – a search for the *conditions* in which such events take place. As far as MAR is concerned we have no evidence whatever since apparently he made no comment. One can equally interpret his actions as either bored by the entire problem or simply playing. The point at issue is whether the children conform to the Piagetian scheme of things and whereas it would be silly to say that these children of 4-and-a-half have a 'tool-kit' of logic comparable to that which some adolescents achieve and a few adults also, it is also impossible to conclude any particular model as an absolute certainty from the protocol given us in *The Growth of Logical Thinking.* As Piaget himself says (p. 279) in reference to the impossibility of detecting through a purely verbal criterion the transition from concrete to formal operational thinking, 'All in all, the subjects' language expresses their thoughts only in a rough way'. How much more must this be the case with very young children with an inadequate mastery of language and who have not yet been systematically socialised into a situation where they tend to be inhibited from any verbal expression of thought except the socially permissible.

The nature of the task exhibits another restricting factor upon the subject and reveals another form of constraint in the mind of the experimenter. For the task itself identifies *horizontality* with equilibrium. But this is a very particular case of equilibrium, which can be manifested by a bar which is at any angle whatsoever to the horizontal. What is actually being asked of the subject is to proceed from one state of equilibrium to another. At later stages, when the task is satisfactorily performed by older subjects it is clear that these subjects have the same built-in assumptions about equilibrium and its identification with horizontality that the experimenter has, and in fact their search can be seen as an inquiry into fewer possibilities than with younger children. The conditions for horizontal equilibrium emerge out of a matrix of actually changing and dynamic processes. Horizontal equilibrium may be a special and very important case of equilibrium in general with its own particular conditions, especially symmetry. But its recognition is intimately connected with all other possible equilibrium situations the balance can demonstrate.

The stage I-B subjects are said to show increasing integration of intuitive representations which are 'moving towards reversible operations'. These are the protocols (p. 168):

MAL (5;8) notes that the arms are not horizontal: *'You have to put another (weight) on the other side. I know what has to be done; put still another one there because there isn't any weight here* (she adds it). *These here must be lighter than those over there. You have to take two that have the same weight.'* Next: *'You could take one off'* (because it is too heavy on one side). MAL does not spontaneously discover the influence of distance, but when a weight is moved in front of her she says: *'You brought that one up closer, that makes more weight. If it were at the end, it wouldn't work and there it makes more weight.'*

GAS (5;9): *'You could put one at the other side: the same* (he takes a weight of the same color but having a very different weight). *That doesn't work: maybe there is a little too much weight there.'*

Piaget's interpretation of this behaviour is that the children have an approximate idea of compensation but not in a systematic way. 'His [GAS's] actions are successive corrections [thus regulations], and are not yet strictly reversible' (p. 168).

There is no evidence here of any combinatorial operations but there are simple implications, especially at the end of the passage, that is, MAL's comment 'If it were at the end it wouldn't work and there it makes more weight'. We have already seen in the case of GOU that even he, at 16 years old, does not include all the possible combinatorial operations. Other stage III subjects also use only some of the possible combinations in working out the solution to the problem. At what point does the use of combinatorial operations become a system? Piaget defines this latter in terms of what is done by successful subjects. However, in terms of a theory of definite stages, the question has to be answered, at what *exact* point does the number of operations used by the subject become sufficient to warrant its being called a system?

Piaget (and Inhelder) interpret MAL as 'not spontaneously discover[ing] the influence of distance'. However, when the experimenter moves a weight she comes quite near to discovering the relation, 'You brought that one up closer, that makes more weight'. What does 'spontaneous' mean in this context? At any stage of life discoveries are always made in the context of something that happens to the subject as a result of 'probing'. MAL is given insufficient credit for her achievements for she has started on the road of an organised attempt to solve the problem in a way which is not fundamentally different from that of older subjects, including adults.

Stage II-A subjects MAS and NEM provide the following protocols (pp. 169-70):

MAS (7;7) begins with E_3 and D_3, then replaces them with G_3 and F_3 (thus equal distance and an attempt to find equal weights), adds two other weights, takes off some, then all, and finally weighs two equal weights (E) in his hands, counts equal numbers of holes (14) and places E_{14} at each side. Afterwards he looks for other forms of equilibrium; he adds the weights, moves them, takes off some, and finally has GED on one side and P_3 on the other: '*That's it* (empirical compensation of weight and distances). *It's just like when there weren't any* (when the arms were horizontal without weight); *it's the same weight on each side.*' He begins again with large weights (for which there are no matched pairs). '*I should have put one on each side. Since there aren't any, I had to put three on one side and two on the other. It stays straight because it's the same weight on each side.*' He predicts that equal distances are necessary for two unequal weights, but he does not find the law: heavier $\rightleftarrows$ nearer. – 'If you put on C and E, where would you have to place them?' – '*I would say one hole and another hole* (= two different distances), *but they shouldn't go the same way* (at equal distances) *or it wouldn't make the same weight.*'

NEM (7;4) discovers empirically that C on the left at a distance of 10 balances E on the right at a distance of 5. We ask him to place C on the right and E on the left, but he does not succeed in inverting the distance relationship. After the experiment, he exclaims, '*Ah! You have to do the same thing as before but in the opposite way!*'

Both these experiments are regarded as showing the emergence of organisational capacity related to learned reactions to situations. Not only is organisational capacity beginning to appear, but so is the quantitative as distinct from qualitative abstraction. Piaget notes that MAS does not draw out general correspondences but, following on the protocol of NEM, he (Piaget) lists a number of things that the subject can now do, including serial ordering, adding weights in a reversible manner, make use of the transitivity of equality or inequality, and in the case of distances his correspondences are said to be oriented in opposite directions, and therefore represent symmetries. The subjects are getting better at this sort of problem and are increasing their organisational capacity and sophistication about how the system works. But the list of achievements reads too much correspondence to Piagetian theory into what the subject says and there is no justification for representing it in symbols (pp. 170-1):

Two equal weights B_1 and B_2 situated at equal distances L_x come into equilibrium by symmetry:

$$(B_1 \times L_x) = (B_2 \times L_x). \tag{1}$$

Thus, one of the weights is conceived of as compensating the other by reciprocity. Two equal weights B_1 and B_2 at unequal distances L_x and L_y do not balance each other:

$$(B_1 \times L_x) \gtrless (B_2 \times L_y) \text{ if } x \gtrless y. \tag{2}$$

Two equal weights B_1 and B_2 at unequal distances L_x and L_y do not come into equilibrium either:

$$(A_1 \times L_x) < (B_2 \times L_x). \tag{3}$$

Moreover, in each one of these relations the subject can substitute for one object an equivalent set of others through additive operations:

$$C_1 = (A_2 + A'_2 + B'_2) \tag{4}$$

and the same holds for distances.

On the other hand, in the case of unequal weights A_1 and B_2 and of unequal distances L_x and L_y, coordination is not yet possible at substage II-A. Even when the subject discovers by experimentation that a large weight at a small distance to the right of the axis balances a small weight at a large distance to the left, he does not know how to invert these relations from one side to the other and discovers too late that he should have 'done the same thing but in the opposite way' (NEM).

Comparing these sentences in symbols with the protocols of the subjects, particularly MAS, shows that they say both too much and too little. Too much, since there is an implication of generalisation and of universality which is not present in the subjects' very particularised responses. Too little in the sense that the subjects' logic is much richer than Piaget gives them credit for. The mention of numbers might well be taken for the first inkling of measurement.

Stage II-B subjects are said to achieve qualitative correspondences bordering upon the equilibrium law.

FIS (10;7) sees that P does not balance F *'because it's heavy: that one* (F) *is too light.'* – 'What should be done?' – *'Move it forward* (he moves P toward the axis and attains equilibrium). *I had to pull it back from 16 holes* (arbitrary) *to see if it would lower twice* (arbitrary) *the weight.'* – 'What do you mean by that?' – *'It raises the weight.'* – 'And if you put it back over there?' (moves P away). – *'It would make the other one go up.'* – 'And if you put it at the end?' (P). – *'It would go up still more'* (F), etc. Conclusion: When you have two unequal weights *'you move up the heaviest'* (toward the median axis). But FIS does not measure the lengths even for the relations of 1 to 2.

ROL (10;10): *'You have to change the position of the sack because at the end it makes more weight.'* He moves the lightest away from the axis: *'No, it's heavier.'* He is presented with G at 2 and A at 14: they balance *'because that one is there* (A at 14) *and it is less heavy than the other one.'* (p. 171)

The same points apply here as with stage II-A subjects, that is, that the logic is richer than they are credited with but the cases are much more particular than the symbolic representation on p. 172 would lead us to believe:

> Thus, the new operation mediating the determination of the conditions of equilibrium is a double serial ordering of weights $A < B < C < \ldots$ and distances $L_1 > L_2 > L_3 > \ldots$ but with bi-univocal inverse correspondences:

$$A < B < C < \ldots$$
$$\uparrow \quad \uparrow \quad \uparrow$$
$$L_1 > L_2 > L_3 > \ldots \tag{5}$$

> which can be translated into reciprocities (expressed in the language of relational multiplication):

$$(A \times L_1) = (B \times L_2) = (C \times L_3) = \ldots, \text{etc.} \tag{6}$$

Everything that has been said about horizontal equilibrium as a special case is still applicable here but needs emphasis at this point since the subjects at stage II-B are nearly 11 years old and are by now very much influenced by cultural assumptions, and also by a tendency to react positively and even anticipatorily to the experimenters' expectations. Every test directs the subject towards symmetrical equilibrium and by now every subject seems to take this for granted.

Stage III subjects are said to understand metrical proportion, to be in possession of the schemata of the INRC group and able to differentiate the general equilibrium schema by constructing the proportions $W/W' = L'/L$. The subjects do show evidence of a lot of influence by ideas of measurement, but whether their acquisition of the proportions stated is achieved as Piaget alleges is not established. The 'reciprocity' alleged in ROG's protocol regarding the game of marbles is also dubious since ROG uses it to give an example of a situation he cannot explain (p. 173), that is, that if you bring the weight half-way towards the centre its 'value' is halved. This halving of the value of the weight by bringing it towards the centre is not an example of reciprocity which is supposed to be compensation without annulment.

> ROG (12;11): for a weight P placed at the very tip of one arm (28 holes), he puts C + E in the middle of the other arm, measures the distances, and says: '*That makes 14 holes. It's half the length. If the weight* (C + E) *is halved, that duplicates*' (P). – 'How do you know that you have to bring the weight toward the center?' (to increase the weight). – '*The idea just came to me, I wanted to try. If I bring it in half way, the value of the weight is*

cut in half. *I know, but I can't explain it. I haven't learned.'* – 'Do you know other similar situations?' – *'In the game of marbles, if five play against four, the last one of the four has the right to an extra marble.'* He also discovers that for two distances of 1 and $^1/_4$ you have to use weights 1 and 4; that for two distances of 1 and $^1/_3$ you need weights 1 and 3, etc.: *'You put the heaviest weight on the portion that stands for the lightest weight* (which corresponds to the lightest weight), *going from the center.'* (pp. 173–4)

CHAL (p. 174) talks of compensation and explains it as 'The distances and the weights; it's a system of compensations'. The emergence of the idea of compensation is a very natural one in the circumstances just as the idea of proportions is bound to come up in the solution of problems of this particular type. The misconception consists in erecting the notion of compensation itself into a central and necessary feature of cognition in general.

CHAL (13;6) quickly discovers that *'the greater the distance, the smaller the weight should be. It's staying up.'* – 'Why?' – *'It is compensated there and there.'* – 'What is compensated?' – *'The distances and the weights; it's a system of compensations. Each one rises in turn. For equal distances you need equal weights, and if it's inclined it rights itself and goes down on the other side.'* – (We propose a test with two weight units at a distance of 5 and one at a distance of 10). 'What will the angles be?' – *'Larger on one side* (he points out the two-unit side) *and smaller on the other* (experiment). *Oh! No, the same angles!'* He outlines them: *'The distance compensates for the weight.'* – 'What distances do they cover?' (heights H and H' are pointed out). – *'The smallest weight covers a greater distance and the large weight a shorter distance.'* – 'And what forces are required?' (strings which can be used to raise and lower the weights are pointed out). – *'For the smallest, there is more distance to pull, for the large one, less distance.'* – 'So where is more force required?' – *'Here* (two units). *Oh! No, it's the same: the distance* (he is speaking of height) *is compensated by the weight.'*

We have looked at the test cases related to the balance experiment after, not before, going through the theoretical interpretation of formal operations. For, although these experiments in *The Growth of Logical Thinking* lead up to the final analysis of the structures alleged to be necessary to a solution of the balance problem, the order we have presented seems much more in correspondence with the chronology of Piaget's own thinking. It should be remembered that while he conceived of the grouping in the 1930s, the 'mathematics' of this structure was worked out in TL in a definitive manner for the first time in 1949. Formal operation theory was not embarked upon fully until the 1950s.

5 The Equilibrium Model of Cognition

Introduction

So far only the mathematical and logical components of Piaget's thought have been examined in detail. These constitute the core of his system, notwithstanding his public image mainly as an experimental and developmental psychologist, and although it is difficult starting material, this is why it was considered first.

Can the logico-mathematics of the theory cope with the problem of genesis and novelty, or the mechanics of change from one form of structure to another? Or does this latter require factors beyond logico-mathematics? Alternatively, do the ambiguities of Piaget's logic and mathematics reflect a fundamental unsoundness in Genetic Epistemology as a whole?

The most general form of the model of cognition is progressive equilibrium, or equilibration, rooted in inherited physiological structures the development of which generates isomorphic psychological structures. In this chapter and the next two this central idea and its component aspects are discussed, bearing in mind the main points of the previous two chapters on Piaget's logico-mathematical core.

It is difficult to decide where to begin any analysis of Piaget's system because there is an inbuilt interdependence of concepts which makes virtually any aspect a justifiable starting-point. We have decided to start with equilibrium, and what might be called its structural expression, reversibility, and to follow this with a discussion of the component aspects of the model. We have chosen this starting-point since Piaget sees equilibrium as the target of the process he calls equilibration. This term encapsulates all the interactional relationships between cognising subject and cognised milieu, or total environment, in which the subject exists and grows. Also, as the target of the cognising process, equilibrium is the principal objective determining the system as a whole. The best order for a critical exposition of Piaget's system is, of course, largely a matter of opinion. A case could be made, especially in respect of the definitive *The Development of Thought*, for doing it almost any way round. We, however, propose to 'move outwards', as it were, from the generalised notion of stability expressed in the most mature stage of the individual's development, that is, general cognitive equilibrium, to the set of activities (if one can refer to them thus) whereby Piaget affirms that the subject's action becomes manifested in the operational structures of cognition.

Essentially, this is about how the equilibrated cognitive structures are achieved and maintained, or, alternatively, how one state of equilibrium 'transforms' into another, comparable state. Thus, a central point of interest in both this chapter and the next must be a concern with Piaget's claim to have discovered a 'transformational dynamics'.

Problems in Genetic Epistemology Attaching to the Identification of Intelligence as a Distinct Zone

It is clear that, parallel with the deep-rooted logico-mathematical features of Piaget's thought, is the ongoing analogy that he sees between psychology and biology. J. H. Flavell places the influence of biological notions very high in the circumstances of Piaget's intellectual development.

> An image of an active organism which both selects and incorporates stimuli in a manner determined by its structure, while at the same time adapting its structure to the stimuli, emerged from these early studies as a ready-made model for cognitive development. In Piaget's view cognitive development must have its roots firmly planted in biological growth, and basic principles valid for the former are to be found only among those which are true of the latter. (Flavell, 1963, p. 36)

Also:

> For Piaget, the one-time biologist, intelligence can be meaningfully considered only as an extension of certain fundamental biological characteristics, fundamental in the sense that they obtain wherever life obtains. (It is indicative of Piaget's biological orientation toward matters intellectual that he sometimes refers to cognitive development as 'mental embryology', e.g., 1947, p. 143.) Intellectual functioning is a special form of biological activity and, as such, possesses important attributes in common with the parent activities from which it derives. (pp. 41–2)

In deriving intelligence from what Flavell calls a 'biological substrate', Piaget shows no particular originality. Ever since the publication of the *Origin of Species,* Mendelian genetics, and still more with modern advances in molecular biology and neurophysiology, there has been a very strong tendency in biological science to make mentality dependent on the physically organic, and sometimes wholly indentified with it. Within such a framework the genesis of novelty regarding mental phenomena, and for that matter the advent of mentality itself, is directly attributed to physiological modification and thereby placed wholly within the physical ambit of biology itself. There are no issues separate or different from the biological ones in such a view. However, Piaget has a somewhat different problem to confront. He has to reconcile the genesis of novelty in mental phenomena, biologically originated, with logical structuration, where the latter is not only regarded as qualitatively different from the former, but this difference is actually the mark of intelligence as opposed to the biological aspects of the intelligent organism.

It is not that such problems are absent from the biologically oriented schools of psychology. But they tend to be buried beneath technicalities and/or jargon in the manner referred to in Chapter 1. Piaget is distinguishable precisely because he rejects such an identification. Dealing with thought-processes and knowledge, which he claims are both rooted in, and 'isomorphic' to, biology, he has to reconcile temporal, or evolutionary, change with an interpretation of the stability of things which is wholly tied to non-temporal, logically closed structures. While there is clearly a new dimension of difficulty in Genetic Epistemology over and above the problems of the dynamics of growth in biology itself, there are also difficulties in this latter area which prompt the question, does biology really offer the secure base for the understanding of mental growth that Piaget's system implies?

Since the 'take off' of biology in the later nineteenth century, its guiding principle has been the search for a satisfactory theory accounting for transformative change and not simply the identification and classification of living things. The classificatory process is reconcilable with axiomatic thought provided that *transformation,* which involves challenging the principles of classification, is excluded. The problem arises when this classification process reveals factors not directly evident in the principles of the original classification. The original axioms of the classificatory system become modified without the change being recognised and/or acknowledged. Flora and fauna may be grouped into ever more precise genera and species by description as Aristotle did. The same technique, but governed by a principle of development from a common source over time such as Darwin adopted, forces into the open the notion of 'self-change', where formerly no change is recognised beyond the original act of creation. The conflicts around geological and biological issues in the nineteenth century are a monument to this problem. The Darwinian paradigm has never solved this. Nor has its neo-Darwinian successors, genetics and molecular biology. Today, we possess vast and increasing data which manifest biological stability ever more precisely, but which do not actually explicate transformation as such.

Additional to the problem of identifying intelligence in terms of cognitive structures, Piaget inherits the uncertainties of biological science itself, both regarding the origins of intelligence and his claim that it 'isomorphically' replicates biology. The unresolved problems of trans-formation in biology are hence carried over into the development of intelligence itself which is embodied for Piaget in logico-mathematical forms that cannot by their very nature admit of an evolutionary factor. Thus he is burdened with two major problems.

These disparate strands, summed up into the logico-mathematical on the one hand and the biological on the other, constitute the source of the main problems within his theory of cognitive growth. Piaget seeks the solution to this problem through 'isomorphism' expressed initially in the relation between what he calls 'specific heredity' and 'general heredity'.[33] 'Specific heredity' refers to what the individual organism receives from the gene pool of the species, that is, actual mechanisms such as sight and touch. 'General heredity' is more subtle. In effect, it is the 'modus operandi' of these received mechanisms, and this activity *alone* generates cognitive structures. In due course the latter appear to acquire the distinctness and separateness of the original special mechanisms themselves.

Thus we arrive at the basis of 'isomorphism'. The behaviour, growth and character of mentality are structurally identical with its biological substrate. The principles of structuration leading to equilibrium (that is, the process of equilibration) parallel the organic world in every respect. By implication these structures become heritable, to satisfy the general idea of universal progress towards ultimate total equilibrium. But how this relates to individual learning at any time always remains obscure in Piaget's system. In sum, we are all born with *biological mechanisms*. We are also born with the specific *way* these mechanisms *function*. The *functioning* itself we are *not* born with but acquire and modify during life. This latter is the *source of cognitive structures*. Here one can see the starting-point of all the subsequent problems to do with the genesis of psychological novelty. There is no clear way of distinguishing between 'way of functioning' and 'function'. There is ample evidence, for example, of the eye seeing what it wishes to see. In effect, the *cognitive* structures, especially their birth, cannot be distinguished from the *biological* matrix which is said to generate them. The situation is comparable to the 'collapsar' feature of Piaget's logico-mathematical model which emerged in Chapters 2, 3 and 4, where, for example, the INRC group 'collapsed' into logical propositions and thence into numbers.

The device of distinguishing between 'special' and 'general' heredity does not really work. It is supposed to reconcile the zone of intelligence with that of biology from which the former is supposed to derive, but from which it is radically distinct. Such a situation produces an unclarity regarding the sort of elements being dealt with – mental or physiological. This is what we shall be calling 'non-terminality'. By this term we mean that interrelationships are devised, or supposedly 'discovered', without reference to stable phenomena. If 'special' heredity means specifiable physical functions like the optical mechanism, and cognitive structures are supposed to derive from these, then we have no identifiable phenomena which are special to intelligence and distinct from physiology.

Piaget's relationship to the biological foundations of his system is, in fact, very ambivalent. On the one hand intelligence in general is understood as an extension of biology, and yet, as in *The Mechanisms of Perception* (1961, Fr. edn) especially, but also elsewhere, the very schemata which are seemingly 'gateways' for the internalisation of action, and hence the process of intellectual structuration, emerge as *distorting*! (Flavell, 1963, pp. 226–36; Hamlyn, 1978, p. 53). Only differentiation and decentering, the processes by which the subject is to become able, as he grows, to order his world intellectually and separate it from himself while including himself in it, can *compensate* for the distortion and thus allow the subject, ultimately, to overcome it.

But distortion plays a rather more subtle role than appears at first sight. While Piaget treats perception (biological mechanisms) as a positively quantifiable process[34] involving a progressive error-correction, the distortion is actually instrumental in carrying over from the perceptual to the conceptual 'level' and provides the foundation for differentiation of objects from the subject and each other, as well as the decentering of the emotions. Hence, in a sense, the *necessary* abstractive process for the foundation of cognitive structures themselves is intimately, if ambiguously, related to error and distortion of perceived sense data in the external world of the subject. The relation, moreover, is hierarchical; the cognitive growth process is without doubt a superior one to the level of physiological sense data and ultimately stands over it in a controlling position. The biological, while being the foundation of thought, must, therefore, also be conquered by thought in order that intelligence can appear. The main problem here is that of identifying the origin of the differentiating and decentering process itself. If we remain within Piaget's frame of reference, differentiation and decentering, the logical ordering of the subject's cognitive and affective experience, must originate *either* out of a biological matrix or possess some independent origin. If the former is the case then 'distortion' is automatically transferred to the cognitive process and must ultimately invalidate the whole of cognition. If the latter is the case then the 'distortion' means that the system fails at this crucial point to reveal the mechanism by which intelligence is actually generated *out* of biology. The ambivalent relationship with biology is contained in this dilemma (see Hamlyn, 1978, pp. 49ff.).

The extensive experimental work on perception itself carried out by Piaget and his colleagues over the years does not exorcise this problem but merely narrows it down to zones of fractionally different concepts, for example, *perception* of space and *representation* of space. The latter is different for Piaget, being an act of intelligence and not, as the former, a 'pure' physical act (Flavell, 1963, p. 232). Even more precisely, the analytical technique adopted in the experiments, which is based on the notion that the act of perception 'adds up' aspects of the object perceived in diminishing quantities in a form of 'convergent series', leaves the final 'jump' to total perceptive recognition of the object unexplicated (ibid., pp. 226ff.). In other words, whatever is done, if one stays within the Piagetian terms of reference, the hiatus or 'gap' of transition from external to internal world of the subject remains. The system is forced to work on the basis of a 'dualised' or bifurcated set of rules which are claimed to be homogeneous but those applying externally are split from those applying internally. The clearest example we have yet seen of this is in the discussion of the balance experiment in Chapter 4 where removal of weights on the balance is simply equated with logical negation.

We can see, then, that there are major difficulties attached to the distinction of intelligence as a separate zone from the biology of the individual within the stipulated terms of reference of Piaget's system. These terms make it difficult to avoid either biological preformationism or the complete separation of intelligence from any biological connection, that is if it is to preserve its developmental character within the lifetime of the individual. It is in the context of these conflicting factors that Piaget postulates the existence of equilibrium manifested in intelligent activity which is 'isomorphic' to an equivalent condition in biology. If this cannot be substantiated then the Piagetian system is rendered unable from the start to substantiate, also, the distinct existence of intelligence with its own laws of growth.

The Nature of Equilibrium in the Piagetian System

The notion of equilibrium is central to Genetic Epistemology. But there are aspects of this concept, especially in relation to problems of the biological–psychological parallelism that must be particularised if the system as a whole is to be appreciated.

The idea of equilibrium certainly does not originate with Piaget. Strictly speaking, the word itself derives from notions of physical balance which came to full fruition during the seventeenth and eighteenth centuries. But the concept of balance, expressed in the qualitative categories of harmony and coherence, is much older. The rise to general predominance of the mechanical understanding of equilibrium embodies the movement away from such qualitativity, and towards a purely quantitative interpretation, which is the stamp of seventeenth-century science and its aftermath. When we look, for example, at the Taoist tradition of harmonious complementarity, there is a qualitative as well as a quantitative element always present. One does not need, however, to regard the oriental tradition as wholly distinctive from the Western tradition in this respect. Notions of harmony and complementarity of a qualitative character such as one finds in Taoism and Buddhism are to be detected in the early Greek roots of the Western tradition. All perfectionist ideals from Plato onwards contain the notion of ultimate harmony either as the objective of the real world or a characteristic of an ideal world lying behind the real world. The precise relationship between 'harmony' and 'reality' in both these situations has always, in the Western tradition, presented difficulties and ambiguities. We are never clear whether Plato sees his republic as a goal or as an ideal prototype in relation to actual society. It is sometimes affirmed that the Aristotelian tradition in the West stands as an empirical alternative to the Platonic in these respects, in the sense that the most harmonious and balanced situation, according to Aristotle, is arrived at by a process of associative, bit-by-bit, construction based on the principle of a search for a mean. Yet for Aristotle as much as for Plato the notion of an ultimte form of stability is always present, if only via the treatment of the mean as itself an ideal. Thus what may appear to be empirical in the first instance reveals a notion of ultimate perfection in its own way. (See below, Chapter 8, for further discussion.)

It is difficult to assess to what extent the emergence of the modern scientific movement from about the seventeenth century onwards actually departs from these early and very fundamental features of Western thought. In its anticipatory and earliest stages this movement certainly associates the search for laws governing physical behaviour and existence with the identification of an ultimate condition of perfection. And this manifests itself in many ways, one of these being the firm belief lasting to modern times that the discovery of the 'right' techniques will yield ultimate and final knowledge. Bacon and Descartes saw this happening in a finite number of generations. Later, Laplace saw 'perfection' as already achieved by Newton. In more modern times the search for a unified field theory in physics suggests the same idea but in a new form.

Alternatively, within the last 400 years or so the embodiment of the principles of empiricism in technique and technology implicitly carries with it the assumption of an indefinite advancement and development standing in sharp contrast to the idea of the completion of knowledge. From the mid twentieth century onwards, this latter view of the world has tended to predominate over the former in Western thought and society. How long this will be maintained has become an open question, especially as deepening uncertainty and critical reactions to the complacency of technical progress are voicing themselves more and more. In fact, 'meta-science', or the discussion of the foundations upon which science itself rests, is now questioning the very premises of science themselves (see Chapter 9).

Although Piaget's first general statement regarding Genetic Epistemology did not appear until the 1940s, there is clear evidence that he was concerned about the major theoretical elements of his system as far back as his adolescence. Without doubt, Piaget was convinced very early of the generality of equilibrium as a condition of nature (Rotman, 1977, p. 18). But he did not see this as an immobile condition of pure existence to which all natural phenomena unchangingly conform, but rather as a goal towards which a moving, evolutionary nature is tending. Equilibrium, for Piaget, signifies much more than a mere feature of human thought. 'The most profound tendency', he writes in *Six Psychological Studies* (p. 70), 'of all human activity is progression towards equilibrium' (see Rotman, 1977, p. 34). The mental structures of which general cognitive equilibrium is composed 'denote the kinds of equilibrium towards which evolution *in its entirety* [our emphasis] is striving; at once organic, psychological and social' (Boring, 1969, p. 256, quoted Rotman, p. 34). Thus equilibrium, when applied to intelligence, cannot fail to dominate every aspect of Genetic Epistemology. It has to be the central, fundamental, necessary and all-determining feature of mental activity (operation).

At first sight it may seem easy simply to equate the features of equilibrium with the logico-mathematical elements of Genetic Epistemology and to identify equilibrium with the group features of cognition. However, equilibrium can be said to derive, at least in part, if not equally, from Piaget's understanding of the principal features of biological dynamics. He is quite specific that it must not be taken in the physical sense of a simple balance of forces alone, although this is not absent from the concept. His view of it has two main features. First, it is always symmetrical in the sense of exact and opposite forces. The manifestation of the 'balance' must always be in terms of recognisable symmetry. Secondly, equilibrium is 'mobile' – a notion which Piaget himself likens to that of 'homeorhesis'. In homeorhesis, the system under consideration is not designed to maintain a *state* of equilibrium but rather 'a steady course of progression, deviations from which are corrected in virtue of the self-regulating properties of the system' (Hamlyn, 1978, p. 50).

Piaget contrasts the idea of homeorhesis, which seems to originate in the writings of C. H. Waddington, with 'homeostasis', which is a conventional physiological concept. Briefly, the former seems intended to convey the idea of the maintenance of the progress of a system governed by self-regulation in the presence of changing environmental conditions. The latter, on the other hand, means the maintenance of a given system *without* the notion of progress, in the presence of changing conditions. The distinction is subtle. Thus in *The Development of Thought* (p. 4), '[Cognitive equilibriums] resemble above all the static biological equilibriums (homeostasis) or dynamic equilibriums (homeorhesis)'. Hamlyn (op. cit.) tends to contrast the two concepts, but in fact their similarity is important to Piaget's idea of equilibrium. The notions are late ones for Piaget and belong to that latter part of his writing life which is considerably influenced by Systems Theory. Nevertheless, the attempt to resolve the perennial problem in Genetic Epistemology is evident. By employing these subtly distinct and extremely close concepts the conflict between the conditions of the developmental and the stable might be overcome.

An initial conclusion from these considerations is that equilibrium is something more than the logico-mathematical framework abstracted from it, although, as we saw in Chapter 2, the identification of (mental) structures with their logico-mathematical expression in group form is certainly affirmed by Piaget. Equilibrium is intended to include that aspect of mentality which is highly structured and logico-mathematically governed on the one hand and that aspect which is dynamically fluid on the other. Latterly, especially in *The Development of Thought,* Piaget has opted to concentrate on the second aspect rather than the first, under the generic heading of 'equilibration'. Equilibrium is thus an extraordinarily elastic concept. Sometimes it includes equilibration and therefore what might be termed the 'apparatus' of cognition. Sometimes it refers only to the 'finished' state of cognitive structures. In fact, one can associate on the one hand ideas of homeostasis, the static, the logico-mathematics of congition with a stress on symmetry and *equilibrium*, and, on the other hand, 'homeorhesis', the dynamic, the apparatus of cognition with *equilibration*.

Flavell (1963) alleges that the theory of equilibrium cannot really be understood separately from equilibration. Yet according to him the former describes 'essentially discontinuous equilibrium states, that is, organised systems of actions (sensory-motor, perceptual, concrete operational, and all the other totalities already familiar to the reader) whose attributes as systems are describable in equilibrium terms' (p. 238), and must be distinguished from equilibration itself. Flavell claims for Piaget that he succeeds not only in elaborating the separate states of equilibrium themselves but analyses the transition mechanisms, equilibration, that produce them (loc. cit.). In particular he stresses that the connection between equilibration and equilibrium is governed by what he describes as ordered differences between different equilibrium states: 'one state may be said to be "better equilibrated" than another, to attain "a higher degree of equilibrium" and so on' (pp. 238–9).

Without doubt equilibrium is an all-embracing concept which may cover up the problem of transition from 'outside' to 'inside' and vice versa in the subject's ongoing interaction with the milieu. To what extent the notion of ordered differences actually explicates this transition is dubious, in the absence of any independent measure of what 'better equilibration' means. But a more complete judgement on this is better left until after consideration of the 'apparatus' of this transition in the next chapter.

How does Piaget himself think of equilibrium? There are of course hundreds of references in his writings to the question and we can only supply a tiny handful here. We have tried, however, to use references that present sharply the alternative views of equilibrium Piaget himself has given at different times.

'First of all, what do we mean by equilibrium in psychology?', he asks in *Six Psychological Studies* (p. 150), and comes back with certain clear answers. 'Equilibrium is notable for its stability' (loc. cit.). 'Compensation [is] . . . fundamental in the definition of psychological equilibrium' (ibid., p. 151). 'Equilibrium is synonymous with activity' (loc. cit.). Flavell's description is a useful extension of these notions. 'Essentially, a system in equilibrium is one which possesses some sort of balance or stability (fragile or secure, temporary or enduring) with respect to the forces acting upon or within it. Forces or perturbations which, unopposed, would lead to a change of state are counteracted in an equilibrated system by equal and opposite forces which guarantee the status quo' (Flavell, 1963, p. 241).

The central constituents here, that is, 'stability', 'compensation' and 'activity', together with the maintenance of the status quo, do not in themselves make clear to what situation they are addressed – to the state of the subject in himself, to the state of the relationship between the subject and his milieu, or to both. A reference from *The Psychology of Intelligence* (1950) goes somewhat further in this respect:

> Every response, whether it be an act directed towards the outside world or an act internalised as thought, takes the form of an adaptation or, better, of a re-adaptation. The individual acts only if he experiences a need, i.e. if the equilibrium between the environment and the organism is momentarily upset, and action tends to re-establish the equilibrium i.e. to re-adapt the organism (Claparède). (p. 4)

This is, in fact, the Claparède Law of Consciousness, expressed here by Piaget, and in general taken up and fully endorsed by him. Immediately following this, Piaget refers equilibrium to what he calls 'functional interaction between the subject and the environment'. Yet it is quite clear in the passage we have given that two *distinct* meanings are to be attributed to equilibrium. These are internal/structural on the one hand and subject/environmental on the other. We know that, following this relatively early general theoretical work, and well-authenticated by the references in Flavell's book, there is an indispensable distinction for Piaget between the activity of the subject in respect of the milieu and the interiorised action which pertains essentially to what Piaget describes as the reflective abstraction of cognition.

Yet when we refer, again, to the notions presented in *Six Psychological*

Studies these ideas do not emerge as distinct at all. The vacillation between distinctness and indistinctness of the different interpretations of equilibrium can be still more precisely identified: 'Unlike physiological interactions, which are of a material nature and involve an internal change in the bodies which are present, the responses studied by psychology are of functional nature and are achieved at greater and greater distances in space (perception, etc.) and in time (memory, etc.)' (p. 4). It is quite clear from this that Piaget understands physiological interaction and any equilibrium pertaining to this physical relationship of the subject with the milieu as dependent upon an actual balance of *phenomena*. It is also clear that he conceives of psychological interaction as to do with sets of relationships the elements (psychological) of which are definitely obscure. The connection with the mathematical 'skeleton' of the system is very apparent here. It will be recalled that the analysis of this showed the indeterminacy of the 'element' in groups, groupings and lattices, permitting a vacillating movement from one interpretation to another, for example, propositional to numerical. Thus, when moving from the outside world to the inside world of cognition, the discussion passes without clear comment from the interaction of *subject and objects* to that of states, or conditions, *within the subject* without clarifying exactly what they refer to.

This transition from the outside to the inside world of cognition is tied in at several points with theoretical characteristics of the system. For example, the relation between subject and object is a matter of time, space and causality whereas the essential feature of the equilibrated structures of cognition is their non-spatio-temporality. Their logico-mathematical character ensures this. The interiorisation of action, so basic to the Piagetian view of individual–milieu relationships, again involves a qualitative change. Such interiorisation leads ultimately to 'reflective abstraction' which in its highest manifestation is reflection upon reflection. The difference between this and the physical experience from which it is to be derived is so radical that there is no possibility of a common element shared between them. The very conditions of the system drive towards such problems. For, in the external world, *things* relate, and even the subject has a phenomenal aspect in relation to objects. In the internal world, however, it is impossible to specify elements in any comparable way at the same time as satisfying the conditions Piaget has laid down for the system. Such non-specifiability is what we have called 'non-terminality'.

Although referred to before, this notion is usefully clarified further. A condition of 'terminality' does not require objects or 'things' as such to be specified in a theory or description. These constitute only one variety of 'terminal'. The most abstract mathematics is 'terminal' provided *elements* are *distinguishable* from *relationships*. The essence of non-terminality lies in the absence of such distinguishability and the consequent inability to determine which relationships refer to which terminals. The problem is very simply illustrated. When I say 'I am running', the terminality is both specified and implied through 'I' and my predicated action of 'running'. I can actually draw a picture of myself running. But the word 'running' itself can neither be illustrated nor conceived without additional 'terminals'. On its own it is non-terminal – in fact it is doubtful whether it is conceivable at all without a terminal extrapolation of some sort. Benjamin Whorf's work on the Hopi Indian language[35] might suggest that it is possible to construct a world-outlook which is basically 'non-terminal'. But careful consideration of the circumstances of that language,. its non-recognition of the categories of time, space and the distinction between subjectivity and objectivity, which underlie all 'advanced' languages and the thought categories they express, does not necessarily imply non-terminality. Rather, terminality is discovered in Hopi freed from its particularisation in logico-mathematical spatio-temporal categories. If one wants an example exposing the wrongness of a total identification of mentality with logico-mathematical categories, Hopi thinking and culture is certainly an excellent, but by no means isolated, one. Piaget's problem is that his particular variety of non-terminality occurs in the context of the strictest insistence on an exclusively logico-mathematical interpretation of mentality as a whole. Because of the essentially 'either–or', character of logic (irrespective of the number of values recognised) and mathematics, the non-terminality of Piaget's system is a most extreme form, especially as he is obliged by the system's requirements and objectives to unite this 'either–or-ness' with the contingency and randomness involved in development.

Do the central concepts of equilibrium, that is, 'stability', 'compensation' and 'activity', themselves express only conditions without relating the conditions to specific referents? All three, in the first place, have to be taken in conjunction as they relate to one another very closely. Piaget is at pains to stress (for example, Piaget, 1968, p. 101) that his conception of equilibrium is not static. What he attempts to do is to encapsulate the fluidity that he sees as an essential part of development with the structural stability that, in cognition, is exactly expressed by groups and lattices. Exactly how he sees this 'mobility' is quite difficult to establish with certainty. Rejecting the dynamical concept of equilibrium in the mechanical sense, Piaget expresses the relationship between 'mobility' and 'stability' in such phrases as 'the more mobile it is the more stable it is . . . it may be likened to the assembly of a subtle mechanism that goes through gradual phases of adjustment in which the individual pieces become more subtle and mobile as the equilibrium of the mechnism as a whole becomes more stable' (Piaget, 1968, p. 4). The notion comes through of an idea of constant motion directed at maintaining an overall stability – to use an everyday analogy, rather like walking up a down escalator. In itself the mobile-stable idea is self-sufficient and self-sustaining. But it is firmly on the non-developmental side of the fence because it excludes contingency/randomness. The problem is still how to link this up with development. One possible way of solving this is to break down the transitional process into a smaller number of steps, and this Piaget attempts particularly in his most recent theoretical development of the system, *The Development of Thought*.

Equilibrium and Reversibility

The connection between the idea of reversibility and equilibrium is extremely important in Genetic Epistemology, but also extremely difficult to clarify. On the one hand reversibility appears essentially to be part of the logico-mathematical framework, connected as it is with the mathematical inverse, and thence to the group core of Piaget's mathematical theory of intelligence. On the other hand it sometimes appears virtually identical with equilibrium itself which straddles the developmental and the structural aspects of cognition. From the point of view of the claimed group character of cognitive structures, reversibility is the king-pin without which there are no groupings, no groups and no logico-mathematical core in general. It is also an essential prerequisite for the growth of the structures since no interiorised action can become operational without becoming at the same time reversible.

Along with the organic growth of Piaget's own thinking go various differing formulations and definitions of reversibility in relation to equilibrium. Yet despite this variability, throughout the period especially since the Second World War the constant feature of the system has been to link the properties of cognitive structures with the apparatus of cognitive development by treating reversibility as a kind of hallmark of equilibrium. Reversibility appears from this point of view as a condition, or mode of existence, of cognitive structures, and is to do with their 'mobility'. Such mobility expresses the *operational* character of these structures and can be identified with negation and reciprocity in the logico-mathematical form Piaget says such structures take.

We seem, then, to be able to get a connection between the ideas of 'mobility' (characteristic of fully emerged structures), 'negation', 'reciprocity', the logico-mathematical manifestation of activity, namely, 'operations', and all with 'reversibility'. From these considerations, reversibility ought strictly to refer to the operations of structures alone, where 'operation' means a logico-mathematical operation not a physical one, and equilibrium ought to refer to the whole of the cognitive process inclusive of notions such as adaptation (assimilation, and accommodation), schemata, the interiorisation of action, the existence, or authentication, of structures themselves, the very notion of operation itself, and so on. In fact, Piaget often presents equilibrium as the *objective* of the cognitive process, and reversibility the acid test that that objective has been reached.

But the issue cannot really be settled so neatly. There are a considerable number of points to sort out as to what Piaget actually means by reversibility with respect to equilibrium. In *Les Notions de mouvement et de vitesse chez l'enfant* (Paris, 1946, p. 260), for example, Piaget writes that permanent equilibrium is 'due to the fact that the intuitive regulations have achieved complete reversibility'. Again, in the same work, he writes that 'Equilibrium [is] finally reached between assimilation and accommodation [which] explains. . . the reversibility of the operational groupings' (op. cit., p. 172). It is clear in the first case that Piaget sees equilibrium as derived *from* reversibility. Here, reversibility is the essence of cognitive structures and equilibrium the form these take. The second viewpoint is not manifestly contradictory to the first, although the order of 'achievement' makes reversibility more derivative of equilibrium than vice versa. In the following year (1947, Eng. edn 1950) Piaget writes in *The Psychology of Intelligence:* 'Reversibility thus characterises not only the final states of equilibrium but also the processes of development themselves' (p. 41). At *all* stages, it appears, reversibility is present in some form.

What we are really considering here is the derivative relationship between the two notions. This is no pseudo-problem for it is already given by the presence of two distinct terms relating to the same 'phenomenon', namely, the cognitive structures themselves. They are both in equilibrium and reversible, and the two concepts are not intended simply to be synonyms for each other. There is still another dimension to the problem, however. In *Six Psychological Studies* Piaget writes:

In short, the stable and final psychological equilibrium of the cognitive structures is confounded [*sic* – compounded?] with the reversibility of the operations, since the inverse operations exactly compensate the direct transformations. But this poses a final problem. Is it the reversibility of the operations that engenders their equilibrium or is it the progressive equilibration of the actions – passing through the stages of simple regulations with their retroactions and anticipations – which ends by engendering their terminal reversibility? Here the results of genetic analysis seemed decisive. Since the 'compensations' which respond to the intrusion adjust themselves only progressively and at first incompletely, the operational reversibility expressed by the complete compensations must be the result and not the cause of gradual equilibration. This, however, does not prevent the operational structures, once constituted, from acceding to the rank of instruments or organs for subsequent equilibration. (p. 114)

Piaget seems to commit himself completely here. Without doubt, and with full logical argument, reversibility is said to *result* from, not equilibrium, but *equilibration*. Equilibration, we must remember, is *not* identical with equilibrium (see the Preface to *The Development of Thought,* and see above, Chapter 2) but is really to do with the 'apparatus' of transition from the external world to the internal world of the subject.

But even here Piaget has not really made up his mind. Notice the last sentence in the above passage which immediately qualifies the *order* of determination. Perhaps even more important is the clear implication that a non-temporal (and non-spatial) condition, the subject's internal world of cognition, is, via its reversibility, *made dependent* on and *derivative from* the spatio-temporal world. This is the more startling when we recall that the former is hierarchically superior to the latter in Piaget's system – a point also reinforced in the last sentence – and is entirely borne out by Piaget's idea of logical necessity (cognitive) arising from the supposed recognition of the increasing likelihood, or probability, of an event occurring (*Six Psychological Studies*, p. 157). Such a sense of necessity is supposed to exercise a control over the more primitive phases of development of subsequent action, interiorisation, and cognitive growth.

Yet, despite the positiveness of the relation between reversibility and equilibrium asserted in this passage, earlier in the same book Piaget writes, 'This growing reversibility assumes progress towards equilibrium since physical equilibrium is defined by its reversibility' (p. 130). It is possible to construct an ever-growing list on both sides of the derivation, equilibrium equilibration from reversibility, reversibility from equilibrium equilibration. The following are only a handful of passages just to make the point.

PASSAGES INDICATING DEDUCTION OF EQUILIBRIUM
EQUILIBRATION FROM REVERSIBILITY

Equilibrium will thus be defined by reversibility. (*Introduction à l'épistémologie génétique,* Vol. I, *La Pensée mathématique*, Paris: 1950)

the system is in equilibrium when the operations of which the subject is capable constitute a structure such that these operations can be performed in either one of two directions (either by strict inversion or negation or by reciprocity). Thus, it is therefore *because* [our emphasis] the total set of possible operations constitutes a system of potential transformations which compensate each other – and which compensate each other insofar as they conform to laws of reversibility – that the system is in equilibrium. (Inhelder and Piaget, 1958, p. 267)

It is worth recalling that equilibrium is defined by reversibility. (Piaget, 1973, pp. 60–1)

PASSAGES INDICATING DEDUCTION OF REVERSIBILITY
FROM EQUILIBRIUM EQUILIBRATION

Here as elsewhere, operational reversibility is an end state of dynamic equilibrium (Piaget *et al.*, 1960, p. 58)

and of equilibration (self-regulation) mechanisms, which make for internal reversibility (Piaget, 1971, p. 62)

The passage already given from *Six Psychological Studies,* p. 114.

The following remark is quite clinching:

Whether we say that the operations are organised into reversible structures or that they tend towards certain forms of equilibrium then amounts to the same thing. (Piaget, 1968, p. 131)

As we said these are only a handful of references, and there are hundreds of such commentaries by Piaget to be found throughout his writings. These are supplied only as an indication of the different stances he takes up in relation to the derivation of reversibility from equilibrium or vice versa.

One might ask, if the identification between these two notions is so complete, why, then, does Piaget employ two concepts? To answer this we have to turn to the issue of dualism in the system again. Both reversibility and equilibrium, like other concepts, occur in both spatio-temporal contexts and non-spatio-temporal contexts, without any clear indication of their respective meaning and significance in the two zones. Reversibility is unclearly related to the physical process of 'back and forth' particularly shown in the analysis of the balance experiment in the last chapter, and equilibrium is unclearly related to the notion of symmetrical balance itself. Yet it cannot be overstressed that in Genetic Epistemology, the non-spatio-temporal character of cognition is an indispensable distinguishing feature marking it off as different, and supposedly superior, to the basic interaction of subject and environment. This is what the whole theory of the development of the individual from the sensory-motor stage through to the formal operational stage is about.

Despite, then, the very close relationship between equilibrium and reversibility, the former is undoubtedly primarily about the *state* of either a structure, or the 'structure d'ensemble', whereas the latter is about an *activity* which is a feature of equilibrium. Although both are firmly on the cognitive side of the subject–environment division, nevertheless they play a role with respect to one another which shows similar signs of the dualism that we find precisely in the subject–environment relationship itself. More than this, since they can both be ambivalently referred to either the cognitive state of the subject internally or to the subject's relationship with the environment (primarily, of course, from the subject point of view), the very circularity of the derivation of one from the other serves in a sort of way to knit up the difficult and incompatible zones of the external spatio-temporal with the internal non-spatio-temporal. In short, the circularity we detect here is itself an indispensable and inevitable concomitant of the dualism generally characteristic of the system. It emerges as a device (not necessarily preconceived) for different and fundamentally incompatible meanings to be ascribed to the same terminology without definite references of any sort.

Not only does this allow a sort of 'free movement' between zones that are different in kind, but such a device carries with it also a deeper connotation. By preserving a pseudo-unity of two such incompatible zones, the system as a whole makes itself, to use Karl Popper's term, 'non-falsifiable'. What is not referable to one of the interpretations of the dualism because it does not fit in with the assumptions of that interpretation is referable to the other in a way that seemingly does not break the axiomatic rules of the system as a whole. The guarantee of the latter, of course, derives mainly from the non-terminal aspects of the system. It is a curious definitive process which accepts establishing the one zone at the expense of the other and vice versa virtually at will.

Compensation and Disturbance in Relation to Equilibrium

A further problem is involved in the concept of reversibility over and above the problem of its dualistic relationship with equilibrium. This is the basic problem of accounting for the origin and nature of reversibility as such. An explanation is needed for the fact that reversibility is given by Piaget as the sole condition for operational thought, yet such a condition is very limited and particularised to form the exclusive basis of logical thinking as a whole.

The origins of cognitive reversibility in the subject are obscure, although limited, unstable and partial forms of reversibility are said to be features of even the sensory-motor period. It seems curious that there is no biological 'isomorph' for reversibility as there is for the general model of adaptation and its components. One is led to think that reversibility, as the criterion for operational thinking, is almost chosen for the exact way in which it fits in with the idea of group inverses as the central feature of the logico-mathematical cognitive structures seen by Piaget as the core of cognition. In the experiment relating to conservation of quantity of liquid, some Stage III subjects, who are said to have acquired conservation of quantity, explain this by the fact that the liquid may be poured back and will reach the same height as originally. This is said to demonstrate (conceptual) reversibility. However, many children do not, in fact, give this particular explanation but some other such as, 'You didn't add any or pour any away so there must be the same amount'. The important point in such comments is that reversibility is not referred to either directly or by implication. In fact, it seems that in a majority of cases like this, reactions are partially qualitative rather than quantitative.

Why, then, is so much importance to be attached to cognitive reversibility and the search for its existence? Of course, in relation to displacement backwards and forwards, it is very plausible to postulate a logical mapping of this in reversibility and a mathematical mapping by inverses. In this way, logic and mathematics map 'the return to the starting-point'. What is invalid is the conflation of the situation in Actuality with these separate mappings, as the discussion showed in Chapter 2. It is also queriable to postulate this as the keystone of operational thinking. At the very least, there are countless other features of displacement in the environment which have an equal claim to significance, the majority of which show irreversible characteristics.

Piaget's earlier writings do not satisfactorily answer this problem, and it is only with *The Development of Thought* that the problem is seriously tackled. On p. 25, in referring to the need to formulate a theory explaining the development of cognitive structures by equilibration, Piaget concludes that 'two conditions must be fulfilled: the reversibility must be shown to be the product of compensation systems of different levels, and the reason why these compensations are inseparable from constructions proper must be discovered'. Thus, reversibility has to be shown to be based upon compensations. This idea is not absent in works written before *The Development of Thought,* but is a very different concept from the early one familiar to most people of a 'return to the starting-point'. The relationship of reversibility to compensation must necessarily involve a connection with disturbance deriving from external intrusion. Once again, reversibility 'wanders' between events in Actuality and exclusively logical phenomena.

In fact, the implicit connection between reversibility and compensation appears as early as 1964 in *Six Psychological Studies* where Piaget writes: '[we] shall define [equilibrium] very broadly as the compensation resulting from the activities of the subject in response to external intrusion . . . we must insist emphatically that external intrusion can be compensated only by activities' (p. 101). Equilibrium is here defined in terms of compensation instead of, as before, in terms of reversibility. It seems as if the two notions are to a certain extent interchangeable, and it must be said that there is a certain correspondence of meaning between them as the sense of 'reversibility' can suggest a sort of compensation if both are referred to the idea of confronting and overcoming an obstacle to recover a former position through a sort of flexible mobility.

The first mention of compensation in *The Development of Thought* is on

p. 5 in reference to a basic 'model' of cognitive systems shown on p. 4 as:

$$(A \times A') \rightarrow B, \quad (B \times B') \rightarrow C, \quad \ldots \quad (Z \times Z') \rightarrow (A \times A'), \quad \text{etc.}$$

Here, A, B, C, . . . refer to parts of cognitive systems and A', B', C', . . . represent elements of the milieu. Piaget writes: 'Consequently, if there is an outside disturbance stemming, for example, from a substitution of B'' for B', either the conservation of the whole becomes impossible and the organism dies (if we referred to a cognitive system, we would say the substitution would be rejected), or there is a *compensating modification* (B is modified into B_2 which remains inserted in the cycle)' (our emphasis; p. 5). Thus, the notion of compensation is clearly that of a cognitive *element* (B) which is modified into, or replaced by another, cognitive *element* (B_2). What is not clarified is:

(a)   the nature of this cognitive element;
(b)   the mechanism of replacement or modification of B by B_2;
(c)   the effect of the substitution and subsequent modification (B to B_2) on the entire set of relationships involved in the cognitive system. As shown, any 'bit' may be changed, apparently with no effect upon the whole. Moreover, the entire model expresses a fragmentary approach to cognition which is portrayed here as occurring element by element with an implied temporal order from $A \times A'$ to $Z \times Z'$.
(d)   the structure is described as cyclic, yet any individual modification does not seem to disturb the *cyclic* character of the whole structure.

These points raise problems with respect to the Piagetian concept of structure which will be further discussed at the end of Chapter 9. The relevant issue here is that the concept of compensation (which is conceived as the basis for reversibility) is one of modification or replacement of each *separate* cognitive element through the influence of a change in a *separate* element in the milieu. What is actually happening is obscure and the nature of the elements problematical, the total description suffering from what has been termed 'non-terminality'. Thus, it is possible for the reader to form any image or 'model' he likes of the Piagetian description of cognitive development. This is especially so since there is no clue to the nature of the interaction between the elements, denoted in the sequence by the sign '×'.

Later on, the situation provides for a further variation of imagery. 'If we call compensation an action in a direction opposite to a given effect which thus tends to cancel or to neutralize the effect, it is obvious that the negative feedback plays such a role as an instrument of correction' (p. 26).

Positive feedback is later linked to compensation through the idea of 'filling the gap' and compensation is seen in this case as an equal and opposite action in relation to a disturbance (which implicitly includes intrusion since the disturbance is described as external – (loc. cit.)). Such a notion is indistinguishable from Piaget's views prior to *The Development of Thought* (see previous passage from p. 101 of *Six Psychological Studies*), and it shows that the attribute of 'feedback' is the only real addition made by this book to extending and developing the idea of compensation (and thus, by implication, reversibility). The trouble with this concept of 'feedback' in cognitive development is that it substitutes a trial-and-error, externally determined process for the subject-determined constructivism that has previously been the basis of the system. Whatever contribution the subject makes in a 'feedback loop', he is inevitably at the mercy of the milieu with respect to what is fed in. On the other hand, if the *source* of what is 'fed' in is external, the selection of what is 'eaten' depends on the selectivity of the subject and must raise very fundamental queries regarding the certainty that cognitive growth will indeed result at all from such a model. In sum, it remains to be shown whether a subject is able to acquire a deeper know-ledge of a reality if this is directly and exclusively derived from a 'feed-back', itself resulting from the subject's own actions and the motives for which are controlled by pre-selectivity. Thus, the notion of 'feedback', even as an analogy, brings the system no nearer to its goal of accounting for the growth of cognition.

Still another image or analogy is given on pp. 162–3 which confuses the issue in so far as it tends to contradict the equal and opposite notion provided by the first of these three characteristics. Piaget writes: 'If the relations between objects are varied, the variations of the independent variable x, in $y = f(x)$, can be called disturbances insofar as they modify the previous state, and the variations of y (dependent variable) will be the compensations which conserve the relation.' The notion offered here of functional dependence (in connection with compensation) is at variance with the 'back and forth' notion suggested earlier. Functional dependence obviously involves a *different quantity* from the original independent variable (x), not only a different *direction* (which conceivably is a 'dif-ference' of sorts in the reciprocal/inversion situation). So, in this presenta-tion of compensation, Piaget has switched to a new and different model without any explication of the connection between the two.

A further exposition appears on pp. 181–2 which sees the issue from yet another point of view. Here the disturbance is seen as that which 'creates the obstacle to reaching a goal–the compensation being what reduces this obstacle and favours reaching the goal'. Such an exposition in terms of goal-orientation has a certain plausibility compared with a model of mathematical functional dependence the symbols of which, as Piaget uses them, say nothing beyond what the words they symbolise convey. But plausibility of imagery is not the issue here. This last example of the explication of compensation gets no farther than affirming literally, what is, is!

It appears, however, difficult for Piaget to escape from his lifelong notion of reversibility manifested mathematically as inversion and reciprocity. When the three main characteristics of compensation are given in *The Development of Thought,* inversion and reciprocity are mentioned first similarly to Piaget's analysis over the previous fifty years. The others are 'a terminal evaluation of their success or insufficiency' and 'the tendency to conservations through transformations' (p. 29). The second is the most noteworthy. The evaluation of success or insufficiency would seem to be different in nature from the other characteristics. These latter are clearly parts of an inherent mechanism; but 'evaluation of success or insufficiency' goes beyond this. If such 'evaluation' involved no more than an automatic, inherent mechanism like the others, then it would be difficult to sustain the view that perfect equilibrium is not instantly attained in the compensatory act, thus throwing the whole equilibration process out of control. Yet by including this disparate, and entirely unlogicisable, characteristic in the list of essential features of compensation, an *erratic* factor is brought in which is quite at odds with the closed character of the other aspects of compensation. Thus, the basic conflict between the 'openness' requirement of growth and the closure requirement of Piaget's logico-mathematical structuration of cognition is not exorcised by the 'new' compensatory explication of reversibility and equilibrium; rather this conflict has become pinpointed in a decisive battle around the notion of compensation itself as a means of reconciling the two requirements.

Can one say, then, that *The Development of Thought,* by its use, or expansion, of the notion of compensation, has resolved any of Piaget's basic problems? We are still left not really knowing the nature of what we are talking about, nor at which points we are referring to the milieu external to the subject or the subject's internal cognitive system. Furthermore, in the case of disturbance, as distinct from compensation, this is consistently treated as a 'thing' (even in the negative case of 'closing a gap' this is so). But compensation is not so treated, normally carrying the meaning 'behaviour', or 'action' as it must if it is to be considered in the context of inversion or reciprocity, or, for that matter, any of the other definitive characteristics. Quite apart from the inappropriateness of treating disturbance as a 'thing' without a relationship, it compounds the error to treat disturbance and compensation as having totally different and distinct natures. So, as well as the non-terminality of the concepts themselves there is a further muddle of category arising out of this all-pervasive problem of non-terminality. When the form of the disturbance is actually an 'external intrusion' then this is even more the case.

A further analysis of compensation in *The Development of Thought,* this time in terms of different types of compensation arising at different stages in cognition, breaks the whole issue down into even smaller 'steps'. Three types are noted: α-type reactions occur early. 'When there are disturbances the re-equilibration, which is produced as a result of the nonbalance, will be obtained by behaviour known as type α', and these 'are only partially compensating, and consequently the resulting equilibriums remain very unstable' (p. 67). The next, more developed type is known as β-type behaviour and, again, this is said to 'consist of integrating into the system the disturbing *element* [our emphasis] arising from without' (p. 67). Now, the new element is not rejected or cancelled but the system is modified by 'equilibrium displacement' so that the 'unexpected fact' is made assimilable. This is still only *partial* compensation but superior to α-behaviour. For example, the subject will introduce 'solidarities' such as perceiving the unity between the extension and thinning of a clay sausage that is being moulded Finally, there is γ-behaviour, described as 'superior' which 'consist[s] in anticipating the possible variations which, as foreseeable and deducible, lose their disturbance characteristic and establish temselves in the potential transformations of the system' (p. 68). Piaget continues (p. 69) to deal with the differences between these three forms of compensation:

> The only major difference between these transformations and that of two actions occurring in opposite directions, each tending to cancel the other and reach a compromise (like a balance of two forces), is that, being part of the same system, all the transformations are sufficiently bound together so that operator T implies the existence of T^{-1} and the product $T \times T^{-1} = 1$. Our understanding of the compensation is consequently that there is a symmetry inherent in the system's organization and no longer an elimination of disturbances.

The compromise idea is new and is at variance with both inversion and reciprocity as forms which compensation must take. To reach a compromise is quite different from cancellation or from reciprocity (that is, compensation without cancellation). The most important point here is the use of mathematical symbolism to restate what has already been said and thus provide what might be termed 'credentials' for the idea of symmetry later in the passage which has in no way been demonstrated or proved. Symmetry lies in the idea of group elements having inverses ($T \times T^{-1} = 1$); but the connection between this and compensation is no more than assertion so long as the elements are not clearly delineated and as long as the referent continually slips from the external to the internal world of the subject and back again. This is very clearly related to the issues discussed in Chapters 2–4.

Additionally, of course, the other 'explications' of compensation, occurring later in the book and referred to earlier, can in no way be re-conciled with this α, β, γ sequence. Whether it be 'evaluation of success', functional dependence, or 'goal' orientation, the notion of symmetry is entirely incompatible with any and all of these concepts as well as 'gap-filling' ones since, however incoherent they are, they all reflect in some way or other *asymmetric* features – that is, in so far as one can apply, at all, this purely mathematical notion which is very doubtful. Even the most mathematical, functional dependence involves a *different dimension*.

Piaget continues by explaining that while the three types of compen-sation do not represent three distinct stages from sensory-motor to formal operational, but are phases discovered fairly regularly, a study of the interrelation between them 'enable[s] the equilibration process of cogni-tive systems to be understood' (p. 69). In short, this is a final 'scientific' solution to the central problem of the origins of equilibrium and, there-fore, of reversibility itself. The issue of the scientific nature or otherwise of his system is discussed in more detail in Chapter 9. It must be said now, however, that quite apart from other points at issue, there is a degree of casualness here beyond which it is impossible to go without rendering it an 'ad hoc' collection of partial theories which can be connected virtually at will. Moreover, the mutliplicity of analogies is no help to understanding because they do not clearly relate to each other and are often contradictory. The noteworthy point is that, whatever new ideas are imported to expli-cate the situation, the general feature of cognition remains the same as it has always been – regulation in terms of compensations which are charac-terised by exclusively symmetric forms and express inversion or recipro-city – in other words, reversibility. Has reversibility been shown to be the product of compensation? Not yet. So far, the connection seems to be no more than replacement of the word 'reversibility' by the word 'compen-sation' with the latter, because of its intuitive connotations in everyday life, endowing the former notion with plausibility.

But there is a further point. On p. 71 of *The Development of Thought,* Piaget writes: 'Thus it remains legitimate, as we have always emphasized, to consider the reversibility as a result of the equilibration as a complex process which takes in the psychogenetic variations of compensating reactions and modes of comprehension or of disturbance assimilation and not as an independent process called upon to explain the equilibrium.' Further, on p. 170: 'The subject's coordinations resulting in the logico-mathematical operations, the final operational structures, achieve a com-pensation in a complete form, as indicated by the fact that they are reversible, and compensation exists between all operations that show relations of inversion, reciprocity, or correlativity (duality).'

Thus, complete compensation is indicated by reversibility. But this is by no means the same thing as showing that reversibility is the product of compensations (that is, the original intention). The problem has been, though, that compensation has either been discussed in the same terms in which reversibility was previously talked of (that is, inversion, reciprocity and the ultimate formation of the INRC group), or in terms of disturbance or external intrusion (with a casual slip-over from one to the other in different passages), or in terms of positive or negative 'feedback' and other ways, none of which are explicative. All these involve the now very familiar problem of non-terminality and a dualistic treatment, and thus fail to solve the original problem set out. Equilibrium, previous to *The Development of Thought,* might be said to have a static bias. Now, in trying to get closer to a solution of the problem of reconciling the logico-mathematical (static) aspects of the system with the evolutionary developmental ones, Piaget adds an extra problem. For in *The Development of Thought* (p. 4) he defines equilibrium simultaneously in static and dynamic terms: 'cognitive equilibriums . . . resemble above all the static biological equilibriums (homeostasis) or dynamic equilibriums ('homeorhesis')'.[36]

Perhaps this is the basic problem in *The Development of Thought* and as such has compounded the conflict already inherent in the system. As we analysed previously, equilibrium and reversibility were defined for many years in terms of each other. Now, equilibrium is defined in terms of compensation. Is compensation a dynamic or a static concept? We do not really have a definitive answer to this and the multiplicity of explications provides alternative answers at will.

Before we leave the issue of compensation one more point might usefully be made. In relation to compensation as a basis for cognitive development, when disturbance or unexpected intrusion occurs, the Piagetian implication is that there is an *automatic* response of the subject due to the inherent character of the mechanism. Thus, there is an inbuilt, and, indeed, probably unconscious, 'absorption' of the disturbance into the subject's structure of thought which, at the formal operational stage, is accentuated by the fact that such disturbances may be anticipated. Piaget writes (ibid., p. 182): (in the compensatory process) 'The obstacle is . . . first felt only as a gap, but it becomes concrete the moment work begins and then, before it is incorporated in a superior whole, *it seems to threaten the preceding completion* [our emphasis]. The special characteristic of these virtual disturbances is the result of *the novelty of what is to be constructed as compared to constructions by simple adjustment* [our emphasis].'

The whole emphasis of this passage on virtual disturbance is a recipe for anticipatory *control* of factors which may overthrow the established system. In effect, novelty becomes 'permissible' *only* if it submits to *already extant* organisation. The social implications of this are extensive and will be looked at in Chapter 10. Here it is worth noting that if Piaget's offering of this as a 'scientific' observation is doubtful, his record of it as an expression of reality is indeed accurate. There is of course a degree of natural selectivity related to survival which lies outside social training. But the latter strongly orients this selectivity towards the requirements of the particular social establishment in which it is taking place. Victorians frequently did not 'see' the poor. White South Africans frequently do not 'see' black South Africans if it is inconvenient to do so. We shall observe the significance of this in Piaget's treatment of the (to him) necessary transition from adolescence to adulthood as he deals with it in the last chapter of *The Growth of Logical Thinking*.

Further on the Dualism of the Equilibrium Theory

We have said a fair amount about the inherent problems in Genetic Epistemology which derive from the persistent attempt to reconcile zones the paradigms of which are incompatible. In the one case we are dealing with the paradigm of change within time, that is, development, involving *unpredictability*. In the other case we are dealing with a classificatory process, or 'nesting' in accordance with logical rules, which is therefore entirely *predictable*. The word 'nesting' as used by Piaget is intended to convey the containing of one layer of a logical system inside another, rather as in mathematics a less general geometry is contained within a more general one (Piaget, 1971, pp. 23ff.). The question is whether Piaget ever really succeeds in reconciling the 'nesting' with the developmental aspects of his system, and if he does, must it be concluded that the notion of equilibrium is void of meaning?

For Piaget himself the 'nesting' concept is virtually universal, which makes his notion of development undoubtedly much more a matter of logical deduction than unfolding evolution. Thus:

> Every structure is to be thought of as a particular form of equilibrium, more or less stable within its restricted field and losing its stability on reaching the limits of the field. But these structures, forming different levels, are to be regarded as succeeding one another according to a law of development, such that each one brings about a more inclusive and stable equilibrium for the processes that emerge from the preceding level. Intelligence is thus only a generic term to indicate the superior forms of organisational equilibrium of cognitive structurings. (Piaget, 1950, p. 7)

Certainly by doing this, by subsuming development under the laws of an axiomatic system which a 'nesting' concept implies, Piaget may appear to have resolved the incompatibility problem. But, as Rotman (1977, p. 105) points out, Piaget's assumption that 'Equilibrium is a concept that can be quantified' is at variance with the notion of equilibrium as applied to dynamic situations: 'Why', asks Rotman, 'should a system . . . moving into equilibrium have only one position to move to?' In fact, applying the logical 'nesting' concept to development depends on the assumption that there *is* only one equilibrium. Once it is supposed that there is a choice of positions, the axiomatic structuration of equilibrium – the 'nesting' of cognitive structures one within the other – is made impossible. In fact the deductive 'tightness' which goes with an axiomatic system, and its quanti- fiability in some form (Piaget always talks of 'increasing' equilibrium), are entirely mutually dependent features. Clearly we are very close to a predestined situation. If the growth of things and phenomena as well as their existence is a matter of pure logic, how can we escape accepting that all is already 'written' before it is done? That this must be avoided at all costs is basic to Genetic Epistemology, especially since, unlike biological evolutionary notions as Piaget sees them, it is characterised by learning within the individual's lifetime.

We may see at this point of the discussion a curious 'cross-reference' situation. As we know, Piaget understands the *function* of organic mechanisms as *innately* given (for example, the optical mechanism involved in the use of the eye–brain link up), and the cognitive *structures* which are built up through functioning, as *learned*. Now, the first is undoubtedly the scene of the 'action' which is then interiorised into (ultimately) equilibrated, operational structures characterised by 'nesting' of a non-evolutionary logical sort. Thus, despite the original distinction between 'function' and 'structure' it looks as if the *functioning* is the source of learning, and the *structuring* is, by definition, impervious to change, once it is established, except by being linked to other similar structures.

Thus, from one point of view (*a*) biological inheritance is unchanging and cognition is an individual learning process; from another, (*b*), the biological is the scene of action (function) and therefore the source of learning and development, whereas that which is learned (structures) is axiomatically organised and therefore is fundamentally non-develop- mental.

Developmental	*Non-developmental*
(*a*) Cognitive structuring	Biological functioning
(*b*) Biological function as the source of 'action'	Cognitive structures (operational) resulting from interiorised 'action'

It should be clear from this 'fluidity' of movement between different points of view how much Piaget's thought in general demonstrates the 'collapsar' features detectable in his mathematics. Such fluidity clearly also depends on either the unspecification, or ambiguity, of elements in all cases – what we have called 'non-terminality'. It is also fairly easy to see how Piaget's special notion of apriorism, whereby a process, including an act of cognition, tends to certainty from uncertainty through convergent probabilities, arises from the same 'fluidity'. In short, the non-terminal and convergent probability aspects of the system enable the central problem to be avoided and apparently allow equilibrium, interpreted as a logico-mathematical phenomenon, to be derived without interruption or qualification from the non–logico-mathematical activity of the subject in his milieu.

Such factors, of course, have not gone entirely unnoticed. Piaget has been accused, for example, of circularity of definition on several occasions and has sought to rebut such accusations. Circularity is quite a tricky question since the containment of conclusions within the premises of any logically ordered system is a bugbear at least as old as Aristotle himself. It is as well to bear in mind, however, that the real goal of any deductive system is not the arrival at conclusions as such but the demonstration to the full of all possible relations between a set of assumptions (axioms) within the rules governing these relations. In the well-known simple syllogism 'All men are mortal; Socrates is a man; therefore Socrates is mortal', the mortality of Socrates can, of course, be shown to be already contained in his manhood. The logic, however, consists in demonstrating the relationship, expressed within the rule applied, of Socrates to manhood in general, and thence to mortality. All this may seem obvious to the point of triviality; however, what can be seen clearly is the necessary presence of 'elements' of different 'levels' among which rational linkages can be established. There is no non-terminality here. In fact, in such a system the original 'elements' constantly reappear in different relationships, and the 'theorems' of the system are embodied in exhaustive exploration of all such possible relations under the rule. Circularity has meaning in such a linear system only if any original assumption emerges again deductively from the unfolding of all the possible relations under the rule.

We saw how this possibility definitely exists in relating equilibrium to reversibility. It is, in fact, the practice of leaving the elements unclear at all levels (that is, non-terminality) that masks the circularity of which Piaget has been accused. Effectively this is like modifying, not the axioms of a logico-mathematical system, but those elements about which the axioms establish the initial self-evident relations *in the course of unfolding all the possible relations*. It is like altering without comment the definition of a point in Euclidean geometry as having position and no magnitude in the midst of the theorem-building process. Quite simply, if a logico-mathematical linear-deductive process is opted for as an exclusive expression of a particular system (in Piaget's case human cognition), then it is unacceptable to indulge in any form in the kind of ambiguity just described. *This* is indeed circularity and derives from the linear-deductive method itself and has nothing in common with the *self-reference* involved in Gödel's and others' work (see below, Chapter 8).

In such circumstances as these it becomes impossible to be certain what is the distinction, or at what point a distinction actually occurs, between the activities of the subject and the nature of that which is acted upon. It is also, of course, unclear how to decide on the nature of the milieu, or environment–subject interaction. In fact, we have arrived at a very serious crisis for the notion of equilibrium. For without clarity of element, and in particular transmutation of such elements, it is difficult to clarify the character of equilibrium at all. It can be *asserted* that a logical notion of reversibility 'corresponds' with an idea and even an actual physical action, of 'back and forth' motion in the milieu. This is the essence and intention of the theme of logical–psychological isomorphism. It can be *asserted* that there is a transmutation (interiorisation, or latterly, self-regulation and compensation) between the external and the internal. The stage theory follows once the assertion is made. But in none of these cases is any genuine mechanism revealed and no evidence of the existence of equilibrium at all.

The attempt to affirm its existence 'circumstantially', as it were, by employing in addition to the idea of isomorphism those of 'recapitulation' (that is, the form of phenomenal existence at the psychological level 'recapitulates' biological forms of existence) and 'convergent reconstruction' (similar to the 'convergent probability' notion we have already looked at) is highly unsatisfactory. This is so especially in the context of strictly applied hypothetico–deductive methods supposedly backed up by experiments. Nor are notions which verge on the oxymoronic like identifying increasing 'mobility' with increasing 'stability' convincing. 'The higher forms of intelligence and affectivity tend towards a "mobile equilibrium". The more mobile it is, the more stable it is, so that the termination of growth in healthy minds by no means marks the beginning of decline but rather permits progress that in no sense contradicts inner equilibrium' (Piaget, 1968, p. 3).

A particularly important point coming out of this latter passage is the idea of equilibrium sustained by the proposition that it always reaches a point of 'termination'. There is no doubt that Piaget understands mental development to have an ultimate and terminative equilibrium. On the first page of *Six Psychological Studies,* he writes:

An essential difference between the life of the body and that of the mind must nonetheless be stressed if the dynamism inherent in the reality of the mind is to be respected. The final form of equilibrium reached through organic growth is more static and above all more unstable than the equilibrium towards which mental development strives, so that no sooner has ascending evolution terminated than a regressive evolution automatically starts leading to old age.

The passage immediately following this one is the one already referred to, including the quotation given above regarding healthy minds. The fact remains that a *final* mental equilibrium is postulated here although different, indeed, from the organic final equilibrium. Later, in the definitive work, *The Development of Thought,* as we saw in Chapter 1, the Preface explicitly talks of ultimate equilibrium.

An important question must be put at this juncture. Does Piaget mean by 'termination' the end of structuration, or does he mean the end of the development of the cognitive apparatus leaving the individual (ideally) in full possession of all the equipment necessary for the acquisition of knowledge at any time in any circumstances and in any form whatsoever (the formal operational stage)? In the passage we give, 'termination' is related specifically to the growth of what is by implication the cognitive structures ('in healthy minds . . . '). But this termination 'permits progress' not in conflict with 'inner equilibrium'. Clearly there is an absolute distinction here between the knowing process (which is to terminate) and what is known (which may grow) – which is quite at variance with the Piagetian position on action as the source of knowledge. But more suggestive still, if progress does not contradict (disturb) equilibrium, then *all that can happen after reaching this final stage is an indefinite repetition of activities achieved at this point without any qualitative change in the nature of knowing and no possibility of knowledge outside that subsumed by the methods of knowing the subject has supposedly achieved by the end of his teens.* The implication is clear: cognitive growth can be regarded as a sort of acquisition of a 'bag of tools' which thereafter are 'used' on the world to produce 'knowledge'. 'Progress' is thus reduced to a piece of mental philately where you end up with a lumber room of 'facts', larger or smaller according to whether you have spent more or less time on acquiring them, together with a simple deductive system of propositional logic.

This all constitutes an expansion on the basis of a particular interpretation of 'termination' as meaning an end to the acquisition of the cognitive apparatus and which regards the latter as a 'bag of tools'. But in this passage, and in *The Development of Thought* Preface, an alternative meaning can be drawn out – that actual *structuration* ends with the completion of the formal operational stage, and that by his or her early twenties the individual is (or ought to be) a completed psychological entity in the fullest sense. Certainly the social treatment of the individual's maturation, as Piaget handles it in *The Growth of Logical Thinking* (the final chapter) especially, carries this meaning. The individual's psyche is only stable when it is completely harmonised with social need via the acceptance by the individual of his or her social role; when the formal operational stage in the individual merges, and is at one with, the individual's social co-operation (see below, Chapter 10).

We are indeed in a dilemma here. *Either* cognition is purely a matter of learning how to learn, which completely bypasses the interactive influence of mode of knowing on what is known (which Piaget constantly shows himself aware of anyway), *or* it is the total process of knowing where the nature of the act conditions the target or goal of knowledge. In either case the notion of 'termination' is quite disastrous. Yet it is probably the most important notion sustaining the concept of equilibrium. All equilibria have 'termination' features at whatever stage they are considered. In fact, if one reverts for a moment to the characteristic of closure, plus all the group-like aspects associated with equilibrated structures, then the notion of termination is virtually unavoidable.

And at this point we leave the question of equilibrium in itself in Piaget's system. There are clearly many incompatible and, in fact, fanciful aspects to the notion, but it is not our job to attempt to tidy these up. Some might say that the analytical survey of the system needs to go no farther – that if equilibrium does not stand up, nothing else will. This is as may be. But one would certainly not be doing Piaget justice if the 'apparatus' of the system were not discussed, and this is what we propose to do in the next chapter.

6 Equilibration I. The Apparatus of Cognition

If equilibrium is the target of cognition, then the mechanism of its establishment is almost as important. Moreover, there must be a mechanism of genesis which at least attempts to couple up with and complement this theory of equilibrium.

The problem is to decide which is more indispensable and original for Piaget; whether he was at first mainly stimulated by a desire to explain thought through its development or its development through its extant forms. His intellectual roots in biology might suggest the first. But equally early he adopted a belief in the central role of logic in intelligence. And even within Piaget's biological experience, wholeness and stability play as important a part as any interest in evolution. On balance, and especially with the Preface of *The Development of Thought* in mind, one can conclude that his principal concern has been with the explanation of the *stability* of things and in accounting for their deveopment in this context. This certainly emerges from a study of the influences on him and the sources of his own treatment of the notion of equilibrium. It certainly accounts for his tenacious adherence to the exclusively logico-mathematical model of mentality embodied in the attempted applications of Group Theory and the lengths to which he goes to maintain this in the face of its manifest inappropriateness to any growth process. It is particularly important, therefore, to examine what might be called the apparatus Piaget has constructed, particularly in the second half of his writing life, aimed at revealing how the dynamics of experience are translated into his view of the logico-mathematical relationships of cognition itself.

Broadly, one can divide the Piagetian world into two major areas, that area lying on the 'inner' side of the subject–milieu dualism and that lying on the 'outer' side of the same dualism. That there is such a dualism there is no doubt, as emerged in the consideration of equilibrium itself. The dualism is especially revealed when one comes to examine the 'frontier' region of the direct contact beween the world of the subject and the world of the object.

In the opening paragraphs of Chapter 5 we opted for considering the state and nature of the inner world of the subject first, and then to proceed 'outwards' as it were to the point of contact between the subject and the external world. Either method, we said, can be justified depending on whether equilibrium or equilibration is treated as prior in Genetic Epistemology. Piaget is entirely undecided on this question. Sometimes equilibrium is paramount and development entirely subordinate to it. In *The Development of Thought,* it looks at first sight as if equilibration is made paramount. Yet even here the ambivalence remains despite the apparent concentration on equilibration. In line with our decision that ultimately Piaget regards the condition of stability as predominant, we are progressing from the internal zone (dominated by equilibrium) to the external zone (fluctuating). This, after all, corresponds closely to the 'activism' with which the system is associated. This line of procedure rather than its alternative (to start with action on objects and progress 'inward' to cognitive structures) does not affect the dualism problems in the slightest degree. Moreover, the 'outward' line is true to Piaget's notion of the subject's actions in the external world. These, after all, remain appendices or extensions of the subject's cognitive whole, not primarily attributes of the objects, although, again, there are problems of ambiguity here.

Following, therefore, the 'inner–outer' direction of discussion, we start with structures as such and continue with operations and transformations. The concept of schemata is a complex one as it hovers between the inner and outer worlds of the subject and also between his innate (functional) bequest and his learned structures. Similarly the very important notion of adaptation (assimilation and accommodation) involves crossing the 'frontier' backwards and forwards as it were from the external world in which the subject is acting to the cognitive world. This also is one of the sensitive concepts in the system. The idea of action is at least firmly situated in the external world of the subject, although, of course, it is always *his* actions that are involved. Such actions must of course be distinguished from operations which are often described as interiorised actions.

It is not intended that these aspects of the apparatus of equilibration be regarded as a linear sequence. Operations do not follow on structures nor do schemata precede adaptation. The best way of understanding these aspects of the system is as a form of hierarchical ordering. Action is undoubtedly 'inferior' to operation in the scale of cognitive manifestation, but although Piaget never actually says so, all the aspects of equilibration are, by implication, happening at once in the mature individual. Of course, the *development* of these aspects through the stages of maturation from infancy to late adolescence involves some notion of successiveness. Also, tracing one cognitive event from its source in the action of the subject to the highest level of structuration inevitably involves some sequential implication. But there is always a 'two-wayness' implicit in the actual activity of the apparatus, and it is this which must offset any idea of simple progressive sequence.

Structures

The notion of structure goes a long way back for Piaget – at least as far as 1928, but it becomes particularly important when he begins to generalise his system, especially in *The Psychology of Intelligence* (1947), basing himself upon experimental and methodological work of the previous two decades. The nature of these structures is not entirely clear and from one point of view they may be regarded as units of cognition. Their association with logical operations is certainly fixed from the beginning (See Flavell, 1963, p. 4, for an interesting discussion of 'logic-in-action' which may be compared with cognitive structure.)

The main question under review is *what* do the cognitive structures, whatever form they are supposed to take, actually structure? Flavell's description (p. 7) of Piaget's earliest developmental model, that is, the *grouping* (see Flavell bibliog., Piaget, 1937b, c, d), is not particularly helpful. 'A grouping', says Flavell, 'is a hybrid logico-algebraic structure, possessing properties of both mathematical groups and lattices, which Piaget uses to describe cognitive structures in the 7–11 year old' (p. 7). Similarly, reference to the group of spatial displacements (see Flavell bibliog., Piaget, 1954a) as an early example in the infant of structural equilibrium, together with the characteristic of reversibility, does not actually lead towards discovery of those elements whose cohesion identifies a structure. In 1968, in *Genetic Epistemology*, Piaget gave the following definition of a structure in general:

> First of all, a structure is a totality; that is, it is a system governed by laws that apply to the system as such, and not only to one or another element in the system. The system of whole numbers is an example of a structure, since there are laws that apply to the series as such. Many different mathematical structures can be discovered in the series of whole numbers. One, for instance, is the additive group. The rules for associativity, commutativity, transitivity, and closure for addition all hold within the series of whole numbers. A second characteristic of these laws is that they are laws of transformtion; they are not static characteristics. In the case of addition of whole numbers, we can transform one number into another by adding something to it. The third characteristic is that the structure is self-regulating; that is, in order to carry out these laws of transformtion, we need not go outside the system to find some external element. Similarly, once a law of transformation has been

applied, the result does not end up outside the system. Referring to the additive group once again, when we add one whole number to another, we do not have to go outside the series of whole numbers in search of any element that is not within the series. And once we have added the two whole numbers together, our result still remains within the series. We could call this closure, too, but it does not mean that a structure as a whole cannot relate to another structure or other structures as wholes. Any structure can be a substructure in a larger system. (pp. 22–3)

It is clear here that 'structure' is seen primarily as to do with the totality of a system. It is also clear that the laws of this totality predominate over the behaviour of any element of the system. By this presentation, identification of elements can be avoided. The case used to exemplify elements is that of the integers and it is implied that the elements are being specified *in cognition* when in fact they are not. But it is precisely this problem of the elements of cognition that is difficult to settle in Piaget's system.[37] In the glossary to *Six Psychological Studies,* four years earlier, Piaget had written that structure (cognitive) was 'a mental system or totality whose principles of activity are different from those of the parts which make it up' (p. xxii). The only clue we have here to the elements of the cognitive strucure is in the word 'parts'.

It could be argued that a search for the elements in cognitive structures is misleading in so far as Piaget distinguishes strictly between structure, function and the content of intelligence (see Flavell, 1963, p. 17). In short, to ask what elements are structured in cognition may be illegitimate in so far as content (that which is concretely involved in mental structuring) is strictly distinct from structure itself. But is this any different, say, from the example of whole numbers? Piaget would distinguish between structure and content for this system too, yet the elements must be clearly known before the system can be seen to be subject to transformation. In fact, element (content) is ignored when considering structure-in-itself; yet without such elements structuration is impossible or meaningless.

We shall also find here the same problem of circularity based upon the non-terminality that we uncovered in considering equilibrium itself, and it is difficult, indeed, to distinguish structures, thus non-terminally conceived, from a 'condition of equilibrium'. The one argues the existence of the other and vice versa.

Now, content, for Piaget, may be thought of as 'raw, uninterpreted behavioural data . . . ' (ibid., p. 17). Here, in association with the notion of function (described by Flavell as 'those broad characteristics of intellectual activity which hold true for all ages and which virtually define the very essence of intelligent behaviour'), we have the determining factors for the subject's action in his milieu. Thus the elements, or content, of cognition can, if we are not careful, be reduced to nothing but 'raw behavioural data' securely related in the last instance to inherited 'functions', or functioning, alone. And here circularity emerges again, indicated in the last passage quoted. For the presence of actually functioning organs (of intelligence) is detectable, ultimately, *only* from the observation of behaviour, but what is actually done by the subject (behaviour) is identifiable *only* through the use he makes of things he is acting on, which is a matter of functioning. Hence, function is deduced from behaviour and behaviour from function.

Another dimension (if one may call it this) of circularity is shown when Piaget's notion of the independent content of intelligent behaviour is brought into the picture. For content one must read the world of objects and their relations with each other external to the subject but including the subject's reaction to them. Such content is recognised by behaviour and behaviour is recognised by the subject's relation to the world of objects. Between this world and the subject's function Piaget postulates cognitive structures (ibid., p. 17). A diagram might help here: see Figure 6.1.

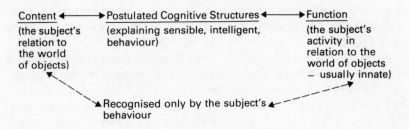

Figure 6.1

The system may be thought to escape from the problems of structures without specified elements as well as from this circularity by a stress on the invariance of function as opposed to the variability of structure and content. By the former, Piaget means that all *functions* embody the *fact* and *necessity* of the individual's interaction with the environment, and are therefore invariant under all circumstances and at all times. Adaptation (assimilation and accommodation), for example, is an existent fact independent of what is adapted to. The contents of intelligent experience are, of course, variable in the sense that the environment, both internal and external, of the thinking organism is constantly changing. But most important, it is the postulated cognitive structures that are regarded as variable because they must satisfy the indispensable principle of epigenesis whereby Piaget claims to avoid both the environmental determinism of a Lamarckian position and the genetic determinism of a neo-Darwinian one (see above, pages 6–10). By these means it might be possible to reach a 'midway' position in which structures are only formed in the *process* of construction by the interaction of function and content (see Piaget, 1971, *passim,* but especially pp. 32ff.).[38] In such a manner structures can be shown to emerge without reference specifically to their elements. These may be referred to generally but need not be spelled out.

But does Piaget really escape from the two traps of environmental and genetic determinism, which is what is involved in the contrast between function and structure? We have seen how he adopts a modified form of apriorism which makes necessity (for the subject) emerge out of probabilities – a notion closely paralleling the one affirming that structures only appear in the course of their construction (Piaget, 1968, p. 147; Piaget, 1971, pp. 127–8) and that no structure can ever be radically new (see Flavell bibliog., Piaget, 1957c; also Flavell, 1963, pp. 83, 114, and Piaget, 1968, p. 149, 'every genesis emanates from a structure and culminates in another structure'). If we look at Figure 6.1 again, bearing this in mind, then in a sense Piaget can be seen as benefiting from an environmental determinist position while not acknowledging its influence (beyond, that is, constant behavioural patterns) on structure formation. The nature of the elements of the structures can thus be left an open question but their existence can always be extrapolated from the subject's behavioural content and function.

But, despite all this, the system remains dogged by the possibility that intelligent growth is only an extension of biology. For whichever way one turns the question cannot be avoided of the mutual impact of that which is biologically inbuilt on what the subject learns in his lifetime. The distinction between 'function' and 'structure' is supposed to cover this, but in practice it evades the issue. The 'doing' of the action is regarded as a phylogenetic problem to do with heritable abilities. 'What is done' is regarded as ontogenetically particular to the individual organism and contingent upon its lifetime experience. But in *both* of these conceptual positions we are left with the *same question with which we began* – how is the act of doing (function) distinct from what is done (structure) and what is acted upon in the course of this (elements/content)? It does not avail to claim, as Flavell does (p. 408), that Piaget overcomes the problem (of relating continuity to discontinuity) by associating the former with 'function' (the subject always adapts) and the latter with 'structure' (the adaptation involves forming cognitive structural wholes). The same questions remain unanswered. Furthermore, Flavell's suggestion that there is an inherent necessity to postulate cognitive structures (p. 409) without which Piaget would have only a learning theory, not a developmental one, begs the question. It is still impossible to identify what it is that is, in fact, developing.

A somewhat different approach to the question of the nature of structures is to be found in a consideration of 'totalities', or wholes, an indication of which was given in the earlier passage from *Genetic Epistemology*. This concept is central to Piaget's notion of structures. In *Six Psychological Studies*, and still more subsequently, he presents structure as basically dependent upon this idea.

> We shall define structure in the broadest possible sense as a system which presents the laws or properties of a totality seen as a system. These laws of totality are different from the laws or properties of the elements which comprise the system. I must emphasize the fact that these systems are merely partial systems with respect to the whole organism or the mind . . . We are concerned with a partial system, which, as a system, presents laws of totality distinct from the properties of its elements. (Piaget, 1968, p. 143)

Piaget goes on to show, using mathematics as an example, and making special reference to the Bourbaki structures, that it is possible to handle 'structures of order and . . . topological structures'. 'Structures of group, field or ring' are algebraic structures and 'lattices, semi-lattices, etc. are structures of order' (p. 143). In all such cases Piaget claims to find a justification for the strict separation of element and structure. This separation is not, moreover, a subsidiary point. Flavell makes the case (pp. 4–5) that Piaget's point of departure from Gestalt psychology rests on the issue of algebraic additivity. Cognitive structures, argues Piaget, are distinct from the perceptive wholes such as are dealt with by Gestalt psychology, since, because they exemplify equilibrium, they are essentially additive. By clear definition, therefore, they *cannot* possess the character of the whole which is not equal to the sum of the parts, as is the case with a Gestalt – 'whole', but must strictly demonstrate mathematical exactitude.

> First, though logico-mathematical structures are without the least shadow of doubt subject to laws of wholeness . . . they are not gestalten, since their laws of composition are strictly additive (2 plus 2 make exactly 4, even though, or precisely because, this addition 'participates in' the group laws). (Piaget, 1971, p. 59)[39]

Yet in the original reference to *Six Psychological Studies* above, Piaget is clearly referring to equilibrated logically operative cognitive structures. Here we come upon yet another conflict of basic position. But at least what is clear from this particular discussion is that 'element' is to be taken as strictly distinct from structure and the latter's laws subsist in themselves and do not need, or have no dependence on, the elements they structure.

It is probably time to try to bring some of these diverse points together. We started by asking a question: if there are (cognitive) structures what is it that they are structuring? The first and perhaps easiest answer, as Rotman suggests 1977, pp. 46–7), is to go straight to mathematics itself and interpret Piaget's structures exclusively in these terms. But second thoughts on this do not reveal a mathematical explanation as very helpful. Neither logic nor mathematics can be regarded as sciences of 'pure' structure. Mathematical structures, however abstract, always have their elements, as does logic, and their invocation by Piaget can serve only to postpone the vital answer. Nor do the structure–function–content arguments lead to clarification; and, indeed, the problems of innateness and apriority, which haunt Piaget's thought on the question of the origin of structures, serve only to raise further problems around the same question. There is also the important circularity of description/definition which is illegitimate in the same sense as we discussed with respect to equilibrium. Here, as in that case, there is a deductive process based on axioms which are *not* independent of each other and which, therefore, can be interchanged at any point.

What is significantly in common among all these notions is that they portray 'states', or conditions of things *to the exclusion of the things themselves*. This is not in any way altered by passages such as the following on the origin of (logical) structures, of which comparable ones can be found throughout Piaget's writings:

> Certainly it is only when actions are exercised upon objects that the logical structures are formed. We have emphasised the fact that the source of logical operations is action itself, which, of course, takes place only in connection with objects. In addition, the stage of 'concrete operations' shows that, before it is applied to pure verbal statements or 'propositions', logic is organised in the midst of practical manipulations bearing upon objects. (*Six Psychological Studies*, p. 127).

What is bypassed here is the *metamorphosis* which must necessarily occur in 'elements' in the transition process from physical objects and features, and the subject's action upon them, to mental ones. And this affirmation of the objective basis to thought gives no answer to the question of what constitutes the mental elements that are subject to structuration. In fact the 'action' offered as the origin of cognition, in a thoroughly non-terminal manner, simply serves to make the issue still more vague. If structures are 'only' formed when actions are performed on objects, that is, by *disturbing* the situation by the actions, then how can it be sustained that the *source* of operations is, in fact, action? This passage bears comparison with one from the first of the *Studies*:

> The logico-mathematical operations derive from actions themselves, because they are the product of an abstraction which proceeds from the co-ordination of actions and not from the objects themselves . . . For

operations to exist, these actions must become reversible and capable of being co-ordinated into integrated structures which can be expressed in such general algebraic terms as: 'groupings', 'groups', 'lattices', etc. (pp. 81–2)

Yet again an 'entitiness' is asserted without any element content whatsoever being specified.

The theme runs much deeper for Piaget than may appear at first sight, and certainly influences all other concepts that we are concerned with. It is also clearly related to his utilisation of Group Theory as a model of cognition. Perhaps if the original question were rephrased in the following form the situation might become somewhat clarified: 'If the elements of the cognitive structures are defined is it not the case that the Piagetian system would then produce the problem of relating these elements to the elements (physical) in the subject's milieu?' There is, in fact, no escaping a clear 'yes' to this question – in which case the problem becomes simply narrowed to the region 'between' the internal and external elements and the relationship between these. This, however, is not a problem peculiar to the Piagetian system but is a fundamental problem of epistemology as a whole. What it does reveal is that Piaget's system does not overcome this central problem of epistemology.

The point relates particularly to what we have called the 'collapsar' notion in the mathematical analysis. With the latter the presence of notational ambiguity allows not only a 'slip-over' from an open situation, impermissible in the terms of reference of Group Theory, to the closure of that theory itself, but the possibility of vacillation from the subject's internal to his external worlds – the system reaping the benefit of both. The cognitive structures proposed allow a similar 'slip-over' to be achieved by avoiding identification of the elements of the structures and by a descriptive definition based *essentially* and *wholly* on relationships internal to the structures alone such as reversibility. From one point of view it is this exclusion of elements from structural thought that generates the ambiguity of the relation of the subject's action to objects which makes it impossible to decide what actually belongs to the mental world and what does not. But as usual with Piaget one can make a good case for taking the generation process the other way round, that is, the unclarity of the relationship between the external and internal worlds of the subject necessitates the 'element-less' thought structures. We find ourselves, in short, clearly in the presence, again, of non-terminality.

Any explicative, scientific, philosophical, or plain common-sensed model must possess *identifiable* elements, *however conditional,* marking the terminal points of the models' relationships. The nature of these elements is irrelevant to this principle. Without such elements specific internal relationships and external relationships which are not specific to the phenomenon cannot be identified or distinguished from each other, beyond, that is, an indeterminate attribution of a 'state' or condition such as 'reversibility'.

The line of discussion pursued here on the character of structure clarifies a difficult point regarding their actual existence or otherwise. From one point of view, openly admitted by Flavell, the cognitive structures are '[postulations] interposed between function and content' (p. 17). They are, in effect, from this viewpoint *interpolatory entities* from given observable data, or the actual response (behaviour) of the organism/intelligence to specifiable stimuli/factors in the milieu, but not possessing any identifiable existence in their own right. But on the other hand we are constantly given to understand by Piaget that such structures, in their logico-mathematical forms, are *actually extant* in the conscious mind – although to what extent their existence relies on neurology, or not, is yet another point of uncertainty in the system. The question all along has been whether or not elements of intelligence exist which are the subject of structuration. Until such time as such elements can with certainty be identified the existence of structures of intelligence cannot be affirmed. We can at best accept them as working hypotheses. This point is particularly important with regard to the *consistency* of Piaget's system. If the consistency stands up then one can say that the system has not been *disproved*. If, however, it does not stand up, if it cannot be used even as a working hypothesis, then there is nothing to fall back on to justify at all a field of investigation. So far the latter seems the more likely result.

Operations

The problematic relation between structures and the elements structured in cognition remains unresolved up to this point. Despite frequent references to 'elements' they never appear precisely in distinctive cognitive terms. The nearest one can get to an element of intelligence (or mental element) is (possibly) a simple proposition of the form $p \implies q$ (that is, 'if p then q'), where p and q are propositions referring to events in the subject's milieu. This, of course, is itself a simple mental 'structure' in Piaget's terms. It is certainly not p and q in themselves. In fact, as we saw before, Piaget's concept of the relationship between the subject and the milieu at the 'frontier' of interchange is that, from the onset, incoming sensory data are 'distorted' by the subject's own selectivity. Indeed, the superior role allocated to structuration in mental growth by Piaget demands this.

The source of the simple relationship '$p \implies q$' is to be found in the subject's action in the world of objects. A causal relation in the physical world is said to change into an implicative one marking the transition to the cognitive world of the subject. The ensuing 'mobility' of the cognitive structures is thus to be understood in a logico-mathematical and not in a physical sense. Yet we are never clearly apprised of the distinct meaning of this 'mobility'. It is always portrayed in *dynamical* terms which are not clearly distinguished from the physical origins of cognition. It is, however, the notion of 'mobility' that goes together with that of 'operation'. If intelligence is 'mobile' and such mobility is related especially to the notion of logical reversibility, which it is, the idea of 'operation' emerges almost inevitably in the system to account for the *movement* of intelligence itself.

We are already familiar with the process of transition, the interiorisation of action or generation of operations. Such a process involves a major and qualitative 'leap', or metamorphosis – a term well justified since Piaget himself constantly stresses that there is an *essential* difference between action and interiorised action. This difference, which we know is between the spatio-temporal, causally governed milieu and the non-spatio-temporal, acausal, cognitive world, is manifested in the characteristic of operations which makes it quite unnecessary, once they exist, to refer them outside the cognitive structural system. As Flavell has put it, 'cognitive actions become more and more schematic and abstract, broader in range, more what Piaget calls *reversible*, and organised into systems which are structurally isomorphic to logico-algebraic systems (e.g., groups and lattices)' (Flavell, 1963, p. 82; see also Piaget, 1968, pp. 81–2). Thus, 'Operations are nothing but interiorised actions whose efferent impulses do not develop into external movements' (see Flavell bibliog., Piaget, 1954c, p. 141). 'In effect, an operation is psychologically an action which has been internalised and has become reversible through its co-ordination with other internalised actions within a structured whole, this whole obeying certain laws of totality' (see Flavell, pp. 82–3; and bibliog., Piaget, 1957b, p. 35).

The same sort of problems arise here as have been encountered already in considering structures and equilibrium itself. Beyond the (non-terminal) notions of 'interiorisation' and 'action' it is difficult to pin down the ultimate source of operations in themselves, which it is essential to know if the metamorphosis is to have any meaning. Perhaps if one turns again to the very basic distinction Piaget draws betweeen function and structure some idea of this ultimate source may emerge.

The former is, as we know Piaget to affirm, not only biologically given, but constitutes 'the basic and irreducible properties of cognitive adaptation which hold true at all developmental levels' – what Piaget calls the intellectual core or 'ipse intellectus' (Flavell, 1963, p. 41). Function makes *possible* the appearance of cognitive structures with their specific feature of operations. Now, we have already seen how much Piaget relies on the idea of function as biological in the first instance. Similarly the action of the subject, occurring as it must via his functional potential, inevitably rests upon a physiological inheritance. Furthermore, the 'qualitative leap' involved in the internalisation of action does not destroy this biological debt. Piaget never says that the transfer to cognition means the end of the biological link. Rather, the direct link gets replaced by the idea of isomorphism, although how this particular transition takes place is not at all clear. It is not for nothing that Piaget refers periodically to the growth of cognition as 'mental embryology' (see Flavell, 1963, pp. 41–2, and bibliog., Piaget, 1947, p. 143).

At this point one might say that 'operations' clearly derive from an inbuilt biological functioning and that because this is so, cognitive activity is purely an extension of biology. But this would be to misinterpret Piaget's intentions completely. We must never forget that, to preserve the basic philosophy of the system, the learning process itself must be detached from innate predispositions and functional mechanism. For without this the basic principle of the convergence of development everywhere on states of ever 'better' equilibrium cannot be sustained.

Moreover, the basic demands on the system compel it towards a new condition of circular deduction. For if one carefully puts together Piaget's references to the necessary factors involved in the origins of action and its subsequent internalisation into operational structures, we get a sequence of connections such as the following: *structuration,* characterised by operations that are *reversible,* derives from the subject's *actions* which themselves depend on biologically inbuilt *functioning.* Since functioning is indefinitely traceable back through biologically ever more simple stages of life, there are *no absolute beginnings to functioning.* As we go backwards towards early infanthood and the moment of birth itself, we pass out of the zone of cognition typified by reversible structures into the *operational-free* zone which, though possessing elementary *structures,* resulting from purely *sensory-motor actions,* are *not characterised by reversibility* and therefore are *not operational.* Consistent with this they are also non-conservational (Piaget, 1968, p. 80). This latter condition closely relates to a predominantly functioning, rather than structuring, organism. The circularity emerges in what follows: '*Because* [our emphasis] the child is . . . above all a conservationist [!] (ibid., p. 80), the absence of *conservation,* and hence all the other characteristics, is due to an *initial lack of reversibility*; 'The young child reasons [sic] only about *states* . . . and neglects *transformations* as such. In order to conceptualise these transformations, one must reason by means of reversible "operations" ' (ibid., p. 81). In order to achieve the breakthrough into cognitive structuration the child must have the equipment which only the break-through itself can supply! Put another way, the reason for non-conservation in the pre-operational child is said to be the absence of reversible operations and the existence of conservation later on becomes a 'proof' that reversible operations exist.

Summing these points up: (*a*) the clear distinction between function and structure is not consistently adhered to by Piaget so that we can never make concrete at any point the foundations of cognition;[40] (*b*) in the light of this situation Piaget gives an essentially circular argument for the cognitive take-off by making reversibility and hence operations derive from conservation and conservation depend on reversibility and hence operations.

There is no doubt that Piaget has been very concerned with this problem. But it is only latterly in *The Development of Thought* that he attemps a detailed theoretical exposition of the transition from the innate to the non-innate. Here Piaget is attempting a final, precise uncovering of the mechanism of the acquisition and growth of knowledge as a whole. There is a smooth transition for the sensory-motor infant from his innate, and hence functioning, behaviour to his earliest structuration. The transition is embodied in the diagram we reproduced in Chapter 1 which is a particular case of a general diagrammatic method used in *The Development of Thought* to explicate the movement of the stimuli to cognition from the subject's environment through to the formation of cognitive structures themselves. Broadly, the technique adopted in *The Development of Thought* is the intrusion/disturbance – (self)-regulation – compensation cycle the detailed analysis of which the whole of this book is about. The cycle is most succinctly embodied in the diagrammatic representation of the mature structuration process which the infantile one (see above, page 15) is supposed to anticipate. Below is a reproduction of this mature diagram (Figure 6.2).

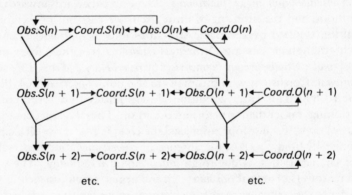

(Piaget, 1978b, p. 56)[41]

Figure 6.2

The Development of Thought is particularly important in considering the genesis of novelty in general (see below, Chapter 7); but here it is relevant to the special question in hand of the existence and nature of operations. The only direct reference to operations comes in the following passage:

The principle of creative novelties, as expressed by the cognitive development of this general regulating structure (which constitutes the most important example of increasing equilibration), explains the very formation of operations. In fact, the operations, insofar as they always appear as pairs of direct and opposite (or reciprocal) operations, constitute the final point of improvement of the regulations and thus represent 'perfect' regulations (pp. 37—8)

Thus, in Piaget's latest estimation, operations are to be identified with perfect regulations whose roots are to be discovered in the initial reaction to intrusive disturbance. The mechanism of the supposedly continuous process is to be found in the interactive behaviour of 'observables' and 'co-ordinations' ('Obs.' and 'Coord.'). The diagram illustrates all these points clearly.

Piaget defines 'observables' and 'co-ordinations' as follows: 'An "observable" is that which experience makes it possible to identify by an immediate reading of the given events themselves whereas a "co-ordination" includes inferences and thus involves more than [an] observable' (p. 43). Immediately following these (non-terminal) definitions comes this highly relevant passage:

However, such a distinction is clear only on levels where the subject is capable of objective observation and of logically valid inferences, whereas their delimitation is less marked when the identifications are in fact inexact and the inferences include false assumptions. It is insufficient, therefore, to define the observable merely by its perceived characteristics, since the subject often believes that he perceives what actually he does not perceive and characterises the co-ordinations by verbal formulation, adequate [inadequate?] or riddled with errors. It is evident that the implicit inferences play a role as great, if not greater, than the partial perceptions. The observables must therefore be defined by what the subject believes he perceives and not simply what is perceivable . . . In other words, an identification is never independent of the recording instruments (hence of an assimilation) available to the subject, and these instruments are never solely perceptive but are influenced by pre-operational or operational schemes capable of modifying or distorting the perceived entity. But as these schemes are, moreover, those used by the co-ordinations, the observables themselves are most often conditioned by previous co-ordinations. If therefore, we consider an observable with co-ordinations at level N, we must remember that such observables do not constitute first facts but themselves ordinarily depend on observables and co-ordinations from the level $N - 1$, and so forth. Even at the elementary levels, apparent[ly] close to the birth of the subject, observables are part of a network of co-ordinations, but these are partly innate (involving reflexes, etc.) and are not only progressively inferred. (pp. 43–4)

It is clear here that the subject-matter of observation as achieved via perception is absolutely unreliable. This is not only true of immediate and contemporary interactions between subject and milieu, but is also to be ascribed to the developmental process from birth onwards. Moreover, the unreliability is directly related to the innate (and functional) conditions of what Piaget calls the 'neonate' which survive as inbuilt structures through-out life. Indeed, elsewhere in the book very great stress is laid on the increasing certainty of knowledge in direct relation to its removal from the unreliable sphere of perception to the reliable one of equilibrated structures.

Now, none of this is entirely new. But we do have in *The Development of Thought* a greater clarification of the exact nature of operational structures in relation to their origins than elsewhere. And what emerges is a re-cognition of the unreliability of the external sources of cognition and, implicitly, the ultimate dependence of knowledge on internal logico-mathematical factors. This is an ironical position for Piaget who stresses the experimental basis of his system. But this understanding of his position makes the nature of operations clearer.

We cannot, in the Piagetian frame of reference, seek for an external explanation for operations for they are *culminatory* rather than points of departure.[42] Yet Piaget does not (in this latest exposition) depart from regarding the source of operations as the 'action' of the subject. On pp. 18ff., for example, 'action' is tied to 'regulation' and 'regulation', leading to 'operation', possesses the same character of interiorised action as before but here it makes the transition to operation a smooth one – and thereby, of course, bypasses the central problem of the system. The 'smoothness' of the transition is embodied in the central role played by 'co-ordinations' which are the *antidote* to intrusive disturbance, elevating thought by *self-regulative compensation* to a higher (absorptive) level of reflective *abstractions* (see Figure 6.2).

Although the notion of 'smoothness' of transition is used to exorcise the 'leaps' inherent in Genetic Epistemology, Piaget does not get rid of these entirely. Immediately following the diagram reproduced as Figure 1.1 above (page 15), he writes: 'The passage from these initial reactions to type IIA interactions (through every intermediary that we can distinguish in detail) corresponds to a rather radical transformation which we have often commented upon and which we have compared to a kind of Copernican revolution.' Without doubt he is still haunted by the problem of un-explained transitions which, indeed, is still present.

What is the effect of all this on the concept of operation? In *The Development of Thought*, co-ordination has assumed a central role as opposed to operational structures. This is not a matter of contradicting the latter, but rather of reinterpreting them in terms of emphasis on equilibration rather than equilibrium – as Piaget indeed stresses in the Preface. Thus co-ordination can be interpreted as dynamically expressing the progress towards ever more effective operational structures. By thus directing attention away from the dualistic problem which interiorisation of action (and, indeed, the group and lattices model of cognitive structures) highlights, the 'new' presentation offers what can only be called a pseudo-solution to the origin and nature of operations themselves. In a sense, *The Development of Thought* as a whole embodies the 'slip-over' technique of earlier expositions such as we find in *Six Psychological Studies* (p. 121) where a tight link is established between logic, structures, operations, reversibility and, of course, co-ordinations.

Logic in the child (as in the adult) is evidenced in the form of operational structures; i.e., the logical act consists essentially of *operating,* hence of acting on things and toward people. *An operation is, in effect, an internalised action which has become* reversible *and co-ordinated with other operations* in a grouping, governed by the laws of the system as a whole [our double emphasis]. To say that *an operation is reversible* is to say that every operation corresponds to an inverse operation, as is true, for example, for logical or arithmetic addition and subtraction.

This is an extreme example of circularity. *The proof of logic* is to be found in *operational structures*; reversible *operations* are shown to *exist via logical (and arithmetical) addition and subtraction.* Over and above this circularity, the 'slip-over' between the external and the internal worlds is manifest and it is this which is later brought to its culmination in *The Development of Thought.*

Increasingly in the later part of Piaget's life, probably from the publication of *Six Psychological Studies* in 1964, he seems to have become concerned with liberating mentality as a phenomenon from dependence in any way upon any non-mental roots. Thus the subject when fully developed mentally attains 'equilibrium to the extent that he is capable of anticipating intrusion by representing it to himself through what we call "direct" operations and by compensating for it in advance by "inverse operations" ' (Piaget, 1968, p. 101). Such compensation in advance of 'virtual intrusion' inverts the relationship of subject to milieu as Piaget envisages it in infancy and is a mark of the self-regulating independence that cognitive intelligence is supposedly destined to attain.

Such is the burden of the emphasis during the 1960s and still more in the 1970s culminating in *The Development of Thought* in 1977 where logical necessity is understood to emerge in the *course* of development rather than as a condition of that development. This emphasis is characterised by an elaboration over this period of the intrusion/disturbance–(self)-regulation–compensation model of equilibration and the acceptance of the sort of circularities we have been discussing. This trend would undoubtedly have some positive aspect were it not for the fact that Piaget never renounces biological-psychological isomorphism, and the rootedness of psychology in biological origins. Moreover, his limitation of mentality to rigidly logico-mathematical confines is still further emphasised in this later period. This is why McCulloch and Pitts have remained his ideal neurologists since they are primarily mathematicians, and present a basically mathematical notion of neurological functions.

To sum up, then, in tracing the origin and character of the idea of operation in Piaget's system, we come again upon the problem of circularity which arose originally in consideration of the principal notion of equilibrium itself and with that of structure. The attendant problem of non-terminality raised both there and in the discussion of structures is clearly also evident here. One of the hidden stumbling blocks in trying to understand what Piaget means by going from the world of experience to the world of operations is that in the former case the activity of the subject is clearly attached to his experience of objects about which there is no question regarding terminality (although, even here, if action is seen wholly as a predominantly subject-related phenomenon there is indeed a non-terminal problem). It is when the interiorisation process results in 'operational structures' which are qualitatively different that the elements of these (that is, operations) are seen to be unclear. It is essential to this unclarity that operations can sometimes be presented as the elements of cognition. But since the structural interrelationship between such 'elements' is also operational, we are left in the dark as to the distinction between 'element' and 'operation' exactly as was demonstrated mathematically in Chapters 2 to 4 especially. Not only do we have no idea how operations are arrived at, but we have no means of establishing their identity assuming that they exist at all in cognition. *The Development of Thought* only changes the 'venue', as it were, of the problem to that of 'co-ordinations' (of operations) and seeks to replace the problem of existence with a discussion of emergence. But it would be quite wrong to leave the impression that Piaget has not considered this aspect of the system. In fact, the theory of transformations is supposed to account for the driving force of cognitive development in relation to the subject's milieu and it is to this we must now turn our attention.

Transformations

The close connection between the concepts of operation and transformation is shown in *Six Psychological Studies:* 'In short, the compensations start by being effectuated by degrees that can end by consisting of pure representations of the transformations with the intrusions like the compensations, being reduced to certain operations of the system' (p. 113). It might therefore seem reasonable that transformations should be treated as simply an extension of operations. It could be argued on these grounds that one might proceed directly through to the notions of 'adaptation' and 'action' without spending too much time on this idea. However, transformation is a concept of quite central importance in Genetic Epistemology. This is so because it purports to be an explanation of the actual 'engine' whereby the circumstances and objects making up the milieu of the subject are translated, through his experience and the interactions of his accumulated structural formations with the milieu, into the crucial cognitive operations and new structures.

Rotman expresses Piaget's intentions rather clearly. Discussing the nature of genesis, he writes: 'The problem, then, [for Piaget] is to find a notion which expresses what is common to structure as an entity and structure as a process, and Piaget finds one in the idea of a system of transformations; a system that both affects [effects?] change and yet leaves certain aspects of what is changed invariant' (Rotman, 1977, p. 48). While this shows Rotman's awareness of the problem attaching to transformation, it is not entirely satisfactory. The concept is used by Piaget in two diametrically opposite ways. Structure, for example, is explicable as *system(s)* of transformation (ibid., p. 49), and the biological substratum of structures, to which the latter are seen to be isomorphic, itself also demonstrates a systematic form of transformation; 'the important analyses of McCulloch and Pitts have revealed an isomorphism between the transformations underlying synaptic connections and the logical operators' (Piaget, 1972b, p. 62). On the other hand, a distinctly different meaning must be attached to the following: 'Between two structures of different levels there can be no one-way reduction, but rather there is reciprocal assimilation such that the higher can be derived from the lower by means of transformation' (ibid., p. 93). Here, there is a *process* involved which must include a temporal or openly developmental aspect. The previous passage on the other hand clearly relates the notion of transformations to logical and/or mathematical type operations and is required thereby to *exclude* open-ended change.[43] One of the most succinct expressions of this dilemma, which begins right away to have a familiar look, is to be found in *Six Psychological Studies* (p. 144). A fluctuation is discernible between the opposite meanings of 'transformation'. Piaget is discussing problems attaching to the idea of genesis and it is in this context that transformation is referred to. When we come to discuss genesis itself below, it will become clear that he was at this time acutely conscious of the problems surrounding the idea of transformation precisely because, as the engine of the system, it is as intimately related to genesis as to operation.

In defining 'genesis', I should like to avoid being accused of constructing a vicious circle so I shall not say that it is simply the process of transition from one structure to another. Rather, genesis is a certain kind of transformation which stems from a state A and results in a state B, where state B is more stable than state A. When we speak of genesis in the field of psychology – and no doubt this is true of other fields also – we must first avoid any definition based on absolute beginnings. In psychology there are no absolute beginnings and genesis is always conceived as stemming from an initial state which may also comprise a structure. Consequently, genesis is simply a form of development. It does not, however, involve just any kind of development or a simple transformation. We can define genesis as a relatively determined system of transformations comprising a history and leading in a continuous manner from state A to state B, state B being more stable than the initial state and constituting an extension of it.

This passage speaks for itself in the light of what has been said but it might be helpful to point out some of the salient features pertinent to the argument. In the second sentence the link between genesis (which is of course a temporal process) and transformation clearly makes the latter into a developmental concept. Sentences two and five specifically indicate this. In sentence seven, transformation is related to a 'determined system' which is conceptually different in kind (this is not abrogated by the word 'relatively') but which is nevertheless in the same sentence described as 'comprising a history and leading in a continuous manner'. Here, the fluctuation appears to be at its most rapid between the alternate meanings of transformation.

In another passage in the *Studies* (pp. 113–14) the same issues arise where the distinct meanings of transformation are even more entangled with each other.

In considering the operational (logico-mathematical) structures, i.e., the most equilibrated structures, we see that each constitutes the system of all possible transformations for a certain class of transformations, such as the classification groupings or the combinatory groupings of propositional logic, etc. Then we see that certain transformations can be envisaged as modifications of the system owing to intrusions. The inverse transformations will thus consist of virtual compensations of these original transformations. The operational system is thus comparable to a system of vector forces in physics whose algebraic sum is zero. But in physics the vector forces are, by definition, not 'real', since they exist only in the mind of the physicist. In the case of the operational system, by contrast, the virtual transformations exist in the mind of the subject. The mind is the proper domain of psychology, so that the virtual transformations correspond to the subject's real operations. This is why the concept of equilibrium is explicative in psychology.

Notwithstanding that the passage begins on a logico-mathematical note, the notions of modification and intrusion introduced here carry with them the same openly developmental features as were seen in the previous passage.[44] This is so since the other transformations referred to, being logico-mathematical operations of the system, cannot modify it but can only interrelate with each other according to its rules. Transformation, then, in the strictly logico-mathematical sense, is brought into direct relationship with transformation in the sense of intrusive modification of the system as a whole with its accompanying features of unpredictable contingency. The third sentence here, clearly intended to be deduced from the previous one, appears to revert to a logico-mathematical concept of transformation but ties this in with the 'original transformations', that is, those 'envisaged as modifications of the system'. Thus not only do we have here a fluctuation between two definitely incompatible concepts of transformation, but also one is made to service the other.

We cannot escape the fact that the conditions of a logico-mathematically determined structure obligatorily exclude open-ended modifying factors as disturbing to the axiomatic foundations and, alternatively, a historical or developmental process obligatorily must *include* the notion of accident or contingency as an integral part of the process. Now and then Piaget comes close to recognising this difference. As he says, the cognising subject not only structures the world but 'transform[s] reality rather than simply discovering its existence' (J. Piaget and B. Inhelder, 'The gaps in empiricism', in A. Koestler and J. R. Smythies, eds, *Beyond Reductionism*, London, Hutchinson, 1969, p. 128; quoted Rotman, 1977, p. 26). Rotman is also aware of the distinction. He continues: 'but the logico-mathematical knowledge so essential for this transformation is itself abstracted from our activity in the world' (loc. cit.).

Of course, linguistically, the word tranformation can be applied to both situations. A change of form occurs in both circumstances. What is illegitimate is the incorporation of both meanings without spelling out the change in the usage of the word itself. More than this, something of key importance in understanding Piaget's system is embedded in this seemingly narrow question, and the passages we have just looked at particularly exemplify this. If a term like transformation is used unqualifiedly in two mutually exclusive contexts, it is always possible that while one meaning is being attributed at one point the other meaning is by implication and association also present. It is as if when the term is used in one context the other, hidden meaning is carried along with the one which is for the moment under open consideration. Such a device, intentionally conceived or not, ensures the non-falsifiability of a disparate system. In fact it would appear to be the only way in which such a system can be made seemingly consistent. The essence of this situation is that we are dealing with a 'gap-bridger' – relating to the very central problem discussed previously in the chapter on equilibrium, the non-terminal problem. In fact one might go so far as to say that non-terminality is particularly relatable to transformation in the Piagetian system.

Transformation is closely linked to a central issue emerging in Chapters 2, 3 and 4. There the implications were discussed of the vacillation arising from the use of the words 'operation' and 'element' each with several distinct possible meanings. We saw how this formed a necessary part of Piaget's presentation of cognition with reference especially to reversibility, conservation and similar equilibrated conditions. The pluralistic use of the word 'transformation' performs a similar function in the general cognitive theory. Looking first at the group theoretic meaning of the word and recalling that the elements of a group need not be actual things or numbers (and in most cases are not), it is very significant that Piaget slides (from the earlier to the later writings) from the use of the word 'operations' to the word 'transformations' as (possible) elements of a group. In fact, in his later writings he often refers to a 'system of transformations' which he sees as 'a system that both affects change and yet leaves certain aspects of what is changed invariant', as Rotman puts it (1977, p. 48).[45] Rotman makes this point very concrete when he says:

> In cognitive terms it is the point at which a child has grasped that number, volume, and weight are invariant under the transformations related to re-arranging, pouring, moving and so on, that signals the beginnings of the final stage of development. His internalised structure of these transformations has, in Piaget's analysis, formed a group. (ibid., pp. 48–9)

But the linguistic ambiguity which attaches as much to 'transformations' as to 'operations' is precisely brought out here. At one time, according to Piaget, the subject has failed to grasp that number, and so on, are invariant under rearrangement, and so on, and that the 'transformations', here relating to rearrangement, exemplify the subject's cognitive goal. It will be recalled that, as with operations themselves, transformations which form a group, and are therefore understandable as logico-mathematical in that particular context, *cannot* involve *genetic* change. It is clear, therefore, that when the whole situation is taken over into the cognitive scene the growth notions and mathematical notions attached to the word transformation are completely confused with one another. We have seen how, by ambiguously using the same term to apply to both element and operation (rule of combination), it is possible to conceal the absence of a group rule of combination. The idea of transformation does a comparable job when cognition is considered as a whole. We can never establish when 'transformation' moves from a genetic meaning into a logico-mathematical meaning and vice versa, as the passages provided earlier amply show. What is certain is that *a mathematical transformation can never accomplish a genetic transformation.*

There is yet another connection between transformation and operation. In *Six Psychological Studies* (p. 7) Piaget writes: 'At any given moment, one can thus say, action is disequilibrated by the transformations that arise in the external or internal world, and each new behaviour consists not only in re-establishing equilibrium but also in moving toward a more stable equilibrium than that which preceded the disturbance.' The 'stable equilibrium' referred to here is a state relating to Piaget's 'structure d'ensemble' which, in the case of cognition, has a group structure at its core. However, in any particular situation, group structure applies only to a *subset* of all the possible transformations of the structure and this subset must be the one which 'leave[s] some particular aspects of the structure invariant' (Rotman, 1977, p. 48). But Piaget's words in the *Studies* reference imply the continuous integration of *all* transformations into an ever more stable equilibrium – a situation exclusive of all forms of conditionality which is a totally unreal one. There is no escaping such a conclusion since Piaget's conception of ultimate equilibrium, both for the subject and as a philosophical premiss regarding all processes whatsoever, is the underlying and determining feature of the remarks made in this reference.

Additionally to the confusion surrounding the meaning of transformation is, of course, the deeper confusion as to whether transformation, or for that matter operation, can be regarded as an element in the normal sense. In fact both concepts are non-terminal. So there are two dimensions of ambiguity to cope with here – a situation which is especially fateful in dealing with this particular concept of the system.

The Schemata (Schemas)

So far we have dealt mainly with the aspects and features of cognitive intelligence in the Piagetian system. These aspects of cognitive intelligence, far from escaping the ambiguities and conflicts typical of the treatment of the general characteristics of equilibrium, spell out the details of this ambiguity. Transformations, perhaps not surprisingly, reveal these problems exceptionally. But it could be argued that in the case of transformations one is nearing the 'frontier' dividing the subject from the milieu, and it is precisely this feature of cognition which admits of a 'janus-headed' position, that is, it is transformations that are intended to integrate the developmental and the logico-mathematical.

Transformations by themselves, however, do not stand up well to the test of uniting the external and internal worlds of the subject. If they collectively constitute the 'engine' of the cognitive process then that 'engine' must be provided with some sort of housing. This may be found in the notion of adaptation with its double aspect of assimilation and accommodation. Perhaps the analogy vis-à-vis transformations would be closer if the idea of 'power' were used and that of 'engine' reserved for the adaptive process itself. Certainly in the sense that an engine manifests and embodies power so also is adaptation intended to manifest and embody transformations.

We are very much in the domain of those 'frontier' circumstances already referred to. If transformations can be thought of as 'power' then adaptation, seen as either a link or a boundary, straddles the external and internal worlds like a bridge. One end of this bridge (external) relates to actions and the other end (internal) relates to phenomena described by Piaget as schemata which he characterises with untypical succinctness, in one case, as 'the catcher[s] of the actions susceptible of being actively repeated' (*The Psychology of Intelligence,* p. 8).[46]

There is a certain linearity in this account which is not entirely satisfactory. These Piagetian concepts intertwine so closely that, as we said before, they should be understood as running 'in parallel' as well as 'in sequence'. In order to maintain some consistency in our procedure we shall look at the idea of schemata next, then adaptation (assimilation–accommodation) and finally the action of the subject in the external world. Pursuing the power-engine analogy, this action plays the role of the 'fuel' of cognition.

It is difficult to know exactly where to start with schemata, but, as is often the case with Piaget, a safe point is at the biological roots. Hamlyn says (1978, p. 48) that Piaget while wanting 'to leave full room for instinct . . . does not want innate ideas' – a central problem that we have seen haunting Piaget's assumptions throughout and which the biological-psychological connections cannot throw off. Rotman, quoting *Biology and Knowledge,* writes: 'thought is a reflection of physiology. Between the two he [Piaget] inserts actions. These start as the literal handling of objects in the sensori-motor period, become internalised to form operations that manipulate schemas relating to concrete situations, and finally shed their adherence to real, particular content and become applicable to any object of thought whatsoever' (p. 45). It is thus that the 'milieu intérieure' is created. Here, the nature of schemas emerges as some form of structure but closely or predominantly related to *non-internalised* action rather than cognition itself. We should not make the mistake, however, of thinking of schemata as exclusively innate although many are obviously intended to be so. As Hamlyn points out, one must presume within the Piagetian system innateness of certain capacities such as the structural relationship between colours (1978, p. 30) (not to be confused with cognitive structuration). Some evidence of this might be deduced from the fact that the blind from birth have a structural notion of colour related to sound (for example, a trumpet sounds 'red'). Again, Flavell refers to Piaget's description of the schema of sucking, of prehension, of sight itself, and so on (see Flavell, 1963, p. 53; also Flavell bibliog., Piaget, 1952c, p. 13), indicating that these must be innate schemas related to the commencement of sensori-motor development. On the other hand, the affirmation of, for example, a 'schema of intuitive qualitative correspondence' referring to a strategy by which the subject in middle childhood assesses 'whether or not two sets of elements are numerically equivalent', together with Piaget's affirmation of the existence of the 'operational schemas' in adolescence, all indicate that the notion of schema is not only related to the innate but also to the ontogenetic structuration process occurring within the subject's lifetime (Flavell, 1963, p. 53; see also p. 222).

Further, 'Schemas are structures, and one of their important, built-in properties is that of repeated assimilation of anything assimilable in the environment' (ibid., p. 78). Perhaps the most complete description is given by Rotman when he says:

> For Piaget psychological structures, like organic ones, are co-ordinated systems of substructures. The simplest type of substructure Piaget calls a *schema*. The schema is a structure of action, the underlying form of a repeated activity pattern, which can transcend the particular physical objects it acts on and become capable of generalisation to other contents. For example, in the first three months of infancy the 'sucking schema' applies only to objects in contact with the mouth. After this, when vision and grasping are co-ordinated, this scheme is generalised to objects of vision and the infant tries to grasp all that he can see in order to put it into his mouth. His visual objects have thus acquired a new meaning and have become 'objects to suck'. This integration of something new into an existing schema Piaget calls *assimilation*. But certain objects (because they are too long, too heavy, and so on) cannot be assimilated into the sucking schema and the infant can only operate successfully by adapting himself to their peculiarities. In general when an attempted assimilation produces hurt or disequilibrating difficulties and a schema has in consequence to be differentiated the process is called *accommodation*. (Rotman, 1977, pp. 38–9)

Rotman assigns these latter processes a central position in Piaget's theory of cognition. In this respect, he may be overstressing the 'physical' in relation to the logico-mathematical. However, there is no doubt that the linked notions of structure, schema, assimilation and accommodation (adaptation) are central to the transition from the external world of the milieu to the internal world of the subject. Certain other points made by

Rotman seem to bypass the central question here. The transition process is *exactly* what is not explained by the notion of schemata. Assimilation of *objects* into schemata (the latter being at best non-terminal relational phenomena) exemplifies specifically the central incompatibility which we are examining. This, of course, does no more than reflect Piaget himself (see Flavell, 1963, p. 56). These schemata in fact seem to play a sort of 'catalytic' role since, like catalysts, they participate in the process of change from outside to inside and emerge after this apparently unmodified.

But one must not push the chemical analogy of 'catalysts' too far. What we have said up to now on this question may have conveyed much too much definition, in the configurative sense, of these notions. In fact, the schemata exemplify to a maximum degree the general problem of non-terminality in Piaget's concepts. One searches in vain if one hopes to find definitiveness in this particular notion. Thus Piaget writes at one point, 'A schema is a mode of reactions susceptible of reproducing themselves and susceptible above all of being generalised' (see Baltro, *Dictionary of Terms*, p. 156); and again (with E. W. Beth) in 'Epistémologie mathe-matique et psychologie (*Etudes d'épistémologie génétique*, Vol. XIV, Paris 1961, p. 251). '[A] schema of an action is, by definition, the group structured by the generalisable characteristics of that action, and that means of those which allow repetition of the same action or application to new contents. Now the schema of an action is neither perceptible (one perceives a particular action but not its schema) nor directly introspectible, and one becomes conscious of its implications only in repeating the action and in comparing successive results.' Here the schema is removed from both external *and* internal identification, and its very existence is detectable only via the *repetition of action*. This last is the source of the 'catalytic' analogy we use and it is about as far as one can go in actually identifying what these schemata are.

But while on the one hand definitiveness is absent, the *role* assigned to schemata seems relatively clear; 'such schemas have the entirely general content and do not characterize simply one or the other of the actions of a single individual . . . they remain unconscious as long as a "reflective abstraction" does not transform them into operations' (ibid., p. 252). This is quite consistent with the view that schemas 'represent actions sus-ceptible of being applied to objects' (Piaget, *The Origins of Intelligence*, 1963, p. 211). They certainly cannot simply be described as structures as Flavell and Rotman describe them, though the latter qualifies this by attaching the notion of schema to that of action. The passage from *Etudes d'épistémologie génétique,* Vol. XIV, referred to just now – and this is probably the best definitive statement we have of schemata – makes this clear. Schemata have to be 'transformed into operations' by reflective abstraction which strictly defines them as suboperations and therefore 'substructural'.

All in all, schemata appear to become evident only when transformed into something else. Yet having said this we are confronted, as is so often the case, with a contradictory rejection of this. There are at least three references of Piaget's to exactly the opposite viewpoint.

An operational schema is a method of reversible composition. (Baltro, *Dictionary of Terms*, p. 159)

An anticipatory schema could not arise from thought alone, because representation cannot predict anything without being guided by the action. It is only at the level where co-ordinated actions constitute a grouping of reversible operations that the system of compositions inherent in that grouping can be translated into psychological terms under the form of an anticipatory schema of an operational nature. (loc. cit.)

Anticipatory schema is [sic] 'nothing but the grouping of operations'. (loc. cit.)

In all of these cases it is clear that the notion of schema *is* applicable to operational and hence structural situations and we are in the midst, yet again, of verbal fluidity that allows the same notion to be employed in strictly, and incompatibly, different modes. Notwithstanding the fluctuation in date for these references there is no evidence that Piaget has clarified this since.[47] Although their role may have been clarified in *The Development of Thought* their nature and specificity have not.

There is, of course, a close connection between the non-terminality of the notion of schemata and its unqualified use in incompatible situations. In fact, the only meaning which can be extracted whatever the circumstances is the idea of repetition.[48] Schemata are (general?) organs (?) of repetition. This is what they both allow and ensure.

But apart from this 'permissive' role, schemata are supposed to behave positively and are also closely associated with the concept of 'groping'. Ostensibly, Piaget rejects the view of 'pure groping', that is, the assertion that the subject's relations with the environment originate in pure chance encounters involving trial and error and that this is *always* a feature of such relations, notwithstanding the development of organised knowledge. The issue for him is whether there is a degree of directedness in the relationship, which, in his view, would modify pure groping. Yet while generally adopting the latter position Piaget leans more heavily towards the pure groping position (see Flavell, 1963, pp. 75–6). And, indeed, this corresponds closely to his preferred apriorism as opposed to empiricism, as he himself affirms (quoted Flavell, p. 75). In his contacts with the world around him, therefore, the subject, employing schemata (sub'structures' of action), 'gropes' repetitively mainly on a trial and error basis with some

internal direction, but chiefly in a manner which is largely *blind*. We have
here the link between schemata and groping and, moreover, possess the
'building bricks' of the notions of assimilation and accommodation (see
the quotation from Rotman above, page 179). This is so since groping, via
schemata, must be seen as a *two-way* process, the essence of assimilation
and accommodation, in order to make sense. We look at this question
next; here the point of interest is that not only is the interchange between
subject and milieu biased towards 'blindness', but at all levels of cognitive
structuration thereafter this element is present if not predominant. It is our
contention that this is an entirely consistent derivation from the overall
non-terminal condition of the system, combined with (or as a necessary
adjunct to) the treatment of the growth of intelligence under two headings
which are never reconciled – environmental-causal and logico-
mathematical. The 'activism' which is so frequently attributed to Piaget
becomes extremely difficult to identify in the light of these points.

Assimilation and Accommodation (Adaptation)

Adaptation in its 'resolved' form, assimilation and accommodation,
derives most particularly from biological sources. From the point of view
of the system as a whole it may be described as constituting the *actual*
'frontier' between the external and internal worlds of the subject as distinct
from the approaches to the 'frontier' from either direction. Until now the
non-terminal, and to a slightly lesser extent dualistic, concepts employed
by Genetic Epistemology have held the centre of the stage. Because of its
'frontier' position, the dualism of the system takes on its most acute form
in the case of adaptation. With assimilation and accommodation, what
might be termed the problem of directionality becomes predominant. By
directionality is meant the exact establishment of the direction of interaction between subject and milieu. To some extent we find this anticipated
in transformations and even in equilibrium itself. It is, however, with this
notion of adaptation that the directionality question becomes urgent.

It has been stressed that a central problem in any attempt to relate
intelligence to the circumstances under which it occurs is that of reconciling spatio-temporal parameters with some sort of parameter referable
to mentality whch does not involve exclusively spatio-temporal measurement. If a purely physical-biological reductionist view of mentality, or
alternatively an 'identity theory' point of view typical of many contemporary neuro-physiologists, is taken, then this particular problem
does not exist, at least not in this form. But Piaget is not an identity
theorist and his explicit distinction between the features of the physiological world on the one hand, summed up in his recognition of causality,
and the features of the mental world on the other, summed up in the idea of

implication, which is isomorphically related to the other but distinct from it, is an indispensable part of his discussion throughout. He cannot, therefore, be regarded simply as a physical–biological reductionist notwithstanding his insistence upon the biological roots of intelligence. Because he occupies this indeterminate position, sooner or later in the exposition of the system in detail the relationship between the physical–biological and the mental must in some way or other be accounted for. This is what the notion of adaptation is designed to do.

The biological substratum of assimilation and accommodation is fairly obvious. The organism must process substances in its environment in one way or another, ingesting them and modifying them so that 'they can become incorporated into the structure of the organism' (Flavell, 1963, p. 45). Such processing is clearly well described by the notion of assimilation. On the other hand, in the course of such an assimilation the organism must also adjust itself to the incorporation of such substances and this happens right through from the initial intake to the final digestion. 'Just as objects must be adjusted to the peculiar structure of the organism in any adaptational process, so must the organism adjust itself to the idiosyncratic demands of the object' (loc. cit.). This latter is also well described by the notion of accommodation.

Similar notions may be generalised into the biological scene as a whole as distinct from the individual organism. Adaptation, in its two aspects, accounts for the process of growth of the individual organism in relation to the phylogenetic character of the species and total environment. Piaget, in line with his biological–psychological isomorphism, regards it as quite legitimate to take over these notions into the field of psychology and intelligence. Thus, 'To assimilate psychologically as well as biologically is to reproduce oneself by means of the external environment' (Piaget, 1964, p. 142; quoted in Baltro, 1973, p. 14) and again, 'assimilation constitutes a process common to organic life and to mental activity, thus a notion common to physiology and to psychology' (Piaget, 1963, p. 43; quoted in Baltro, 1973, p. 14). Similar considerations apply to accommodation.

It is worthwhile paying attention to the biological parallelism that is of such importance to Piaget. Considering the step–by–step process by which an organism ingests and digests, one thing is obvious. In all cases there is not simply a 'break-up' of substances, but also a 'transcendental' change from the original level of the substances outside the organism to a qualitatively *different* level of chemical composition necessary for the absorption of these substances.

In Piaget's comparison of biological with mental assimilation there is a problematic conflict in this respect. In 'Logique, langage et théorie de l'information', p. 123,[49] biological assimilation 'is an incorporation of the substances and energies in the organisation of the body itself', an entirely unexceptionable statement in the level terms we have just referred to.

Compare it, however, with this comment in which elementary mental assimilation is described as the 'incorporation of objects into the schemas of the appropriate activity . . . '; and again, with the '*incorporation of objects into the schemas of behaviour* [our emphasis], those schemas are nothing other than the catcher of the action susceptible of being actively repeated'. Similarly, speaking of rational assimilation, Piaget now describes it as the '*incorporation of objects into the system of operations*' (our emphasis) (ibid., p. 15) – an even more radical difference, considering the substantial gulf separating the logico-mathematical realm of operational structures and the external world of physical causality. Still more confusion arises in the following:

> all needs tend first of all to incorporate things and people into the subject's own activity, i.e., to 'assimilate' the external world into the structures that have already been constructed, and secondly to readjust these structures as a function of subtle transformations, i.e., to 'accommodate' them to external objects. From this point of view, all mental life, as indeed all organic life, tends progressively to assimilate the surrounding environment. This incorporation is effective thanks to the structures or [*sic*] psychic organs whose scope of action becomes more and more extended. Initially perception and elementary movement (prehension, etc.) are concerned with objects that are close and viewed statically; then later, memory and practical intelligence permit the representation of earlier states of the object as well as the anticipation of their future states resulting from as yet unrealised transformations. Still later intuitive thought reinforces these two abilities. Logical intelligence in the guise of concrete operations and ultimately of abstract deduction terminates this evolution [!] by making the subject master of events that are far distant in space and time. At each of these levels the mind fulfils the same function, which is to incorporate the universe to itself, but the nature of assimilation varies, i.e., the successive modes of incorporation evolve from those of perception and movement to those of the higher mental operations. (Piaget, 1968, pp. 7–8)

The introduction to this passage makes clear that all concepts are at the service of assimilation and accommodation and that not only *things* but *people* can be, and are, incorporated into activity; moreover, structures that we know to be logico-mathematical are accommodated to external *objects*. Even the notion of 'psychic organs' is an extraordinary encapsulation of object–non–object notions into one concept. What is at issue is the absence in the notions of assimilation and accommodation of *necessary level transcendence* manifested through the metamorphosis of the phenomena of one level into those of another. To pose assimilation and accommodation without some model of the mechanism of level change is not explicative. Nor does it offer any descriptive advantages. At least in the biological assimilatory/accommodatory process the resolution of one level into another can be followed even if the mechanism remains elusive.

By now, perhaps, one should not find this surprising, particularly at this 'frontier' point. However, there is another dimension of difficulty attached to the assimilation/accommodation notion. Flavell writes: 'However necessary it may be to describe assimilation and accommodation separately and sequentially, they should be thought of as simultaneous and indissociable as they operate in a living cognition. Adaptation is a unitary event, and assimilation and accommodation are merely abstractions from this unitary reality' (1963, p. 48). In a long passage from *The Psychology of Intelligence* Piaget makes the position clear:

If intelligence is adaptation, it is desirable before anything else to define the latter. Now, to avoid the difficulties of teleological language, adaptation must be described as an equilibrium between the action of the organism on the environment and vice versa. Taking the term in its broadest sense, 'assimilation' may be used to describe the action of the organism on surrounding objects, insofar as this action depends on previous behaviour involving the same or similar objects. In fact every relation between a living being and its environment has this particular characteristic: the former, instead of submitting passively to the latter, modifies it by imposing on it a certain structure of its own. It is in this way that, physiologically, the organism absorbs substances and changes them into something compatible with its own substance. Now, psychologically, the same is true, except that the modifications with which it is then concerned are no longer of a physico-chemical order, but entirely functional, and are determined by movement, perception or the interplay of real or potential actions (conceptual operations, etc.). Mental assimilation is thus the incorporation of objects into patterns of behaviour, these patterns being none other than the whole gamut of actions capable of active repetition.

Conversely, the environment acts on the organism and, following the practice of biologists, we can describe this converse action by the term 'accommodation', it being understood that the individual never suffers the impact of surrounding stimuli as such, but they simply modify the assimilatory cycle by accommodating him to themselves. Psychologically, we again find the same process in the sense that the pressure of circumstances always leads, not to a passive submission to them, but to a simple modification of the action affecting them. This being so, we can then define adaptation as an equilibrium between assimilation and accommodation, which amounts to the same as an equilibrium of interaction between subject and object. (pp. 7–8)[50]

What we have called the 'directional' problem begins to emerge. One has to ask the question, to what is accommodation actually being applied and whence does assimilation derive? This question is far from redundant since 'directionality' here is of major importance. In fact, the unitariness suggested by Flavell of assimilation and accommodation is actually achieved (as the passage from *The Psychology of Intelligence* shows) by assigning responsibility for accommodation to the *outside* world and responsibility for assimilation to the *inside* world, contrary to what one might expect. Is there then no priority in this directionality? Actually, closely examined, the combination of *assignment of responsibility* in both cases of assimilation and accommodation *to that which is 'the other' factor* (in the binary combination of subject and environment) to the one to which the notion directly *applies*, is a means by which the system aims at avoiding the problems of terminality and dualism – the problem of identifying the element and what happens to it in the vital transition from the outside to the inside. Diagrammatically, we can show the implications of this clearly (Figure 6.3). Here, by careful separation out of four factors, A, B, C and D ('modification' counts as two because of opposite directionality), and

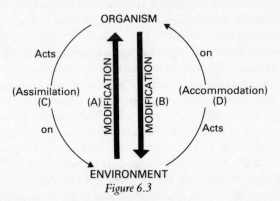

Figure 6.3

concentrating on their *directionality* they are turned into 'pseudo-elements' that are *even countable* but which are not *quantifiable or delineable in any way apart from this directional notion*. It is really a quasi-vector notion which appears in Piaget's writings several times in varying forms.[51]

It can be seen that the question about priority was a misleading one to ask in the first place. One cannot establish any priority in the absence of specified quantity or quantifiable delineation. There is no answer *in Piagetian terms* to the questions, to *what* does the subject accommodate, and *what* does the subject assimilate? Indeed, there is similarly no answer to the question about the priority (in the causal sense) of biology or psychology in the formation of the isomorphic parallelism between them. The biological and psychological (in the general sense) cannot be distinguished from each other in the specific form of the transition from the external to the internal worlds of the subject, and, indeed, action and operation themselves are similarly indistinguishable. The relationship between assimilation and accommodation is the most extreme expression of 'concept fluidity' to be found in the Piagetian system. But this fluidity enables the central problem of the multi-level relationship between intelligence and circumstance to be bypassed or 'absorbed'.

The issue runs deeper than this for the central philosophical problem of the relation between the discrete and continuous is evaded by this approach which ignores the important distinction between the *circumstances* of being and being itself. An analogy can be found by considering the way in which the high-speed sequence of 'stills' in a film simulates the actual movement of real life. The 'stills', like objects, exist within their own level matrices. The speeding-up in sequence (which corresponds to interaction among objects) generates new level matrices, producing a new mode of 'object-ivity'. In both situations, the distinction between level matrix and mode of being, or object-ive manifestation, arising from the matrix must be strictly maintained. With Piaget, the situation alternates. Either the movement is reduced to a collection of 'stills' or the 'stills' (objects) are dissolved in pure relationship.

An important link between the structuration process and the world to which it is supposed to relate is easily missed here if one is not careful. Both assimilation and accommodation constitute the 'vent' by which the world is transformed into cognitive structures in some way or other. But the key question is the nature of the world which is thus transformed – or rather this world as Piaget sees it through the eyes of the subject. Piaget constantly speaks of 'object' but we know from, for example, *The Mechanisms of Perception* that the very character of these objects themselves – their 'object-ness' – is at least partly dependent upon the already extant structuration pattern the subject brings to bear upon them. In fact, it is very difficult to know at what point Piaget intends us to take the term 'object' as an absolute starting-point. He frequently refers us to raw sensory data, and a considerable section of *The Mechanisms of Perception* is spent in examining the 'distorting' effect of subjective factors in perception on that which is perceived. A case can be made for the object being entirely subjectively determined within Piaget's terms of reference. What is more pertinent is that the boundaries of the object are indeterminate in Piaget's estimate and that such indeterminacy can only contribute to the ephemeral character of the cognitive element – whatever this might be.

In relation to the priority problem, such non-terminality leads to an implied abandonment of any serious consideration of assimilation since the subject relates to an indeterminate milieu. We are (surprisingly?) left with the predominance of accommodation in such a situation – a not inconsistent position with respect to Piaget's subjective apriorism. Notwithstanding this, there is no real solution to the problem of priority, for the more evanescent the external world becomes the less determinate become the elements, or potential elements, and the more remote the possibility of a specific terminality. This consideration of the uncertainty of the object serves only to reinforce the overall hesitancy of Piaget's position at this point in his system. As he, himself, succinctly expresses it:

> Assimilation can never be pure because by incorporating new elements into its earlier schemata the intelligence constantly modifies the latter in order to adjust them to new elements. Conversely, things are never known by themselves, since this work of accommodation is only possible as a function of the inverse process of assimilation. (quoted Flavell, 1963, p. 49; also Flavell bibliog., Piaget, 1952c, pp. 6–7) [52]

Perhaps the vital question that has to be answered regarding adaptation is the actual progress of assimilation and accommodation towards an ultimate equilibrium for the subject in the milieu – biologically or psychologically. Flavell's discussion of this (p. 49) exposes very clearly the problems surrounding the question in the light of Piaget's characterisation of assimilation and accommodation. 'First of all', Flavell writes, 'accommodatory acts are continually being extended to new and different features of the surround. To the extent that a newly accommodated-to feature can fit somewhere in the existing meaning structure, it will be assimilated to that structure.' One has to ask, what is the drive or motivation for such 'extension'? It cannot be included in the assimilation–accommodation–schemata system, because these in the immediately preceding state of the organism or subject are presumably in an *equilibrated* condition. Thus, we are forced to alternative conclusions. Either the organism or subject *seeks out a condition of disequilibrium* relative to its present state, or such a condition of disequilibrium is forced upon it by environmental conditions outside its control. In the first case there is nothing in the Piagetian mechanism to account for such seeking – in fact, the emphasis is the other way, a constant trend towards ultimate equilibrium, and in fact the relationship, if anything, between the subject or organism and the milieu is a *blind* one expressed in the concept of 'groping', as we have already seen. In the second case, the initiative for the process of extension is transferred *outside* the subject or organism and the responsibility devolves on the environment for either biological or psychological progress. This is entirely at variance with Piaget's fundamental thesis that the individual plays a determining role in cognitive growth. In fact, anything but this would force Piaget back into a preformationist position and cancel the structural theory, as he himself is quite aware.

So, when the mechanism is actually put to work we plunge into two alternatively unacceptable positions (in terms of the Piagetian system, that is). And notwithstanding affirmations by Flavell that 'Systems of meanings are constantly becoming reorganised internally and integrated with other systems . . . [a] continuous process of internal renovation . . . [which is] . . . a very potent source of cognitive progress', the key question remains unanswered – how does the progress of cognitive growth actually happen? (quoted Flavell, 1963, pp. 49–50; also Flavell bibliog., Piaget, 1952c, p. 414).

Further to a possible solution of the problem, Rotman refers to certain passages in Piaget (Rotman, 1977, pp. 100–1) which develop the notion of the interrelationship between 'need' and 'interest'. According to Rotman, Piaget approaches the possible reconciliation between the idea of energy (biological) and value, the latter connected closely by Piaget with the notion of 'interest'. In this context, Piaget writes, 'All needs are manifestations of disequilibria' (quoted by Rotman, 1977, p. 101), and Rotman stresses that, for Piaget, the condition of disequilibrium is more basic than the condition of need. 'Durable disequilibria constitute pathological organic or mental states' (quoted Rotman, p. 101). Thus, if we can link some of these notions together we may arrive at something like this: Need (biological/psychological survival) derives from the absolute necessity to equilibrate; interest constitutes a further (higher?) development of need involving a system of values. Since Piaget sees the most basic drive in this sequence as related to energy output in its most fundamental form, we have a supposed '*level*' sequence ranging from the most basic biological activity through to the most rarefied cerebration. Now, as a descriptive hierarchy, this model may be no better or worse than others. However, as Rotman correctly indicates, nothing in such a sequence determines what, in the world that is encountered by the subject, is specifically disequilibrating him, 'and, indeed, why it should impinge on the subject's cognitive system at all' (ibid., p. 101). We are still as far away as ever, after having related disequilibrium, need and a notion of cognitive development together, from actually being able to specify the way in which assimilation and accommodation constitute together an 'engine' of change.

Piagetians themselves have not been unaware of this problem. H. Furth, an entirely sympathetic Piagetian commentator, is critical precisely on this question. The discussion occurs around the exact meaning to be attributed to the well-known term (in the French original) of 'intériorisé' – variously described as 'internalisation' or 'interiorisation' of action. Here, this 'internalisation–interiorisation' concept is the nearest we come to something resembling an engine of change. Now, Furth regards Piaget's terms (in the French), especially in their usage, as vague, and his answer to this problem is intended to help Piaget by distinguishing between the notions of 'internalisation' and 'interiorisation'. By so doing Furth intends to overcome the problems that we have been discussing. Rotman, referring to this question, writes:

Furth makes a separation between internalisation as part of symbol formation whereby an imitative action becomes internalised as a 'mental image', and internalisation in the sense of abstracting the general features of actions. He suggests that 'We could use "interiorise" for the functional dissociation between general schemes of knowing and external content, and the word "internalise" for the real literal diminution of imitative movements that according to Piaget lead to internal images or internal language'. (Rotman, 1977, p. 112; quoted Furth, 1969, p. 28)

Here is a sort of two-stage rocket which takes off and jettisons the first stage (interiorisation) to get into orbit. But, pursuing the analogy, we have to suppose a common force to the internalisation and interiorisation stages which means that we still need to discover some way of straddling the gap between the content or external world situation and the general schemes of knowing or the internal situation. Furth shows himself clearly and sharply aware of the problem through his use of the phrase 'functional dissociation' by which he means precisely the *disjunction* involved in passing from outside to inside.

Does Rotman agree that this is a solution, and if he does, do we agree with him as well? After further discussion, he says: 'The ambiguities here [in the passage quoted on pp. 112–13 of Rotman from Piaget's *Developmental Psychology,* p. 142] suggest that Piaget really does want his verb *intériorisé* to refer to a transfer of actions, a movement from outer to inner, rather than the purely internal process of functional dissociation Furth suggests for him.' Thus, Rotman has no faith in the Furth solution. Nevertheless, while crediting Piaget (quite unjustifiably) with rejecting the literal internalisation idea (knowledge as a copy of reality), Rotman says that

he [Piaget] seems caught between avoiding such mimetic simplicities and nonetheless wanting to use words like 'reversibility' which are appropriate to action, to describe mental entities as well as speaking of actions being 'reproduced in thought'. The result is a certain confusion. There is the domain of real actions and the domain of thought. By conceiving of mental operations as internalised actions which 'are comparable to other actions that are reversible' Piaget extends the words [sic] action into the second domain illegitimately. For while the metaphor behind the term mental activity is indispensable and unobjectionable in normal speech it carries too many unexamined assumptions about the nature of thought to be the basis of a cognitive theory. (Rotman, pp. 113–14, and Piaget, *Genetic Epistemology,* p. 14)

Rotman continues by observing the misuse Piaget makes of 'transformation'. But while aware of the acute incompatibilities of Piaget's position, he unfortunately stops short of specifying their exact nature. These cannot, in fact, be understood without spelling out the fluidity of element and relationship in the system – a condition at its most embarrassing in the adaptation–transformation area. *The Development of Thought* hints that Piaget might have been considering towards the end of his life opting for the primacy of assimilation over accommodation.[53] It is true that this notion occurs in a discussion of the relation of cognitive subsystems to each other. Nevertheless, in the context of the concentration in *The Development of Thought* on equilibration, it would not be surprising if assimilation tended to outweigh accommodation (always keeping in mind of course the 'source' of each). At this late stage, Piaget seems ready to move towards a more environmental emphasis and to assign a greater weight to assimilation in the internalisation–interiorisation process. The implications of this are important in the light of the protracted struggle Piaget had over the years to reconcile the innate (biological) with that of the learned (psychological) in the growth of intelligence by means of various devices such as the mathematical notion of isomorphism and the directionally opposite concepts of assimilation and accommodation.

This is without doubt a most fundamental level of his thought which is, as we have seen, evidenced by the influences that have played a part in his own development stemming from the major trends of nineteenth-century thought on 'nature versus nurture'. We talked just now of the 'processes' of assimilation and accommodation. Actually, the word is misplaced since it necessarily carries with it a terminality which means the activity taking place among a number of specified things or elements. But as we are about to see, assimilation and accommodation, like the idea of schemata, is based exclusively on a notion of action which is severed from a linkage with any specific things or elements whatsoever. This is not gainsaid by Piaget's reference to 'action upon' objects, things, and so on. For although it might normally be argued that action is inconceivable separated from the 'acted upon', Piaget's specific definition of thought deriving *only* from action, actually relies upon this severance.

Action

It may seem odd to affirm yet again the importance of a particular concept of Piaget's. This is somewhat mitigated if we recall that while hierarchy is a deep-rooted factor in Piaget's thought, on the other hand the reconciliation of the closure of cognitive structures with the openness required by cumulative growth involves a cyclical aspect to the system due to an inability to assign prior responsibility to any one of the concepts he deals in. Even equilibrium itself is an 'umbrella' condition rather than a source or origin point (although, of course, its goal aspects are undeniable). Hence, despite the significance assigned to other ideas, 'action' is the foundation of Genetic Epistemology because it is the source of knowledge although it is not the cause of it.

The origins of its importance are traceable to the basic idea of psychological-biological isomorphism. As Rotman puts it, 'Piaget's theory of child development, then, provides a simple and brilliant elaboration of the fundamental hypothesis of *Biology and Knowledge* that thought is a reflection of physiology. Between the two he inserts actions' (p. 45). Describing what these are, he continues:

> These start as the literal handling of objects in the sensori-motor period, become internalised to form operations that manipulate schemas relating to concrete situations, and finally shed their adherence to real, particular content and become applicable to any object of thought whatsoever. All the other elements in Piaget's account, the recapitulation of cognitive structure from stage to stage, the decentrations that remove successive layers of subjectivity from thought, the creation of a kind of *milieu intérieur* of internal actions, and the sequence of progressive re-equilibrations, are contingent on this conception of action as the prime mover in the creation of thought' (loc. cit.)

Because of the character of Piaget's basic assumption of the logico-mathematical nature of intelligence and his elaboration of a structural theory of cognition especially in its relation to adaptation, the insertion of action between physiology and thought simply narrows the 'frontier' area to a zone between the external and the internal world without which the same questions must be posed but in more specific terms.

Piaget's problems with the relation between the biologically innate and psychologically acquired, which stem directly from his requirement that thought must not be preformed, have brought him to consider several linkages between the external and internal worlds, one of which is the neurological one. On the assumption that the brain is the source of mental processes (see Rotman, 1977, p. 38), Piaget has become interested in the particular thesis put forward by McCulloch and Pitts, which purports to demonstrate an isomorphism between the 'on–off' switching-circuit logic of the synaptic connections in the brain and the structure of logical propositions. The fact that Piagetian theory takes relatively little account of developments in knowledge of the brain, apart from this rather specialist reference, is a comment on the system's firm adherence to an aprioristic bias in its conception of mental growth. It is perfectly possible that Piaget and his colleagues have been unwilling to pursue this line too deeply just because of their fear that it may lead inevitably towards, for them, a preformationist conclusion especially in view of their imprisonment within a closed circuit of logico-mathematics.

Certainly, of the many references to action that arise in Piaget's writings the following strongly indicates an anti-preformationist stress: 'All action applied to objects accommodates itself to them, i.e. it undergoes as a negative the imprint of the things on which it moulds itself. The *essence of the action* is naturally not this imprint; it is the *modification imposed on the object,* i.e., the assimilation of the latter to the schemas of the subject' (our emphasis) (Piaget *The Child's Conception of Space,* 1956, p. 455). Similarly the concept of action as primarily emitting from the subject not the object is confirmed by this remark of Piaget's: 'Definition 1. Action is all behaviour (externally observable, including the clinical interview) seeking a goal from the point of view of the subject under consideration.' And again: 'Action [has to be] defined as a re-equilibration of behaviour in the event of change of environment' (loc. cit.).

Clearly, too great an emphasis on the neurological foundation of psychological activity must seriously affect an idea of action which stresses the impingement of the subject on the object rather than vice versa. Nevertheless, the isomorphism between the subject's psychological equipment and its biological roots carries an opposite implication to that which Piaget stresses here. Once again the typical conflict situation emerges between the *directions* of determining sequence, that is, on the one hand, the sequence from the biological to the psychological and, on the other, the psychological structuring activity directed by and from the subject towards the milieu. These opposite directions within the sphere of action are the most irreconcilable of all Piaget's conflicting theories. Because they refer to action (which is *physical*) they must be *either* mutually exclusive *or* reciprocally co-existent. If the latter is so, then some specified and delimiting relation has to be established such as is the case in Newton's equal and opposite law – what one might call a principle of coherence. This is certainly in doubt in Piaget's system.

Actually the bifurcation now very familiar between the zone of spatio-temporal causality and the zone of logico-mathematical inference is highlighted by the very use of the word 'action' itself, for on the one hand we have to conceive of action 'upon' something when dealing with the external world; but it is simply 'action' which is deemed to be the source of knowledge. Thus, in the first of the three preceding passages one has to accept something essentially inconceivable. How is it possible for a *logico-mathematical* phenomenon (for such is the accommodation aspect of action) to receive a 'negative imprint'? Nor is the notion of 'modification' (of the object) specifiable because this modification is described relative to the private experience of the subject alone, via assimilation. 'Imprint' and 'modification', in other words, are illegitimately carried over from the spatio-temporal causality world to the logico-mathematical world.

The nature of the conflict between the two 'directions' can be seen from another point of view. The external world is space- and time-governed as well as causal. The logico-mathematical world of operations is neither space- nor time-governed, as Piaget himself frequently avers. Trying to reconcile these without benefit of any notion of qualitatively different levels of existence is bound to produce the sort of conflict we see surrounding the notion of action. Piaget's 'one level universe', or alternatively 'level-less universe', attempting to encompass two such disparate conditions of existence, must always be fraught with inconsistency, notwithstanding his attempt to overcome this by the notion of isomorphism. But isomorphism is, after all, a mathematical concept and does not, and cannot, refer to qualitatively different states of existence.

It is pertinent here to refer back to Chapter 3 on the groupings of the concrete operational stage. The discussion there examined the 'collapsar' process involved in the element of the grouping and it was noted that Piaget vacillates between three different notions for his 'element'. To save referring back, here is the essence of the argument again. At the level of operations, the element is given its primary definition as the whole equation-sentence. At a subsidary level this is reduced to $(+A)$ or 'set down the class A', thus moving into the action situation. Finally, and in the *actual* description of particular groupings, Piaget treats the element as the class alone, that is, A or A' (and in groupings of relations reduces this to difference). Thus the vacillation ranges from operation to action and thence to the external object itself. It might seem here that Piaget recognises three different *levels*. But the outstanding feature of the three possible treatments confirms that this is not so, for, no matter how we range from operation to action to object and back again, the object, 'A', remains utterly untouched and untransformed. We are aware that it is a necessary built-in feature of mathematics that its elements (as mathematical elements) must reman unchanged in themselves no matter how they are manipulated. This feature characteristic of *all* mathematics reveals immediately and distinctly that this treatment by itself can never reveal the 'jump' from level to level, and can only *describe* what has happened *after* the leap has occurred. This is a central reason why a mathematical model such as Piaget offers can never deal with the situation he wants it to apply to, namely, the jump from the zone of the spatio-temporal to the zone of mentality. Reduction of mentality to logico-mathematical operations alone, which appear to correspond with spatio-temporal causal relations, simply destroys the qualitative difference and becomes another form of reductionism.

However, the question of action raises more than these issues. Allied with action in Piaget's thinking is the idea of 'need' to which we have referred before, which seems to play a rather important part in underpinning the notion of action itself, especially in his later writings. Flavell says: 'For Piaget . . . the need to cognise is not fundamentally an extrinsic motive, separate from intellectual activity and pushing it, as it were, from behind. The need is an intrinisic, almost defining property of assimilatory activity itself; it is indigenous to this activity from the outset' (1963, p. 79). Piaget has written: 'Need manifests the necessity which the organism feels or any organ which uses some exterior data for its own functioning,' (Piaget, 1963, p. 45; Baltro, 1973, p. 115). Furthermore, with his inbuilt problem of reconciling two incompatible zones (described by Rotman, p. 100, a little unclearly as 'spheres . . . of equilibrium and energy' on the one hand and 'significance and value' on the other), Piaget seeks to find some substratum of support for action which may divert the incompatibility problem elsewhere. It appears at one point that he believes he may have found it in the notion of need related to interest. But, as Rotman stresses, if we pursue this we have to investigate the idea of interest. Rotman quotes Piaget thus: ' "interest is, in effect, the prolongation of needs" when combined with the belief that "all needs are manifestations of disequilibria" . . . [this] takes us back to the original question of what determines whether an encounter with the world is disequilibrating; and indeed . . . why it should impinge on the subject's cognitive system at all' (Rotman, p. 101, and also Piaget, 1968, pp. 34–5).

The hope is perhaps that since 'interest implies a system of values which in the vernacular constitute [ordinarily] "interests" ' (loc. cit.), there is a link between affectivity, or emotional life, and need, which removes the problem away from the cognitive area, dominated as it is by logico-mathematical categories. Thus the problem of the source of action vis-à-vis the external world may seem to have been 'pushed back' into an area in which we do not have to consider the inconsistency referred to originally. The difficulty here is that affectivity, far from being independent of the logico-mathematical structuration in the Piagetian system, is subsumed in this system under the same logico-mathematical forms. As Piaget says at one point, 'affectivity is always the incentive for the actions that ensue at each new stage of this progressive ascent, since affectivity assigns value to activities and distributes energy to them. But affectivity is nothing without intelligence. Intelligence furnishes affectivity with its means and clarifies its ends' (Piaget, 1968, p. 69). Thus there is no escape this way. Actually Rotman records this when he says:

It is axiomatic for him [Piaget] that 'durable disequilibria constitute pathological organic or mental states' . . . for Piaget the achievement of equilibrium is even more basic than a 'need'. In his system needs are 'manifestations of disequilibrium' so that, without incurring an infinite regress in his analysis equilibrium cannot itself be a need, but must precede all needs as a necessary precondition for existence; it is the 'intrinsic and constitutive property of organic and mental life [*sic*]'. (Rotman, pp. 101–2; Piaget, 1968, p. 102)[54]

But if equilibrium is to occupy this substantive position then we have to return, yet again, to the problem of non-terminality in a major form. Indeed, neither 'need' nor 'action', themselves, escape this problem. Returning to the earlier point that the notion of action alone distinct from 'action upon' is particularly meaningless, then the non-terminality can be understood very clearly. It is particularly damaging since action even from the subject's point of view is firmly within the realm of the spatio-temporal and is *undetectable* except via the agency (object) in which it terminates. 'Loose' action is an inconceivable notion in the physical world. There are no circumstances in this world in which action is not deduced from its physical results. A beam of light in a completely massless vacuum is a total incompatibility.[55] Notwithstanding the generalisation of laws of action, such generalisation is really a way of summing particular *'terminal'* embodiments of this action.

When the obvious comparison is made with the logical frame of reference, into which Piaget's notion of action separate from its terminals must fall, a very decisive issue emerges. Whatever particular logic one is dealing with, three basic rules apply,[56] and all three possess the feature of 'anyness' intrinsic to the logical process as such. We have here, then, an insurmountable incompatibility between the action situation and the logic situation. The action situation cannot be separated from action-upon but logic is based upon universal applicability. It is not that there is no connection between logic and action, which is manifestly absurd; but we have to accept that there is a metamorphosis from action to logic which precludes the isomorphic correspondence so necessary to the Piagetian theory. One may say that there is an essentially asymmetric relationship to be detected between the 'zone' of action and that of logic in so far as action is 'logicisable' but logic is not *uniquely* 'actionisable'. (See below, Chapter 8.)

One may see this still more specifically. Action belongs to the world of spatio-temporal causality and therefore is always subject to an element of irreversibility. Even the repetition and/or 'inversion' of an action, in all respects, is a new action in this sense. Only logic involves reversibility although one must be careful to distinguish between logic in itself and the logical act carried out by the mind. In the latter case there is undoubtedly a factor of irreversibility involved as well. Thus with action there is a *non-repeatable order* of occurrence with each event which is not the case with any system of logic taken in itself. Any such system may be reordered 'at will', in the sense that deductions may be changed into postulates and the previous postulates may emerge as deductions. The important role of the logical process as part of the threshold of mentality is obvious here. One is not condemning logic because Piaget uses it as if it were exclusively equivalent to intelligence.

We shall be discussing this type of asymmetric relationship below as it underlies both the ordering of the external world and also the unique capacities of mentality in handling this natural ordering. Such asymmetry has something of the nature of difference of 'dimension' about it in the sense that relating three dimensions to two or one involves a process of *projection* in mathematics. It is also, to some extent, analogous to the relation between the real and complex domains. In fact, the latter may be conceived of as a quantitative projection of this asymmetrical but co-existent relationship. (See below, Chapter 8).

In the light of these considerations, therefore, action cannot be a *direct and unmediated* source of knowledge exclusively embodied in logical forms, simply because two asymmetrically related but co-terminous 'zones' are involved. The device of isomorphism which Piaget employs does not solve the problem precisely because of this asymmetry. Logic by virtue of its 'anyness' partakes of the infinite whilst any action is, by its very nature, finite and particular. The finite and particular cannot be summed into the infinite and thus cannot produce an isomorphism between the two. And here we discover what is in effect a restatement of the non-inductivist character of knowledge and at the same time find Piaget exemplifying such an inductivist position, particularly in the relationship of action and logic, notwithstanding his general anti-empiricist point of view. Even 'reflective abstraction', which is a major concept in Piaget's progress from the external to the internal world of cognition, says no more than that in some unspecified way one moves from the realm of action to that of logic.

7 Equilibration II. Cognitive Growth

The Stages

Piaget's treatment of the actual development of human cognition from birth to adulthood is one of the best-known aspects of his thought, and is embodied in the theory of stages through which the individual necessarily passes over this period of his life. The sources of the stage theory are quite distinct from those of the structural theory of cognition. Actually, Piaget's lifelong search for a science of epistemology has occurred 'reciprocally'. The greatest pressure on him originally seems to have been the search for a union between experimental psychology and philosophy, and even his earliest views show a constant interaction between conclusions drawn from what are claimed as the experimental situation and a preconceived logico-mathematical model (see Boring, 1969). It is from the former that the stage theory is principally derived whereas the structural theory is largely attributable to the latter. Piaget's working life seems to have alternated somewhat between these two positions. Strongly influenced as he was by theoretical considerations when young, his first five principal publications relate to work carried out with children. The period from the later 1930s through to the early 1960s seems to have been one of extensive theoretical elaboration, although experiments continued to be carried out in large numbers. More recently, experimental activity seems to have become increasingly prominent again as the overall trend of Piaget's work and writing in later life has been to concentrate increasingly upon the deeper implications of his experimental work. This is borne out by the relatively recent publications *Success and Understanding* (1975), *The Grasp of Consciousness* (1977), and particularly *The Development of Thought* (1978).

It is difficult, therefore, to be decisive as to whether the structural apparatus is more determining of the stage theory or vice versa. There are strong arguments on both sides. Apriorism certainly plays a role in what Piaget claims to be 'independent evidence' – as much for the stage theory as for the structural theory. One can almost speak of 'cumulative apriorism' in describing the stage theory and how it works.

'Piaget', writes Rotman, 'sees the development of intelligence as a dialectic of temporary resolutions or impermanent equilibria between them [assimilation and accommodation]. He describes this dialectic as passing through three major phases of development, the *sensori-motor* stage, the *operational* stage and the *formal* stage, before it reaches adult thought where it continues its progression within scientific and mathematical knowledge' (1977, pp. 39–40). These three stages are what are normally associated with Piaget's system, together with the additional subdivision of the pre-operational or intuitive stage (from about 2 years to about 7 years). This gives four major stages. But this number is not stable. In *Six Psychological Studies* (pp. 5–6) six distinct stages are indicated which are clearly to be regarded as major ones.

> Each of these stages is characterised by the appearance of original structures whose construction distinguishes it from previous stages. The essentials of these successive constructions exist at subsequent stages in the form of substructures onto which new characteristics have been built. It follows that in the adult each stage through which he has passed corresponds to a given level in the total hierarchy of behaviour. But at each stage there are also temporary and secondary characteristics that are modified by subsequent development as a function of the need for better organisation. Each stage thus constitutes a particular form of equilibrium as a function of its characteristic structures, and mental evolution is effectuated in the direction of an ever increasing equilibrium. (p. 6)

The 'non-terminality' features of these views are quite evident. The notion of 'characteristic' comes closest to being a sort of element and this is not definitive but a descriptive generality. This non-terminality is specified in the three (or more) possible delineations of stages given here. The first interpretation characterises stages 'by the appearance of original structures'; the second describes 'each stage' as 'correspond[ing] to a given level in the total hierarchy of behaviour'; and in the third, each stage 'constitutes a particular form of equilibrium as a function of its characteristic structures'. Each of these is quite a different set of circumstances from the others but all are given equal status. Furthermore, each stage, said to be typified by specific structures none of which can be identified, gets carried forward into subsequent stages equally unidentifiable in the form of substructures. Now, if there is no certainty about the identity of each stage, there is equally no certainty about the number of stages nor of their structures or substructures. Corresponding to every stage there is an indefinite number of substructures which is made definite only by reference to the division of the previous stages. This can go on indefinitely, back to the point of origin, or birth of the individual. In the end there may be as many stages as there are structures and substructures, and any significant and reliable distinction between the different stages disappears.

The absence of terminality when it comes to a theory of development has thus particular significance. It becomes very difficult to establish the existence of development at all under these circumstances, beyond an ordering of concepts in a time sequence and even this is, to a degree, arbitrary. Non-terminality in the field of developmental analysis acts to exclude the essential distinction between phenomena and the circumstances under which they come into being. The problem has definite echoes of Zeno's paradoxes and involves similar problems.

How does Piaget's claim to demonstrate the link between the development of the individual's cognition and his experience fare in the light of these points? His ideas on *decentration* and *differentiation* are especially relevant to this issue. Piaget elaborates on these very fully throughout his writings. We have chosen *The Principles of Genetic Epistemology* (1972b) in particular as it is a relatively recent work and is very comprehensive in its treatment of these concepts. Discussing the world of the very young child (pp. 20ff.), Piaget comments on the 'adualism' which he says is characteristic of the very early stages of mentality. He claims that at this early period there is no fixed boundary between 'data given internally and those given externally' nor any awareness of self (the experimental work of both J. M. Baldwin and Th. Gouin-Décarie is cited as having confirmed this). Continuing, he says: 'Clearly, a structure of reality with neither subjects nor objects provides only one possible link – action – between what will later become differentiated into a subject and objects' (pp. 20–1). Hence, action is placed completely at the centre of the development(al) stage model.

> In the field of space as well as in the different perceptual ranges in process of construction, the young infant relates everything to his body, as if it were the centre of the universe – but a centre that is unaware of itself. In other words, primitive action exhibits both a complete indifferentiation [*sic*] between the subjective and the objective, and a fundamental centring which, however, is basically unconscious because connected with this lack of differentiation. (p. 21)

The notion of developed action is *identified by* differentiation and a departure from centration, or egocentricity.[57] Furthermore, the idea of action is elaborated by the concept of co-ordinations (as we saw in Chapter 6): 'In short, the co-ordination of the subject's actions, inseparable as it is from the spatio-temporal and causal co-ordinations which he attributes to reality, is the origin both of the differentiations between this subject and objects and of the decentring process on the level of physical acts; and this latter in combination with semiotic function is going to make possible representation or thought' (ibid., p. 22). At this early sensori-motor period it is stressed, because of the supposed restriction of action to the purely physical, there is an epistemological problem with regard to co-ordinations. Piaget suggests that this is overcome by the beginnings of reciprocal assimilation, that is, the beginnings of structures assimilating to each other internally. Such a notion is an important element in under-standing what he means by co-ordination. To settle the issue Piaget writes that 'from the sensori-motor level onwards there are two aspects to the growing differentiation of subject and object, viz. the formation of co-ordinations and the distinction within them of two kinds: on the one hand, those which relate together the actions of the subject, and on the other, those which concern the actions of objects on each other' (ibid., p. 24).

Summarising the central ideas in this sequence of references, the fol-lowing emerges. Basically, the notion of action pervades all; differen-tiation and decentration emerge as the identifiable 'forms' in which this all-pervasive action ultimately shows itself by virtue of the co-ordination of actions; such co-ordinations are specifically identifiable in the form of reciprocal assimilation which is an internal structural process. The two kinds of co-ordinations, those relating the actions of the subject and those relating mutual actions of objects, are responsible for the separation of subject and object. The whole gives us the road along which the subject must pass to achieve operational thought.

The first point needing attention is the assertion that action is the only structure of reality available to the young infant. But note that it is action 'between what will *later* [our emphasis] become differentiated into subjects and objects' (ibid., pp. 20–1). In short, there are no terminals for this action at the stage at which the infant is. The absence of terminality in the later concepts is traceable to this deficiency in the first instance. This is most important in considering co-ordination which is treated as the actual transformative force – that which actually generates thought. While other concepts certainly are necessary, they are in themselves insufficient to account for the growth of thought according to Genetic Epistemology. It is the co-ordinations which ultimately make reversible systems of opera-tions possible. Later, in *The Development of Thought*, this is particularly emphasised.[58] Without co-ordinations, it is said, there can be no move-ment from sensori-motor through to concrete operational and thence to formal operational thought. But a closer look at this idea of co-ordination, which is always attached to action or operation, fails to reveal any devel-opmental element.

In any attempt to provide a theoretical model for development it is impossible to avoid the problem of reconciling the extant stabilities of the changing situation with the overthrow and transformation of those stabi-lities. Both the logical and mathematical extractions from the process can only record the *fixture* of any given phase of this change. Even a repeated record of different phases only provides a series of static pictures. Bearing this in mind, the logico-mathematical 'extract' from the given situation has all the characteristics of the conclusion being contained within the premisses that strictly logical and mathematical situations always possess. Thus one can legitimately speak of the logical 'unfolding' of the logico-mathematical reflection of a process, but cannot specify this in the emergence of the process itself.

This latter has, of necessity, to include all unforeseen factors generated by the encounter of the process with the milieu in which it is occurring. There is a *contingent* aspect here not reflectable within logico-mathematics except in non-contingent forms. We can describe these as 'incrementally additive' although this does not do justice to the transformations of the whole by the absorption of the novel factors that the emergent movement of the process itself necessarily entails. The best we can do in a logico-mathematical 'map' of the growth process of Actuality is a combination of logical *unfolding* and *incremental additivity*. Only the record of novelty is contained here, not its explanation.

The concept of the 'co-ordination of actions' claims to reflect logically the actual novelty involved in the development of thought. But following what we have just said, nothing new is added by 'co-ordinating actions' other than their 'displacement' within the same (logico-mathematical) frame of reference. They cannot *in themselves* involve novelty. Put in another way, 'co-ordinating actions' serves to obliterate understanding of development, not explain it.

We can see, then, that the 'co-ordination of actions' is to be equated with differentiation and decentring, themselves the *formal* manifestation of action, and the whole intended as the full explication of the stage process. This is not, however, simply a matter of individual (personal) development but in part is a function *within* each individual of a condition common to mankind.

Piaget distinguishes very specifically 'between the pyschological subject whose source is the conscious ego, and the epistemic subject which represents what is common to all (psychological) subjects at the same level of cognitive achievement' (Rotman, 1977, p. 135); 'decentring leading to objectivity is but a decentring in relation to the ego of the observer, and is correlative with a logico-mathematical structuralization due to the activities of the epistemic subject and proceeding from the co-ordinations of actions (whence "groups", etc.) and no longer from isolated actions which are sources of possible illusions' (Piaget, 1973, p. 56).

The difficulties of non-terminality, manifest in the notion that pure action is the source of subsequent subject-object differentiation, is supposedly resolved by the use of the notion of 'co-ordinations'. But this is not really sufficient. A second sheet-anchor for the system is the notion of the epistemic subject – a sort of generalised or universalised (idealised?) subject possessing all the required features of perfect stage development. Co-ordinations offer security regarding a sort of common (inherited?)

feature of humanity. The stage process is thus supposedly protected from empiricism and although learning is an individual matter achieved in a lifetime, or the early part of it anyway, it is nevertheless endowed with a certain inbuilt destiny referable to the species as a whole.

> Reflective abstraction starting from actions does not imply an empiricist interpretation in the psychologist's sense of the term, for the actions in question are not particular actions of individual (or psychological) subjects: they are the most general co-ordinations of every system of action, thus expressing what is common to all subjects and therefore referring to the universal or epistemic subject and not the individual one. (quoted Rotman, 1977, p. 136, from Piaget and Beth, 1965, p. 238)

This can be described as a 'non-terminality' of 'non-terminality', as it were, which corresponds very well with the Piagetian notions of operations upon operations, co-ordinations upon co-ordinations, actions upon actions. There is no doubt, as well, that the epistemic subject is to be regarded as the definitively superior manifestation of cognition, as we may see from the last lines of the reference from *Main Trends* (the reference before the last). It is clear that we have come a long way from notions of development. The discussion around the nature of both co-ordinations and the epistemic subject is about essentially *logical* procedures without even the benefit of propositional concepts.

The fact that Piaget opts for an identificaton of thought with logical procedure (or at least an isomorphism between them) cuts off his system from the internal–external interrelationship essential in any developmental process, and leaves it internally with only one possibility of accounting for thought, namely, logico-mathematics. Such a view entails the principle of inclusion of the simpler in the more complex structures in a hierarchy of classification, in which there is no means of distinguishing development as such from co-existence or simultaneous behaviour. There is no reason in Piaget's system why the stages, substages, and so on, should not have the same 'nesting' relationship as the structures and substructures, which all co-exist at any instant. There is no certain means of distinguishing the stages as a developmental sequence beyond the affirmation that they are so. The conclusion emerging straight out of this is that the theory of stages involves a series of time-ordered discontinuous plateaux with no explanation at the very point at which it is needed, that is, at the points of transition. It is unhelpful that Piaget, at various points, breaks down the major steps into a multitude of minor ones. We are still left with the discontinuity of explanation – only the number of points at which this occurs has increased.

In the course of his study over the years it obviously became clear to Piaget that the plateau notion, interpreted as all-inclusive at each stage, was unsatisfactory. On the other hand, he has always affirmed that while the chronological ages of stage development can vary (that is, they can stretch over longer or shorter periods), the order is invariant. Now, in the course of their practical investigations of the stage theory, Piaget and his colleagues concluded that stages and substages identified by specific structures did not always correspond to the sequence. This constituted a severe challenge to the invariant order view. For example, the ability to map a given area (say a room) was registered as coming later than the physical ability to position things in it.[59] Since the structures involved were said to be similar it was surprising that there should be a gap of perhaps several years between the emergence of the two features. Again, the subject sometimes appeared to possess at the same time structures in one area well in advance of structures in another (for example, conservation of weight as compared with conservation of quantity). Both these characteristics came to be described as 'décalage', the first case being 'horizontal décalage' and the second 'vertical décalage'.

Certain results follow from this. If invariant order is a definitive feature of the stage theory and, at the same time, the variability of chronological age related to vertical and horizontal décalage is accepted, then enough theoretical 'equipment' is present to account for every possible manifestation that may arise under whatever circumstances. In other words, these concepts between them can account for *anything* that actually happens and thus render the stage theory untestable because its 'truth' can always be affirmed by one or other of these principles. The process of development is thus not identifiable since this can be varied at will. It is not certain, even, whether the sequence of plateaux is reliable since, in the event, if the sequence is not demonstrable it can nevertheless be accepted without disturbing the 'theory'. Trouble and difficulties with the stage theory have not been resolved by these devices. Possibly an awareness of its inability to account for the origin of novelty lies at the root of the theory of recapitulation, a fundamental notion in Piagetian thought which often does not receive the treatment it deserves. This may be partly because it exists only as an implication in a large part of his writings. For example, the isomorphic relationship between the psychological and the biological is a covert manifestation of 'recapitulation'.

Piaget is not particularly original in his adoption of this viewpoint. Recapitulation theories abound in the nineteenth century and have influenced Piaget through Lamarck and Spencer and to some extent von Bayer and Haeckel. Mammalian and human embryology is a favourite field for biological recapitulationist theories. As recently as Maynard-Smith's *The Theory of Evolution* (1972) recapitulationism has been deemed important enough to oppose with the alternative theory of neotony 'the widespread and important evolutionary process whereby adults retain embryonic characteristics of their evolutionary predecessors, so that for example human adults resemble young apes' (Rotman, 1977, pp. 127–8).

The issue here is not the truth or falsity of some form of recapitulation but the use of the notion as a substitute for explaining the genesis of novelty. This is recapitulation*ism* – a theory which affirms that at different (usually more complex) levels of organisation, the features of a previous level are restated.[60] The most important question mark against any theory of recapitulation in biology derives from the fact that, embryologically speaking, the phases of foetal development reflecting earlier stages of evolution do *not* mature but are 'bypassed' en route to the point of birth of the particular organism or unit of the species concerned. Thus, no representative of a species can be regarded as simply a recapitulation of previous phases of evolution. Notwithstanding such questions, it is the affirmed 'isomorphic' correspondence between different life 'levels' (that is, biological, psychological), and also between different supposed stages of intelligence, that Piaget makes the basis of his concept of recapitulation (Rotman, 1977, pp. 43–4). Using this notion, the essentially non-developmental, and logically nesting view of the stages-plateaux can convey the illusion of development through the temporal arrangement of these plateaux according to a recapitulation theory.

The most recent attempt to resolve the stages question is to be found in the theory of compensatory equilibrium, the core of *The Development of Thought,* to which we have already given considerable attention. It is enough to add here that by changing the emphasis to 'equilibration' rather than equilibrium and to compensatory mechanisms rather than operational structures, the place of stages in Genetic Epistemology is thrown seriously into doubt. We do not believe that Piaget resolved any of his fundamental problems by switching from structural stability and equilibrium (both reconcilable with his stage theory) to a concentration on transformation. He seems never to have found time to resolve the relationship between the two.

In view of these cumulative and unresolved problems surrounding the stage theory, it is not surprising that Flavell identified it as one of the most difficult of Piagetian concepts to deal with. At the end of his comprehensive and meticulous book he writes:

> We conclude chapter and book with a brief discussion of one of the real posers for developmental theory and research: the possible meanings and applications of the concept of 'stage', or its various synonyms 'period', 'level', etc. Although Piaget (1955(d)) and others (e.g., Braine, 1959; Kessen, 1960; Werner, 1957) have discussed the problem, there are still many ambiguities and unresolved questions. The philosopher Mario Bunge (1960), for example, has given us a poignant reminder of these in distinguishing no less than nine separate meanings of the concept 'level'. We shall limit our treatment to a particular, but

particularly important, segment of the general problem, using Piaget's findings as the empirical context for possible resolutions.

> An obvious, but almost insuperable difficulty which bedevils anyone trying to make a stage analysis of human development is the fact that a given stage, however defined, is typically a function not only of chronological age but also, or so it sometimes seems – of everything else under the sun. There are independent variables consisting of the specific tasks and testing procedures by which the stage assignment was arrived at and of the particular setting and conditions in which the testing took place. And there are also variables residing in the child himself: his over-all intellectual ability; his enduring personality and current emotional state; and his background as regards sociocultural and family milieu, education, previous experiences with this sort of test or with testing in general, and so on. With this potpourri of influences, the argument runs, how can statements like '6 – 9 years is the stage of such-and-such' have any determinate meaning? And more generally, can the construct 'stage' really serve any theoretical purpose and intra-age homogeneity which is just not to be found anywhere in developmental reality? (Flavell, 1963, p. 442)

Flavell continues by affirming that any attempt to define developmental 'stage' is bound to be somewhat vague and equivocal, or alternatively to be a 'data statement' so concrete as to rule out the need for the concept of stage. Yet Flavell finds a justification for the notion in its 'usefulness' in designating a 'step' or 'level' and/or an 'overall state'. We have looked at these ideas in the foregoing comments and do not find it possible to accept that 'usefulness' outweighs the indeterminacy of the notion (in fact there is a strong argument that such 'usefulness' is actually misleading).

But there is a further consideration as to whether the stage theory stands up even to a logical analysis of its inherent assumptions, which follows directly out of the remarks made by Flavell. If two abstract 'stages' are posited, say A and B, where B follows A, and it is assumed that all such stages are structures divided into substructures, namely, a, b, c, d, etc., for A, and a', b', c', d', etc., for B, then certain results follow. It should be remembered, first, that Piaget affirms *necessary* sequence or invariant order. Also, one condition for a stage to be identifiable is that an *interdependence* exists between the structures comprising it. Now, in examining the transition from stage A to stage B, if either a or b, etc., *separately* transform into a', b', etc., then the *interdependence* of the structures at the previous stage is *violated*. If, on the other hand, the transition to stage B involves the *simultaneous* total transformation of all the structures, a, b, c, d, . . . into $a', b', c', d', \ldots$, then the question of *initiation* of change becomes entirely unspecified. In other words, the mutual interdependence of structures at any stage renders the initiation of change to a new stage impossible, and vice versa. Yet, in Piagetian terms, *both* of these conditions have to be satisfied. The problem can only be resolved if it is postulated that the *subsequent* stage *B* plays a role in determining the change from *A* to *B* – a position which Piaget actually entertains elsewhere, as has already been noted (see Piaget, 1968, p. 157). In fact, his notion of *logical* necessity arriving as a result of the developmental process and not antedating it, is very relevant to this. Thus, by this 'backward' reflection of necessity the non-developmental character of the stage theory is confirmed. The procedure is governed by two mutually exclusive deductions. You either go from stage *A* to stage *B* by violating its very essence, or stage *A* goes as a whole to stage *B* and is thereby rendered indistinguishable from it.

If, in fact, the discussion of 'groping' under 'The Schemata' above is recalled, the essentially *blind* character of this activity, allied with its vital role in the system in passing from stage to stage (or sub-stage/structure(s) to sub-stage/structure(s)), ties in closely with the ambiguities associated with this transition. Putting all the relevant components together: Piaget's logico-mathematical constraints dictate the *type* of transition, with its unresolved conflict, as we described it above; the *necessary* (for the system) outcome of this, if it is offered as a 'developmental' theory, can only be a form of blind *activity* – a notion which is, in fact, well accounted for by Piaget's idea of 'groping'. The fact that he opts *on balance* for a greater role for internal decision-making (cognitive direction) in this activity, rather than external chance-governed encounter, only serves to increase the ambiguities already present.

Moreover, as emerges from the stage *A*–stage *B* discussion, the role of *initiative* in propelling development forward is unresolved. If individuals contain different stages for different concepts at any one time (the 'décalage' situation) they are clearly not *integrated* within the Piagetian terms of reference. If, on the other hand, they are *required* to be integrated to be indentifiable at a *given* stage, then they cannot be at different stages regarding individual concepts. All this adds up to an inability of the system to account for initiation of novelty. The absence of initiative on the part of the subject means that he cannot actively introduce a transition and is *therefore not actively related to his environment* – the one feature of the system which is supposed to be definitive of it. This ultimate passivity of the subject, which conforms closely to the blindness of 'groping', is clearly a direct product of the constraints and conditions inherent in the basic stage/structure theory of development. Yet experience of learning, even ungoverned by experimental controls, repeatedly affirms that if one pathway to a new concept is 'blocked' then another can and will be found. Whatever developmental theory may be adopted in the end, this initiative, or 'probing', relationship with the environment must be an integral part of it.

The objection may be raised to all the foregoing criticisms that the sheer weight of evidence over decades of individual and team work on the experimental front, and embodied in literally hundreds of publications, is not adequately dealt with by a critique of this sort. The reply to such an objection can only refer the reader to the original terms of reference of this examination of Piaget's thought. It is not the need for an adequate theory of development that is questioned; it is the claim that the stage analysis with its attendant equipment of assimilation and accommodation, etc., etc., is, in effect, not only a *theory* of development but the development *itself* objectively existing and uncovered by Genetic Epistemology. The criticism is of the inherent incapacity of the hypothesis to do what it sets out to do. This criticism can never be substantiated simply by experimental challenges, although these are of great value in demonstrating the inbuilt assumptions in Piaget's experimental methods.[61] It can only be achieved by examining both the assumptions and the fabric of thought of the system. Thus, in arriving at the viability or otherwise of Genetic Epistemology as a whole, it is such factors as these that must be the foundation of criticism and not a mountainous sifting of claimed 'evidence'. This point applies as much to the stage theory as it did to the 'apparatus' of cognition and the notions of equilibrium/reversibility.

As a tail-piece to this discussion, Piaget himself (perhaps in an unguarded moment) has committed to paper a view which, in our opinion, has gone a long way towards destroying the value and meaning of his stage theory:

One of these problems, for example, is the problem of genius, for while it is still an unsolved question of general psychology how scientific or artistic creation operates, it is an even greater mystery to understand what constitutes the secret uniqueness of an individual creator. It is when we find ourselves in close touch with such questions that we best realise the probable limits of *structuralism* [our emphasis]: whereas Newton, Bach and Rembrandt, when they were children, probably went through stages of development [!], the possible structures of which we can form an idea, and whereas it is or will be possible perhaps to explain their creative work by means of new combinations of structures that they assimilated and then far surpassed, the actual process of such reorganisation and then of surpassing them will probably long elude structural analysis, because occurring in exceptional if not essentially individual cases. (Piaget, 1973, pp. 52–3)

A theory of psychological development which resigns responsibility for one type of extreme case and refers to this as a 'mystery' *while still affirming its own conceptual equipment as generally relevant and applicable,* is indeed committing hypothetico-deductive 'hara-kiri'! Non-conformity is deemed to be *inferior to the norm,* that is, the subject is 'backward'. If it is superior, however, it is placed quite unwarrantably outside the system.

Perhaps the assessment of the stage/structure theory of development in regard to genius is a most suitable point at which to turn to the last, and probably the most unmanageable, notion in Piaget's system – the genesis of novelty.

The Genesis of Novelty

It could be said that the phrase 'the genesis of novelty' is what the Piagetian system is about from start to finish, and that all the other categories and notions are simply elaborations of what is enshrined in this idea. We have Piaget's own confirmation of such a viewpoint. 'I fear I have given the impression of a man who has touched many fields. But in fact, I have followed a single goal that has remained always the same: to try to understand and explain what a living development is in all its perpetual construction and novelty and its progressive adaptation to reality.'[62] Furthermore, 'I consider the main problem of Genetic Epistemology to be the explanation of the construction of novelties in the development of knowledge' (Piaget, 1970, p. 77). And indeed these views well express an important side of Piaget's thought. Despite this orientation of interest and the characterisation of the system in its very name Genetic Epistemology, discussion of genesis as such is strikingly rare.[63] In *Six Psychological Studies* there is a fairly full discussion. But this degree of detail is unusual. Of course its meaning must be assumed within other contexts all the time. Its central importance is such that it warrants a separate analysis in its own right.

In the previous two chapters discussion of the principal basic Piagetian notions has indicated a division in his thinking between the zone of cognition itself, internal to the subject, and the zone external to the subject, or the subject's milieu. There is a dualism here in the sense that when we come to look at each 'component' of cognition as a whole, an unbridged gap exists between the two zones, and although the two zones differ fundamentally in their nature, the same principles are applied to both. This gap manifests itself, one way or another, under every notional aspect of Genetic Epistemology. The principal means which allows Piaget the illusion of reconciliation is the various forms of 'collapsar' symbolisation, centrally the mathematical, but also the actual terminology employed by Piaget in his descriptive passages. The term used to describe the whole system, Genetic Epistemology, itself suffers from the same disjunction. Relating to growth and hence involving contingent relations and randomness, the word 'genetic' cannot be reconciled within the same parameters as 'epistemology' which is related, at least by Piaget, to a logico-mathematical structure of knowledge free by its very nature of all indeterminacy. Thus, the gap between growth and structure centres on the emergence of the new. It is the genesis in particular of the new which is the last and perhaps most sensitive area of Piaget's thought that needs consideration.

In *Six Psychological Studies* genesis is related to the achievement of greater stability but at the same time always 'stemming from an initial state which may also comprise a structure'. Thus, 'genesis [is] simply a form of development . . . a relatively determined system of transformations comprising a history and leading in a continuous manner from state A to state B, state B more stable than the initial state and constituting an extension of it' (p. 144). This immediately poses the question: at what point does the genetic process actually start? Piaget's answer is categorical. There is not, and cannot be, 'absolute beginning'. 'Genesis is simply a transition from one structure to another, nothing more' (Piaget, 1971, p. 141). Again, 'Genesis emanates from a structure and culminates in another structure' (Piaget, 1968, p. 147).

A new problem arises when we relate these notions to Piaget's concept of objects: 'Objects certainly exist, and they involve structures which also exist independently of us. But objects and their regularities are known to us only in virtue of operational structures which are applied to them and form the framework of the process of assimilation which enables us to attain them. They are therefore only arrived at by successive approximations, that is they represent a *limit never itself attained*' (our emphasis) (Piaget, 1972b, pp. 90–1). Hence, under the conditions given we cannot arrive at the 'object' at all. It plays something like the role of a mathematical limit in a convergent series. This is what Piaget actually says: '[the] independent nature [of these objective structures] become[s] in its turn a limit never attained though one in whose existence we are compelled to believe' (ibid., p. 91). 'On the other hand', he continues, 'every causal explanation also presupposes the attribution of our operations to objects, and consequently is evidence of an isomorphism between their structures and ours' (loc. cit.). He agrees with P. Franck in being unable to 'decide between the two conceptions of causality as a law of nature or a requirement of reason: this disjunction appears to us to be both non-exclusive and reduceable to a logical conjunction' (loc. cit.).

The conflict here with respect to the object is very obvious. On the one hand, it is seemingly never actually attained by the subject; on the other, Piaget affirms the isomorphism just quoted in the clear *absence* of the object. Taking each 'side' of this conflict separately, neither can provide a basis for a theory of genesis. Genesis involves the emergence of objects/ events/processes into a distinct identity whereby new phenomena are distinguishable from old. If this cannot be done, and the confusion between the 'limit' and the 'isomorphic' approach in Piaget's treatment of the object shows that it cannot, then there is no possibility of identifying, either subjectively or objectively, what is actually new.

By affirming the independent existence of objects on *logical* grounds alone, Piaget creates an unbridgeable gap. In this passage, causality (which Piaget frequently affirms does not belong to logic) is presented as a law of nature. But the 'lawfulness' of natural phenomena is restricted to logical and mathematical extraction. Causality, on the other hand, as a feature of Actuality, is indissolubly linked with contingency which it generates. The way in which causality and contingency are mapped into logico-mathematics is discussed below in Chapter 8. It is vital not to confuse the nature of the connectedness of Actuality with its mapped parallel in logico-mathematics. For the former the definitive character of *self-movement* can only be reflected in a combination of *axioms and implications* in the latter. The former is capable of producing the 'unexpected' (novelty) which this latter, in itself, cannot do but only map. By 'drifting' between Actuality and logic, Piaget evades the issue of the interaction of causality and contingency in the growth process, and hence slides out of the real question of genesis and into an essentially logical, acausal, non-genetic situation where he can utilise non-exclusion and reduction without regard to the changed terms of reference.

The allusion to non-exclusive disjunction demonstrates the 'slide-over' technique. Contingency cannot arise, and reduction forces the conclusion of logical conjunction. By such methods it is possible to remove growth or genesis entirely out of the realm of indeterminacy that accompanies it and into the predictable realm of logic. If everything, the external as well as the internal worlds, is thus contained within a logical frame of reference alone, nothing is left of Actuality but 'unreason'. This is, paradoxically, the irrational element that Piaget's method retains – concealed by drifting between Actuality and logic.

The evanescent character of Piaget's conception of the object complements the notion of genesis as simply a movement from structure to structure. The non-terminality of structural interrelation is again amply revealed by this evanescence. Without any possibility of grasping the object as such but only approaching it in the sense of a mathematical limit, newness can never even be detected, let alone delineated. The idea, for example, of logical 'nesting' together with the recapitulation model referred to earlier, contains no sense of newness beyond that of restatement. The cycle of intrusion/disturbance–self-regulation–compensation (see *The Principles of Genetic Epistemology,* pp. 60ff., and *The Development of Thought* in its entirety), even in the context of 'homeorhesis', cannot solve the problem. Homeorhesis, especially in respect to homeostasis, in any case raises what might be called relativistic problems. The latter describes the *maintenance* of a given system in respect of a fluctuating environment; the former describes the *modification* of a system in respect of a fluctuating environment. The distinction is extremely subtle. Deciding which is the situation in each case depends entirely on the frame of reference, so that there is no sense of an absolutely necessary increment of development.

Again affirming the isomorphic relationship between psycho-genesis and bio-genesis and attempting to show how the subject progresses from physically handling the world to operational techniques applied to this manipulation, that is, psychological novelty, Piaget puts forward the view that, despite the moulding of the elementary forms of such techniques by a definite physical system, they are not 'limited in advance and restricted to the physical world, since in gaining access to *the non-temporal world* [our emphasis] of possibility and of the unobservable, they completely transcend the former' (Piaget, 1972b, p. 62).[64] Here, although the notion of transcendence is brought into the explanation of the genesis of novelty, it is used hierarchically to relate the psychological to the physical world, which is again a form of logical inclusion. But more than this, an unexplained gap in the movement *from* the physical world *to* the psychological is very obvious.

Yet another attempt to cope with this problem is to be found in the last pages of *Six Psychological Studies* (pp. 154–7). Here, Piaget in a section called 'Case Study' examines the process of continuous equilibration whereby 'the subject passes progressively from an unstable to a more and more stable state of equilibrium, up to the stage of complete compensation which characterises true equilibrium'. This advance is undoubtedly to be equated with the genesis of novelty in the light of the general feature of Genetic Epistemology which is the achievement of ultimately complete equilibrium. Here, Piaget distinguishes what he calls four phases, each described as a 'strategy' and associated with which is a 'probability'. The idea is that the subject passes through these four 'strategies', each one of which is related functionally in the mathematical sense to the previous one. The thesis is exemplified with the well-known example of the manipulated ball of clay.[65] At the end of the discussion, he writes, in a passage referred to here more than once, 'Equilibration is thus a process with sequential probability which finally results in a necessity at the point where the child comprehends compensation and where equilibrium is manifested directly by the system of implication which I previously called reversibility . . . It is in this manner . . . that an extra-temporal structure can develop from a temporal process' (p. 157).

It is in *The Development of Thought,* however, that Piaget has attempted a final treatment of the genesis of novelty in the context of the emphasis on equilibration rather than equilibrium. It is principally developed around the idea of compensation, with *over*-compensation playing an important role, elsewhere described as 'dépassement', or 'convergent reconstruction with overtaking' (*Biology and Knowledge,* quoted by Rotman, 1977, p. 126).

One thing should be clarified here before proceeding. Evidence of novelty in cognitive development is not in dispute. When a subject shows conceptual extension in, for example, the ball of clay experiment (see, for example, *The Development of Thought,* p. 118), expressed in the realisation that 'long and thin' can be equated with 'short and fat', or similar cases of conservation, there is no doubt that novelty is present. Something has happened which is inherently new in the sense that it was not simply contained within the premisses of the early conceptual phase. But this is the essential problem with Piaget. If the purely logico-mathematical characterisation of intelligence is maintained, then such containment is inevitable. Newness is reduced to the simple difference between before and after the 'unpacking' of what is there all along. Even this difference, itself, lies outside the logical 'nesting' that is, for Piaget, the construction process, since the motivational drive to develop is not identifiable in the layers of the 'nest' (see *The Development of Thought,* p. 56).

The situation is very similar to the one we encountered in relation to rearrangement or consumption of sweets in Chapter 2. Newness can only arise in the context of the interaction of a system (causal) with the milieu in which its presence generates contingent relationships. In other words, it is the circumstantiality or conditions under which an event occurs which is the scene of novelty both physically and psychologically. The invariance of quantity that appears to be absolute in Piaget's presentation of the relation (in the manipulation of the ball of clay) between 'long and thin' and 'short and fat' is in fact not absolute but relative. If the ball is pressed flat and moulded into a hollow container, then the entire experience is transformed. Piaget is concerned with presenting progress in terms of the discovery of absolute conservations. Actual progress, however, concerns itself with relative conservations and also with the nature and circumstances of non-conservation. It is very often a matter of surprise even for sophisticated subjects that a plane shape of constant perimeter has a variable area and that a plane shape of constant area has a variable perimeter. What emerges is that newness in the sense of non-containment is dependent on (a function of?) the relationship between a given system demonstrating a particular causality unique to that system, which can be mapped logico-mathematically, and the milieu encountered by the system. Now, the notion of 'milieu' is not of some void or 'etheric' medium but always consists of a structure of systems of the same order each of which relates necessarily, at all times, to *all* the others taken together. The encounter of systems with their milieus involves, therefore, a multiplicity of frequently conflicting interactions in which the 'either–or' character of logico-mathematics is only a limited and final expression of this encounter. Any system must in the end absorb into its causal framework the *relations* it forms with the milieu in the sense of positive, actively sought adjustment. Piaget might call this adaptation, but his combined concept of 'groping' and unmediated transformation of action into logico-mathematical cognitive structures inverts the relationship affirmed here of an active search on the part of the subject (probing) linked with a continuous, contingent encounter with the milieu.

It is, thus, in the operation of the *mutual relations and positive adjustments* multiplied uncountable times that novel phenomena/independent causal systems get generated. This is so primarily as a result of a *generalised negation* – a general rejection of adjustment from many directions. This is why it is valid to affirm that mutual encounter *has no option* but to generate new phenomena in direct response to the contingent interaction of systems. These new phenomena enter into the general encounter situation, of course, with the same generative possibilities.

A line of thought such as this makes it clear that novelty – the emergence of new relational–phenomenal entities – derives its drive in the first instance from the contingent not the causal aspect of actuality. It is also clear that this is not random in the probabilistic sense. It is certainly not a conflationary connection between 'probabilities' and 'necessity' such as Piaget suggests. In fact, the unpredictability associated with probability is, in reality, a function of a viewpoint of the external contingent interactions of the system from *within* that system.

But most important of all, Piaget's subsuming of novelty under exclusively logico-mathematical categories means from the viewpoint affirmed here that it must cancel itself out of existence. For without freedom from the 'either–or-ness' of logico-mathematics, and the causality of the system(s) that this maps, which guarantees contingent interactions between systems in their mutually influencing milieus, there can be no generation of things as such because the indispensable things–relations connection has been reduced to things alone. For Piaget, arriving at defined phenomena, including his cognitive structures, is a convergent process ending up with rigid entities unmovable except as permutable, indivisible units. There can be no novelty in this – only the 'unpacking' of what was already packed up in the first place. Novelty demands relative not absolute invariance. It is the relative 'part' that permits the appearance of new relational–phenomenal manifestations. The exclusive absoluteness of Piaget's system puts a stopper on all possibility of newness.

Thus, while novelty is involved with the internal unfolding of systems, the only way in which it can be distinguished as an independent and separate process is through its external, non-system and contingent aspect. To make it a product of an ever more abstract 'nesting' hierarchy is to retreat farther from this understanding. The history of any invention or discovery process exemplifies this. While the constructional principles of

Watt's steam engine are logico-mathematical in character, and constitute, in the case of this engine, a map of its *causal system,* the bringing together of wood, iron, coal, oil, and so on, in relation to this system in the particular way this was done derives from the engine his predecessor Newcomen built, in its contingent interaction with the general miliieu of mechanical power and its application. The simple existence of elements of a system, in the presence of each other, must not be confused with the causal inter-connections always 'mappable' into a logico-mathematical organisation between them. Likewise, the 'encountered' systems are contingent on the original system by virtue alone of their *relationship with each other through the medium of this system.*

With all this in mind, the way Piaget approaches the question of novelty in his last theoretical treatise shows some noteworthy modifications. The emphasis of *The Development of Thought,* it has been noted, is upon equilibration rather than equilibrium. Hence, because the process of arriving at equilibrium is regarded as key, the genesis of novelty must occupy a central position. Hitherto, with the concentration on the extant manifestations of equilibrium, the dualistic split between the external and internal worlds of the subject has been fairly easy to identify. The non-terminal character of Piaget's conceptual equipment appears at first sight to provide a plausible solution for any problem arising from this dualism. In *The Development of Thought,* however, the retention of the dualism and its resolution become more difficult to handle. If Piaget had abandoned the notion of the finality of equilibrium, genuinely followed by Bertalanffy, and accepted an open-ended development for cognition, then the problem of accounting for novelty might have solved itself. But, in effect, this would have meant abandoning the logico-mathematical king-pin of the system which no temporising with the problem of genesis could possibly justify. If the growth of knowledge is to continue to be characterised exclusively by logico-mathematics, then the knowledge-forms must achieve finality for logic cannot supersede itself. Thus, however novelty is designate   must come to an end and be resolved into a *permutative activity* whereby the same knowledge-forms are repeated over and over again (the 'bag of tools' approach). This is the essence of the 'nesting' concept and is clearly shown in the formal operational stage, the logical operations of which have no other possibility than permutation.

But with the stress on equilibration in this later work characterised by the intrusion/disturbance–self-regulation–compensation cycle, Piaget is found expanding on a very un-Piagetian theme – the theme of 'more-or-less' or alternatively 'overtaking'.[66] Strictly speaking, 'more-or-less' is primarily a spatial matter and is developed mainly in connection with the seriation experiments (that is, the ordering of sticks of different lengths: see *The Development of Thought,* pp. 172ff.). It connects closely with another important notion which Piaget broaches here, namely, the 'going beyond' process. Thus:

> the essential driving forces of the cognitive development being the
> external nonbalance (from application difficulties and the effects of the
> operations on the objects) and internal nonbalance (difficulties of com-
> position) as well as the reequilibrations which this nonbalance involves,
> sooner or later the equilibration will be increasing and *constitute a
> going-beyond process as much as a stabilization* [our emphasis], thus uniting
> the constructions and the compensations within the functional cycles.
> (p. 40)

The idea put forward here of 'overshoot', combined with an alternating
notion of 'more-or-less' which involves a 'convergence' on to exactness
(you judge more or less the correct sequence of lengths and then adjust this
more and more), together produces an idea of novelty which seems
primarily dependent on non-logico-mathematical factors.

Let us return to the quite surprising theme of the first few lines above
which challenge the fundamental assumptions of the system. On the
previous two pages Piaget provides a line of argument quite in violation of
his lifelong presumptions which always regarded the achievement of
equilibrium as the essential stimulus and motor force of novelty, not its
opposite, non-balance – especially when this is external to the subject.

In the progress to what he describes as a 'better equilibrium', Piaget
writes:

> It is . . . impossible to distinguish what in these increasing equilibra-
> tions is due to compensations, that is, the equilibration as such, and
> what offers constructions proper. Constructions are indicated by new
> compositions of the extension of the field, and in principle are capable
> of proceeding from the subject's *spontaneous initiatives* [our emphasis]
> (inventions, etc.) and from chance encounters with the objects in the
> environment (discoveries, etc.). (ibid., p. 38)

He then affirms that constructions and equilibrations (both 'new') are
'bound up with each other'. So far so good, except for the curious
introduction of 'spontaneous'. But within the next few lines, Piaget writes
of the research work carried out by Inhelder, Sinclair and Bovet that 'In a
study of the relations between learning and development, these authors
showed that *the most fruitful factors in the acquisition of understanding were the
results of disturbances producing conflicting situations* . . . which once handled
in a systematic manner *involve the excesses and new constructions*' (our
emphases). He continues:

> Of special interest is the fact that a device was found to create conflicts

only on certain given levels for the structure in question. In other words, a device is not a disturber in itself, but, on the contrary, is conceived as a disturbance or is not one according to the elements that have been acquired by the structure in formation. Such facts are highly significant for an understanding of the close union of constructions and compensations. (loc. cit.)

If this thesis – the 'more-or-less' or alternating notion – is connected with that of 'overtaking' (an indispensable component of convergent reconstruction leading to ultimate equilibrium), we have what looks like a new theory of Genetic Epistemology which *rests itself primarily on the irrational increment involved in disturbance and the resultant conflict, with rationalisation (systematisation) as a derivative not a primary source of cognition.* This is particularly reinforced by the distinction of assimilation and accommodation from each other when hitherto they have been inseparably related. Assimilation is connected with extension of the field (effectively intrusions) and accommodation with adjustment to this extended field (effectively *systematisation*), the whole embodying *conflict*, notwithstanding Piaget's affirmation that the 'two orientations are bound up with [each] other in an indivisible whole' (p. 40). At first sight the roles of assimilation and accommodation do not appear to have changed at all, but this is deceptive. The roles may not have changed but their relationship has. Mutual reinforcement, if not actual interpenetration, has been replaced by confrontational antagonism. This is the source of the 'irrational gap'.

the assimilation and the accommodation constitute two poles, and not two distinct behaviours, it is clear that the new assimilation plays the construction role (extension of the scheme field, introduction of new articulations in the cycle, etc.) and the new accommodation that of compensation (new adjustments in reciprocity or inversion of the objects' unforeseen characteristics) . . . even in a sensorimotor scheme, the assimilation and accommodation, although from a certain viewpoint opposed to each other, necessarily involve each other, so that the conflict situation between the subject's action and the resistance of objects is immediately accentuated. (pp. 39–40)

Once the significance of the 'irrational increment' is admitted, moreover, it becomes acceptable to introduce the 'overshoot' notion with respect to compensation. In fact, the overall balance idea that runs throughout Piaget virtually demands it, and we have this idea referred to several times in *The Development of Thought*. A notable example occurs in the discussion of the transition from the innate situation immediately postnatal to the earliest cognitive structuration (pp. 84ff.). Elementary constructions 'consist of novel actions' (p. 89), and in the consolidated states built upon the innate schemes, 'compensations do more than satisfy momentary needs' (loc. cit.). This notion of 'doing more than', related to compensation, introduces another incremental notion, this time in association with systematisation itself. In a very subtle way Piaget has blended together in *The Development of Thought* ideas of irrationality and 'over-shoot' with logico-mathematical closure, which is entirely incompatible with them. This is no accident, for he shows himself acutely aware of the implications:

> Generally speaking, we can thus say that not only do the opposed mechanisms attract each other like opposite charges of electricity, but they also produce each other, which implies a closed cycle capable of increasing and enriching itself while conserving its cyclic form . . .This explains the fact that the constructions and compensations are insepar- able, for if the whole is to conserve the parts, and vice versa, during each modification, there must be simultaneous production and conserva- tion. (ibid., p. 41)

Does Piaget solve the problem of the genesis of novelty by this 'unity of opposites'? In a discussion relating to the stages of compensation (ibid., pp. 64ff.) he writes:

> Another behaviour will consist of integrating into the system the disturbing element arising from without. The compensation then no longer consists in cancelling the disturbance or in rejecting the new element, so that it will not intervene within the whole set already organised, but in modifying the system by 'equilibrium displacement' so that the unexpected fact is made assimilable. The description will thus be improved; the classification will be recast to co-ordinate the new category with the others; the seriation will be extended or distri- buted in two dimensions, etc. Or a causal explanation contradicted by an unexpected fact will be completed or replaced by another explana- tion which takes the new factor into consideration. In short, what was disturbing became [*sic*] a variation within a reorganised structure, thanks to the new relations which make incorporating the element possible. It is these new characteristics of the structure which ensure the compensation – here again there is definitely a form of compensation. (ibid., p. 67)

Virtually every problem that has come up in connection with the genesis of novelty is to be found here. There is confusion between element and operation; on the meaning of integration regarding assimilation and accommodation; it is unclear what the relation of 'action' is to 'things' (elements) as a source of knowledge; it is unclear what the relation is between 'elements' and 'disturbance', which is a *state* or *condition* and not an element. This is one of the most comprehensive examples yet of the conflation or 'drifting' of Piaget's thought, which has been our principal object of attention hitherto. Far from resolving the problems already revealed in the earlier writings in this respect, *The Development of Thought*'s emphasis on equilibration offers fewer possibilities of solution than ever.[67]

In the course of discussion in this chapter and the previous two, we have attempted to show how the mathematical ambivalence and ambiguity in Genetic Epistemology are reflected throughout the system. The epistemology (Chapters 5 and 6 above) appears to us to fail, beyond a descriptive level, and the genetic theory (current chapter) does not offer any explication of growth. But the questions at issue are not simply the revelation of the inconsistencies and shortcomings of the Piagetian system. The central characteristics of Piaget's thought relate to major issues in epistemology – the connections and alignment of logic, mathematics and Actuality, especially in relation to the origins and development of novel objects, events and processes. It is this alignment which is the principal concern of the remainder of this book.

8 Problems of Logic and Mathematics

Introductory

At all points in this critical analysis of the Piagetian system the central problem to emerge has been the relation of logic and mathematics to Actuality and to each other. This is the form in which we have expressed the nature of the object of epistemological study, that is, the relation of knowledge to being, involving, too, the relationship of subject to object. The problem emerging from this has been centrally important in one form or another throughout the history of Western thought.

The foregoing analysis has found Piaget 'slipping' from logic to mathematics and vice versa and from either or both of these to Actuality, in his terms of reference.[68] This always occurs without acknowledgement of the change of reference and without a change of axioms. This 'slipping' or 'wandering' or 'collapse' or (sometimes) 'conflation' is often difficult to detect because we, in our Western cultural tradition, are conditioned to accept such 'slipping' so that it has become an unconscious habit of thought. Piaget's apparent impregnability results from his combination of descriptive accuracy about the trained condition of individuals in our society blended with a seemingly sound analytical model. This has raised major obstacles to criticism from other workers in the field, and partly explains why no detailed critique has appeared of the Piagetian use of logic and mathematics or of the system as a whole.

Piaget is not unique in these respects. The history of Western thought, especially in its later phases, demonstrates the same features, that is, a difficulty in maintaining the distinction between logico-mathematics and Actuality and between logic and mathematics, so that very often one is mistaken for the other. This is not at all surprising, since the struggle to liberate abstract thought from spatio-temporal constraints in order that they may be related to each other in a predictive and calculative manner constitutes the essence of the growth of intellectual thought in general and is particularly significant in Western culture. The process can be understood from two viewpoints. The subject either 'wanders' conceptually with a blind 'groping' action with no certain criteria of form and content of wholes and their parts; or, alternatively, he explores with a 'probing' action, guided by past abstracted models (and theories) and prepared for what Popper calls 'falsification' at every stage. The confusion between these two situations is the essence of the problems of the Piagetian system, although it is found throughout contemporary epistemology. The next section looks at this problem in its historical context, and aims at providing a brief background to the wider discussion of its contemporary manifestations, essential to an all-round critique of the Piagetian system. A further problem is whether the Piagetian system is 'scientific' – a point often raised by Piagetian critics and highlighted by Piaget's own claim to have created in Genetic Epistemology a 'new science' (see especially *Insights and Illusions,* 1966). Two auxiliary and closely connected questions must be faced here: (1) Does Piaget achieve a genuine model in the accepted scientific sense? (2) Does the means he adopts to represent the system in sign form constitute a genuine symbolic system? These issues form the axis of discussion in Chapter 9 which closely follows on the argument in the present chapter.

Finally, in Chapter 10 the mechanism is explored whereby Piaget is enabled to view human mentality as dominated by logico-mathematical parameters and to equate, through conflation, the social and individual zones of existence. This last is particularly important since it is the combination of the exclusively logico-mathematical interpretation of human personality together with this conflation which is the direct and immediate cause of a feature of personal life unique to the contemporary world – the 'infantilisation' of the individual which renders him or her convinced of his or her helplessness, dependence on the social structure and hence loss of all identity separate from it. The whole of the foregoing critical analysis of Piagetian thought can be regarded from this viewpoint as a case study in the manufacture and application of the tools for this infantilisation process in the more sophisticated societies of the modern world and now increasingly in other areas as well.

Sources of the Problem of Conflation

A central distinguishing feature of Western thought from at least the sixteenth century is the preoccupation with establishing a satisfactory link between 'appearance' and 'reality'. The inevitable outcome of this search is the unprecedented development of abstract thought, separated from Actuality and experience, yet seeking to reflect it exactly, especially the development of logico-mathematics related to the world itself.

Certain central concepts have emerged in the foregoing analysis of Piagetian thought. Most prominent among these have been the notions of 'collapse' or 'conflation' or 'non-terminality'. Before looking at possible explanations as to why Western European culture in general shows such characteristics, it is advisable to clarify these notions and certain others connecting the logico-mathematical world and the world of Actuality.

Although not unique to human beings, the activity of *exploration* of the circumstances under which one lives is a major feature of human life. All human beings naturally and from birth onwards *probe* the milieu in a constant search going beyond mere survival. Unless there is some mental block and/or brain damage, such exploration always yields identifiable objects/events/processes and this discovery is invariably dependent upon recognising the wholeness of phenomena together with a grasp of the articulation of their structure. There is a universal oscillatory relationship between these two aspects which is easily recognisable in the notion of the whole-and-its-parts. It is the essence of the logico-mathematical process – the combination of *abstraction* from defined phenomena and *projection* from the external and internal relations they possess – that this *oscillation* is mapped into the *alternation* that is a fundamental feature of logic and mathematics resulting from its 'either–or-ness'.

What has emerged from the study of Piaget's thought is some idea of how these concepts can be distorted and misused. We have seen how the subject, instead of exploring his milieu by probing, is said by Piaget to 'grope' – a blind, dependent activity. Such blind groping naturally results from the 'non-terminality' (that is, indefiniteness) of reference between the logico-mathematical and the Actual, the whole situation being manifested in the *collapse* of logico-mathematics into Actuality or the *conflation* of logico-mathematics and Actuality into each other. The effect is a theory which 'wanders' between the internal and external worlds of the subject without recognition of the distinction between them. Piaget, as we said above, is by no means unique in this respect. This is a deep-seated and longstanding feature of Western thought in its struggle to achieve the separation between the zones of Actuality and of logico-mathematics so that they may be clearly related to each other. The roots of this struggle lie at least as far back as classical Greece. But Greek thought is not the only constituent in this process. The other ingredient derives from the even older notion of universal creation specifically manifested in the Judaic and then the Christian tradition.

Very little is known of pre-classical Greek logical and mathematical thought. But the nature of Pythagorean thinking makes it arguable that it very probably had characteristics in common with oriental philosophy, notably Zen and Tao. This sect rooted itself in a number mysticism which had not yet achieved the status of an abstracted and projected map of Actuality such as logic and mathematics were later to become. The deepest origins of number concepts lie in physiological and other rhythms, expressed in dance, rituals, and so on. Pythagorean number mysticism, however, has a special quality which derives from the recognition of pattern and regularity, later to become the basis of what was seen as inherent law. It is the acceptance of this inherence of law in number regularity that is a particular manifestation of the classical Greek world outlook. When the Pythagoreans established that the sum of a certain number of odd numbers is equal to a square number their method was inductive but the implication of inherent law strongly implied the co-existence of a deductive proof.

By Plato's time a distinction had been established between *logistica* and *arithmetica*, logistica as calculation conceived of as relations between numbers (regarded as a multitude of things or of 'pure' units) and arithmetica as the theoretical study of such numbers in themselves and especially different kinds of numbers (species, *eidos,* that is, forms). The most 'advanced' concept of number is reached by Plato in terms of a plurality of 'pure' (non-extended) units, or monads. The *Parmenides* reveals the main thrust of Plato's position, for while his thought is still tied to physical involvement it is already struggling for a non-extended interpretation. The doctrine of 'eidos' as applied to both quantity and quality is a 'non-object-ive' one. The ongoing discussion in the *Parmenides* ranges from the distinction between 'inside' and 'outside', 'big' and 'small', and comparable contrasts, to the proof that if there is '*one*' there is '*number*'. The problem of the relation of the whole to its parts arises again and again in Plato's writings. The line of descent from the Pythagorean stress on the inherence of law in number is clear. With Plato, the behaviour of number has become a sphere of existence in its own right.

In opposition to Platonic thought the Aristotelian outlook rejects the separation of number from things (for example, *Metaphysics,* Vol. II, p. 205), and although it affirms the extraction of logic and mathematics from things and phenomena there is a contant reference back of this extraction to the Actuality from which it is derived. Aristotelian thought is unqualifiedly linear and 'object-ifying', and in contrast to the Platonic 'eidos', which sees the being of things as co-existent with their structure, understands being as a summative result of the assembly of its parts. Hence, Aristotle's emphasis on the classification of things as the key to world-knowledge.

The theme of dependence, upon 'things', which is Aristotle's mark, makes any extraction, quantitative or qualitative, always referable back to phenomena. This provides a foundation for logic and the classificatory basis of natural science but at the same time opens the door to the conflation between idea and phenomenon which is so misleading. Plato's approach, on the other hand, leads directly towards a distinction between the extracted zone and the zone of Actuality which invites a view of the latter based on self-reference and paradox in which the whole is *not* equal to the sum of the parts nor is it necessarily in the same dimension. Particularly in his acceptance of paradox, Plato contributes to the foundations of later mathematical thinking and goes beyond the constraints of Greek thought in contrast to Zeno whose 'paradoxes' are a very Greek rejection of the notion as unacceptable within the linear restrictions of this tradition.

If one major source of Western thought and culture lies in the Greek tradition of axiomatic deductive and inductive thought, the other major contributory strand is to be found in the extremely ancient Middle Eastern tradition of cosmic consciousness. The Judaic manifestation of this cosmic consciousness is particularly significant for Western thought since it directly yields the Christian derivation. The significant notion here is of an unseen, universal God, responsible for all creation but with a special and personal relationship with the Hebrews. A deity such as this, which is universal but unseen and yet permeates everything material, is entirely self-referential, and it is this self-reference which is at the root of the Judaic and subsequent Christian tradition. The nature of the Law in Judaism is such that the spirit must always be distinguished from ritualistic mani-festations of the spirit at the same time as infusing them. Recurrent crises in Judaism relate to the separation of spirit and letter in the observance of the Law. Jehovah emerges (from about 800 BC onwards) as a paradoxical personal–cosmic deity, demanding what appears to be almost trivial re-cognition in rituals which nevertheless, properly seen, reaffirm Jehovah's cosmic role in the creation and maintenance of the universe.

It is possible to speculate from this as to the source of the power of the derived Christian message. On the one hand, the constant struggle to maintain the integrality of the Law and its ritual – the personal life of the believer and the law of the universe – yields a history of repeated 'redemp-tions'; on the other hand, the recurrence of this pattern means that it is cyclical and does not fit in with the Messianic element which sees the relationship between man and God as moving towards a perfectionist climax (the conflict is fundamental between the repetitive and the pro-gressive). Thus, Christian thought is, on the one hand, rooted in the conflict between the spirit of the Law and its letter, and on the other, grasps the need to move 'outside' the Hebrew ethos to the Gentile world in order to resolve this particular conflict. The deity is now both fully universal and yet present in each and every human being.

How does this particular religious development contribute to Western thought? It is in the Judaic-Christian tradition that the preoccupation is to be found with resolving the relation between the interactions of the cosmos and the phenomenal manifestations of these interactions. The notion of spirit, of immanence, of immediacy coming from this tradition is to be contrasted with the preoccupation with matter, abstraction and causality deriving from the Greek intellectual heritage. The 'balance' between material spatio-temporality and the immeasurable, contingent interaction between God and the universe, both fundamental to Western thought after the sixteenth century, is traceable to these sources.

This century is important for a deeper reason than the reintegration which it is normally credited with of Greek and Judaeo-Christian thought. A new and essentially European factor is added to these. This factor, which is revealed by a cultural upheaval, including economic and social transformations is a new manifestation of thought independent of authority. The self-generation of mind fully comes into its own. If the Judaic-Christian and Greek strands provided the basis for the complementary structural and phenomenal aspects of the European world-outlook, then Europe itself provided this element of *self-reference*. It is this that enabled thought to be set free for autonomous discovery. In the Copernican system the pre-ordained fixity of the geocentric cosmos is replaced by a 'free-floating', self-operating frame of reference, a self-reference which releases energy directed against entrenched thought, Greek as well as Judaic-Christian. Descartes strips everything back to the basis of active thought and reconstitutes the cosmos from this starting-point. It is not surprising that his mathematics embodies the new freedom – a moveable system of co-ordinates the point of reference of which is the curve to be described and not some absolute framework, and which is based upon an algebraic symbolism at last liberated from physical constraints. Pascal creates the basis of probability theory – the mathematics of the 'uncontrolled' – but expresses through the *Pensées* the new isolation of man in a universe grown vast which has, at the same time, lost the personal touch of God. There is a close connection between chance and the alienation of Pascal's thought.

Such is the character of this new 'arena'. Neither the Judaic-Christian nor the Greek tradition alone could have provided it since both in their different ways are externally referable, the first in the cosmic-personal deity and the second in the determinism and preformation inherent (especially) in logic. The self-generation of thought in conjunction with the two ancient strands of Western thought create what might be called the necessary and sufficient conditions for the modern 'lift-off'. The character of philosophical presumptions is altered and, notwithstanding their differences, later philosophical figures have in common the search for an adequate self-referential basis for epistemology, psychology and experience of the world. By the late eighteenth century even Euclidean presuppositions are under fire. Goethe evidences the disturbance of the Genesis concept, later to be embodied in Darwinism. The nineteenth century sees the explosion of problems in the foundations of mathematics culminating (so far) in the work of Frege, Dedekind, Cantor, Russell, Hilbert, Brouwer and Gödel. Above all, physical science is fraught with problems from the end of the nineteenth century onwards and the heart of the entire new movement contains the possibility of a new understanding of the relations of thought to Actuality and experience.

A Presentation of Actuality

In the course of what follows a considerable number of terms will be used the conceptual meaning of which will be made clear as we go along. The first among these is 'Actuality'. This is sometimes referred to as 'reality' or 'fact' and it has been fashionable recently to regard this notion as inadmissible within the terms of reference of any rigorous epistemological system (unless, that is, one is influenced by some variety of materialism or existentialism). Despite his structuralist leanings in later life, Piaget has never rejected 'fact' as the basis of thought and we, too, affirm that by 'Actuality' we mean an externality to the subject which, even if it is treated as a projection of the perceptive self in Berkelian fashion, nevertheless exists as one of the polarities of a subject-object relationship. Before discussing the foundations of logico-mathematics and its companion, the structure of science, our basic position on 'Actuality' needs to be made clear; and because of the severe limitations of space this must occur without elaborate argument.

In the ongoing debate around the priority of the 'objective' or 'subjective' it is affirmed that, in the circumstances of existence as experience finds them, the point of departure must be the recognition of the separate identity of things, however these are found. Major considerations in distinguishing different interpretations of this separateness are: how awareness of this evolves in the individual; and how it is affected by time, place and circumstances.

But this is not the principal concern at the moment. All we are talking about as a base position is the common possession by mankind (and not only by mankind) of direct, immediate and unmediated appreciation of 'self' and 'the world' as *different* from each other. We regard this as taking first place and the notion of *similarity* as derivative. The appreciation of difference is experienced, in its minimal form, as the distinctness and separateness of 'I' and 'not-I'. The primordial sense of separateness has been a persistent central concern in the evolution of human thought. It is to be found, at least in an incipient form, in every culture in the world. It is intended here to take as the basis of experience and thought the *interaction* in its totality between 'I' and 'not-I', including 'It' and 'not-It'.[69] This is a point of departure only and no reductionism or non-terminality is implied.

Following this, we can say that, whatever other differences may be recognised in 'the world', it possesses the basic feature of *quantisation*, that is, the dual presence of *separateness* and *interrelationship,* in which the independence characterising the former, and manifested in what we call Quanta, derives from the latter. The term General Quantisation is used to express this. General Quantisation shows itself in both intelligent and affective life as the distinction between 'I' and 'not-I'. The recognition of the relation between 'It' and 'not-It' within the 'not-I' part of the 'world' is one expression of this intelligence and affectivity. There are implications here regarding the relation and evaluation of discreteness and continuity – the mathematical 'mapping' of separateness and interrelationship respectively. At the moment it only needs to be affirmed that *both* the reality *and* the relativity of *both* discreteness *and* continuity are 'mapped' aspects of the world. What is continuous in one frame of reference is discrete in another and vice versa.

It may be asked whether the separateness–interrelationship of things is always the case for all things at all times? Clearly this is not so in the light of coming into being and disappearance, the birth and death of things. We, too, are subject to this process of growth and decline, but are uniquely distinguishable by our self-awareness. This self-awareness is a function of the interaction between, on the one hand, the growing separation–interrelation of the self and the world – the emergence of 'I–not-I' – and on the other, a grasp of this same feature in the world itself – the 'It–not-It' of the world.

What then happens to the holistic relations 'I'–'not-I', 'It'–'not-It' in the development of phenomena? At the beginning of the life-span of all things (including ourselves), there is neither a discernible 'I'–'not-I' nor 'It'–'not-It' distinction.[70] All is given together, immeasureable and non-spatio temporal. But as being unfolds, the thrust of General Quantisation generates such a distinction and produces an 'interactive separation' in accordance with the conditions under which any particular object/event/process shows itself. The holistic relationship 'I' and 'not-I' and its derived companion 'It' and 'not-It' emerge. The interaction between them is both a 'milieu-to-phenomenon' and a 'phenomonon-to-milieu' one. However, the relationship between these is not symmetrical. For no growth process is reversible and, at the very least, the increase of entropy ensures non-symmetry. In all cases of discernible entities (objects/events/processes), this intimate holistic relationship replaces the unspecification of such entities at their origin.

The unfolding of the life-span of any object/event/process involves its quantised, separated identity which is reflexively manifested as it matures in its interactive connections with the milieu from which it was originally indistinguishable. The physical contact with the world of the subject consists of an uncountable number of interactions each of which involves giver, receiver and the connection between them. This relationship is both ongoing and altogether in a complete integrality. We have adopted the word 'holisms' to describe such interactive connections. These must be seen as open-ended but at the same time distinguishable with specifiable interconnections between phenomena and milieu. Such interconnections are always receptive to modification and are never reducible to logical, mathematical, or verbal forms.

We use 'holisms' in the plural to convey the multiplicty of every one of these special relations, which involve the phenomenon, wholly and/or partly (including self-conscious subjects), the milieu to which it relates and the link between them, and also the susceptibility to transformation which is dependent on the *non-additive* character of the whole-and-parts structure of all Quanta.[71] If the whole-and-parts structure were additive, then further 'additions' would result simply in enlargement or displacement but not transformation. If the whole-and-parts structure *is not* additive, any 'addition' alters all relationships and hence leads to transformative change. (The latter is also possible by simple alteration, without addition.) The word 'holism' always refers to a Quantum in its milieu. A physical object and its (physical) surroundings possesses a multitude of holistic connections. Intelligent and emotional activity constantly involve holisms in respect to the chosen milieu. Also one has unconscious and involuntary holisms operating continuously between one's self and one's body.

There is a tension in holisms between the differences of 'I' and 'It' (and 'not-I' and 'not-It') and their complementarity. In the case of intelligent and affective life, holisms involve the whole subject and not just the rational–cognitive aspect. In human holisms many factors are interwoven – spatio-temporal, aesthetic, affective, basic physiological (unconscious), learned and genetic. One can regard them as the most fundamental form in which a mentally oriented organism like Man relates in a living manner to his environment.

Holisms provide a working basis for identifying 'Actuality', particularly in its relation to logic and mathematics. The discernible differentiability between phenomena (objects/events/processes) is a central feature of a Quantised world so the concepts of 'causality' and 'contingency' play a key role in identifying Quanta. 'Causality' is used to indicate the internal structural consistency of objects/events/processes. It is characterised by a certain 'closure' in the sense that unrestricted movement from one point to another within the structure is allowed, provided this movement does not go outside the system. 'Contingency' is used to indicate the interactions between phenomena of the same order, generated by the presence of such phenomena in their own milieu. These interactions show characteristics of the *unforeseen* from the viewpoint of the causal system of the phenomenon. Neither causality nor contingency should be confused with different orders of phenomena such as wood-cell, molecule, atom, sub-atom, and so on, all of which are 'contained' within, for example, a table, just as this object itself is contained within the room, building, city, planet, galaxy, and so on. Causality and contingency are not 'things' but (in the same way as holisms) are an intimate expression of things and their relations. Granting this, however, the distinction between the phenomenon and its relations must still be maintained, otherwise there is a conflation between the circumstances of existence and existence itself. Any such conflation makes it impossible to distinguish different orders of phenomena from each other.

Causality and contingency can be regarded as another way of presenting General Quantisation, for Quanta derive their existence from the intimate interaction of causality and contingency as a universal characteristic. On the other hand, causality and contingency have no meaning except in and through Quanta. In effect, the indissoluble link between causality and contingency expresses that open-ended-ness of Quanta-in-their-milieus which the concept of 'holisms' embodies.

The causal and contingent way of understanding General Quantisation is not a substitute for the whole-and-parts interpretations of it, however. The latter is indispensable for an understanding of Actuality which is the foundation in experience for both logic and mathematics. This under-standing can be presented as follows. If all objects/events/processes, whether mental or physical, are only fully expressed as holisms, and these holisms include indeterminate factor(s) deriving from their connections elsewhere, then the whole-and-parts structure of these phenomena must always be non-additive. And when any phenomenon is broken up, the parts in themselves lose the significance they possessed *in situ*. Their 'partness' depends exclusively on their relations with other parts in the whole, in other words, their orientation. This orientation not only refers to the internal circumstances of the whole but also to the whole in relation to its milieu. These internal and external relations are realisable only through the whole phenomenon in all its aspects. Hence, the 'whole-ness' and the 'part-ness' possess a difference of 'dimensionality' in relation to each other which is entirely *paradoxical*. (If the parts add up to the whole they shouldn't; if the parts do not add up to the whole, they should.) One can express this relationship as 'the presence but unseenness of one dimen-sion of being within another'. Although the word paradox is used here, there is in experience no sense of incompatibility. The 'given-ness' of whole-and-parts, far from evincing any notion of contradictoriness, *requires* the 'complementarity' of the paradox.

This manner of viewing Actuality is directly related to the concepts of 'appearance' and 'reality'. The setting free of the premises of thought and knowledge from the dictates of external and unquestioned authority after the sixteenth and seventeenth centuries generated this central question of modern philosophy which, although present before, was not self-referential. Appearance and reality correspond respectively to Quanta, or wholes as they present themselves on the one hand (appearance), and the structure of Quanta related to their parts on the other (reality). Appearance and reality are not primarily conditions of Actuality but of the subject's experience of it. Reality is produced by an analytical process and is usually (and wrongly) identified with a 'level' of existence underlying and sub-stantiating that of appearance and wrongly conceived of as involving parts of the whole. The persistent emphasis on appearance as illusion and reality as true (notwithstanding that there is always another echelon of 'reality' to be uncovered) has generated the modern world's certainty that logic and mathematics especially embody this 'truth', and the world from which they are drawn is made meaningful only in their terms.

Contrary to this view, Actuality is presented here as the fully rounded being of things and thought; that while logic and mathematics are essential in arriving at the structural possibilities of the world, they are 'mappings' of it not replicas of it, and as such cannot yield the creative transformations which only the multi-dimensionality embodied in the quantised, whole-and-parts universe can show. The assumption that logico-mathematics is the true essence of being, indistinguishable from it, which is to be found exceptionally expressed in Piaget's system and thought, is revealed generally in the way in which logic and mathematics have been extracted from Actuality. By examining the mode of this extraction, the relation of logic and mathematics to Actuality may be seen without ambiguity.

Concepts attached to Actuality

It is the constant ambiguity of being simultaneously actor and audience in a culture that has become self-referential that results in the powerful drive to distinguish rigidly between subject and object and hence to transform all holisms into 'object-wholes' – hard, solid, alienated objects characterised by isolation and force in their interactions. Only in Western society is the subject-object division seen as an exclusive basis for relationships so that all holisms degenerate into an almost pure subject–object exchange dominated by the problem of communication.

Despite this cultural emphasis, however, the natural fluidity of holisms survives this rigid division between subject and object. As a result, there is a sharp conflict between the formal structure of thought and the living holistic flow between subject and milieu, resulting in a constant pre-occupation with the problem of what is appearance and what is reality. Such a preoccupation is manifested in an ever-pressing need to treat explanation as reality, where the latter is thought to lie 'behind' appearance. The relation between appearance and reality normally emerges as a hierarchy of classification with the most inclusive categories being regarded as absolute and the less inclusive as relative. The former is identified with reality and the latter with appearance.

The usual supposition going with this, that 'every*thing* is relative' but that somewhere 'outside' such relative phenomena an absolute frame of reference exists, has its roots a long way back and precedes the upheaval of the seventeenth century and afterwards. Despite the emergence at that time of self-reference as the implicit basis of thought, what might be called a 'fish-tank' notion of the relation of phenomena to their frame of reference, very characteristic of pre-Renaissance thinking, reappears in a new form. This view treats all things (the fish) as purely relative but simultaneously referable to an absolute framework external to themselves (the tank). This applies to such notions as matter, mass, energy, or simply co-ordinates in space which, once chosen, acquire an absoluteness of their own. Logic and mathematics have in a similar way acquired the status of absolute frames of reference in their own right.

How can the self-referential basis of modern science be squared with this 'fish-tank' view of absolute and relative? The answer depends on recognising that the *self*-authority and *self*-generative nature of post-Renaissance Western thought, which sought to be free of unquestioned external authority, was essentially subversive and in order to become transformed into an establishment in its own right this self-reference must be 'split' between a new frame of reference which was deemed unchallengeable, for example, Newton's Laws of Motion, on the one hand, and the objects/events/processes referred to it on the other. This must occur in a way which preserved the freedom of self-reference, or the *raison d'être* of the new establishment would disappear. It had to happen in terms of separating the absolute from the relative, blurring the distinction between the existence and the circumstances of existence of phenomena, and by making ambiguous where the ultimate point of reference lay, thus allowing the reintroduction of arbitrary authority.[72] For example, the confusion in priority between curve and co-ordinate axes in analytical geometry still exists at least at the teaching stage. It appears here that curves and equations are ultimately referable externally to co-ordinate axes, yet the latter are essentially relative. The curve and its equation are thus self-referential in the sense that they are given in themselves. It is the axes which are moveable. The point illustrates how originally self-generated scientific/mathematical objects may be turned, at least partially, into an external frame of reference against which all subsequent similar phenomena within their ambit are judged. Even with Relativity, which seemingly redresses the absoluteness of Newtonian physics, it can be argued that it is the absoluteness of each inertial *frame* that is asserted and not its relativity!

A similar confusion occurs with the notion of 'level' and phenomenon, the latter being analysable into the 'whole' object and its 'parts'. The meanings attached to these concepts have acquired an 'overlap' such that they appear simultaneously the same and yet different. Apart from its everyday connotation, 'level' is now a common scientific term (see M. Bunge, 'Levels: a semantic preliminary', *Review of Metaphysics,* vol. 13, 1960, pp. 396–406) deriving from the urge of Western science to divide and subdivide the world into smaller and smaller separate fragments in the search for an ever more elusive ultimate reality. Molecules, atoms, sub-atomic particles are typically referred to as representing different 'levels' which are pictured as hierarchical layers rather like a Neapolitan ice-cream. Thus, an entirely acceptable notion of the *circumstances* under which phenomenalisation occurs is conflated with the equally valid but distinct notion of *phenomena themselves* whose wholeness delineates their existence. Any modification of this wholeness necessarily raises the question of new circumstances or conditions of phenomenalisation – a new level. We affirm that to distinguish between a whole-and-its-parts on the one hand, and the circumstances making possible the coming into being and continued existence of this whole – its level matrix – on the other, is essential to preserve the self-referential principles underlying modern thought including scientific thought.

Departure from, or the blurring of, this distinction has created a continually recurring authoritarianism in science and epistemology. Yet it is this very distinction deriving from self-reference which is the greatest contribution of the West to human culture as a whole. And this is so because it comes closest of all forms of thought to *mapping* Actuality. The notion of level matrices and the wholes-and-their-parts born out of levels is the closest representation of the extant Actuality. Without a clear distinction between them it is impossible to relate phenomena to their origins. From this distinction it can be seen that the notion of absolute properly belongs to the phenomenon and not to the circumstances of its being whereas the notion of relative is meaningfully applied only to the latter.

The 'object' view of levels deriving from the ambiguity between levels and wholes-and-their-parts gives rise to its own problems. The search for an ever more 'ultimate' truth through fragmentation, related to the notion of authority *external* to phenomena as they are found, generates a scientific impasse since it involves an infinite regress of explanation. Hence technological expansion comes to be equated with scientific maturation. The hierarchical form in which this mode of the search for explanation shows itself is also problematical for no criteria can be established for deciding whether, for example, 'bigger' and 'smaller' should refer to 'higher' and 'lower' or 'lower' and 'higher'. The simultaneous *co-existence* and *co-terminousness* of different phenomena within the same object/event/process is difficult to reconcile with their hierarchical, 'layer-cake' interpretation. By co-existence and co-terminousness we understand that in the case of any such phenomenon, for example, a table: (*a*) every 'level' of its existence, and every possible whole-and-parts into which it may be divided, exist together, but: (*b*) such different levels and wholes-and-parts are subject to distinct spatio-temporal parameters. From this viewpoint, for example, it is not just inappropriate but meaningless to use the spatio-temporal parameters of 'everyday life' in the region of sub-atomic particles.

The notions of levels and of wholes-and-their-parts are, of course, not restricted to physical phenomena. Every object/event/process has its own level matrix, including all social phenomena. Moreover, as far as mental activity is concerned, transformative change is connected with a continuous 'breach' of level relationships and (totally?) free dismemberment and reconstruction of the world's Quanta as given. This additional dimension of being reflects the levels and Quanta of the external world and also manifests in itself its own internal levels-wholes-and-parts character unconstrained by the limits associated with non-mental objects/events/processes.

Generally, Actuality is given in the first place for the subject in terms of the manner in which he or she selects wholes-and-their-parts and only secondarily in terms of the way in which these present themselves.[73] Western society is distinguished by the solid-object-ness of the selective process by which the wholes-and-parts of Actuality are appreciated. This has given rise to the accompanying and increasingly significant problem of whether the parts do or do not add up to the whole. One of the ways in which Plato presents the issue (*Parmenides* 131b and c) is in this form: if several men are covered by a sail, is a particular man covered by the whole sail or only by a portion of it?

The question may be put differently in relation to an object with what appear to be indisputable parts, for example, a table. First, the parts may be thought to be 'molecules' or 'atoms' which are conceived of as the units of which the table is constructed. That this is not so is immediately clear on two counts:

(a)   'Molecules' and 'atoms' are models resulting from analytical fragmentation and refer in the first instance to materials and only secondarily to what is constructed out of such materials. Different types of 'molecules' cannot therefore be made the *necessary* basis for tables since there is a wide range of possible materials a table may be made from and a wide range of possible articles that can be made from a particular material. They may, however, be regarded as contributory. In other words, 'molecules' are beyond or at the margin of what may be described as the *limits of relevance* of the parts–whole relationship defining 'tableness'. Thus, molecules (still less atoms) cannot determinately be made the 'parts' of tables.

(b)   Assuming the 'viewpoint' of a 'molecule' or 'atom' inside a table, the table itself becomes undetectable. This is so since the circumstantiality (level matrix) of the 'molecule' whole-and-parts is distinct from the circumstantiality of the table (the laws ensuring the coherence of the molecule are not the same as those securing the coherence of the table – even if there is some common ground, or overlap, to these laws). The molecule-whole is thus incompatible with the table-whole, the two representing distinct dimensionalities.

Hence, the *parts* of the table are referable only to the *level* of the table itself. They are not even distinguishable as 'wholes' themselves as long as they are functioning as parts. 'Tableness' can exist only at table-level. It is this that makes the object (the table) self-referential in the last analysis, and any reference outside itself it not an affirmation of *its* existence but only an indication of what it is *not*.

The self-referential nature of the 'entitiness' of any object/event/process may hence be expressed as existence referred to the *frontier* of what exists understood/seen as a whole – a seemingly paradoxical notion but which tallies with the proposal made before that the absolute always lies in the phenomenon itself, not in its frame of reference. There is, of course, a certain indeterminacy attaching to such a frontier. This indeterminacy is constantly manifesting itself in daily experience when we find difficulty in establishing where one thing 'ends' and another 'begins'. (There is even a neurological–optical mechanism which establishes edges by an alternate visual–neural response on *both sides* of a sharp colour or line contrast.) But such indeterminacy is never 'resolved' by reverting to 'molecules' or 'atoms' because the very act of attempting this takes the observer outside the zone of the original object to be determined.

This all helps us to understand the 'whole' side of the phenomenon; but what of the 'parts'? Formerly it was said that the 'parts', in so far as they are so considered, or function, are refereable to the 'whole' (table) of which they are a part. This means, in effect, that 'partness' is only realisable through its expression in and through the whole. But the latter should not be conceived of as some sort of 'container'. The connection can be expressed thus: the whole emerges from the particular, or unique, orientation of each part to every other part and the 'wholeness' derives from these orientations which, because they are not simply quantitative, cannot be summed. The 'wholeness' makes the 'partness' possible and vice versa; they are distinct yet indissoluble. The table example is again helpful. If one considers its structure (and there is a virtually infinite range of possibilities here) then it is not simply the well-turned condition of legs, struts, top, and so on, which constitutes the 'partness' of the object. It is also the non-extended as well as the spatio-temporal connections established between all these factors if 'table' is to include aesthetic, historical, economic, even religious features. As a socially produced and used object this is perfectly possible and normally unavoidable. The problem, then, of the summation of parts into wholes is not a question of summing mathematically conceived 'molecules' or even legs and struts and their connections into tables but a question of the parts of the table in their unique relationships with, and orientations to, each other and this is clearly not a simple summation procedure. This is even more obvious when the 'whole' is not tied to spatio-temporal constraints such as a musical composition, or better still a musical performance.

Although it is to some extent anticipating the discussion below, a comment on the relation of level matrices, and the manifestation of these in wholes-and-their-parts as mapped into the logico-mathematical notion of necessary and sufficient conditions, is appropriate now. The latter may be understood as a *projection* into the logico-mathematical zone of the level circumstances, or matrices, whereby any whole-and-its-parts can come into existence. The term 'projection' is used quite deliberately here and refers to what is *relational* in Actuality as distinct from what is phenomenal. The 'necessary' side of this (projection) corresponds to the general level circumstances which permit a given *range* of phenomena to exist and are, so to speak, the 'negative' *sine qua non* of their existence. 'Sufficient' corresponds to those level circumstances which determine a *particular case* of such phenomena. These latter circumstances can be regarded as 'positive', that is, what brings this and no other phenomenon into being. Thus level matrices constitute an inclusive expression of the generative circumstances of objects/events/processes in Actuality, mirrored in the necessary and sufficient conditions of logic and mathematics. The connections between the parts uniquely oriented to each other, and to the whole, maps into these logical forms. The phrase 'wholes-and-their-parts' has deliberately been written in a hyphenated form so that both the separation and indissolubility of the concepts contained is conveyed as far as possible in the language used.

If summation is inadmissible regarding the relation between wholes and parts, how can we describe this relation in order to convey the stability and (relative) permanence of objects/events/processes in actual experience? The notion has been adopted of 'oscillation', interpreted as an immediate, paradoxical fluctuation between the polarities of 'partness' and 'wholeness' of phenomena. This notion is paradoxical in the sense that parts and wholes are always given together but at the same time are essentially distinguishable. Clearly, table-parts and wholes taken together terminate in tables; yet the partness and wholeness remain distinct from each other. Thus, 'oscillation' should not be identified with physical oscillatory motion. It should be thought of as a generalised hyper-spatio-temporal (and hence immediate) built-in feature of the quantised world of Actuality. Pulsation, that is, the general rhythmic aspect of the world, shown for example in the rhythm of the seasons, or physical oscillation as with a pendulum or radio signal, is a particular, spatio-temporally detectable manifestation of this general oscillation. Oscillation can be regarded as a 'point of convergence' of the causalities and contingencies of all the relationships involved in the existence of Quanta. It is the manner in which objects/events/processes manifest relative stability. It expresses the unity-in-diversity of things and is a guarantee of their 'thing-ness'. Oscillation thus unites 'appearance' and 'reality', wholes-and-their-parts with their level matrices and makes concrete sense of the concept of the absolute within the relative. It also underlies all holistic relations every subject/ phenomenon has with the milieu.

The immediacy, or co-existence and co-terminousness, of oscillation in its general form points directly towards a notion which is of great importance in grasping Actuality. This notion is expressed here by the term 'complex' which is used to summarise the idea referred to earlier as 'present but unseen' in relation to what were described as the different 'dimensions' of being. The word 'complex' has been chosen in order to utilise the mathematical meaning of the relationship between dimensions, represented by perpendicular co-ordinates, one of which corresponds to (ordinary) real numbers and the other to the complex element of the completed complex numbers.[74]

Mathematical complexness can be regarded as a mapping of the oscillating nature of Actuality which derives from the dimensional distinction between wholes and their parts. The term 'complex' is regarded as the most succinct way of expressing the non-summability yet inseparability of the part-whole relationship. Thus, it is always the case that from the point of view of the parts the whole must be postulated as present, but cannot be 'seen'; from the viewpoint of the whole the parts must be postulated even though the whole is 'lost' in and through their identification. This definition of 'complexness' encompasses whole*ness* and part*ness* and fully expresses the relationship between level matrices and the wholes-and-their-parts which manifest them. The nature of level matrices – that is, their non-phenomenal character – makes the concept of 'complexness' inappropriate and inapplicable to their relationships with each other.

The 'complexness' of Actuality, expressing its multi-dimensionality, may be regarded as the origin of constantly observed and experienced paradox. But although the notion of paradox is reserved for Actuality itself, we cannot completely escape the problems which arise through the verbal and logico-mathematical mapping of Actuality. Both the notions of 'complexness' and 'paradox' are intended to come as close as possible in word-concepts to the direct experience of Actuality lying beyond language. However, both these terms still carry with them a suggestion of *incompatibility* which only fully emerges with the law of non-contradiction in logic and mathematics. This suggestion of incompatibility derives from the necessity in both these zones to reject the multi-dimensionality of Actuality because it involves an indeterminacy (due to the non-summability of wholes-and-parts) which is inadmissible in logic and mathematics. The latter must function *as if* the world they are extracted from is uni- or zero-dimensional. It follows that great difficulties arise from the conflation of Actuality and logico-mathematics, difficulties still further enhanced by the frequent identification of 'paradox' and 'contradiction' (see the discussion of Russell's views below, pages 264–70. It is only in the context of this conflation (which even the word 'paradox' itself does not fully escape) that *incompatibility* becomes a central issue. Living Actuality involves no such incompatibility since co-existence and co-terminousness are norms of being.

Some illustrations of the meaning of oscillatory 'complexness' may be helpful at this point. For example, in ordinary two- and three-dimensional experience the 'present but unseen' feature of complexness is there. Every point on a straight line is *potentially* capable of having a perpendicular drawn through it. Third dimensions must always be inferred because they cannot be 'seen' directly (even perspective is a form of inference). 'Higher' dimensions (for example, duration) are obviously 'unseen' in a similar way. Every piece of music demonstrates the same principle, as every note relates to its 'present position and to the unseen' whole at the same time. In this case the whole-and-its-parts complex relation is time-ordered, but this makes no difference. The examples can be multiplied without limit. Complexness always calls for all aspects of the complex composite whole to be 'given together' and all to be present (unseen) *in* each of the others.

It is natural in the light of all this to ask what role the Gestalt view plays. This view, repeatedly revived despite repeated rejections, is very relevant since it affirms a belief in the non-summability of wholes and their parts. Basically, a theory of perception, the Gestalt view, while approaching the problem, tends to confuse the direct immediacy of experience with the linear form knowledge of it must take. While linearisation is unavoidable in the mapping process, it is the old story of conflation which must be guarded against. In a sense Gestalt would fare better if it did not attempt to reduce the whole-and-parts relation to such a linear relationship. Gestaltism does not really break free of the 'linearising conflations' to be found in the concepts of being, not-being and becoming, for example. Dating back to Plato, at least, these concepts have been widely employed, particularly by Hegelians, Marxists and Existentialists, as fundamental tools of their world-systems. Such notions have not been particularly helpful, however, because the parallel linear collapse of Actuality into basic logical forms which this conflation always involves restricts any capacity to express the multi-dimensional and multi-level nature of Actuality. The resulting systems, expecially all forms of Marxism, have generated distortions particularly of the view of man, himself, and man in society. Piaget's outlook in these respects places him firmly within this category of system-building.

The Attributive Extraction from Actuality

No human being experiences Actuality in the form of 'pure' holisms. The basic subject–object separation combined with the particular form of holisms produced in any society results in a special map of Actuality generally acceptable to that society. In our own culture, the expression of holisms predominantly as 'objects' has influenced the type of logico-mathematical model we construct and made it predominate in our world-outlook. The primary source of the *need* for making the model undoubtedly lies in the subject's initial separation from the milieu and the mode in which this occurs. The bridging of this gap demands an expression which fits it, and the 'object-ivised' form of holisms emerging in Western culture has resulted in the logic and the mathematics familiar to us today. The process has shown a reciprocity between the subject-object separation on the one hand and the model(s) on the other with an increasing perfection of the latter reflecting back on the former and intensifying it. Ever more powerful drives have been generated leading towards new forms of logico-mathematical experience. A similar reciprocity has marked the relation between the overall intensification of logico-mathematical modelling (of subject–object relations) and holistic relations with the milieu. What were formerly free-flow holisms between environment and subject have now become 'problems of communication' and, in the extreme, totally subordinate to mechanical connections enshrined in computer language.

The word 'mapping' has already been used. Here its application to the forming of a model has been very deliberate because it results in a 'map' which has a relationship to Actuality closely resembling the relationship between a geographical map and the terrain it represents. Each has a distinct *zone* of existence in which the signs of one correspond to phenomena in the other. Graphical representation plays a similar role in relation to the actual situations it mirrors. But as with the geographical map, the curves, lines, or points must never be identified with *actual* wages or populations, for example, but must be kept quite distinct in their separate zones or it will be impossible to set up a correspondence and a calculative and/or predictive relationship between them will not be achievable.

The basis of logical and mathematical models is logical *classes* and mathematical *sets* respectively, both of which are *constructed* out of the *attributes formed by extraction* from *phenomena* in Actuality seen as *wholes-and-parts*. The major force for the extraction of attributes lies in the *object*-ifying drive, particulary emphatic in our culture but not unique to it, which demands rigorous definition. From this comes the increasing preoccupation with mathematical and logical foundations and an expanding emphasis on both logical and mathematical models especially in the last hundred years.

In order to create the attributive basis for the logico-mathematical zones, two mechanisms are required. First, undifferentiated wholes are *abstracted* and *represented* by a *sign* (word or logical sign), *symbol* (general and particular number), or *diagram* (for example, geometrical, graphical, chart) and this representation is treated as *manipulable* in its own right (not always validly). The identification of wholes, with abstraction in view, is intimately connected with the process of *fragmentation* involving the dissociation of given wholes into a number of sharply differentiated units, deemed to be the 'parts' but which have, in effect, lost their 'partness' and acquired their own independent 'wholeness'. This (analytical) process precedes the abstraction. Secondly, and entirely dependent on the first procedure, the original part-whole relations disappear in the fragmentation process and appropriate relationships have to be constructed in the fresh situation of abstractedness. The term *projection* has been reserved for this construction. This is a modified use of the mathematical term and retains the notion of invariance of relations under some form of transformation, as when a circle is projected into an ellipse or vice versa. Abstraction and projection are to be distinguished – the first derives from objects/events/processes and the second from the relations between things. They constitute the mappings of the fluid or moving relations of Actuality all of which are undetectable apart from the phenomena they connect. They are, moreover, represented by different signs/symbols in logic and mathematics. The logical and mathematical mapping of the working, or motion, of things (projection and abstraction) can be expressed in a different way. The universal external–internal relations, or movement, of things which we have described as General Quantisation can be said to map in the zones of logic and mathematics, into inference and strict implication.

As careful a distinction must be maintained between abstraction and projection as between Actuality and the logico-mathematical mapping of Actuality, for it is on the basis of this distinction-within-unity that the attribute itself is formed. The attributive mapping of Actuality thus contains both the 'thing-ness' and the 'relationality' of Actuality and this corresponds to the *propositional/predicative* manifestation (in for example, 'John is a teacher') of the attribute, which itself derives from the things as such (that is, objects/events/processes) and their properties.[75] There is, in short, a close parallelism between *attributivity, predicativity and propositionality*. The first and the third of these belong to logic and mathematics and their differences with each other will emerge presently. The second is really restricted to language/grammar, although there is a certain looseness in its use and application in logical situations. The interrelation of language and logic is an important extension of the present discussion but cannot be given space here (see note 109 of the present volume).

It can be seen, then, that the mapping of things and their relations/

interconnections into abstraction and projection lays the foundation for the identification of the attribute which is an essential first stage in the logico–mathematical process. Consider the statement 'John is a teacher'. Treated attributively, 'John' expresses the phenomenality of the actual situation and 'is a teacher' expresses its relationality. The distinction between the attribute and the Actuality it derives from is clear here. In Actuality 'John' and 'teacherhood' are not *necessarily* conjoined for John is not necessarily a teacher. To obtain the connection in the form of an attribute they must be regarded as inseparable, as being necessarily linked. This necessity is, of course, ultimately referable to the axioms employed for attribute-extraction – but discussion of this is reserved for a treatment of what is described as Phase 2 of the logico–mathematical process below. In short, abstraction and projection, and hence an attribute, can only occur as a result of an assumed provisional (relative) *inseparability* in the world external to logic and mathematics. This inseparability is absolute for the time being, for that which has no relationship cannot be identified in the phenomenal (quantised) sense, and 'loose relationships' without terminals or moorings are equally inconceivable since they also must remain unmanifest and therefore undetectable.

It may occur to some that problems arise in the case of purely numerical statements, for example, 'there is one triangle', 'the triangle has three sides'. As far as the derivation of the attribute in numerical statements is concerned, the same reasoning applies as with logic. A statement like 'the triangle has three sides' or just 'there are three sides' is clearly predicative. What distinguishes it from logic is its *computativity* or calculability. Such computativity is not to be identified with quantisation as such. While Quanta are certainly phenomenal they are also relational. Quantitative statements such as the last example isolate the *countable/measurable* aspect of Quanta as the designated attribute as distinct from statements such as 'the triangle is red', which isolate qualitative aspects.

What then is meant by the notion of quantitative attribute?[76] First, it lacks the specificity of the qualitative attribute because it is universally derivable. *All* Quanta have a countable aspect. Secondly, and because of this countability, it maps the *wholeness* of Quanta exclusively. It expresses first and foremost the separateness of things in and through their *discreteness*. Their interconnection is, in practice, a construction of continuity out of this discreteness. The example of the mathematical definition of a limit (a concept primarily to do with continuity) illustrates the point. This definition is strictly in terms of discreteness and from it comes the ambiguity between discreteness and continuity in this very definition.[77] Mathematical elements are unaffected by manipulation, which is a basic condition of mathematical operations. This is probably the most general manifestation of the exclusive extraction from wholeness which typifies the quantitative attribute. This undividied unitariness, shown most completely in the system of whole numbers, is the foundation of computatitivity. It is neither possible nor relevant in the case of qualitative attributivity. It is the hallmark of the quantitative attribute that its extraction occurs on the basis of an assumed undivided wholeness in Actuality, and the mathematical objects that emerge as a mapping of this are treated initially as indivisible. Subsequent divisibility is a matter of definition and entities emerging from this are initially regarded as 'indivisible'. Thus, when the quantitative attribute is extracted (by abstraction and projection), this means that the *quantised-ness* is 'taken out of' the separate identity of things, without consideration of their construction or content. Their internal–external relations, moreover, are also rigorously subordinated to quantised mapping. It is this that makes computation and countability possible.

In the light of these points, if quantity is to be identified with the basic quantisedness of wholes, what is meant by qualitative attributivity? Since there is undeniable truth in Descartes' implication that quantity is what is left after all quality has been exhausted, the latter must refer to the 'non-quantisedness' of wholes. Alternatively, this latter can be described as their interconnected 'flow' and is therefore to do with that which is *not* the whole, or the 'not-thingness' of things. Quantisedness provides the possibility of counting and can always be ultimately expressed by mathematical elements that are manipulable in their own right. But 'redness' or 'roundness', while possessing their own integrity, nevertheless relate *outwards* to what is not them. We run up against this all the time in the marginal decisions that have to be made in identifying qualities. The distinction between the exclusive-whole-condition of 'quantisedness' (which number never departs from), which is universally derivable, and the fluidity of qualitative derivation lies in the fact that the latter must always be extracted from particular phenomena. There is no ultimate common basis for 'roundness' and 'redness' as there is for 'two-ness', 'three-ness', '*n*-ness'.

One final point: although logic clearly maps out of the qualitative aspects of the world, it, itself, possesses an 'either–or' character. But this 'either–or' character should not be confused with the specific quantitative attributivity that lies at the root of mathematics. Logic, in other words, cannot be identified with mathematics although mathematical statements can be given a logical form. The development in the modern era of symbolic logic has tended to obscure these points. But the test we can always apply is whether the symbol/sign system is manipulable in its own right or is it meaningful only by reference to the sources of the system from which the map comes? If the former, it is genuinely mathematical; if the latter, it belongs to logic. (See ★ below p. 282)

The Nature and Formation of Logical Classes and Mathematical Sets

The first question to pose is: what is a logical class? This needs prior consideration of the derivation of a collection. Both the collection (Phase 1) and the logical class (Phase 2) are formed around particular aspects of the attribute (see Figure 8.1). A collection of animals is obtained from all living beings by comparison of the attributes of living organisms as a whole with the attributes of animals, bearing in mind the mechanism of attribute formation discussed earlier. This collection cannot itself be a logical class. If we examine the proposition 'this dog is an animal', while the predicative structure of the proposition places it on the 'logic side' of the Actuality–logic division, the statement involves the (non-logical) objects 'dog' and 'animal' in and through the cultural and linguistic meaning attached to these terms. These concepts already satisfy the abstraction-projection formula which marks the transition from one zone to the other. Nevertheless, there is still, at the collection phase, a phenomenalistic emphasis in the enunciation of the attribute. In the logical class relating to the collection which is identified attributively by '. . . is an animal', it is this phenomenalistic aspect which recedes. The way in which this is revealed is by a change of emphasis from the existence of animals to the *conditions* of being an animal, that is, 'animal-ness'. For example, '. . . has a circulatory system' or '. . . has four legs' could be taken as conditions of 'animal-ness'. These statements also have a certain phenomenalistic aspect except that the emphasis is on the conditionality of the attribute and not on phenomenality itself. This is why the term (in this case) 'animal-ness' is a highly suitable expression of the *condition* of the original attribute '. . . is an animal'.

The logical class, therefore, does not consist of a countable/identifiable number of elements, but provides the conditional basis of 'animal-ness' for the countability/identifiability of the collection. It should be noted that the phenomenalistic aspect has not entirely disappeared in the logical class. In 'animal-ness', 'animal' is still detectable. But it is also the case that the conditional aspect is not entirely absent from the collection as the predicative form of its enunciation shows.[78] This, in fact, is a specific demonstration of the 'co-existence' of collection and class. But it is of major importance that the two phases (Phase 1 = collections; Phase 2 = classes and mathematical sets – see Figure 8.1) are not confused or conflated. If they are (as is normally the case) then there is no bar to falling into the error of treating Actuality itself as the same as logic and vice versa. Actuality is expressed as much through contingency and paradox as through causality and consistency. It is, therefore, not subsumable under the Law of Non-Contradiction. The co-existing zones of logic and mathematics are referred to below as Phase 1 (for collections) and Phase 2 (for classes and sets) as a means of distinguishing them.

Schematic summary of the broad relations of Actuality with logic and mathematics.

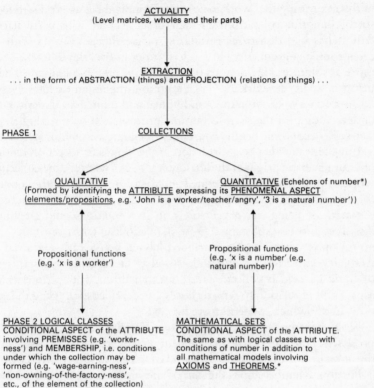

ACTUALITY
(Level matrices, wholes and their parts)

EXTRACTION
. . . in the form of ABSTRACTION (things) and PROJECTION (relations of things) . . .

PHASE 1   COLLECTIONS

QUALITATIVE   QUANTITATIVE (Echelons of number*)
(Formed by identifying the ATTRIBUTE expressing its PHENOMENAL ASPECT
(elements/propositions, e.g. 'John is a worker/teacher/angry', '3 is a natural number'))

Propositional functions   Propositional functions
(e.g. 'x is a worker')   (e.g. 'x is a number' (e.g.
                                         natural number))

PHASE 2 LOGICAL CLASSES   MATHEMATICAL SETS
CONDITIONAL ASPECT of the ATTRIBUTE   CONDITIONAL ASPECT of the ATTRIBUTE.
involving PREMISSES (e.g. 'worker-   The same as with logical classes but with
ness') and MEMBERSHIP, i.e. conditions   conditions of number in addition to
under which the collection may be   all mathematical models involving
formed (e.g. 'wage-earning-ness',   AXIOMS and THEOREMS.*
'non-owning-of-the-factory-ness',
etc., of the element of the collection)

Figure 8.1

* See diagram of mathematical 'pathway', Figure 8.3 below.

Key to Figures 8.1, 8.4, 8.5, 9.2 and 10.1
   ⟶ **Does not mean mechanical derivation. Does mean predominant directional movement which does not exclude mutual interaction.**
   ←‖→ **Indicates a combination of 'in parallel' and mutual interaction' resulting from this parallelism,**
   ---→ **Indicates 'is the predominant source of '. (This is so for cognition but not so for mentality as a whole, including the affective.)**
   ←--→ **As above but with an added element of mutual interaction/penetration.**
All our diagrams are intended to be descriptive and not analytical.

Considerable confusion can, in fact, arise if the attributive extract of things is either explicitly or implicitly identified with the things them-selves, or alternatively the conflation is the 'other way' and attributes are made equivalent to logical class conditions. If this identification occurs then logic is destroyed as an abstraction-projection from Actuality and 'collapses' into it. What emerges is a universal distortion, in which neither logic nor Actuality is discernible with certainty. Take the concept 'working class' and its normal identification with a collection of individual people, treating them as totally identifiable with this description, instead of distinguishing the 'worker-ness' of the individuals as expressed in their socio-economic roles from all their other aspects. This particular conflation has had disastrous results in socio-political analyses with quite catastrophic consequences in modern times in the establishment of elites more absolute and tryrannous than any in the past. No individual human being is totally 'a worker' – such a notion implies an exclusively socio-economic view of the human individual and ultimately undermines the understanding of the socio-economic process itself by rejecting all other *non*-socio-economic factors constantly operating within this sphere.

But there can also be a distortion in the 'opposite' direction unless the phenomenalistic origin of the attribute '. . . is a worker', the collection of workers thus attributively defined and the identification of the conditions for the attribute, are all separately kept in sight. Such a distortion reduces the state of being a worker solely to its conditions, and attributivity dissolves into an insubstantial 'mist' of relationism with conditions having no meaning whatever. The attribute, having been clearly extracted from Actuality, must be carefully understood as 'facing both ways'. It is a tool of logic by which collections are formed through its phenomenalistic aspect and in relation to which classes are identified expressing the conditions under which collections are formed.

Now, it is impossible for either a collection or a class to exist without the presence of the other. So every element of a collection has a class aspect and the *membership* of the class is the class aspect of every element of the collection. Membership is the *state* of an element considered from its class aspect. Whilst collection and class must never be identified, this view of membership (and member, provided that this is taken as non-individuated) guarantees them simultaneous co-existence. The problem arises because it is so difficult to relate the 'extended' to the 'non-extended' aspects of these notions. A collection has an extended aspect unlike a class which is predominantly non-extended. The following are possible conditions of *membership* of the logical class related to the collection attributively defined as '. . . is a worker': ★

'x is a worker'	(True or false?)
'x is sackable'	(True or false?)
'x gets up at 7 a.m.'	(True or false?)
'x invests in unit trusts'	(True or false?)
'x does the pools each week'	(True or false?)

★ This treatment is not intended to reduce formal logic to empirical statements but presents particular examples of *sources* of the former.

'*x* belongs to a trade union'   (True or false?)
x is etc.   (True or false?)

A problem here is the virtually unlimited number of conditions which may be asserted for the conditions of the attribute. The solution of this problem lies in ordering these functions such that one is taken as a general propositional function (premiss) and the rest as dependent or derived propositional functions (the relation between these is paralleled by an equivalent relation in mathematics between axioms and the terms of proof of any theorems). It is as if the above list of propositional functions were ordered such that '*x* is a worker' (premiss) is followed by '(because) *x* is sackable'; followed by '(because) . . .', and so on. It may be seen how difficult this would be if, for example, '*x* invests in unit trusts' were taken as the first derived propositional function but not if certain others were chosen. A purely logical case can be made for *any* order, but suitable ordering allows the conditions to be found which are *relevant* to the original premiss(es) or axiom(s). The object of the ordering is to identify those conditions which are minimal (necessary and sufficient?) to establishing the membership of the class of any case of '*x*'. In effect, this is a decision mechanism. For every one of these minimally necessary conditions for the particular logical class (each expressed in a propositional functional form as above), the question 'true or false?' must be put. The answer to this question identifies whether '*x*', the actual individual in real life, collected according to the attribute ' . . . is a worker', possesses membership of the class exemplifying 'worker-ness'. We need to clear up a possible terminological confusion. In the foregoing each statement has been described as either a general propositional function or a derived propositional function. On the other hand, the term propositional function is used below to indicate a 'connective' between Phases 1 and 2. These two uses need to be reconciled; but before attempting this, it would be best to examine what exactly this 'connective' notion means.

' . . . is a worker' is, of course, a grammatical predicate. But in logical terminology, this word has a wider meaning. For example, the predicate ' . . . is a real number' when supplemented by a place-holder '*x*' becomes a propositional function, that is, '*x* is a real number'.[79] Although a propositional function is conventionally seen as (almost) indistinguishable from a class, it is important to make a distinction, however subtle this may be. Considering the propositional function '*x* is red', this differs from a collection of red things (Phase 1) as well as from the 'red-ness' of all 'red things' (Phase 2) and may be seen to represent something like an 'alternating link' between Phases 1 and 2.

The distinction between propositions and propositional functions may be summarised as follows. The statement 'the triangle is red' is fully attributive and identifies completely an element of a collection which might be 'all the red things in this room' or 'all the red shapes in the world'. It is also, in fact, an actual proposition, distinct from a propositional function, which nevertheless from one viewpoint comes close to it. The distinction is clear, however: propositions (for example, 'John/Fred/ Brenda is a worker') are Phase 1 phenomena as distinct from propositional functions, since propositions are absolutely specific and propositional functions which they satisfy are general (indeterminate).

Are propositional functions to be equated with classes then? Because '*x* is a worker', if treated as a premiss, delineates the 'arena' in which the conditions can be assessed, one can say that the propositional function comes close to identifying the class. This, of course, is not so with what we have called the derived propositional functions. But for all of these, both general and derived functions (all of which constitute the alternative presentation of Phase 2 from an 'aggregate' of conditions), the subject is indeterminate with respect to the predicate. There is, however, at least one *concrete proposition* that can be substituted for the function in every case. It is in this sense that *all* the propositional functions, general and derived, constitute a collective connection between Phase 2 and Phase 1, that is, the collections of elements each of which corresponds to a concrete specific proposition.

We can see Phase 1 and collections in a somewhat different light through this approach. It is clear that any collection such as the one being con- sidered based on the attribute ' . . . is a worker' can be paralleled by other collections related to this, like ' . . . is exploited' or ' . . . is paid in wages'. For every derived propositional function there is such a parallel collection as much as for the general propositional function: see Figure 8.2.

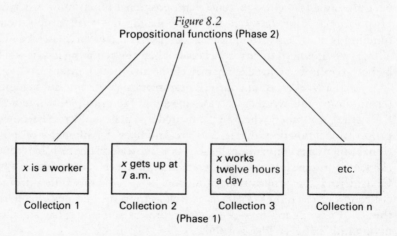

Figure 8.2
Propositional functions (Phase 2)

| x is a worker | x gets up at 7 a.m. | x works twelve hours a day | etc. |
| Collection 1 | Collection 2 | Collection 3 | Collection n |

(Phase 1)

Among these collections, some will coincide and some will only overlap, according to the *premiss(es)* in operation *and the general condition defining the class* (in the given case, '*x* is a worker' and 'worker-ness' respectively), as shown in Figure 8.3. What we have here is the Phase 1 parallel to the *ordered* propositional functions of Phase 2. That is to say, the *strict implicative connections* among the derived propositional functions and the relation of these functions to the general propositional function (premiss) reflect the *coincidence of distinct collections* at Phase 1. This coincidence, together with the strict implication going with it, is similar to what are called *sufficient conditions*. It is also clear how the chosen premiss(es) and strict implicative ordering limits the argument or proof process by identifying this coincidence of associated collections at Phase 1. These points need to be kept in mind during the discussion below of the Russell 'paradox' and its proposed resolution and also in the consideration of Gödel's Incompleteness Theorem.

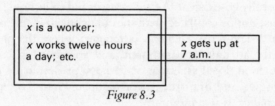

Figure 8.3

Propositional functions can thus be understood as 'flowing between' collections and classes, Phases 1 and 2, and constitute the embodiment of the *alternating 'co-existence'* of collections and classes (or sets) which is an essential way of 'binding-up' the logical zone without conflating Phases 1 and 2.

So far the formation of logical classes on the basis of the conditionality of the attributes extracted from Actuality has been the centre of attention. Sets and classes are often treated as if there were no distinction between them. In the context of what has been said already the nature of a mathematical set is easily clarified. Let a collection, C, consist of all the positive integers less than 5, i.e. $C = \{1, 2, 3, 4\}$. Just as a distinction has been drawn between a class and the collection associated with it a similar distinction must be drawn between a set and a collection. Thus, in the above collection a set associated with it may be written:

$$S = \{x/x \ \varepsilon \ Z+, \ x < 5\}.$$

It might be argued in opposition to this distinction that computation invariably occurs with numbers and that such a distinction is meaningless since the numbers and their attributes are given together. However, the set given before is not the only one relatable to the given collection. The set,

$$S^1 = \{x/x^4 - 10x^3 + 35x^2 - 50x + 24 = 0, \ x \ \varepsilon \ R\},$$

also relates to the collection, $C = \{1, 2, 3, 4\}$, since the solutions to the equation are $x = 1, 2, 3, 4$. Hence an indefinite number of sets correspond with the collection $\{1, 2, 3, 4\}$, each consisting of a different 'ensemble' of conditions relating to these numbers. It is not possible even to deduce a particular set from a given collection simply by the latter's presentation. Thus it is clear that set and collection must be distinguished.[80]

Hence the set *cannot* consist of the *number-'objects'* 1, 2, 3, 4, but of the *positive-integral-less-than-5-ness* of the numbers 1, 2, 3, 4. This is what constitutes the membership of the set and this does not refer to the numbers in themselves. Considered in this latter way, they are the elements of the collection corresponding to the set *S*.

The situation is clarified by referring to the membership of, for example, a club. Such membership is normally based upon a number of rules. Any individual, without reference to his distinguishability as an individual, satisfying the rules, is a member of the club. As in the case of classes, there is no priority or hierarchy between collections and sets. They are reciprocally co-existent. As with classes and collections, 'membership' of sets must not be conflated with the containment of 'elements' within a collection.[81] The term 'element' is retained where the phenomenalistic aspect of the attribute is paramount, and 'membership' (and 'member') where the conditional aspect or ' . . . ness' predominates characterising the fully logical and/or mathematical nature of Phase 2 where any form of 'phenomenality' is at a minimum.

'Membership' has been described as principally to do with expressing the conditions of the attribute, that is, a Phase 2 formulation of it. 'Elements', on the other hand, also refer to the attribute but emphasise the phenomenalistic aspect of it. In an assembled collection of children 'wearing yellow socks', the attribute ' . . . is wearing yellow socks' has two faces: (*a*) *wearing yellow socks* (collection) where individual children are identifiable; (*b*) *wearing-yellow-sock-ness* (class) which summarises various conditions like '*x* wears socks'. With reference to the question of what is usually called 'class (or set) inclusion', it is clear that this notion can only refer to collections.[82] Member*ship* (Phase 2) of classes (or sets) can be seen as 'fading into' inclusion as a sort of 'limit' since membership involves *participation* (that is, members 'participate') in the class or set just as elements can be said to *belong* to collections and sub-collections are *included* in collections. The relationship is perhaps clarified by reference again to the role of the propositional function in alternating between Phases 1 and 2.

It must again be stressed, in distinguishing Phase 1 and Phase 2, that they are co-existent and that, although they cannot be identified, they are nevertheless indispensable to each other. Collections are not 'lying about' waiting to be formed into classes or sets. The essence of their distinctness from each other lies in the 'closer proximity' of Phase 1 to Actuality – a relationship not to be construed hierarchically. This will be important in considering number when it will be seen that one-to-one correspondence is a mathematical state and in no sense a physical activity. Phase 1 might thus be said to be 'quasi-extended' whereas Phase 2 is virtually non-extended. There is not an absolute exclusion of phenomenality from Phase 2 nor is there an equivalent exclusion of conditionality from Phase 1. Either of these exclusions would isolate logic and mathematics totally from Actuality. The distinction is decisive in differentiating Phases 1 and 2 while maintaining their interconnection. It is a distinction which takes precedence over that between classes and sets which relates primarily to the distinction between the qualitative basis of the logical attribute and the quantitative basis of the mathematical attribute. This last refers membership (of sets) to computability which is the distinguishing characteristic of mathematical collections; the former refers membership (of classes) to a qualitative identity distinguishing the logical collection. To confuse Phases 1 and 2 by importing spatio-temporal parameters into the non-extended zones of mathematics and logic commits a major act of conflation.

Has the subject–object differentiation, characterising reflective thought, disappeared in Phase 2 since this phase is principally marked by non-extension? The survival of a degree of phenomenality in the 'thing-ness' of this phase suggests that this is not so, but there is a high degree of 'movement' between the different conditional presentations of attributes which is not so evident in Phase 1 and is very circumscribed in the level-whole-and-parts relationships of Actuality. This 'movement' has to be seen in the overall context of the 'either–or' state of inference, mathematical or logical. Thus, there is a high degree of fluidity between subject and object in Phase 2 and a dwindling of alienation (impenetrability to communication) perhaps almost to zero. Provided that the logico-mathematical condition, in its Phase 2 form, is not equated with the totality of human mentality; and provided that the affective-aesthetic aspects of mind are allowed to intermingle with logico–mathematical Phase 2, then the immense power of mind to grasp the universe can be released, appearance and reality become flexibly interchangeable and that which is understood as absolute can be appreciated also as the absolute within the relative.

A Characterisation of Logic

A brief summary at this point might be useful. Actuality, governed by General Quantisation, can be identified as a multiplicity of wholes-and-their-parts manifesting specific level matrices. The phenomenality, or 'entity-ness', of the world derives from these wholes on the one hand, and the internal and external relationships of phenomena derive from the conditions or circumstances of existence generated through level matrices. These are respectively the sources of the logico-mathematical extraction from Actuality; abstraction relates to phenomenality and projection to internal–external relationships. Abstraction and projection each provide the foundation of the attribute expressed in the predicative form '*x* is *y*' where '*x*' refers to the phenomenon-abstraction and '*y*' refers to the relations-projections. It is this process of passing from Actuality to logico-mathematics which is marked by the formation of logico-mathematical collections (Phase 1).

The notion of 'mapping' has been used to describe the link between logico-mathematics and Actuality and it is assumed that nothing occurring in Actuality is without its mapped 'reflection' in logico-mathematics. General Quantisation, being the most general level matrix of existence in the known cosmos, maps into the generality of inference in logico-mathematics. General Quantisation affirms the universal possibility of the appearance of Quanta. Similarly, as the mapping of this, inference affirms the universal possibility in logico-mathematics of the appearance of implicative/computational connections. On this basis answers to certain problems of mapping can be approached.

In Actuality it is difficult to identify frontiers of things because of the complex, non-additivity of the whole-and-its-parts. This problem is mapped into the problem of defining the limit distinguishing one collection from all others. The fact that no collection belongs to itself is related to this and is further considered below. This can, perhaps, be made clearer by an example. It is easy enough to appreciate a collection being formed of concrete objects/persons through an attribute (for example, 'children wearing yellow socks', 'triangles that are red'). It is not so easy to see this applied to a given whole-and-its-parts (for example, a table or chair). It will be recalled that the discussion of the 'part-ness' of parts is referable solely to the whole in terms of their unique orientation to each other and that dissociation of these parts involves the disappearance of the original whole, and hence the 'part-ness' of the parts, which assume a 'whole-ness' in their own right. Now, if the extractive process is applied to such objects and an attribute is sought in the manner described, then in the case, say, of a table, the 'partness', relative to the 'wholeness', emerges 'logico-mathematically' as the *elements* and the *collection*. Once in the logico-mathematical zone we are not concerned with the unique orientation of the parts but only with the mapping of this into the common and equivalent characteristics of *belonging* as an element to a *collection* of elements attributively identified, in this case, as '*x* (the legs/top/etc.) is *y* (part of the whole table)'. It should be noted that what comes out of this analysis is that the phenomenality of any thing is only realisable in the context of its internal–external relations with everything else, or, that the *whole* is only *fully discernible* in the context of *its being part of another whole*. Alternatively this can be expressed as the notion that the existence of any object/event/process involves the 'not-object/event/process' which has a determining, or at least a limiting relationship to it.

If such a mapping occurs at Phase 1, can any equivalent mapping be detected at Phase 2? It has been affirmed that Phase 2 constitutes the fully logical and fully mathematical spheres of classes and sets respectively and that these are to do with the conditional aspect of the attribute and not its phenomenal aspect (Phase 1). In short, Phase 2 identifies the conditions under which Phase 1 may be set up. Thus, if 'children wearing yellow socks' is attributively set up as a collection, then the Phase 2 or *class* associated with this collection may be described as defined by the *condition* of 'children-wearing-yellow-sock-ness'. As we have noted this is as close to being a 'non-extended' statement as any comparable verbal statement can get.

The question still stands as to whether the phenomenality of the world and its internal–external relations are to be discovered in any mapped form whatever in Phase 2. In the phrase just cited, if it is compared with the previous Phase 1 form of the statement, the detectable differences are the presence of hyphens and the addition of ' . . . ness'. But these differences are very significant. First, the hyphens indicate a merging of the attribute and that which is identified by the attribute (that is, the predicate with the subject). Secondly, the ' . . . ness' indicates that one is not dealing with phenomenality, even in a logically mapped form, as is the case with Phase 1 but with a 'state' which is what the word 'conditions' means. But there is still an ongoing *selective* operation. It is this selectivity which is related to the *premiss* (axioms in mathematics) by which the Phase 1 collection is itself attributively formed. When we attempt to list the features of Phase 2 the first thing we note is that they cannot be meaningfully considered separately from Phase 1. The condition(s) of the attribute sets out what might be called the *rules of membership* by virtue of which the elements of the collection belong to that collection. Membership clearly has no meaning separate from members. It is, however, different from actual members. The abstract entity (member) emerging from the rules of a club is not equatable with an actual individual belonging to that club. The ' . . . ness' feature, again, is meaningless apart from what it is applied to. Its significance lies in its (concealed?) laying down of the 'limits' beyond which it is not possible in the example to identify children wearing yellow socks. First, only children are allowed (what is a child?); secondly, wearing socks assumes that this is on the feet not the arms; thirdly, it must be possible for the socks to be yellow, that is, suitable dyes, no allergies, and so on. These and many others are all decisions which are 'buried' in the conditions and involve the assumptions of the premiss or premisses.

In sum, then, we can say that the premisses which permit the conditions by which the collection and its elements are put together such that these elements participate, by their membership in the logical class associated with the collection, represent in Phase 2 a mapping in the fullest logical form of the phenomenality or wholeness of Actuality. Similarly, the *participative* membership of the class maps at Phase 2 the internal–external relationships, or partness, of Actuality. There is, of course, no hierarchical relation between the mappings of Phases 1 and 2. Also, logic and mathematics do not involve exactly the same process since the former rests on a qualitative and the latter on a quantitative attribute.

On the basis, then, of the necessary reflection of every aspect of Actuality in a mapped form in logico-mathematics, it can be said that

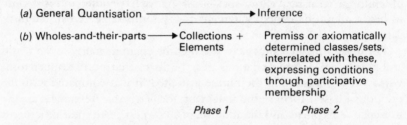

Clarification is needed on the reflection in logico-mathematics of causality and contingency in Actuality. Causality and contingency have been discussed as the active expressions in Actuality of the evolution, maintenance and demise of Quanta. Causality aligns with the internal, structurally consistent *systems* of wholes-and-their-parts and expresses the *internal activity* of these. In the case of, say, a chair, the simplest Newtonian analysis assumes that the internal 'forces' are active in character. 'Internality' and 'system' do not imply that what is being referred to are only *objects* in the directly apprehended way given by the senses. Also implied are *events* which involve a systematic temporal organisation of objects, and *processes* which involve the development, unfolding and evolution of the embryonic into the mature. Objects can be resolved into either events or processes and vice versa.

Interaction of the phenomenon with the milieu generates contingency which, from the viewpoint of the causal system, is 'unexpected'. Causality and contingency should not be equated with different level matrices. 'Molecules' are not the potentially contingent milieu of macro-objects, for they are the manifestation of a different level matrix. Causality and contingency must be referable to the same level. Contingency (as such) is generated by the encounter of objects/events/processes with other manifestations of the same level matrix, that is, manifestations of the same order.

Considering the logico-mathematical reflection of these aspects of Actuality we can be guided as to what to look for. In brief, we need to identify the 'equivalent' or mirror of the interaction between causality and contingency. We understand causality to be active in terms of a definitive system. The internal motion, that is, activity of a car-engine/dynamo/

organism/this particular essay, must all conform to certain basic organisational principles deviation from which involves the ending of that specific
activity. The logico-mathematical reflection of this is indicated as an
axiomatically or premiss-guided, aprioristic deduction – an 'unfolding'
process (on the basis of implication) where the former (deduction) maps
the systematic relationships of the whole-and-its-parts concerned and the
latter (unfolding) maps the directionality of the causal links of the
system.[83] The causal system in its encounter with the milieu experiences
unexpectedness and must show itself flexible enough to absorb or
eliminate that which is encountered by modifying its systematic format.
This interaction is contingency. The logico-mathematical extraction from
contingency is a non-aprioristic induction – an 'enfolding' process (again
on the basis of implication), where the former (induction) maps the
non-systematic (that is, not in the given system) aspect of the whole-and-
its-parts and the latter (enfolding) maps the contingent absorption of the
system.

Causality and contingency can thus be aligned with deduction and
induction respectively. The interaction between causality and contingency which guarantees the coherence of the whole-and-its-parts is
mapped in the strict implicative relations of specific proof processes in the
zones of logic and mathematics. These processes are special cases of
general inference and provide a structural logico-mathematical mapping
of the relevant Quantum in Actuality which a given proof process refers
to. Logical proof thus lies in the zone of such a mapping and its loose
application to Actuality (that is, 'proving fact x to be the case') is a
conflationary distortion (see Chapter 9). The deductive connections of
such a proof-structure set the bounds to the limits of application of the
premisses/axioms.

A simple case reveals the relationship of deduction and induction
clearly. The proposition expressed as 'if the kettle is placed on a heat source
then the water will boil' is a deductively presented statement of an event
that can as well be expressed inductively as 'n kettles have been heated and
water has boiled; the $(n + 1)$th kettle will also boil on this basis and this will
continue if $n \longrightarrow$ infinity'. The mistake frequently made in a case like this
is to identify this last inductive form of the statement with Actuality. This
is yet another form of 'wandering'. Both deduction and induction are
logico-mathematical mappings of the event and the sign that these are
mappings is that neither reveals the creative novelty involved in transformation into another type of event. To map creative novelty requires
that the axiomatic assumptions of the implicative structure, whether
treated deductively or inductively, should *undergo a discontinuous break*.
Water boils at sea level at approximately 100°C. At higher altitudes this
boiling point is lower. The deductive-inductive relationship of the event is
modified by this change in conditionality which is shown in the *sharp*

alteration of the premises or axioms. This is the only way transformative novelty in Actuality can be recorded in either logic or mathematics and, as we have seen, it is one of the principal conflationary points in Piaget's system.

We can now consider the problem of transformation in Actuality itself. Quanta have been presented from two aspects: the level-whole-and-parts, which might be described as the static aspect, and the causality-contingency or dynamic aspect. Complexness or dimensional variation is involved in the relation between the whole-and-its-parts. Now, the origins of any Quantum are inseparable from its growth and trans-formation (metamorphosis). Despite this, one has to try to distinguish these origins in order to grasp the nature of the level circumstances giving birth to the Quantum. It is here that the problem of 'inter-level' relations appears. Clearly a living cell, for example, is not a simple composite of macro-molecules. Not only does the 'cell-ness' derive from the special relations within the cell that the macro-molecules do not possess separately, but also the origins of the cell, notwithstanding the enorm-ously expanded technical knowledge now associated with DNA and RNA, *occur in accordance with the laws of behaviour of cells and not macro-molecules*. Problems of the origin of life as a major 'level-jump' are obviously involved in this. Both in this general case and in every particular case of fertilisation and organic growth, the *distinctiveness* of the organic level matrices from those of the chemical constituents or organisms is well known – but the nature of this distinctiveness is still difficult to identify. The view here of the problem is to relate it to the non-summative nature of the whole-and-its-parts and the fact that their complex association involves a different dimensionality making the generation of wholes manifesting a particular level referable to that level only. This is descrip-tive rather than explanatory but it narrows the field of thought regarding the origins of Quanta, the first feature of which is their *non-reducibility* to the level matrices of other Quanta.

What emerges from this is the notion of a 'level-leap' associated, but not identified, with the complex relation of whole-and-parts. The system of a given Quantum causally 'unfolds' and contingently 'enfolds' all the *dis-crepant* variations generated in the relations it establishes with its milieu. It is, however, built in to the limitedness that goes with quantisation that a point of non-absorption must be reached, and the Quantum faces only two alternatives. Either it 'dies' absolutely or it enters into relations with other Quanta involving some 'surrender' of its separateness in a new structure manifesting a new level matrix. In a sense, it stays 'alive' by 'dying'. These are the circumstances of a 'level-leap'. The new Quanta present a new complexness and dimensionality which is not fully realised and stable until such Quanta are self-sustaining and self-reproductive. The 'level-leap' is thus inseparable from what might be called a 'crisis of discrepancy' and it is this crisis which generates novelty. The 'scale' of novelty is irrelevant. It occurs instantaneously and infinitesimally as measured on our everyday spatio-temporal scale and also infinitely and over incalculable eras as recorded by that scale, with every variation in between. The oscillatory feature of the world in general referred to earlier is particularly well shown in the way these extremes interact in the impact of high velocity sub-atomic transformations on galactic and intergalactic changes over billions of years and vice versa.

It is thus quite clear that the logico-mathematical mapping of trans-formative change, or novelty, cannot do more than record this change. The 'either–or' character of general inference itself rules this out. Instead, oscillation and the non-additivity and complexness of wholes-and-parts is extracted in the abstracted-projected form of alternation and undecida-bility, which is the mapping of the indeterminacy going with trans-formative change. Undecidability is the particular concern of 'meta-logic' (that is, propositions about the truth or falsity of propositions), further discussion of which occurs below.

In terms of a complete grasp of transformation in Actuality the roles of affectivity and conscious or unconscious will or desire cannot be left out. By considering these aspects of the persona a fuller understanding of the holisms referred to previously as the basic and universal interactive forms of subject–milieu relationship is arrived at. One aspect only of this is the general inference of logico-mathematics. As we said, this can only record transformation (and hence novelty) as a change of reference of premises or axioms.[84] Moreover, concepts central to Piaget's thought, namely, reversibility, equilibrium, conservation, signify, like the change of premises, the essentially *non-transformative* character of logico-mathematics as the discussion in Chapter 4 showed; especially of some of the experimental 'evidence'.[85]

When the three basic laws of classical logic are looked at in the light of the foregoing, that is, the Law of Identity ($A = A$), the Law of Non-Contradiction (A and not-A cannot hold simultaneously) and the Law of the Excluded Middle (either A or not-A must hold), then the distinction between logic on the one hand (and mathematics in so far as it is governed by these laws) and Actuality on the other is quite obvious. In fact, it is in the nature of Actuality that A and not-A should co-exist, that A should constantly not be identical with A and that the 'excluded middle' is a continuing feature of concrete existence. The abandonment by the Intui-tionist School of the Law of the Excluded Middle constitutes a struggle to formalise the unformalisable, to subsume in a limited sense Actuality under logic. Apart from this variation, however, which is merely a change in emphasis as to which aspect of Actuality is regarded as basic, the norm has been to treat the three basic laws as if they were equivalent to Actuality rather than a mapped extraction from it. The important bearing this has on the problems arising from Russell's 'paradoxes' (closely related to the work of Cantor and Dedekind) and the work of Gödel should emerge presently.

Finally, the view of the classical syllogism presented by Descartes and J. S. Mill, that it cannot reveal novelty since the conclusion must always be contained within the premiss, is worth looking at from the viewpoint we have been advancing. The standard example is:

> All men are mortal.
> Socrates is a man.
> Therefore Socrates is mortal.

This syllogism is given 'altogether' and, from one viewpoint, the conclusion may be said to be contained within the premiss. But approached with the foregoing in mind the conclusion may not be so totally anticipated as appears at first sight. We may begin with either:

(A)	(B)
'All men are mortal '(that is, '*x*' is mortal'); then all men possess the *necessary conditions* of the *attribute of mortality*.	'*x* is a man'; then *x* possesses the *necessary conditions* of the *attribute of manhood*.

It follows that Socrates fulfils the attributive conditions of mortality if the attributive conditions of manhood imply the attributive conditions of mortality. There is a 'double tier', as it were, of attributivity concealed in the syllogism and the end-point is not simply a containment of the conclusion in the major premiss. It is an axiomatic shift from *A* to *B* which maps the transformation (novelty) involved. This transformation is not illusory since mortality, which is a common attribute of all living things and not just men, must be attached to the man Socrates. This is what the 'double tier' of premiss accomplishes.

As an end-piece to this section, Figure 8.4 is a rather more elaborated scheme of the relation of Actuality to the logical zone.

Notes to Figure 8.4

(a)   At Phase 1 (collection) the concrete proposition '*A* is red' (the Phase 1 form of the propositional function '*X* is red'), expresses the attribute and requires a clear distinction between Subject and Predicate and involves a stress on the phenomenal aspect of the attribute.

(b)   At Phase 2 (logical class) the conditional aspect of the attribute emerges as 'red-ness' where subject and predicate have lost their distinction, signifying the non-extended or *conditional stress* of this phase.

(c)   Note that in both cases it is a matter of stress, not complete absence of the other feature.

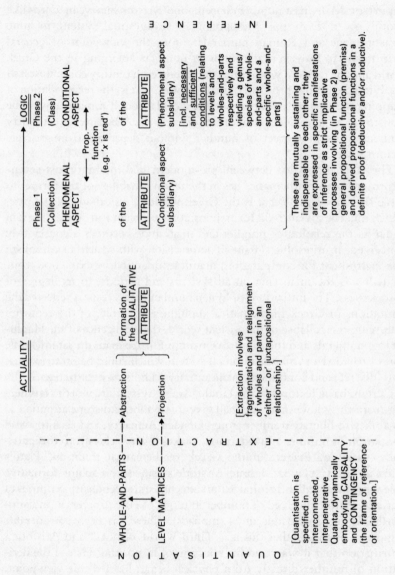

Figure 8.4 The logic 'pathway' (detailed schema).

A Characterisation of Mathematics

So far we have concentrated on the connections of logic and Actuality. The distinct but related link of mathematics with Actuality is at least as important. Many past number concepts and systems survive in words like 'score' or 'dozen', the Mesopotamian sexagesimal system in time measurement and Roman numerals. From the viewpoint of general quantitativity, however, the kinds of numbers emerging in the Greek world and the modern world since the seventeenth century come closest to resolving the central problem of mathematics, that is, the reconciliation of mapping the separate entity-ness of the world through *discreteness* with the 'construction' of *continuity* out of this discreteness. The latter must satisfy connectedness in respect of number without departing from discrete quantitativity.

The chief difference between pre-modern and modern (post-seventeenth-century) mathematics lies in the relative inability of the former to solve this problem. Yet it is the Greek world, classical and Hellenistic, which must be given credit for arriving at the problem and delineating it in so far as the relation of number and magnitude becomes a consciously conceived, if unresolved, issue. The precision with which a symbolism (the instrument for computation) manifests quantitative extraction from Actuality is the main clue, in all systems and periods, to its degree of abstractness. The limitations of Ionian number in this respect reflected the limitations of Greek mathematical thought as a whole. In the centuries following the collapse of the ancient world, the emergence of the Hindu-Arabic numerals and their improvement in Europe from the later Middle Ages provided a symbolic numeral system which could begin to express both discrete and continuous quantitativity without any restriction.

Certain basic features of the Hindu-Arabic system are worth considering from this viewpoint. We shall give this symbolism some attention as its ability to liberate number from extended Actuality, and thus to avoid conflation of number and extension, makes it very relevant to this particular study of Piaget. In the Greek mathematical tradition, Plato's 'monad-ology' played, despite Aristotle's criticism, a major formative role which was still influential in the sixteenth and seventeenth centuries of our era. Plato conceived of number in terms of pure, universal, indistinguishable and indivisible units (monads). There has been considerable argument as to whether this is a 'Third World' or not,[86] and Aristotle's affirmation that it was, and his rejection of it, positing instead the derivation of number directly from physical being, has fed this viewpoint. There is some support for this criticism to be found also in the parallel Platonic problems of the 'participation' of Forms in each other. But for our purposes it need only be noted that the 'monad' notion generates and reflects a composite view of number (apart from the original state of indivisible unit-ness) which falls short of the holistic aspect of number so important for its manipulability. In a simple statement like $1 + 3 = 4$, the holism of each of these numbers (of course we can also see them as aggregates of units if we wish) expresses more absolutely the quantitatively extracted attribute of Actuality than if they are seen as composites of units, when only the notion of the unit itself is a fully quantitative extraction. Perhaps this is the real meaning behind Plato's affirmation in *Parmenides* that if there is one there is number. The Ionian letter and word symbolism for number (and operation where it was recorded) did little to alleviate this and concealed a word–symbol confusion which obstructed the development of manipulation beyond a certain point and was hidebound by a hierarchy (expressed in the monadic structure) which denied it the 'mobility' required for unlimitedly precise and controlled calculation.

These are the specific problems that are resolved by the Hindu-Arabic system. Considering any collection of numbers, for example, $C = \{1, 2, 3, 4\}$, the symbols themselves may be used in any three distinct ways: *instrumental* (objects in computation); *attributive* (for example, two-ness, three-ness, even-ness, square-ness; the Greeks referred to this 'number-typing' as 'arithmetica' (or classification of numbers) as distinct from 'logistica' (or simple calculation)); *operational* (for example, the use of the symbols to raise to a power). Such flexibility shows the virtually unlimited freedom conferred by a system which is structured from (ten) symbols which are infinitely permutable. This last is particularly important for appreciating how, in combination with decimal place-value, the Hindu-Arabic system really begins to approach a complete representation of all number. In any infinite decimal such as $0.293875492 \ldots$, for example, two things are immediately obvious. First, the movability of the position of the point shows the *conditionality* of the indivisible unit for *any number*. This is an extraordinarily difficult, if not impossible, task to express in other systems. Secondly, the right-hand side of the decimal point actually represents irrationals (a Greek bug-bear). Thirdly, rationals are truly shown as 'fragments' and not simply 'little wholes' (as with Egyptian fractions). Finally, the representation of the real numbers in terms of the integers is made possible, opening the door to foundational studies and modern theories of infinity. Only the Hindu-Arabic system makes it possible to establish fully operational relations between numbers. In repetitive systems, for example, addition is little more than a form of rearrangement and its fundamental distinction from multiplication cannot emerge.

Significantly the Hindu-Arabic system allows the quantitative mapping of the complex relation between the whole-and-its-parts notably demonstrated in, for example, the calculus where the 'integral' maps the non-summativity of Actuality. Of course, other systems made major advances in these directions. But only modern Hindu-Arabic-conditioned thought is able to approach *all* of them. The representing of the real numbers in terms of natural numbers, that is, continuity in terms of discreteness, is one of the major achievements of the system. Hence, in their respective reconstructions of the rationals, Dedekind was able to emphasise the discrete aspect of the 'real number line' and Cantor its continuity aspect. Both of these achievements rest on the Hindu-Arabic system in the first instance.

With this background the Hindu-Arabic system enables us to appreciate the 'wholes-and-parts' relation in its mapped numerical form. Consider the 'two-ness' of a number pair and the 'one-ness' of the individuals making up the pair. In the pair, the 'two-ness' is a totality in its own right and the 'one-ness' of the separate individuals are both contributory and distinct. While the 'two-ness' is thus distinguishable, it is also dependent on the 'one-ness' of its 'contributors', and reciprocally we can see that the latter itself needs the 'two-ness' to bring it fully into existence. It is the Hindu-Arabic symbolism that reveals the distinction between, say, 'three-ness' and 'four-ness' as 'whole numbers'. A repetitive system fails in this respect. Very simply, 111 and 1111 differ only in degree. But considering $3 + 4 = 7$ it is clear that the symbolism reflects the 'over-and-above-ness' of 7 with respect to 3 and 4, which has characteristics beyond those of 3 and 4. (The Ionian Greek system achieves this to a large extent but fails in other respects.) This seems similar to the non-additivity of the parts into the whole in Actuality and has to be explained in the case of a mathematical mapping to avoid conflation. Such an explanation rests on the distinction between quantitative and qualitative extraction. The quantitative attribute has a quasi-object-ivity resulting from number being both a mapping and existing in its own right as a mathematical 'object'. Underlying this is the *indivisibility* conferred on the quantitative attribute through being extracted from the *wholes* of Actuality.

The distinction between quantitative and qualitative attributivity needs more clarification. Qualitative attributivity, which characterises logical class, arises from the particularity of objects/events/processes. Being a worker, wearing yellow socks, being a red triangle, and so on, are all unidentifiable unless particularised. Quantitative attributivity, on the other hand, is universal in that it extracts from the separate and countable feature of *all* objects/events/processes. Quality always relies on the particularity of, and difference between, phenomena which provide the initial Actuality foundation for identifying a boundaried collection. But the foundation of quantity lies only in the quantised state of the world and nothing else. The identification of a collection is thus more difficult to establish in this case. The difference lies at the root of the essential distinction to be drawn between logic and mathematics. Computability is inherent in the collection–element relation deriving from quantitative extraction, unlike the qualitative collection–element relation which underlies logical classes. Despite appearances 'symbolic logic', although useful as an abbreviation, is *not* computative in relation to the statements/ propositions it encapsulates as numbers are in relation to theirs. It might well seem that, for example, $x + y$ and $p \vee q$ are both computative. It can easily be shown that this is not so; x and y are general numbers and $x + y$ embodies all possible additions of such numbers, for example, $3 + 2 = 5$, a result different from 3 and 2 respectively. On the other hand, although p, q are general propositions, embodying all possible concrete propositions, their disjunction (or 'logical sum') can never be extended beyond these separate propositions to yield a *new* one.

Thus, the central problem arising from the extraction of quantitative attributivity is its initial 'unlimitedness' or universality. This is another aspect, grasped by Plato, of that same notion we referred to earlier from *Parmenides* – 'if there is one there is number'. In effect, one can say if there is one there is *all* number. The identification of *particular* number is, there-fore, a major problem. One of the more sophisticated solutions to the problem is the Frege-Russell definition of natural number as 'the class of all classes similar to a given class'. If the conflation between set and collection, similar to the conflation between class and collection, is erased and 'set' is taken in the same sense as 'class' to be concerned with the conditional aspect of the attribute, in this case *quantitative* attribute, then the Frege-Russell definition can be restated as 'the *n*-ness of all *n*-nesses similar to a given *n*-ness'. The original intention of the Frege-Russell definition was to provide a definition without any distinction between particular and general number. Thus, for example, 3 should be defined as the 'set' of all 'sets' of things 'similar to' (that is, in one-to-one corres-pondence with) a given 'set' of three things. This is, of course, an example of particular number which should be restated as for general number, that is, 'the threeness of all threenesses similar to a given threeness'.

Returning to the distinction between 'set' and 'collection' and under-standing the former as the conditional aspect of the attribute of which the latter emphasises the phenomenal aspect, then the original Frege-Russell definition must be modified and for the following reasons: first, we are dealing with the quantitative, not the qualitative attribute. The latter is 'given' in a way that the former is not. The attribute '. . . is red' is obvious which ' . . . is a quantity' is not. It is the latter's universality which distinguishes quantitative from qualitative extraction and which calls for a modified Frege-Russell-type definition in terms of the 'collection of all collections similar to a given collection'. This is Phase 1 and co-exists with the 'set of all sets' at Phase 2 and between which and Phase 1 there is reciprocal interaction, as always. The Frege-Russell modified definition requires some clarification. It is the universality of the quantitative attri-bute which requires the setting up of a 'given collection'. Only thus does it become possible to identify absolutely all aggregates of *n* things. This is the only possible means of fixing in a purely quantitative manner that from which the attribute is to be extracted. In this light the 'given collection' plays the role of a *tool* for selecting *n* things on the basis '*n*' alone. It is an indicator as to what quantitative attribute is *to be extracted*. But of course no attribute can be extracted from one example alone. Hence, the tool of the 'given collection' enables the indefinite formation of aggregates on *n* things and lays the basis for the extraction of the attribute *n*. It is at this stage that the Echelon notion is introduced. First a collection is formed (of, say, three things or *n* things) at Phase 1 and this is referred to as Echelon 1 and is the instrumental act of selection. Echelon 2 (Phase 1) is the stage of formation (or postulation) of the collection of all collections similar to (in one-to-one correspondence with) three things or *n* things. It is this Echelon that may be characterised as 'the *collection* of all collections similar to a given collection'.

Parallel with these collections are sets expressible generally as:

Echelon 1   The set(s) manifesting the condition(s) of a given collection.

Echelon 2   The set of all sets manifesting the conditions of all collections similar to a given collection.

Thus it is clear that it is not enough to have one 'stage' of extraction of the attribute as with quality. So the number 'three' not only requires 'the threeness of all threenesses corresponding to a given threeness' (Phase 2 Echelon 2), but also needs at Phase 1 'the collection of all collections similar to three things' (that is, Phase 1 Echelon 2). Another way of presenting this is that since all collections of three things are taken, this very universality involves the presence of all *qualities* and there is no chance on qualitative grounds of being able to distinguish any particular collection of three things. The identification of any such collection is hence compelled to turn to something like the Echelon structure. This Echelon structure should not be confused with the difference between particular and general number. General number always behaves and is treated 'as if' it were particular number. Hence, the Echelon structure of Phases 1 and 2 must apply to *both* general and particular number.

Turning again to the more general question of the relation of Phases 1 and 2, there is, if anything, an even stronger case for not conflating these in the mathematical zone than in the logical zone. This is particularly so in reference to one-to-one correspondence, which is applicable only in Phase 1, emphasising as it does the phenomenality of the attribute. In Phase 1, one-to-one correspondence involves an alignment of elements which can be listed:

$$\text{e.g. } C = \{ 1/2, 2/4, 3/6, 4/8 \dots \}$$

The corresponding Phase 2 definition reads thus: For a set S,
$$S = \{p/q/q = 2p, p, q \, \varepsilon \, Z^+\}.$$

It is clear from this that to present, for example, the rational numbers as a 'subset' of the reals is conflationary, deriving as usual from the unclear use of the 'set' concept. The rationals form a collection under a different quantitative attribute from the reals, and the conditionality of the respective collection, 'rational-ness' and 'real-ness' respectively, are equally distinct in Phase 2. Any identification of the reals with the 'real number line' (Euclidean) is also misleading as is any identification of the latter with space.

Furthermore, the distinction between 'computational numbers' (Phase 1) and 'mathematical numbers' (Phase 2) also emerges from the example. What is also clearly shown is the illegitimacy of conflating number, either general or particular, with Actuality. '3-ness' or 'n-ness' involve conditions removed from any 3 or n objects/events/processes. Even unity or '1-ness' is removed in the same way in that it does not reflect the 'thing-ness' of things but their *separation,* what they are *not* – the source of the initial discreteness of number.[87] It follows that logic, arising from the qualitativity of Actuality, cannot be reduced in any way to mathematics although mathematical statements may be given a logical form. The fact that both logic and mathematics possess an inferential structure is also misleading. Mathematics often uses the same form of inference as logic but, in addition, possesses its own *calculative inferential structure,* determined by the nature of the elements and the operation under consideration. This is one of the key conflationary aspects of the Piagetian system discussed earlier, particularly in relation to his 'logical' treatment of the INRC group of transformations.

It is in this context that the invaluable role of the Hindu-Arabic symbol system is again revealed, for this system allows free movement between different species and aspects of number to occur while enabling a clear distinction between them to be maintained. There is, of course, always a problem of the distinction between calculative and mathematical number where the use of the same symbols for computational and mathematical number can obscure the literal difference of 'being' between monistic (holistic) number with which computation occurs and the 'number-ness', that is, '3-ness' or '4-ness' or 'even-ness' or 'odd-ness' or 'square-ness' or 'prime-ness', which is the 'object' of mathematical theory. The distinction corresponds approximately to that drawn by the Greeks between *logistica* and *arithmetica*. But it is only the Hindu-Arabic system that is able sufficiently to represent the independence of number from its source in Actuality to allow the free movement without ambiguity between computation and mathematical meaning. There is always the possibility of conflation between such meanings but this is minor in comparison with the accompanying advantages of the Hindu-Arabic system of carrying its representation through to Phase 2 and thus able to account for both Phases 1 and 2 in its instrumentality. Repetititive and/or pluralistic systems (including Ionian Greek) could not achieve this fulfilment which only the non-repetitive, monism (holism) of the Hindu-Arabic system accomplishes. The schema for the mathematical pathway (Figure 8.5) is equivalent to the one for logic (Figure 8.4).

Paradox and Contradiction

The discussion of the relations of logic and mathematics to Actuality and to each other cannot be left without reference to certain problems of 'paradoxicality' (or, rather, contradiction) which have a definite bearing on a critique of the Piagetian system. It can be shown that they are related to the types of ambiguity between the zones of knowledge and Actuality which have been referred to as 'conflation' or 'collapse'. Hence, the issues of paradox/contradiction are especially relevant to the Piagetian system. The case of logic and the logical class is considered first.

The so-called Russell paradox is a natural starting-point and the popular presentation of this runs as follows (note that the notion of 'class' is used here in the orthodox manner in which elements of a collection are described as members of a class):

Consider the class which is the class of all classes which are not members of themselves. To do this, consider first a particular class which is not a member of itself such as a class of horses. Clearly, this is not a horse, and the class of horses is not a member of itself. Now consider the class of all such classes. If this class is a member of itself it should not be because it contains all classes which are *not* members of themselves. But if it is not a member of itself, it should be because it contains *all* classes which are not members of themselves.

Commenting on this in a mathematical form of the 'paradox', S. C. Kleene (1967, p. 186) writes:

> Russell's paradox . . . concerns the set of all sets which do not contain themselves. Call this set S. *Suppose* (a) S contains itself. Then by the definition of S, S does not contain itself. So by *reductio ad absurdum* (rejecting the supposition (a)), we have *proved*: (b) S does not contain

Note to Figure 8.5
Echelon structure = a required addition over and above logic because the universality of the quantitative attribute demands an extra method of specification of number, whether particular or general.

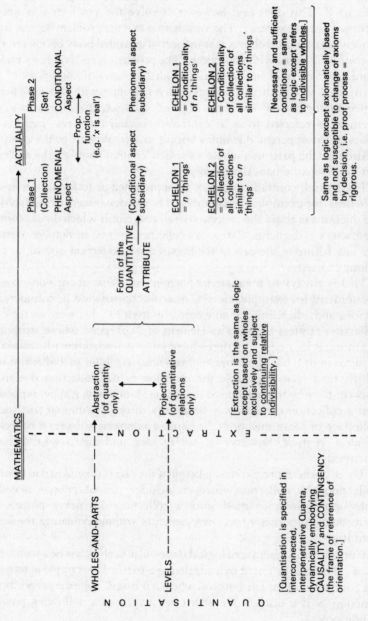

Figure 8.5 The mathematics 'pathway' (detailed schema)

itself, but then by the definition of S: (c) S does contain itself. Together (b) and (c) constitute a proved contradiction or paradox.

Russell believed he had resolved this problem by the Theory of Types which allows a class to be a member only of a class of a higher logical type than itself. This does not, however, resolve the problem – it simply defines it out of existence. The view here is that the problem derives from conceiving of logical classes as some sort of extended body of objects, that is, confusing them with collections. The problem is resolvable by understanding 'class' and 'set' as non-extended systems of conditions of the attribute(s) which these concepts express. In line with this specifically logico-mathematical understanding of class/set, the Russellian-type dilemma is referred to as a 'contradiction' and the term 'paradox' is reserved for apparent dilemmas arising in Actuality from the complex relation of 'the parts to a whole' of which 'contradiction' can be regarded as a logico-mathematical mapping.[88]

The Russell contradiction may be approached as follows: in terms of *collections* (for example, the assembly of horses designated a 'class' above), the dilemma is about the collection of all collections which do not contain themselves as elements. Can such a collection ever be an element of itself? We saw before in the case of the horses that a collection cannot, in fact, belong to itself.

This is always so for material phenomena. What about non-material phenomena, for example, ideas? Can a collection of ideas be considered as an idea and, therefore, be an element of itself? If this were so then the collection of ideas becomes an element of a collection whose attributive definition is idea-ness. But the element under consideration (the collection of ideas itself) has the extra, *differentiating* attribute of collection-ness which renders it unsuitable for inclusion in the collection due to its non-conformity to the required conditions. Intuitively, it appears possible that a collection of ideas may be an idea through assuming that such a collection of ideas must be in the mind of a thinking subject. A collection of ideas in itself, however, is not an idea, and this is what is being discussed.

There is, therefore, no contradiction if the case is formulated in terms of collections. No collection whatever, including the collection of all collections, can belong to itself since a collection can never possess the equivalent properties to its own elements without violating the initial definitions.

Consider now the case of logical *classes*. Can such a class be a member of itself? This can be tested by considering a particular example in terms of the conditions of the attributes on which it is based. Take the propositional function 'x is a teacher' for which we may list the following possible conditions:

x starts work at 9 a.m.
x has three months' holiday a year
x works with students
x writes on a blackboard, etc., etc.

The 'membership' of the class is established by selecting the appropriate conditions, *not all of which are necessary*. If we change them from the (predicative) propositional function form in which they are expressed and put them into an 'attributively conditional' form, we get (note the substantive-verbal grammatical structure indicating the condition or qualification of the subject):

. . . starting-work-at-9a.m.-ness
. . . having-three-months'-holiday-a-year-ness
. . . working-with-students-ness
. . . writing-on-a-blackboard-ness

Now, if the general propositional function 'x is a teacher', corresponding to the identification of the class, be considered as only another condition, and is restated as

. . . being-a-teacher-ness

it becomes clear that because of the non-extended character of all the conditions (including the general propositional function now stated as one of these conditions), it is impossible to separate any one of these out in any ordered manner such that particular conditions become distinguishable from a general condition. Similarly, if the propositional form is retained or reverted to, *any one* of the conditions, now stated as propositions, may serve as the premiss from which an implicative 'chain' may start (logical, of course, not Actual). Important also is the fact that, because a qualitative attribute is under consideration, the conditions/propositions are not rigorously ordered as in a mathematical implicative sequence. From all of this it becomes clear that it is a *matter of decision* whether the propositional function (or general condition) which 'states' the class is or is not a member of the class it identifies.

This treatment was related to a particular example, 'x is a teacher', for reasons of clarity. It would not be as easy to see the possibility of decision-making with respect to the propositional functions embodying the conditions for the class if generalised conditions only had been considered. This does not conflict with the nature of logic as 'contentless' provided that such 'contentlessness' or 'formal independence' is not taken as signifying total isolation from Actuality. Such formal independence is certainly a requirement of logic (and mathematics) which must be treated 'as if' they were contentless from one point of view, but in the final analysis they both depend for their existence on extraction of attributes (qualitative and quantitative respectively) from Actuality. It is, in fact, this duality that is the source of conflation in both their zones unless it is clear that their detachment from Actuality is always simultaneously accompanied by attachment.

Plato understood this and used the concept of 'participation' of things in the ειδοτ to express it. Aristotle, misunderstandng the nature of the ειδοτ, and treating it like a phenomenon, criticised Plato for creating a separate 'third world'. Aristotle's own form of expression for logic and mathematics in relation to Actuality was as 'abstractions from' but 'dependent on' the world. Our treatment of this is embodied in the Phase 1 and Phase 2 analysis.

In applying this to the Russell contradiction, that is, the class of all classes which are not members of themselves, the classes which are members of this overall class have each been identified by this particular decision. In the class of all classes which are not members of themselves, the 'not-members-of-themselves-ness' identifying this membership is the *only* condition that all these classes have in common. Whereas the collection has collection-ness, the class cannot have class-ness because it is not a phenomenon and attributivity may only be extracted from a phenomenon. Conditions cannot be extracted from a basically nonconditional situation. So the class itself (defined by 'not-a-member-of-itself-ness') *cannot be a member of itself.* There is no contradiction here any more than in the case of the collection of all collections. In all examples in this case it is *the decision on conditions* which must precede the identification of membership. The same can be shown with classes that are members of themselves (by decision) as in the case of 'teacher-ness' given before.

It only remains to consider mathematical *sets*, and again, the question to pose is: whether a set can be a member of itself or not? Unlike the case of a class, which is based on the extraction of a qualitative attribute, the conditions for the attribute are very precise in the case of a set. For example, in the set

$$S = \{x/x \ \varepsilon Z^+, x < 5\}$$

the conditions for the attribute are:

> x is quantitative
> x is positive
> x is integral
> x is less than 5.

Because we are dealing with a quantitative attribute each of these conditions *must* be present to satisfy membership of the set. If this is so, the presence of each one and the presence of all are equivalent and the 'quantitative-positive-integral-less-than-5-ness of x' is as much a member of the set as each condition for x taken individually. The set's resultant membership of itself is a product of the exactitude which is an expected feature of quantitativity. Hence, *all* sets are members of themselves. The only exception to this is the obvious (trivial?) case of the empty set. Thus, 'the set of all sets which are not members of themselves' reduces to the empty set and, since by defnition this is not a member of itself, the contradiction does not arise at all.

The issue is different with classes. Here all the conditions of the attribute need not be present. For the class defined by 'x is a teacher', for example, each of the following, 'x works at a blackboard' or 'x belongs to the NUT' or 'x wears a cap and gown', may or may not be conditions of the attribute. The general condition expressing the attribute itself may include all or only some of the conditions. This is an additional illumination of the fact that, for logical classes, membership is a matter of decision. For sets, all the conditions have to be present or the set does not exist at all. This distinction between the two is ultimately referable to the nature of the extracted attribute in each case. Quantitativity necessarily relies exclusively on the wholeness of Actuality since it is inseparable from enumerability and enumeration. The mapping of Actuality by the set is thus a fixed and absolute one related to a precise reflection of the frontier of a whole. Qualitative attributivity, on the other hand, must map not only the partness of the whole-and-its-parts but also the interaction (oscillation or complexness) between whole and parts (for example, 'teacher-ness' and 'working-at-the-blackboard-ness' possess just this interaction relation).

The popularised version of the Russell contradiction runs like this: 'the barber in a certain village shaves all and only those persons in the village who do not shave themselves. Question: Does he shave himself?' (see Kleene, 1967, p. 186). Considered from an Actuality viewpoint the problem is simply solved by discovering what happens. But in the realm of logic more has to be said. The essential point with respect to the barber is that *he* is neither a *collection* nor a *class* nor a *set*. The *man* who is the village barber must be distinguished from the *collection* (of barbers), attributively arrived at ('is the village barber'), which contains only the one member. Further, the logical class interrelated with this barber-collection manifests the conditions relating to 'barber-ness'. These conditions might be listed thus: (*a*) skilled/experienced in hairdressing, shaving, and so on, (*b*) tends beards (original meaning of the word 'barber'), (*c*) receives money for his work, and so on. As before, we can decide whether 'is a barber' is to be included in these conditions or not. (Alternatively we can decide whether 'x is a barber' is a premiss, a derived propositional function and/or a conclusion.) If '. . . is a barber' is to be included then we can say that the logical class (related to the collection also attributively designated '. . . is a barber') is a member of itself. Alternatively we can do the opposite and produce a logical class which is not a member of itself (and replace the suggested premiss with another proposition like 'is skilled in hairdressing, shaving, and so on' as a new premiss, treating the first proposition as derived).

The Russellian contradiction relates only to this situation not to the '*man* who is a village barber'. For when this man picks up a razor to shave himself, he ceases to be a barber as defined by the formation of the collection of barbers, and also, in relation to this collection, the formation of the logical class of 'barber-ness'. The 'paradox' that is normally presented is thus invalid. Put simply, having in his capacity as barber shaved everyone who does not shave himself, if the man who is normally the village barber then shaves himself, he does *not* do so in the capacity of a 'barber', but in an *individual* capacity. To think of him under these circumstances as a barber is a covert way of identifying the man with the class (which has a single member). This is a conflation of Actuality and logic.

Alternatively, we can *decide* that conditions (*a*), (*b*) and (*c*) above *do* apply when the man (barber) shaves himself (for example, he 'pays himself' by putting money in the till!). Such a situation applies in the case of any self-employed man who, *from the point of view of the economic system* of employer (capital) and employed (labour), appears to pay himself wages. If he uses *all* his returns this way he will be bankrupt. But if he uses part of his income to pay wages, to buy new equipment, and so on, then part of what appeared at first to be some sort of wage emerges as capital investment. The operative economic distinctions can only be understood on the basis of logically distinct categories such as arise in the barber example. Karl Marx actually discusses such a situation and distinguishes between the individual person as such and the economic functions of that individual (K. Marx, *Theories of Surplus Value*, Vol. IV of *Capital*, Moscow, Progress Publishers; London, Lawrence & Wishart, 1969, pp. 408–9). Such distinctions have become familiar under the modern description of 'structuralism' in many fields of inquiry.

A contradiction which looks the same as Russell's problem but actually refers to quite a different situation was uncovered by Kurt Gödel in his paper of 1931, 'On formally undecidable propositions of Principia Mathematica and related systems'. In this paper Gödel proved that if the axioms of arithmetic are consistent they are incomplete and he achieved this through the construction of an undemonstrable arithmetical formula (corresponding to an undecidable self-referring proposition).

G. T. Kneebone (*Mathematical Logic and the Foundations of Mathematics*, 1963) describes Gödel's procedure thus:

What Gödel realized was that . . . Any formula, which is simply a finite string of symbols, [can] be represented by a corresponding string of numbers, and by using the key to code we shall be able to get back from the string of numbers to the formula. The coding can be arranged, however, in such a way that the rules which govern both the formation of well-formed formulae and the arrangements of such formulae in derivations can be expressed in terms of simple arithmetical operations on the representative numbers. When this is done, the metamathematical assertions that we are mostly interested in no longer require formulation in terms that refer specifically to the particular formal theory to which they relate, but they are all of a single uniform type, being without exception arithmetical propositions. Thus metamathematics, no less than the mathematics which forms its object, can be formalized, and it then becomes much more sharply defined than it was previously, when no limitation was imposed on it beyond that of being finitary.

When the new metamathematical technique is applied with formalized arithmetic itself as the primary theory, the way is made open for a most significant development. Since the metamathematics is now of the same nature as the mathematics both of them consisting of arithmetical propositions, every metamathematical assertion can be expressed within the primary theory (provided that this is sufficiently comprehensive); and in this way the metamathematics of the formal system becomes formalized within that system itself. A situation is thus created which allows of the sort of exploitation of self-reference that formed the basis of Cantor's proof that no class is equipotent with the class of all its subclasses, and also of Richard's paradoxical argument . . . and of the even simpler paradox of the man who declares 'The statement that I am now making is untrue'. Seizing upon this circumstance, Gödel was able to show that, if a a system of formalized arithmetic is wide enough, then (i) the system is necessarily incomplete, in the sense that there exists a formula **11** of the system such that neither **11** nor its negation is derivable, and (ii) if the system is consistent, then no proof of its consistency is possible which can be formalized within it. (pp. 230–1)

A crucial passage from the beginning of Gödel's paper (see van Heijenoort, 1967, pp. 597ff.) presents a central epistemological problem. He writes:

Of course, for metamathematical considerations it does not matter what objects are chosen as primitive signs, and we shall assign natural numbers to this use.[7] Consequently, a formula will be a finite sequence of natural numbers,[8] and a proof array a finite sequence of finite sequences of natural numbers. The metamathematical notions (propositions) thus become notions (propositions) about natural numbers or sequences of them;[9]

[7] That is, we map the primitive signs one-to-one onto some natural numbers. (See how this is done on page 601).
[8] That is, a number-theoretic function defined on an initial segment of the natural numbers. (Numbers, of course, cannot be arranged in a spatial order.)
[9] In other words, the procedure described above yields an isomorphic image of the system PM in the domain of arithmetic, and all metamathematical arguments can just as well be carried out in this isomorphic image. This is what we do below when we sketch the proof; that is, by "formula", "proposition", "variable", and so on, *we must always understand the corresponding objects of the isomorphic image*.

Logic and mathematics have already been distinguished, especially by identifying the fundamental difference between the connectives of the former and the operations of the latter. It follows that the term 'isomorphism' is not applicable between logical and mathematical systems. An isomorphism is possible if and only if the connectives have been redefined and the predicate expressions (and quantifiers) of the logical system identified solely as quantitative elements. In this case, no change of notation is necessary. Gödel does not do this here and proceeds 'as if' he had, in fact, carried out this redefinition. It is the absence of this latter process that allows him the flexibility to argue from the system PM (*Principia Mathematica*, etc.,) to its isomorphic image and back again.

This is so because metamathematics is a *naming* not an *enumerating* process and is thus a part of logic not a part of mathematics, notwithstanding the apparent mathematical content. It is concerned, in short, with qualitative attributivity. The statement that 'It is impossible to prove theorem T' refers to a theorem whose *name* is 'T' and is not a mathematical proposition. Also, in a proposition of the type '$Wn(n)$ is a theorem of the formal system', $Wn(n)$ is clearly a *name* and 'is a' involves a logical predicate (which may or may not be true) and it cannot simply be translated into number which is then *treated* as number, since this involves a switch, in mid-stream as it were, from qualitative to quantitative attributivity.

There is, therefore, buried in the Gödelian proof what might be described as an 'illegitimate leap' from logic to number. Notwithstanding this, however, 'Gödelisation' provides a technique of exploiting logic to reveal arithmetical statements demonstrating contradiction/undecidability. By thus 'forcing' the 'freedom of decision' of logic into the rigour of mathematics, Gödel exposes, in the mapped form of contradiction/undecidability, that feature of Actuality expressed as the paradoxical co-existence of the separateness and interconnection of Quanta. In the final analysis Gödel's Theorems are quasi-logical not arithmetical. At the decisive 'switch-over' point from metamathematics (logic) to mathematics, the signs are treated 'as if' they were calculable symbols.

One might be forgiven for identifying Godel with Piaget at this point in terms of conflation. But Gödel, unlike Piaget, draws all his conclusions *after* having made the transition, through the Gödel numbers, from logic to mathematics. Piaget, on the other hand, like many others, conflates Actuality, logic and mathematics by drawing conclusions in one zone and using these in an unacknowledged and undefined way in another.

A final thought on the Godelian contradiction might suggest that it can be resolved in the same way as was indicated for the Russellian variety. To find out if this is so consider formula G which represents the metamathematical statement, 'The formula G is not demonstrable'. Proceeding to apply the previous analysis, the statement 'The formula G is not demonstrable' derives from a propositional function, 'x is not demonstrable'. There is only one condition for this:

i.e., 'x is not demonstrable'

This is the only condition provided here precisely *because* it is relevant *only* to proposition G itself. There is in consequence no room for manoeuvre in the (axiomatic) decision of the definition process. Such a presentation may lack formal 'rigour' but it intuitively shows the inevitability of the Gödelian contradiction. It is the *self-referring* nature of this proposition in which the 'x' is itself an undemonstrable proposition, that compels the contradiction and prevents a resolution as in the Russell case. The ultimate source of this contradiction is the 'frontier' character of the Gödelian self-referring proposition G: 'G is not demonstrable'. As the statement is asserting its own undemonstrability, there can be one case only of a proposition deriving from the propositional function. The formula G simply asserts undemonstrability of itself.

In other cases, where a formula is not asserting undemonstrability of itself, 'x' may refer to any number of other propositions. In 'x is undemonstrable' if x is referring not to itself but to another proposition, there is no contradiction and a decision of definition may be made. But in the self-referring formula used by Gödel there is no room at all for a solution in terms of a decision of definition. It is an unresolvable contradiction revealed by an 'excursion' into mathematics from logic and back again.

The undecidability revealed by Gödel's Theorems involves a reflexive proposition which maps in the formal system the self-reference of Actuality. Such self-reference in Actuality is demonstrated by Cantor's work on infinite sets which are defined as sets which have the *same power* or cardinal number as proper subsets of themselves. Any problem in respect of this vanishes on the basis of a conditionally attributive understanding of a set. It can also be seen to vanish if 'infinity' itself is seen as a *relative* condition, dependent on the level matrix under consideration. The 'infinity' understood from *inside* a boundaried everyday object occurs in terms of the level matrix of (say) the 'molecular structure' of the object and has no meaning referred to the level matrix of the object itself. The 'points-of-view' are radically different. The indeterminacy of its boundary, which is mapped in a formal system of mathematics by the undecidability of a reflexive proposition (itself dependent on extracting the *whole* aspect of Quanta as a quantitative attribute), disappears. As we directly apprehend or grasp it, any boundary, be it of the moon, a chair, or a molecule, is absolute. But this absoluteness is itself relative to the frames of reference of other level matrices than the one we are operating in this particular case. The Gödel contradiction, revealed in a reflexive proposition mapping self-reference in Actuality, exposes an indeterminacy of a boundary which derives from our attempt to make it more 'precise'. The search for this precision involves (paradoxically) a progressive failure to attain it. Gödel's Theorems can hence be characterised as mathematical reflections of the *continuous connnection* of *separate* things in Actuality. The emergence of such contradictions is a mathematical 'signal' that a level 'leap' in Actuality is in progress. A new 'dimension' of wholes complexly related to their parts is coming into being. This approach begins to explicate Zeno's Paradoxes in a way that no amount of linear logic or mathematics can achieve. Paradox does not mean that an absolute boundary to knowledge has been achieved or that the field is exhausted. It signifies no more than that another 'dimension' has been arrived at. As we saw previously, 'incompatibility' is only the result of treating the different dimensions of being of a phenomenon as if they were reducible to one dimension only. In fact, Gödel's Incompleteness and Consistency Theorems (the latter refers to the impossibility of proving the consistency of a formal system from within it) adequately reflect and record the fundamental state of Actuality whereby the 'measurability' of objects/events/processes is, from an 'interior' frame of reference, always subject to limiting circumstances. The limit itself is only 'achievable' by making the 'dimensional leap' and going 'outside' the phenomenon.

Further Reflections on the Piagetian System

This chapter began by discussing the formation of logico-mathematical models in relation to holisms and has analysed such models in relation to Actuality. The 'quasi-isomorphic' but asymmetric relationship between logic and mathematics has also had some attention. The separation of the logico-mathematical model from Actuality is an ongoing process as is the distinction between logic and mathematics. At any point these relationships remain only relatively stable, and the distinctions drawn here between them need constant reinforcement and extension for only through such distinction can different levels of existence and the Quanta (wholes-and-their-parts) manifesting them be related to each other in a coherent epistemology.

The ability to relate logico-mathematics to Actuality and logic to mathematics can occur only in the context of such distinction. This is not a mere academic exercise for it involves, when coupled with the affective-aesthetic aspects of mentality, the totality of the thinking-feeling being's relation with the milieu. The exploitation of this varied, holistic relation with the world by social establishments of all kinds through the conflation of life and abstraction is universal. The helplessness and dependence most people experience behind whatever social façade they have adopted, derive from an inability to decide on the boundary and distinction between thought and action. The first condition for such undecidability is con-fusion between what is Actual and what is an abstraction-projection from this Actuality. Because of the immense power of external decision-makers, this confusion is a central means by which the individual is rendered malleable and manipulable by social authority.

The struggle to maintain the distinction between model and Actuality is very much an ongoing process and alternates with (is a response to) periodic conflation. The process has been with mankind for a very long time; but only in the last 300 years or so has it been forced fully into the open by the emergence of the essentially logico-mathematical self-reference on which modern thought rests. The ultimate reference of thought to authority in the form of custom, belief, deities, and so on, in earlier epistemologies obscured the necessity to maintain such distinc-tions. The compulsions of universal and unconditional self-reference, however, leave no room for such obscurity; the distinction between model and Actuality must be rigorously maintained or there is a danger of the stability of thought either dissolving into indeterminacy or congealing into a rigid self-justificative mass. Of course, thought in the last 300 years has not escaped the assault of self-styled 'authority'. Scientific and philo-sophical establishments, with their political and social counterparts, have emerged through the expedient of turning self-reference into unchallenge-able truth endorsed by them, thus destroying the very essence of self-reference itself.[89] The principal instrument in this process has been (through conflation as we have been dealing with it) a capitalisation on the axiomatic aspect of logic and mathematics. The latter is presented as being hierarchically related to Actuality (experience) and is therefore an ultimate, undisputable and superior point of reference. Needless to say, these 'axioms' conform remarkably closely to the desires, interests and world outlook of the establishments which advance them. The process is subtle compared with the old gods, demons and traditions. In the con-temporary world the objective is to convince, logico-mathematically, that the power and control of an external authority is an integral part of the natural order of things. The aim is to encourage loyalty and obedience not simply to an external compulsive force but to make such devotion derive seemingly from an inner *rational* conviction of the intrinsic rightness of such power.

The ongoing epistemological process based on self-reference, which is best characterised by the struggle to maintain the distinction of the logico-mathematical zones from Actuality, itself intensifies the subject–object separation which generated the original need to model Actuality in a logico-mathematical form. Reciprocally, the act of model-making intensifies the subject–object separation. The relationship is comparable to the one referred to earlier as between 'oscillation' on the one hand and its mapping in the form of 'alternation' in the general inference of both logic and mathematics on the other. The more epistemology moves away from external 'supports', the more self-dependent it becomes, the more does the oscillatory, self-referential relation of wholes and parts predominate and hence the greater the significance of the mapped form of this in logico-mathematical alternation. And always, stable points of reference – the axiomatic delineation of the model itself – must be understood as relative and temporary.

In the previous analysis of the Piagetian system, four main strands emerged: First, it is asserted that psychology is derived from biological roots. Secondly, this derivation is 'proved' by affirming an isomorphism between biology and psychology. Thirdly, and contradictorily, Piaget assigns psychology an independent role by identifying it as a *learned* process within the childhood and adolescence of the individual. Fourthly, and again contradictorily, the structural character of this psychology is identified as inherently logico-mathematical and hence distinct from the learning activity in acquiring it. The central conflict underlying all four strands, however, is the incompatibility between psychological-biological dependence linked to psychological structuration on the one hand and the notion of psychology as an independent learning process on the other, the latter having a decidedly self-referential flavour.

It is clear how Piaget's system has remained basically unchallenged – especially in the context of the growth of scientific establishments in the last hundred years or so. Genetic Epistemology indeed 'sails very close to the wind' in so far as it converges on a solution to the main problems of the mind–milieu relation but without actually getting there. This is no particular credit to Piaget since any attempt to 'scientise' a field like psychology must rely, at least in part, on a self-referential frame of reference. But in all fields, scientific establishments are in danger from any unrestricted application of a rigorously maintained self-reference. The answer for any such establishment is a subtle transmutation of self-reference into authority, achieved largely by some form of model–Actuality identity. This is exactly the point where Piaget ceases to converge on a genuine solution to the problem of the mind–milieu relationship. However genuine his system may seem in its approach to a grasp of the mind–milieu connection, this is more than offset by the negative effects of his particular forms of conflation together with the erection of logic and mathematics into unchallengeable authorities equivalent to any other establishment. These forms of conflation allow Actuality to be defined at will and to change, without acknowledgement, from this 'Actuality' to 'model' and thence to 'theory' and back, seemingly 'proving' a conclusion already contained within the original preconceived 'Actuality'. 'Proof' is hence removed from its legitimate zone of logic and mathematics and confused with physical demonstration of what is effectively a 'status quo ante'.

As a final summarising exercise in the present chapter, it would be useful to bring together the principal features of Piaget's methodology, elaborated earlier, within the ambit of the view of logic and mathematics expressed here. Earlier chapters (2, 3, 4) concentrated on Piaget's conflation of logic and mathematics with Actuality. Milestones in this conflation have been shown to be that of logic and mathematics with each other; in the case of the INRC group of tranformations, a 'layered collapse' is effected and this group is 'collapsed' into logic and then into number; the latter is then treated as a 'department' of Actuality. The Klein-four group is central to Piaget's logico-mathematisation of thought and to those ephemeral but crucial entities of Genetic Epistemology, cognitive structures. Any group is defined as a set together with a binary operation marked by special (group) conditions. Formerly, when we identified Phase 2 as the conditional aspect of the attribute, we did not distinguish any particular sort of condition beyond, that is, identifying the premiss(es) (or general proposition) or in the case of sets, the axiom(s). Groups are in the first place exclusively mathematical, and this is another ambiguity in Genetic Epistemology in that Piaget confuses them with logical structures. They are identifiable as such by special conditions (see Chapter 2) and may be considered as a sort of 'flatland' mapping (through the collections they are connected with) of the *integrity* and *symmetry* of wholes in Actuality. Thus, *closure* can be said to map the boundary and stability of a particular whole and its resistance to transformation, either into another whole manifesting the same level matrix, or involvement in a completely new level matrix; *associativity* maps the flexibility of alternative 'routes' within the 'boundary' of a given whole, that is, the internal causality of the whole (cf. the discussion above on causality and its logical mapping); *inverses* map the internal 'activity' of the whole which manifests its 'life' without destroying its structural balance; the *identity element* maps that aspect of the whole guaranteeing the stability, symmetry and resistance to precipitate change which is mapped by closure. All of these relate to organised internal movement/structure, and the *operation* itself – critical in distinguishing whether a collection with its set can be mapped as a group or not – is a map of this movement. All of these conditions are quantitative and also belong to Phase 2 of the mathematical 'pathway'. But as they relate to special quantitative collections it is necessary to refer to group-sets and group-collections.

Piaget's alignment of mental phenomena and group structures to the point of equating them eliminates the possibility of grasping this foregoing relationship between the group and the whole which depends on understanding the difference between conditional attributivity (in this case group conditions) of Phase 2, the phenomenal attributivity of Phase 1 and the Actuality from which attributivity itself is derived. That same alignment, on the other hand, creates a logico-mathematical strait-jacket for mind and mental activity which distorts its true character of combining stability with susceptibility to change. For, the mathematical group is not absolute (as Piaget presents it) and it is always possible to arrive 'outside' the group by means of the right operation. Although such a process has an 'either–or' character, it nevertheless maps (as indeed does the change of axioms referred to earlier) the transmutational possibilities of Actuality – a feature which is lost in Piaget's use of the group.

In fact, a conflation is detectable which underlies all the specific ones hitherto encountered. At the core of the 'collapse' of logic, mathematics and Actuality into each other lies the 'collapse' of Phases 1 and 2 – or rather the failure to distinguish them in any form. Piaget is not unique in this respect but he does pursue it very elaborately especially in connection with the sharp separation of Groupings I–IV (of classes) and Groupings V–VIII (of relations) (see above, Chapter 4). Further, Chapter 2 saw the collapse of 'action' (physical) into 'operation' (mental). These categories can be connected with the General Quantisation of Actuality on the one hand and its mapping into General Inference on the other. This major conflation is reinforced still more by the central concept of reversibility which moves without constraint or qualification between logic (negation), mathematics (inverses) and Actuality (return to the starting-point), drawing conclusions in one zone which are said to apply in others.

The same criticisms can be levelled at another central concept in Genetic Epistemology, that of 'conservation'. Here again, the ultimate conflation is between Phases 1 and 2. The most detailed practical discussion of 'conservation' arises in *The Child's Conception of Number* (Fr. edn 1941; Eng. edn 1952) and the whole of the book is relevant to the point (Phase 1-Phase 2 conflation) we are considering. Condemning Russell's definition of number as 'too simple' (p. 182, see also references in chs III–VI), Piaget puts forward a hypothesis which affirms that if number is both (logical) class and asymmetrical relation (qualitative separations, in Piaget's own words, that is, *A* is bigger than *B,* and *B* is bigger than *C, A* is bigger than *C*) – which is what he claims to demonstrate – it comes not from logic alone but from their union, that is, the reconciliation of continuity with irreducibility (pp. viii–ix, Foreword). The idea is a clever one, but rests on a 'merging' of logic and number. This merging itself relies on the accepted notion of class and set as entirely conflated with collection. Classes and sets are compared in terms of one-to-one correspondence and *members* are obtained from them by bringing in 'a new operation from outside which is not contained in the logic of classes as such' (p. 183). Thus quantification is 'only achieved by disregarding all the attributes (e.g. brownness, roundness, woodenness in the case of the counted beads in the experiment Piaget cites) in question, i.e. by disregarding the classes' (loc. cit.). This attempt at explaining the origin of number is a confusion of categories. Classes, sets, attributes, quantitativity, qualitativity, are all muddled up. Out of this, actual numbers, 2, 3, 6, etc., are supposed to emerge together with a concept of quantitative 'conservation'.

In essence 'conservation' is said to have been achieved when the spacing of the counters or beads scheduled to be counted no longer affects the perception of their total number. The observation of this event is not, of course, being challenged. Children do, in fact, go through such a conceptual phase and Piaget's *observations* in this regard certainly possess their value. It is, however, another case of treating the observation and record of a situation as if one had explained it. Such 'conservation' reflects a socialisation process which increasingly directs attention on to the exclusive *object-ivity* and hence *exclusive computability* in the situation. The subject is encouraged to see 'truth' as residing only in the presence or absence of the phenomena (counters) not in their relationships (spacing). But of course the existence *and* relationships are both required to extract attributivity whether qualitative or quantitative and thus the ability to identify Phases 1 and 2 in relation to it. To form the collection (Phase 1) of the counters, their 'counter-ness' (Phase 2), which is certainly not only their shape, size, and so on, but also, *in this case,* their relative positions (on the table, off the table, next door, in the next town, and so on), have to be established. This is the true significance of eating the sweet or destroying the counter which creates an *irreversible* situation violating conservation. Such an event constitutes a basic change of conditions associated with a novel situation in Actuality, that is, a 'level-leap'. *Reversibility*, as we said earlier, is entirely conditional, entirely a Phase 2 matter and linked, as far as number is concerned, with the *relative indivisibility* (that is, what is taken for the moment to be indivisible) of a *countable* unit. It cannot be presented in absolute alignment with *counting* itself, which is a Phase 1 affair, without conflation.

Piaget's notion of absolute conservation obscures the obvious fact that for all people, irrespective of age, once there is any degree of subject–object separation, there is a difference only of degree in the perception of (relative) conservation. This very difference relates mainly to the person's field of experience. A child of, say, 4 years old knows perfectly well that he/she does not grow more toes by jumping astride or more fingers by stretching his/her arms out. If a group of such children run from the centre to the corners of a playground, they know that there are not more children at the end than at the beginning! Furthermore, if an adult is presented with six counters and one is removed and taken to the moon, then if he/she were asked how many there now are, some aspect of conditionality must arise immediately in the form of whether to count the one removed *a long way away*. The conditionality is specified as a consideration of *distance between* the counters and not only of the act of counting itself. The question of *countability* (a matter of conditionality) is thus raised and any satisfactory analysis of this simple problem can clearly be seen to require Phase 2 as well as Phase 1.

The absolute treatment of the conservation of number, with its concomitant conflation of 'counting' (Phase 1) and 'countability' (Phase 2), links with Piaget's actual definition of number. Number is regarded by him as a synthesis of ordination and cardination where neither of these can exist without the other (p. 122). But despite Piaget's contribution to the question through his recognition of the need for the presence of both ordinal (dependent on the act of counting which is a Phase 1 feature) and cardinal (the 'how-many', that is, dependent on the collection of numbers being *given together* – also Phase 1) in reciprocation to each other, he, like Russell, still conflates collection and set which is the foundation for the confusion between 'counting' and 'countability', the 'how many' and 'how many-ness', in the event itself.

Not only in number and mathematics generally but in cognition as a whole, Piaget's treatment produces what might be described as 'two absolutes'. The conditionality or relativity disappears out of the act itself. This disappearance is revealed by the wandering movement between Actuality, logic and mathematics embodied in the ambiguous relation of 'action' to 'operation'. Such movement enables an absolute identity to be established between number concepts and the act of counting. Secondly, by treating the 'object-ifying' tendency, that is, 'differentiation' and 'decentring', as inherent in human psychological development and ignoring the fact that this is a special feature of Western and Western-influenced cultures, Piaget creates the second absolute, that is, that of social 'norms'. The latter takes up the position of overall determinant – the goal towards which 'the child' must inevitably, and by natural law, move. The last pages of *Six Psychological Studies* (particularly p. 157) show clearly that, for Piaget, the *goals* of cognitive development possess an a priori determining effect on the pathway of their development – a reflexive control that rules out any consideration of conditionality and makes the process *socially absolute*.

It becomes clear, then, that it is basically by collapsing Phase 1 into Phase 2 so that the latter simply fails to appear, and by ambiguous 'wandering' between logico-mathematics and Actuality, that the Piagetian system appears to 'work'. In fact the subject explores and probes the oscillatory relation of wholes-and-parts in Actuality. This is mapped into logic and mathematics by alternation between, for example, deduction and induction. But instead of this, the Piagetian system fails to recognise the distinction between the frames of reference of thought and Actuality and a blind (helpless) 'groping' is put forward as the only means by which the subject can communicate with the milieu. The latter deteriorates into pure relativism; if we take the world to be *nothing but* logic and mathematics, that is, if Phase 1 is collapsed into Phase 2, then we are reduced to pure conjecture as to our place in it and our knowledge of it dissolves into nothingness. It is not surprising that 'non-terminality' is a universal feature of this alienated world. Definitive clarity about *what* is related, interconnected, and so on, would expose the non-viability of an explanatory system which cannot decide what it is talking about.

This, indeed, is one aspect of Piaget's thought. But if there is a collapse of Phase 1 into Phase 2 in his system, there is also a collapse of Phase 2 into Phase 1 (these are not simply to be identified as forms of conflation since they represent two different processes, not two phases of the same process). Distortion of premisses/axioms (Phase 2) into unchallengeable, authoritative 'truths', together with the collapse of Phase 2 into Phase 1, enables a strong hierarchical organisation to dominate the Piagetian system. Phase 2 is not as easily subsumed under a hierarchy as Phase 1 may be if it (Phase 1) is presented as the exclusive *modus operandi* of cognition. In fact, it is this direction of collapse that makes a superior-inferior ordering in cognition inevitable. For, if a Phase 1 view of the attribute is treated as exclusive (even covertly) this makes the phenomenal aspect of the attribute dominant and logic and mathematics become *dependent* on the authority of that which exists. What exists, in other words, becomes under these circumstances the indisputable and absolute premiss of all argument against which what *might* exist cannot prevail. In the final analysis this must encourage the view that Actuality itself is hierarchical and power-controlled. For the relation between the collection and its elements, shorn of the conditionality of Phase 2, is arbitrary. There is no necessary or implicative connection between the collection of yellow-socked children and each and every one of the children so collected unless there is a clear and independent specification of the conditionality here. If logico-mathematics is made *equivalent* to this (by omitting Phase 2) and also, as in the Piagetian system, there is no clear demarcation between logic, mathematics and Actuality, then the way is open for inferring any given order of Actuality by virtue of the (claimed) logical necessity of the system which either exists or is being imposed. The significance of this in relation to social order is explosive, for manipulation of the *individual* becomes effected through the *manipulation of his or her attributes*. Consider just one example of the mobilisation of a nation for war. Some of these implications are considered further in Chapter 10 below.

The collapse of either (or both) of Phases 1 and 2 into each other is thus

the irreconcilable enemy of human thought and any adequate understanding of it. For it destroys the self-referential revolution which is the
triumph and best contribution of modern European–American thought to
the awakening consciousness of mankind. It is the implication of Gödel's
work especially that refers us back to Actuality in a new way in this
respect. For Gödel compels us, through his mapping of Actuality in
undecidability, to see that indeterminacy is a built-in part of that
Actuality. It is this indeterminacy relating to openness and the holistic
interrelation of the thinking-feeling subject to the milieu which Piaget's
system denies.

⋆ Note that logical connectives are not in themselves to be identified with mathematical
operations (just as predicate expressions and quantifiers are not mathematical entities as
such). These connectives may, however, be treated 'as if 'they were such operations if and
only if the necessary change in connotation is defined in advance. Hence, propositions such as
'the set of logical propositions under exclusive disjunction is a group' is meaningful if and
only if 'v' (exclusive disjunction) is redefined operationally and the given propositions have
also been redefined as quantitative elements of a *mathematical*, and not a logical, system.

9 Scientific Method and the Piagetian System

Actuality and Science

So far the mathematics and conceptual-logical mechanism of the Piagetian system has been analysed with reference to individual mentality. Another and more common form of criticism is concerned with the system as a whole, namely, the complaint that it is not 'scientific'. This is a serious allegation in the light of the claim of Genetic Epistemology to be a new science. Piaget is said not to have considered sufficiently large samples, to have based his conclusions on insufficient evidence and, moreover, not to have used proper sampling techniques nor subjected his results to proper statistical analysis.

This lack of scientific method is referred to by Flavell (1963, p. 425) as ' "bad habits" in Piaget's theoretical and research activity; not indigenous to any particular segment of the system'. However, they are 'recurrent shortcomings which may crop up in any segment'. Flavell has a still more definite view regarding some of Piaget's specific techniques. 'On the one hand, habitual shortcomings of procedure, data analysis, method of reporting findings, etc., leave one chronically uneasy about the empirical end of the superstructure . . . On the other hand, inadequacies in technique of theory-making and of theory–data coupling summate with this unsteadiness in the empirical foundation to evoke corresponding uncertainties about the theoretical aspects of the system as well' (p. 426).

A more recent critical study (Brown and Desforges, 1979) culminates with the view that 'this body of criticism clearly suggests that the theory, where testable, proves inadequate. More seriously, it is in many respects untestable' (p. 162). These and other views are those of writers whose notions of scientific method are quite orthodox in so far as their criteria for a valid scientific theory are rooted in the scientific ideology of the last 300 years. It is such unease as this that has given rise to a massive outpouring of written commentary on Piagetian theory. In this latter sense, write Brown and Desforges, such untestability 'acts as a spur to the accumulation of "literature" but not to the accumulation of understanding' (loc. cit.). Before we dismiss Piaget's work as unscientific on the basis of such orthodox criteria for scientific method, some examination of these criteria is needed in order to assess the scientific status of Genetic Epistemology.

Chapter 8 began the discussion of subject–object separation by affirming that all phenomena, even inanimate ones, relate to their milieus in terms of 'holisms'. This term was adopted to describe the total inter-active relation between phenomena in a quantised universe and was deli-berately expressed in the personalised form of 'I' *and* 'It' in order to underscore the *immanence* and *primacy* of the relation, and to stress that holisms are *inclusive of both the relation and that which is related*. For thinking-feeling beings the notions of perception and conception taken together embody such holisms which, as working hypotheses, can be treated as Actuality. 'Actuality' here means the identifiable objects/events/processes, communicated as wholes-and-their-parts and manifesting the level matrices conditioning their existence and all according to time, place and circumstances. Such 'Actualities' are bound to be private to individual experience even though there is some general agreement on common features. One of these features is the constant recurrence of a paradox – the combination of stability and transformation – which we all take for granted without any sense of incompatibility. The latter involves logical contradiction, and contradiction is an aspect of cognising intelligence which *maps* paradox and is distinct from the total thinking-feeling subject. This exclusively cognitive response to the world tends to impose contra-diction (and incompatibility) on to it on the supposition that existence depends on non-contradiction. The effect is distortive because it identifies the 'either–or' feature of logic with the world itself.

In the evolution of a thinking-feeling species (and of the individual), the increasing separation of 'I' and 'It' has generated the combination of symbol[90] and myth (the former standing in place of the world's phenomena and the latter an unmediated and mutual connection between them) as compensations for the tendency to lose the early holistic inter-action, both of the species and of the individual, with the milieu.[91] Rationalistic as well as mystical forms of this abound in the history of human thought. The symbol-myth view of the world carries with it its own 'bridge' of the 'gap' between subject and milieu. But the need to bridge this gap has become an increasingly pressing problem as the para-mountcy of symbol-myth in human thought and feeling has given way to a more absolute subject–object separation. The latter has only become dominant in modern European-inspired culture within the last 300 years or so, although its roots are much deeper than that.[92] But although the symbol-myth is at present at a discount, it has by no means disappeared. Through the long course of the growth of society itself (and manifested also in the duration of every individual's life) there has been, and is, a perpetual struggle to reunite 'I' and 'It' – to regain the fluid one-ness of the unflawed holistic relations of the 'dream-time' of mankind – the childhood innocence of Blake.[93] The symbol-myth is instinctively grasped at as the only way to accomplish this. The survival of the sense of symbol-myth is, indeed, a threat to the logico-mathematical contemporary world, which is one reason, apart from profitability, why this world seeks to capture and exploit it in all forms ranging from Hitlerism to 'true romance' stories.

But the most significant way in which the latter has been implemented is in the handling of the 'scientific revolution'. As the ancient forms of pre-scientific symbol-myth began to be overthrown from the seventeenth century onwards, a new, heightened subject–object separation, based on a self-referential and a strong logico-mathematical foundation, extended throughout the study of nature and society and thence to the organisation and running of society itself. In response to this, and within the heart of the scientific process itself, new establishments emerged with the aim of turning this new science into a new form of unchallenged authority. Thus the 'double-take' of the twentieth century has been to produce pseudo-symbol-myths using irrationality in the service of hyper-rationality. How else can the incredible mixture of high technology and science with totally barbarous ideologies which actually carry out or contemplate genocide (the Nazi phenomenon is only one example of this) be understood? Genghis Khan at least did not offer a logico-mathematical scientific base for building a skull-pyramid!

It is because of such social nad human rationalisations that it is important to grasp the limits and relevance of 'science' and its relation to logic, mathematics and Actuality. Above all, science has come to be associated, quite falsely, with a totally logico-mathematical interpretation of the world. Within the scientific process this is revealed by the decline of individual creativity under the pressure of bureaucratic impersonalisation.

A first step in assessing science may be made by clarifying its relation with symbol-myth. Symbol-myth is an open-ended, transformation re-flection of being and becoming, phenomenon and interrelation, in the individual's interaction with the milieu – a mode of seeing and grasping one's own relation with this milieu and a mode of seeing and grasping how this milieu relates to itself. This mode is not predominantly rationalistic although it may contain rationalist elements. Symbol-myth has, thus, something in common with the abstraction/projection of logico-mathematics but must not be reduced to it. Similarly science, one aspect of which is a modified form of symbol-myth (all forms of scientific insight possess an affinity with symbol-myth), involves logico-mathematics deeply but, unlike the latter, handles defined phenomena and depends upon a 'fragmentation' of Actuality, or the holisms existing beween observer and milieu. But whereas logico-mathematics is based on an isolation or identification of attributes describable as extractive predi-cation, science operates on the basis of fragmenting holisms into scientific 'events' or 'facts'. The latter are delineated on the basis of an accompanying model and theory which are reciprocally related to these 'events'/'facts'.

From the start, then, science retains some of the 'extended' aspects of the Quanta of Actuality, which the attributive extraction of logic and mathematics does not retain, although the latter shows certain phenomenal characteristics in Phase 1. Part of the 'participation' of science in the world of Quanta is a retention also of something of the symbol–myth relation of the subject's holistic links with the milieu. But while scientific 'facts' closely resemble the Quanta of Actuality, their specific difference from these lies in their dependence for their existence (and cognition) on the application of logic and mathematics to the field under observation. It is the possibility of setting up quantitativity and qualitativity with respect to such events/facts and not with respect to attributes alone which introduces the distinctiveness of science from its adopted and necessary tools in logic and mathematics. In the latter it is the 'yellow-sock-ness' or 'x-ness' which is the essence of attribution; for science it is the yellow-socks as such and their relation to the children as such wearing them, and/or the quantitativity of these phenomena, which is the corresponding focal point. The scientific event, therefore, is an 'intersection' between the flexible and contingently active holisms of Actuality (either between observer and milieu or between objects/events/processes in relation to each other) and the precise, deductive–inductive, inferential relations of logico-mathematics. From such an 'intersection' paradoxical/contradictory situations emerge in which the *extended being* of the world of Quanta is both retained and at the same time covertly reinterpreted in an increasingly abstracted and projected logico-mathematical, that is, *non-extended*, manner.

The possibility of 'wandering' in science is, hence, particularly dangerous. The indefinite fragmentation of Actuality, uncertainly related to logico-mathematisation, develops easily into a hierarchy of 'explanation' in which the 'smaller' is considered to be the most basic and determining even of the most macroscopic events like the conjectured 'big bang'. A contradiction inevitably emerges between the unending character of scientific knowledge and the necessary assumptions at each stage that the next layer of 'smaller' or 'larger' phenomena may be or will be the *ultimate* end-point of scientific explantion. Going along with this contradictory process has been the growing conviction that explanation itself is becoming increasingly meaningless. Science turns away from generality, becomes wary of comprehensive theories and is more and more involved in narrow fields and high technology.

If all subject–object divided experience originates with holisms and experience is compounded of an uncountable totality of such wholes, how does science relate to this situation? Science possesses three principal components. The first is the scientific *fact or event*. The second is the general *model* which to be viable must allow the facts or events to be related to each other in a measurable/deductive-inductive manner. Thirdly, from the interaction of the first two and related specifically to the solution of problems thus arising, there are *theories* (and laws) which must be statable in logical and/or mathematical terms. It is clear that the scientific fact/ event is not simply a 'raw element of reality' but a highly selected segment of Actuality, the selection process being predominantly influenced by the prevailing overall model (T. Kuhn's 'paradigm').

The interactions of the first and second components of science and the transformations involved are extremely tortuous and go way beyond the circumscribed limits of any particular field. For example, considering the progress of astronomy between Copernicus and Newton, we can learn something about this relationship. Copernicus is credited with a 'revolution' which he was certainly unaware of himself. Ptolemy's system with its stationary earth had produced complications in celestial prediction and was replaced with a moving earth and a stationary sun *but without altering the cosmic model* which still accepted the plenum of Aristotle. It required more than a century of the combined socio-intellectual experience of the Reformation, political absolutism and rebellion, economic upheaval and philosophical disillusionment to generate new *self-evident truths* which expressed themselves through a self-referential mathematical and mechanically operating model of the universe. Such a change of model cannot be purely rationally understood. There are too many factors involving emotion and matters of faith (and being) for this. In other words, the *change* of model but not the model itself is a *holistic* matter. Thus, in reference to the interaction of components 1 and 2, what emerges in a change such as the one just described are transformations in what is deemed to be scientific 'fact' and also in what is considered to be a valid mode of isolating this 'fact' out of Actuality (the methodology going with the model).

We can also say that in the purely logico-mathematical zones, '. . . .ness' (for example, 'fullness' for the Aristotelean model; 'emptiness' for the Galilean-Newtonian model) is the focal point of attention. But for any scientific model (that is, the 'science of the day'), it is the notion of '. . . ability' which above all governs the issues, that is, 'testability', 'falsifiability', 'verifiability' – notions expressing the *active interference* of observer in the milieu in accordance with a specific method of fragmenting its wholes into 'parts' and the (re)arrangement of the latter in a logico-mathematically determined linear structure directly derivative from the model. This last is the *domain* (at any moment) of scientific fact/event, which is intimately related to what may be called the *co-domain* consisting of the model and the scientific theories and laws directly emerging from the application of this model.

There is clearly a close affinity between the scientific and logico-mathematical zones. Neither of them may be conflated with Actuality without totally confusing the nature of both as modes of knowing the world. Nor may they simply be equated with each other. Both logic and mathematics are based on attributive extraction and operate in an inferential 'ethos' paralleling or mapping the General Quantisation of Actuality. We referred to this before as general inference, with each specific logico-mathematical structure exemplifying this general inference by particular (strict) implicative connections.

Because of its necessary involvement in the 'extension'[94] aspect of Actuality, science is not based on pure attributivity but requires controlled interference where the control is logico-mathematically 'tailored'. Thus the 'ethos' associated with science is an inferential quantisation process (that is, inference related to quantised facts/events) embodying that 'intersection' referred to earlier between holistic interchange between observer and milieu and the logico-mathematically attributive extraction out of that milieu. Inferential quantisation is a notion designed to express the state in which any object/event/process in Actuality is transformed into a scientific fact/event through measurement, enumeration and implication. The distinction between scientific facts/events and the Quanta of Actuality they relate to is clear. The former are *absolutely* dependent on measurement and enumeration and in so far as they fail in this respect, as they must do sooner or later (falsification), they require to be 're-fragmented' according to a new model in which process logico-mathematics plays a key but not conflationary role.

The subtle but important distinction between logic, mathematics and science is quite absent from Piaget's Genetic Epistemology, as indeed is any distinction between either of them and Actuality. Pervading his system is an impermissible confusion between holisms, models and laws and logico-mathematical structures of implication, all of which must be clearly distinguished in order that they may properly relate to one another and function unambiguously in their own right towards the common benefit of epistemology as a whole.

The similarity between the zone of science and that of logico-mathematics is obvious and hardly surprising. The scientific domain closely parallels Phase 1 and the co-domain parallels Phase 2. A possible objection might be raised that the extraction of attributivity (logico-mathematics) and the delineation of scientific fact are artificially distinguished since both involve some form of observation and selectivity. There is some ground for this objection in that an enormous amount of 'experiment' supportive of a new theory is frequently *thought*-experiment. However, the distinction we have drawn between attributive extraction and active interference *altering* the given field and manipulating the relations of phenomena cannot be gainsaid as a significant difference between science and logico-mathematics.

The Domain and Co-domain

The content and tools of science are grounded in the ongoing and continuous interference of the observer with Actuality from which scientific 'facts' are either extracted or constructed. But the total holistic link between the observer (subject) and the milieu is governed by the socio-historical circumstances in which he finds himself. Social and individual experiences of many kinds are witnesses to this. How many can recall a perception-conception in childhood which is transformed at one point, producing a definite sensation of revelation – a sense of sudden clarity of vision, either literal or metaphysical? The specific forms belonging to different periods/cultures illustrate the same point. The absence of perspective (or the use of a 'distorted' perspective) signifies primarily that this way of representing the world is holistically adequate for both artist and observer in a much wider sense than the art object itself. Any sense of *inadequacy* already contains contrasting (paradoxical/contradictory?) holistic relations between subject and milieu.

This, in fact, is very close to the circumstances involved in the transformation of the scientific model referred to earlier. The conditions of inadequacy – the growing unacceptability of a particular whole-and-parts relation, and the consequent rejection of a hitherto unquestionably accepted level matrix – must be present before an overt struggle to change is embarked on (although the 'probing' relationship of the subject with the milieu, with its attendant contingency-generating feature, is a source of initiation of the new in this respect).

The implicit or explicit modifications in the assumptions of Actuality lying behind models all demonstrate this. The scientific facts of the Ptolemaic universe and those of the Copernican-Newtonian and then Einsteinian are all *facts* but all relate to a different holistic mesh of experience – different general Actualities. G. J. Whitrow in *The Nature of Time* (1975, p. 92) makes the point succinctly when he writes in reference to the Michelson-Morley experiment: 'Indeed, if it had been possible to make the experiment in the days when the Copernican theory was still in dispute, it would have been regarded as conclusive evidence that the Earth does not move at all, but stays at rest at the centre of the universe!' So Actuality – the holistic 'web' of interconnection between and including subject and milieu – is both physiologically and culturally induced. The (philosophical) issue as to whether such an Actuality 'exists' or not is either irrelevant or resolved by recognising that the 'given' at any moment is the Actual of that moment conditioned as it is by the Appearance–Reality duality of that moment.

Western society's concept of Actuality in general has been influenced overwhelmingly by the notion that the boundaried object, one of whose central characteristics is *precision,* is the indisputable starting-point of the subject–milieu relation. Thus, the extraction underlying Western science from this specific Western form of Actuality may be characterised in the following way:

(a)   The domain, in conjunction with the co–domain, is generated by the observer out of the culturally/physiologically determined Actuality. The form taken by this domain constitutes the 'universe of the particular era'. This concept corresponds to many changing images in science, for example, the Bohr atom of 50–60 years ago (tiny solar system) and the contemporary view of the same phenomenon as a haze of probability; again, the analogy of brain structure and tele-phone exchange in the 1930s as against the computer model of the brain today.

(b)   The domain is distinguishable from Actuality in so far as it depends on *precise delineation*, that is, description leading to measurement. This is not the same as the calculable exactitude of the quantitative attribute in mathematics because what is handled by the scientific domain are wholes or Quanta, considered in their wholeness in the first instance, and not simply from the viewpoint of enumerable quantitativity as the extraction of number and mathematical relations. The notion of precise delineation is close to mathematical attributivity but not identical with it. This view of scientific entities, or 'facts', can help to clarify certain significant distinctions between different fields and modes of inquiry, for example, physical and behavioural/social studies. The natural sciences have to contend with only one 'dimension' of observer interference in forming domains, that is, the cultural and physiological restriction of observers themselves. In any human field two 'dimensions' of observer interference are involved, the first being the same as in the natural sciences and the second being the self-aware response of the object over and above that of the observer. It is this that makes the applicability of delineation and mathematical modes questionable in behavioural studies and requires a different approach – perhaps a fuller interchange between holistic Actuality and the proposed domain.

(c)   The domain cannot be generated on its own. It requires the guidance of the co–domain, or model of the universe of the era, and the theoretical expressions of the connections of that universe (for example, the rectilinear, vacuum and rigid body assumptions of Newtonian space). A natural question to follow this would be whether the co–domain emerges from the domain or is the domain decided wholly by the axiomatic framework of the co–domain? In the last analysis each possibility is an aspect of the interrelation of domain and co–domain provided that the word 'wholly' is replaced

by 'predominantly'. For at any specific time or period in the epistemological process, the decision as to what are wholes must
ultimately derive from preconceived theory up to, and at the point
of, delineation. It must be stressed that this is to do with delineability, not with 'reality' or 'existence'. The circular orbits around a
stationary earth of the Ptolemaic system are delineable and, up to a
point, subject to precision. So are the orbits around the sun of the
Copernican–Galilean solar system. Neither are absolutely 'real'
although both are absolute *in themselves* in the sense that, under
specific conditions, they express working and workable models.
Thus, in the *reciprocal interaction/interpenetration* of the domain and
co-domain, the origin is always the whole, or the pure Quantum
aspect of phenomena. It is the decision as to what this (these) is (are)
which is critical in the construction of the domain at any stage and,
indeed, in its transformation/modification into a new domain.

The domain–co-domain relation clearly suggests a parallel to the
logico-mathematical zone and this can usefully be firmed up. The model
determinants in the co-domain clearly have a certain resemblance to the
premisses/axioms and conditions/argument of Phase 2 in the logico-
mathematical zone (for example, Newton's Laws depend on the concept
of a rigid body). Conditionality is also a feature of the co-domain as well as
of Phase 2 but, unlike logico-mathematical conditionality, it is tied to
model-determined delineability rather than attributivity. The difference is
subtle since both can be expressed in propositional form. With the attributivity of logic both 'partness' and 'wholeness' are in view, and the latter
is mapped into the limits of the collection formed; the scientific case is
closer to the extraction of the quantitative attribute deriving as this does
from wholes. In the scientific process the domain is extracted from holistically presented/encountered phenomena – a process of extraction involving either the division into, or grouping together of, provisionally
indivisible and exactly defined 'things'. This is a 'fragmentation' of the
complex whole-parts into a non-complex, in clearly arranged juxtaposition of (scientific) facts. The original part–whole relation of Actuality
is not lost, however, but is transformed by this fragmentation into a series
of whole sub-units equally exact and indivisible. The arrangement of these
into a definite structure constitutes the basis for the derivation of the
model, theory(ies) and laws of the co-domain. Once this is agreed, these
begin reciprocally to influence the *mode* of fragmentation of the domain
itself.

This important distinction between logico-mathematical and scientific
methodology is lost in Piaget's conflationary involvement of group, logic,
number and psychological 'structures' into one indiscriminate mass. The
precision aspect of scientific fact is, of course, not purely quantitative, as is

the attributive basis of mathematics, but refers to the combined logical and mathematical aspects of delineated facts. Science is thus open to a degree of description as distinct from *calculation* without losing its scientific character.

It can be seen that the mutually modifying relation between domain and co-domain closely parallels (almost isomorphically?) the relation between Phases 1 and 2 of logic and mathematics. The identification (in terms of precise delineability) of the specific field is comparable with the formation of the logico-mathemaical collection. Similarly, the co-domain is characterised by the general model of the particular field in question (or, in its widest form, of the view of nature as a whole). The theories and laws expressing specific and exact relations in terms of this model parallel the conditionality of the attribute of Phase 2 in logico-mathematics and are specified in the axiom(s)/premiss(es) related to a general propositional function and the particular propositional functions deductively derived from it. It is important to note that theories do not have to be consistent with each other within a given mode.[95] There is, for example, an 'inconsistency' between the laws of inertia and gravitation, the one affirming the dependence of change of motion on external factors and the other that it is inherent in bodies in terms of attraction to each other. Despite this 'inconsistency', inertial and gravitational mass are the same – in Relativity Theory as much as in classical Newtonianism. The co-domain must not, however, be treated as identical with Phase 2 in logico-mathematics for, like the domain, it reflects a complete (whole) mapping of Quanta in Actuality including their qualitative aspects.

How do we know if we have a viable scientific model? The critical analysis of the premisses of Genetic Epistemology pushes this essential question to the forefront. In its most general form it can be put thus: what are the necessary and sufficient conditions for the establishment of model-determinants of *any* scientific model (that is, the parallel to the axioms/premisses of Phase 2)? The notion of abstraction-projection, summarised as extraction, was adopted for the establishment of logico-mathematical zones out of Actuality and a similar process is involved in the delineation of a scientific field. The target here, however, is somewhat different. It was argued that logico-mathematics extracts, in the form of abstraction and projection combined, from the *structure* of phenomenality, or the quantised universe; science, on the other hand, is primarily concerned with the identity of *whole* objects/events/processes *in and through* their structure. Thus the principal aspect of domain extraction is the identification of wholes from which abstractions can be constructed. This affects what is being called necessary and sufficient conditions. There is a closer alignment between these conditions and the circumstances of Actuality than is the case with either logic or mathematics. Broadly, we can say that the *necessary* conditions for model determinants, and hence a viable model, are expressed as ' . . . without which, nothing', and these map very closely the level matrices of Actuality. Similarly, *sufficient* conditions can be expressed as ' . . . with which, something', and involve the constraints of 'at least' and 'not more than' on the quantitative side, and closely map the whole-and-its-parts which *manifests* the level matrices of Actuality. *The necessary conditions*, not in order of importance, for the formation of a genuine co-domain model are thus:

(i) existence of an identifiable domain and co-domain distinct from each other without conflation or reductionist collapse;

(ii) consequent clear distinction between *model, theory and laws* (co-domain) and *precise quantitative and qualitative delineation*, that is, scientific fact (domain).

(iii) a process of extraction from wholes-and-their-parts, and the level matrices of Actuality which they manifest allowing a clear expression of the reciprocal interaction of co-domain and Actuality specifically manifested in the reciprocity of model, theory, law(s) and precisely delineated field.

The sufficient conditions for establishing model determinants should follow. These must involve constraints to do with 'at least . . . ' and 'not more than . . . ' and correspond to a 'positive' form of the necessary conditions. They must demonstrate (in a general manner) the positive ability to delineate the field and model it, yielding identifiable theories and laws which can be spelt out and applied within the domain. Sufficient conditions can thus be particularised as : (i) calculability, (ii) predictability and (iii) regularity (or repeatability). The *overall and inclusive* sufficient conditions can be expressed as (*a*) verifiability and (*b*) falsifiability. All of these criteria must be present. If either verifiability or falsifiability is taken on its own it loses its significance as a criterion. Verifiability alone is meaningless since no finite number of experiments, however large, can ever exhaustively 'prove' a theory; there is always at least one more experiment that can be performed. Similarly, falsifiability alone is an insufficient criterion for any scientific theory or statement since there is no provision by itself for any form of correspondence in Actuality.[96] Together, however, they provide an overall summary of sufficiency. The mutual dependence of these conditions or criteria can be expressed in the single notion of *testability*, a term expressing the totality of sufficient conditions for any scientific statement (theory or law). If one wanted one single concept and term marking off scientific knowledge from all other forms it would be this one.

What is the link between testability and the precise delineation of the domain? First, it is clear that the domain is not restricted in any way to being an 'object' nor is it restricted in scale but may refer to any object/

event/process up to and including the cosmos itself. Consider, for example, a plate. The seeming completeness of the plate at the everyday level is to be contrasted with the apparent behaviour of its 'fundamental particles' observed from this everyday level. Its completeness, manifested in 'low velocity' solidity (subject to its being broken), is apparently in absolute conflict with the motion of its 'particles' at velocities approaching that of light. There is clearly a 'frontier' to the acceptable domains related respectively to these two levels of the plate. The theories applicable to these levels become testable only if such frontiers are precisely delineated and recognised as such. Part of such delineation is the recognition that the relationship between the two domains cannot simply be a linear one of indefinite extension but must reflect the complex and multi-dimensional character of Actuality.

At a cosmic level, a useful thought-experiment further illustrates the point. An empirical result incorporated into the Special Theory of Relativity is that, relative to all observers in frames moving with uniform velocities relative to each other, the measured velocity of light is the same (approximately 300,000 Km). This apparent anomaly for observers with different relative velocities can be turned round: from the viewpoint of an 'observer' moving *at* the velocity of light, the measured velocities of all the (previous) observers will appear to be the same (186,000 mi/sec.). Thus, relative to the 'frame of reference' of the light, all these observers will appear to be *at rest relative to each other*. It is *as if* this observer, moving with the light, were 'outside' or on the frontier of the cosmos which would appear as 'solid' and unitary as the plate does at the everyday level. Of course, the everyday 'separateness' of the plate (from ourselves and other things) is connected with this 'outsideness' and makes the distinction between domains, marked by delineated frontiers, an indispensable constraint on theories (and models) relating to these domains.

It is arguable, then, that for any field of science ranging from individual objects/events/processes to all of natural science itself, there is always a specified domain the limits of which correspond to a definite boundary of measurement and which may be identified by the possibility and means of precise delineation. The arrival at such a boundary is heralded by an increasing failure of testing and hence of the particular criteria of testability. Testability itself becomes increasingly uncertain together with the actual ability to delineate the objects/events/processes of the particular domain. Ultimately the domain itself becomes unidentifiable. The important implication that derives from this is that scientific work proceeds in any field *as if* its domain is universal, even if the boundary of this domain has not yet been reached or clearly identified. A final point in this survey is that it must be emphasised that test*ability* (and, therefore, verifi*ability* and falsifi*ability*) are co-domain issues whereas test*ing* (and, therefore, verific*ation* and falsific*ation*) are domain matters. Any confusion between these (sufficient) conditions and their application is tantamount to a confusion between domain and co-domain which is a major example of conflation.

The ultimate termination (and/or transcendence) of any model formed under the aegis of these necessary and sufficient conditions is built into the scientific process as such. Popper's argument for a falsifiability as opposed to a verifiability criterion is a welcome extension beyond the latter but does not establish its supersession and ends up by saying no more than that one model must always replace another. Further discussion of this and related issues are to be found, for example, in I. Lakatos and A. Musgrave, *Criticism and the Growth of Knowledge,* in which a central interest is Lakatos's development on the Popperian viewpoint. Our only comments here are that:

(*a*) the Popperian discussion treats the scientific enterprise by 'absorbing' the domain into the co-domain, although falsifiability is carefully maintained as a logical criterion;

(*b*) Lakatos's hierarchy of theories is another hyper-logicisation, in which domains, co-domains and theories are strung together in a linear sequence of preferment. Such a linear hierarchy contradicts the actual multiple co-existence of different, apparently inconsistent, theories (for example, we live each day according to flat-earth, geocentric assumptions,while recognising – especially if we are astrophysicists or astronauts – a helio-centric, galacto-centric and curved-space universe, as co-existing with our Ptolemaic everyday view).

The parallel between domain and co-domain and Phases 1 and 2 has already been noted. The co-domain, like Phase 2, is non-spatio-temporal while the domain, like the collection, exhibits a partially spatio-temporal character.[97] Here, the indivisibility/completeness of the mathematical and the logical proposition revealed by the 'unbreakable' character of the element of the collection (relative to the attribute) is paralleled precisely by the identification of the scientific fact by delineation in the domain. In both cases, the relation of these epistemological categories to Actuality involves recognising a distinction between *exactitude* and *approximation*. In effect this distinction marks in a mapped form (in science as much as logico-mathematics) the region of 'impact' of contingency on causality in Actuality. It is this region within which lies creative novelty. It belongs completely to the holistic side of subject–object and object–object inter-action and is mappable in science only as a *change of precise delineation,* comparable to the change of premisses/axioms in the case of logic and mathematics.

This is the central problem area that Piaget begins to approach in *The Development of Thought.* Here, he applies a corrupted version of General

System Theory (Bertalanffy), and hopes to gather up under a notion of 'approximative compensation' logico-mathematical structuration, scientific development and creative novelty. The discussion of this attempt has revealed how he has failed as much in this as in his original enterprise.

Piaget's Claim to Have Founded a 'New Science'

How does Piaget's system stand up as a 'new science' in the light of such perspectives? We began by noting that Genetic Epistemology shares many of the characteristics of orthodox scientific theory and methodology and many of the criticisms of it have been on grounds that it holds in common with other scientific theories in other fields. It has been challenged for failing to use statistical methods. But there are many cases, particularly in behavioural and social fields, where statistical methods are used and although the calculations are 'correct' in themselves, the relation of number to substantive concepts and/or the Actuality of the field is frequently circular, tautologous, or at best ambiguous. There is, in short, a reification of number with an attendant distortion of meaning. A comment by Lakatos on the view that 'Newton's work was hindered by false astronomical data' might apply favourably to Genetic Epistemology in this respect precisely because of the absence of statistics: 'The unreliability of empirical evidence was not then concealed by the ritual of statistical decision procedures' (*Mathematics, Science and Epistemology*, p. 79).

As far as the 'patching up' of paradigms (models and their dependent theories and laws) with 'ad hoc' hypotheses is concerned, all fields are 'guilty' of this. And, as Feyerbend has very adequately shown, all scientific theories are 'falsified' the moment they are formulated (1978 *passim*). So Piaget's system is not unique in these respects. 'Falsification' by alternative experiments or 'verification' by replication is by no means decisive regarding the scientific viability or otherwise of Genetic Epistemology. No finite number of observations/experiments can ever 'prove' or 'disprove' a theory. Theories can be more or less rich in empirical *potentiality* (that is, the possibility of yielding precisely delineated domains or extensions of the same), but the concept of 'empirical content' as Popper and others conceive it is not supportable because of the implied conflation of domain and co-domain contained in this notion. It is the view here that a valid scientific treatment of any field is judged by whether or not there is a real search in progress for the necessary and sufficient conditions for a scientific model without conflation of domain and co-domain.

In the first place, the domain must be extractable in a precisely delineated form. This is clearly not satisfied by the Piagetian system.

Consider the stage theory. From one viewpoint this looks like no more than an (acceptable) 'ad hoc' hypothesis. But there are other features which fail to produce a clearly distinguishable domain and co-domain and do not satisfy the required search for and establishment of the necessary and sufficient conditions for a model. Stage and age are not connected with any degree of certainty (not even relative) by the 'model' (including the assertion of the invariance of order). Thus, it is perfectly possible, as was shown in Chapter 7, for anyone to be at any stage at any age. Again, when a subject is tested, there is no *option*, he/she *must* appear *somewhere* on the stage spectrum. The 'model/theory' is not selective as far as the 'domain' is concerned, and the 'experiments' conducted in this 'domain' are thus inevitably self-confirming. Conversely, there is no way under these cir-cumstances by which the 'model/theory' could be falsified. The domain, in short, is infinite (that is, interminable – a condition quite in keeping with the non-terminality of all Piaget's notional entities, like 'structures'). The exclusion, moreover, of unmanageable elements like 'genius' (a Bach, Rembrandt, or Einstein) reinforces the non-falsifiability of the theory when this is taken together with its infinite boundary. The conclusion from these points is that the particular (sub)field of Genetic Epistemology which is how the stage theory might be described is not only not de-lineated, but is quite *undelineable*. It follows that the supposed inferential Quanta – the scientific 'facts' – claimed by Piaget are entirely pseudo-morphic. At best they have a possible descriptive value although this is offset by the extra effort involved in deciphering them. The same criticism may be made of the equilibrium model which is similarly self-confirming. A sort of 'perfect' equilibrium is already pre-ordained in the inevitability of a process which provides the same goal for every subject. Any variation reflects only a 'falling short' of this goal and there is no possibility of the process itself being theoretically falsified.

Apart from this, it was the object of Chapters 1–7 to demonstrate that all necessary conditions are constantly violated, and although this emerges with particular force in the 'mathematics' discussed in Chapters 2–4, it is clear also from the discussion of Chapters 5–7. The co-domain constantly 'collapses' into the domain or, alternatively, zones are conflated. The premisses/axioms of different zones are perpetually interchanged without acknowledgement and it has been shown conclusively that Piaget's use of conventional mathematics, far from carrying out the abstraction-projection of Actuality into a symbolism distinguishable from the subject of symbolisation, is no more than an alternative to verbal description. Some of it (see *The Growth of Logical Thinking* especially) involves a form of projection but without abstraction, and the later, purely contrived, 'mathematics/logic' (see *The Development of Thought* especially) involves abstraction but no projection.

As regards sufficient conditions, Piaget's model and theory are also unsatisfactory. For as we have seen from the necessary conditions the only constraint on the meaning of 'stage' and 'equilibrium' is the private decision of the inquirer. Hence, there is no realistic means of interpreting the 'data' yielded by the method. In these circumstances, neither predictability nor unpredictability, regularity nor non-regularity, have any meaning because calculation and propositional inference are ruled out by the non-terminality of substantive concepts, such as decentring, differentiation, assimilation, accommodation, action and operation. Any regularities must be tautologous or circular, providing (at best) only mirror-like copies of social–individual relations but no analytical progress in either sociological or psychological terms beyond this. The stop-gap character of *décalage* illustrates this most effectively.

Perhaps the least unsatisfactory aspect of Piaget's work is the clinical method (a very full exposition of this is to be found in *The Child's Conception of the World,* 1929) which, despite its shortcomings, is a potentially fruitful method of investigating mentality, the essence of which is direct verbal exchange between observer and subject. It is a satisfactory way of overviewing mentality, because properly reviewed, with attention paid to the *un*selfconscious and non-verbal aspect of the subject's response, it can include holistic investigation as well as logically analysed verbal response, and can bypass (partially at least) the problems of self-awareness which intrude into any human inquiry. Prejudice on the part of the observer, as much of Piaget's own clinical method shows, is not obviated, however. Apart from this drawback, the method has the advantage of having no pretensions to quantitativity and makes no attempt to apply this attribute where it is inappropriate. Nevertheless, it is constantly misused (not, in this case, by Piaget) by being artifically 'quantified' ('grading' of responses), such quantification then being subject to 'statistical analysis'. This is not a fault of the method itself, however, but of researchers attempting to gain quantitative 'credentials' for their work in a context in which quantification is not only inappropriate but actually distortive.[98]

Piaget's use of the clinical method is not beyond criticism. First, there is his hierarchical assumption that the adult world is the final reference point and that this is absolute and always superior. The judgement of children's responses is thus inevitably related to this alone. Consistently with this the scene is set by the experimenter who is simultaneously part of and outside the experiment but whose inevitable interference is not (genuinely) taken into account. Piaget's discussion of the question put to the child of 6, 'Does the sun move?' (1929, p. 125), for example, demonstrates the point. For this question is extremely profound and may be very difficult to answer. It might require both an awareness of different views of celestial motion and a judgement about preferential 'realities' (that is, Actualities). Is the Copernican-Newtonian view, which is held as an article of intellectual faith today, 'truer' than the Ptolemaic, which is the actual assumption we all make in following through the ordinary day (the sun 'rises' and 'sets' and the earth remains 'still' while we walk on it)? The decision as to which is 'true' and which is 'false' is a matter of social authority and immediate relations with one's milieu and not of scientific judgement. If the latter were so we should be obliged to take account of both solar movement within the galaxy and galactic motion within the cosmos, thus introducing an increasing uncertainty about our daily decisions and movements. Moreover, there is a case for saying that if we base our judgement on immediate experience (as Galileo advises us not to do) we should reject all but the Ptolemaic view. (We actually live our lives on the presuppositions of a flat earth and a geocentric solar system.)

Despite some claim to avoid it, Piaget's question and answer method exercises a continuous form of social authority and also persistently disturbs the 'observed' situation. The description of responses and their categorisation are all products of the *experimenter's* frame of reference and not that of the subject. The disturbance is thus always in favour of the questioner. States of 'disequilibrium' emerge as failures to conform to the criteria of equilibrium conjectured by the experimenter. Child subjects are treated solely as small logico-mathematical abstractors, possessing no sense of rebellion or humour, or points of view of their own independent of the questioner – in fact, as non-human beings.[99] Such 'aberrations' as do crop up are treated as non-serious interruptions or derogated as 'mythomanic', 'fallacious', 'romancing', and so on (Piaget, 1929, p. 8).

Thus, we are led back to the original question here: Is Genetic Epistemology a 'new science' as Piaget claims? In the sense that physics and biology are sciences it clearly fails to meet the criteria and the answer to the question must be 'no' if science is to be taken in this sense. This rejection of Genetic Epistemology as a science is not based upon lack of statistics or even on the existence of ad hoc hypotheses such as *décalage*. Quantum physics itself has many such ad hoc hypotheses (Feyerabend, 1978, *passim*) and the history of science is full of equivalent examples. Nor does the rejection rest on the results of different experiments which either attempt to replicate those of Piaget or are built on different assumptions (notably those of J. Bruner). Replication has produced conflicting evidence, and experiments based on alternative assumptions (models) naturally extract different domains and must be seen as related to an alternative theory. There is no hierarchy of preference between such theories, and the experimental results corresponding to each *together* constitute (relative) absolutes deriving from the conditions on which each is based, that is, the axiomatic or model-determinant basis of each theory.

The main reason for rejecting Genetic Epistemology as a science is its conflationary character which has been our constant theme throughout this book. As we have already emphasised, Piaget is not alone in this, for there are many theoretical pretenders to scientific status who must be queried on the same grounds. In all such cases conflation is normally linked with a 'symbolism' which itself embodies the conflation. This is often regarded as providing mathematical (and logical) credentials for fields of study aspiring to 'scientific status' but which have failed to transcend reflective description. This issue is sufficiently important within science, logics and mathematics to need further, more detailed discussion, especially in the context of rejecting Piaget's claim to have created a 'new science'. The crucial significance of the issue relates not only to whether valid mathematisation is essential for any science but also to whether (if this is so) science is anything more than a special department of knowledge with no more claims to superiority and final answers than any other. The principal feature of the contemporary scene is to drive all knowledge towards an exclusively 'mathematical-logical' form irrespective of its field. It is this context which makes the Piagetian system so sharp a case study in the process.

Symbolism, Science and Genetic Epistemology

Central to the question of whether either science or logico-mathematics holds a particular lien on truth is the *operative form* of propositions and the deductive/inductive connections they are supposed to embody. It is worth examining the extent to which mathematisation or symbolism expands knowledge seemingly otherwise unobtainable.[100] In order that a system of mathematical signs should constitute a viable symbolism, certain conditions have to be satisfied and these conditions have some degree of similarity to the necessary and sufficient conditions for a scientific theory. In the first place, such a symbolism must be demonstrably extracted from Actuality by abstraction and projection, reveal exclusively quantitative attributivity and be expressible in both collection and set forms, such that these are not conflated. It must also be possible to demarcate the collection or set so represented. These conditions approximate to the necessary conditions for a scientific model/theory. For the signs to constitute a symbolism, they must also be manipulable in computation, normally with operational signs, and be joined into meaningful propositions connected by implicative argument. Finally, they must quantitatively mirror the relationships as well as the phenomenality of the relevant wholes in Actuality.

Many sign-systems presented as symbolisms do not satisfy these criteria and it is with these that we are concerned in this end-piece to the discussion of scientific epistemology. A vivid but simple example of spurious symbolism is revelaed in a court scene in a very old film (mid 1930s), featuring Gary Cooper as one of the Depression's unemployed who inherits a fortune and wants to give it away to his friends ('Mr Deeds Goes to

Town'). A psychiatrist has been employed by Mr Deeds's relatives to prove that he is a manic-depressive. The psychiatrist opens up a chart and presents a 'graph' (see Figure 9.1). Pointing to the chart he says: 'When he is elated, he is up here [points to "High"] and when he is depressed he is

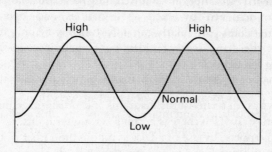

Figure 9.1

down there [points to "Low"].' The 'analysis' is loaded with polysyllabic, technical-sounding words which add nothing to the original simple piece of nonsense but which is intended to lead the listener to believe that some new 'facts' have emerged from the operation; so extensive is this pheno-menon that we decided to adopt the term 'Deeds' to describe certain types of 'mathematics' and 'scientific' terminology. Piaget constantly uses 'Deeds' symbolism and jargon but he is by no means unique in this respect.

What is wrong with 'Deeds' mathematics? There are, of course, many occasions when a diagram or signs, abbreviations, and so on, can reveal what lists of figures or verbal description cannot. Those are not the situations being referred to. What one is concerned with is the diagram and/or notation which claims mathematical characteristics and yet is no more than an abbreviated description of the event it is said to be derived from. Such 'mathematisation' is then seemingly manipulated and seems to 'prove' the proposition relating to the event and this sense of 'proof' is then transferred to the event itself as a causal connection. 'Deeds' mathematics is not simply descriptive. Because it consists of such abbreviations, it remains in the same zone or field as the (often holistic) concepts from which it seems to have been extracted. However useful such abbreviations may be, they are not *symbolic* in so far as they do not constitute a manipul-able (calculable) model yielding results not obtainable directly from either the concepts or the objects/events/processes they refer to. Again, standard operational symbols are frequently used implying a calculability of the sign-system in cases where this does not apply as in the type of behavioural situations Piaget constantly deals with. No 'Deeds' model has any predic-tive capacity or inherent necessity nor can inferences be drawn from it. If a theory is put forward and expressed in 'Deeds' mathematics it is no more and no less than a statement in another way of the beliefs or assumptions of the particular theoretician. 'Deeds' mathematics muddles number itself with the proposition involving the number, that is, quantity with the conditions of quantity and then, in a second phase of confusion, quantity is identified with Actuality. Notwithstanding such confusion, much prestige can be achieved by such abbreviations and operations, and non-mathematicians particularly can unfortunately be only too easily intimidated by these apparently faultless but actually pseudo-scientific and self-fulfilling 'credentials'.

We can characterise 'Deeds' mathematics in the following three points:

(a)   It is always, in terms of the diagrams and/or language underlying it, descriptive. In itself there is nothing wrong with this.

(b)   But it purports, by use of a false symbolisation (that is, the symbols are only abbreviations) to add *something new*, that is, to reveal an inner *necessary* relationship of a calculative character.

(c)   It embodies this in a model, in a false co-domain, claiming to be predictive but which is not so. It is, in fact, self-fulfilling.

Closely related to 'Deeds' mathematics is 'Deeds' language or terminology, that is, words and phrases used in an accepted scientific manner but which do not move from the field of the event to represent an independent model in any way. The sign that 'Deeds' language is operating is its non-terminality which allows it to be indeterminately referred to at least two situations different in kind and making any form of test impossible. In essence, 'Deeds' language is quite arbitrary and any form of 'test' that may be applied to a theory expressed this way resolves itself into an assertive restatement of the original proposition (again, a form of self-fulfilment). 'Deeds' language or terminology can never expose discrepancy and/or falsification but only function to facilitate a self-fulfilling prophecy. Where 'Deeds' mathematics confuses quantity, quality and Actuality, 'Deeds' terminology confuses logical propositions with Actuality. If there is any notion that it might relate to the holistic interaction of subject and milieu, this is out of the question as, above all, 'Deeds' formulations deny paradox in any form because of their *self-fulfilling* aspect. There are also 'Deeds' diagrams, which embody the same features as 'Deeds' mathematics and 'Deeds' language.

'Deeds' characteristics are found extensively in social studies which provide the sharpest examples but by no means the only ones. Economics is fruitful in this respect. It may even be found in science itself, especially in the discussion of its foundations. The *necessary conditions* for a genuine mathematical symbolic system are: (i) only the quantitative attribute may be extracted from the signified Actuality considered as a 'collection' of wholes; (ii) the system, and its signs must be separately identifiable, so that signs and relations on one hand and signified and connections on the other embody distinct spheres of existence. It must also not be possible to confuse the symbols with any other object or phenomenon; (iii) it must be capable of optimally revealing in a progressive way all quantitative manifestations and relationships inherent in its own zone through its computivity; (iv) the generality of the symbols must adequately reflect the quantitative generality of the signified objects/phenomenon and their relations, permitting an adequately general methodology.

The necessity of these conditions may be said to derive from the principle, 'without which, nothing' and may be said to guarantee the system's viability in a general form. We may likewise consider the *sufficient conditions* of a viable symbolism as deriving from the principle, 'with which, something', that is, those conditions which ensure the specificity of the system as distinct from its generality. These sufficient conditions relate to the system's communicability and are mainly exemplified as: optimum, standardisation; lack of ambiguity; immediacy of comprehension; facility of computation.

The essence of all these cases is the absence of level recognition and this omission is strikingly demonstrated in a central Piagetian concept, reversibility, related to the group. Chapter 2 opened the discussion of Piaget's use of the mathematical group and began to show how its misuse results in substantiating the notion of absolute logical 'reversibility' and 'conservation'. It is now possible to look more fully at the mechanism which does this. Piaget, over and above everything else, 'wanders' between a group interpreted as a collection (Phase 1) and a group interpreted (conditionally) as a set (Phase 2). There was some discussion earlier regarding the special characteristics of groups in relation to standard sets/collections. It will be recalled that, conventionally, a group is a special sort of set together with a rule of combination. Following the Phase 1–Phase 2 analysis this means that a *group-set* (Phase 2) related to a *group-collection* (Phase 1) has to be identified. In short, *extra* conditions make a set into a group, and these are expressible in the form of propositional functions, just as ordinary set conditions are. As with an ordinary set–collection relationship, these propositional functions *alternate* between the collection and set phases of the group, but the difference between ordinary sets and group-sets is that the propositional functions for the latter necessarily involve predicates with two or more arguments and those for ordinary sets do not. For example, the property of closure can only be expressed as a propositional function with three arguments.

Now, a notable feature of the Piagetian analysis is its undifferentiated transition from Actuality to logic, logic to mathematics and back again in all cases, without qualification. This is shown most clearly, perhaps, in his treatment of 'reversibility'. The notion implies the possibility of absolute or 'pure' repetition, which is valid if reversibility is defined in, and restricted to, the logical zone but is not valid in Actuality itself. Here logical reversibility is distinguished from that which reversibility maps in Actuality by referring to the latter as 'backwards and forwards movement', that is, a basic aspect of 'action' which constitutes the world of the subject's Actuality according to Genetic Epistemology. It is this movement which Piaget conflates with logical reversibility. Such 'backwards and forwards' motion is, in fact, a very limited part of the subject's action on, or observation of, his/her milieu. More important, the apparently repetitious motion in Actuality always involves unique and novel features and is, therefore, never totally repetitious and never *purely* 'backwards and forwards'. If anything is 'pure' it is the mapping of the movement as *reversal/reversibility* in logic (Phases 1 and 2 respectively). Scientifically, this involves the identification of a domain and a co-domain. While the logical mapping of 'backwards and forwards' motion is *reversal/ reversibility,* the mathematical parallel to this is to be found in the *inverses* of the group-collection and in *invertibility* which is a membership condition of the group-set. All groups, including the INRC group of transformations, the culmination of the Piagetian system, are mathematical and not logical entities. It is quite illegitimate to move without qualification from a mathematical to a logical interpretation as is done in the Piagetian analysis.

Thus, starting with the unacceptable identification of *logical* reversal/ reversibility with the non-reptitious 'back and forth' movement of *Actuality,* and continuing with an equally illegitimate identification of reversibility with invertibility and hence logic with mathematics, one can see more clearly how the employment of various 'Deeds' expressions becomes absolutely indispensable if the system is to appear to 'work'.

Is group theory to be taken as definitely mathematical and not logical, then? One of the central ways in which one can test whether an inferential system is primarily or wholly mathematical, or primarily or wholly logical, is the presence or absence of *computativity in any form*. And in the most general sense, groups and their conditions wholly satisfy this. It is clear, then, that the whole group-method Piaget employs in relation to his 'cognitive structures' is an entirely illegitimate transfer of mathematics to logic.

Returning to 'reversibility' and 'conservation', which are regarded in their most general form in Genetic Epistemology as key features of the final formal-operational (that is, adolescent-adult) stage, marked by the appearance of the INRC group in cognitive structural form, and using again the now very familiar counters or sweets example, we can 'lay out' the Actuality–logical–mathematical relations in a non–conflationary manner. Assuming that the counters/sweets are 're-placeable' (that is, can be returned to their starting point after being moved), then repeated actions revealing this in Actuality can be *logicised* in the normal attributive-extraction manner into *reversal* (Phase 1). The attribute in this case can be stated as 'things (counters/sweets) which can be re-placed' and the collection (reflecting the *phenomenal* aspect of the attribute) derived from this must satisfy this attribute (the previous discussion of removing a counter to 'the moon' and the subsequent discussion of the circumstantiality of any organised piece of Actuality will be recalled). The *conditions* of the attribute in this case (that is, Phase 2) can be stated as 're-placeable-ness' (or 're-place-ability' if one is considering scientific theory/law rather than logic) or *reversibility*. Is the pathway here from Phase 1 to Phase 2 exclusively logical? Clearly not, for the attribute itself can be considered more a quantitative than a qualitative one (although the qualitative feature is not entirely absent), that is, movement 'back and forth' is a measured process and in the final analysis is reducible to this.[101] What, then, is the mathematical, Phase 2, aspect of reversal? This is without doubt one of the four conditions signifying the group, that is, possessing *inverses* or 'invertibility' or 'invertible-ness', indicating that in this case we are dealing with a special type of set, the group–set, aligned with which is a group–collection. The elements of such a group–collection can be stated as 'elements possessing inverses', or the property (condition) of invertibility. The whole of this logico-mathematical extraction relates to the cicumstances of Actuality which allow 'back and forth' movement without destroying the integrality of the particular Quantum or whole-and-its-parts embodied in the original assembly of sweets/counters, none of which is destroyed, eaten, or removed to unfeasible distances in the process of movement.

We saw in Chapter 3, in the case of the 'grouping', how Piagetian concepts are put into mathematical symbols which are then 'collapsed' into standard mathematics, enabling vacillation in interpretation. Generally speaking, Piaget uses two sorts of sign to imply mathematical characteristics. The first (discussed in Chapters 2–4) relates to groups, lattices and propositional logic. The second (used particularly in *The Development of Thought* but also in *The Growth of Logical Thinking*) is not related to such systems but consists of Piagetian concepts expressed in signs that look mathematical but in fact belong to the category of abbreviation. The fluid, or vacillating, interpretations of these various signs is achieved principally through the confusion of element and operation and the use of these notions in quite distinct ways. 'Operation' can mean mental operation (an element of the system?) and be taken as either a 'term' in an equation-sentence or the entire sentence. Again, operation can mean the implicit 'rule of combination'. The net result is a cycle in which Piaget ends with the same conceptual assumptions with which he began.

In Chapter 4, the INRC group was found to fit in with Piaget's theory of proportionality if and only if it is 'collapsed' into logic, whereupon it ceases to be a group. The logic itself is said to replicate the subject's actual thinking. But this 'collapse' of INRC into logic, which is indispensable if the hypothesis of cognitive structures exactly embodying logical relations is to be supported, eliminates the indispensable distinction beween the INRC model, propositional logic and the experienced world along the lines we have indicated. A further 'collapse' of everything into pure number occurs at the end of the exposition which reduces the experienced world itself at its most basic level to the exclusively quantitative.

In a comparable manner the lattice of sixteen binary propositions is alleged to be 'collapsable' into one proposition (no. 15). In Piaget's own treatment, therefore, there is a vacillation between the sixteen propositions seen as a model and the identification of them as actual cognitive events. The case of GOU (see the Appendices to Chapter 4) showed clearly how this was not acceptable. Thus, neither the 'mathematical' nor the 'logical' apparatus used by Piaget embodies any viable model of the event of cognition. The systems which emerge are themselves not genuine models but each and every one – grouping, INRC group and lattice – 'collapse' into the Actuality experience from which they are supposed to be analytically derivative and distinguishable. The instrument for this is the creation of a sign system peculiar to Genetic Epistemology, the abbreviation of its concepts into a 'Deeds' system, the 'collapse' of these into standard mathematical forms, a distorted use of mathematical methods and, finally, the implicit transformation of these standard forms into 'Deeds' mathematics which ends up as an abbreviated sign manifestation of the original concepts masquerading as deductively revealed novelty!

All of this is the case where Piaget adopted conventional mathematical forms to embody his hypothetical constructs, that is, in the earlier phase of the theoretical exposition of Genetic Epistemology, associated with *The Growth of Logical Thinking* and the *Traité de logique*. The second 'mathematical' method used by Piaget is a directly 'Deeds technique' without any intervention of standard mathematical forms. In *The Development of Thought* (p. 4) he writes:[2]

> Like the organisms, the cognitive systems are actually both open in the sense that they undergo exchanges with the milieu and closed insofar as they undergo 'cycles'. Let us call *A*, *B*, *C*, etc., the parts forming such a cycle and *A'*, *B'*, *C'*, etc., the elements of the milieu required to feed the system. We can then formulate a structure whose diagram is:[2]
>
> $(A \times A') \rightarrow B$, $(B \times B') \rightarrow C$, . . .,$(Z \times Z')$ [*sic*]$\rightarrow (A \times A')$, etc.
> [2] With naturally the possibility of varied short circuits or inter sections, etc.

This is 'Deeds' mathematics par excellence. The diagram is intended to be a model of biological and cognitive systems in their exchange with the milieu and in which the characteristics shared by both are manifested, that is, *openness* of exchange and *closedness* of a cyclic character. The diagram says no more than this. The mathematical signs $(A, A', x, \longrightarrow)$ add nothing to the verbal exposition and the diagram remains firmly in the same zone as this verbal exposition (see pp. 5ff.). The cycle appears to consist of separate 'bits' such as $(A \times A')$, B, etc., where each 'bit' is unaffected by any other. What happens, for example, to A, A', etc., after combining to result in B? More important, there is no compulsion inherent in the 'symbolism' for there to be a return to $(A \times A')$. The point illustrates most clearly the 'Deeds' character of this example. The danger lies exactly at this point since the mathematical-type 'symbolism', both 'elements' and 'operations', suggest the usual inbuilt *necessity* associated with computativity of standard mathematics which is entirely absent in the actualities of the diagram. In fact, the *alphabetical sequence*, itself, *A, B,* . . . *A,* hints obliquely, in a 'Deeds' manner, at the necessity of such a return (to $A \times A'$). The cyclic return in the diagram to $(A \times A')$ is no more than an abbreviated representation of what was asserted in words in the previous paragraph. The point is not unimportant in the light of the now very familiar problem in the Piagetian system of trying to combine closed structures with the openness demanded by the genesis of novelty. $(A \times A')$ has to end the diagram for 'closedness' to be satisfied. This 'closure' in *The Development of Thought* is a complete departure from the group closure previously used to define the cognitive process in Piaget's earlier works. It admits *any* elements into the system whereas group-type closure 'preselects' the elements through the rule of combination. In effect, in the case of group closure, the rule of combination is determining, but in this case (cyclic closure?) the elements determine the closure. This is quite consistent with the general line of *The Development of Thought* which changes the emphasis in Genetic Epistemology from the identification of established structures (equilibrium) to the genesis of structures (equilibration). *The Development of Thought* effectively abandons groups, 'groupings' and lattices which receive virtually no mention. The cyclic model seems very influenced by Systems Theory (see Bertalanffy, 1971). The type of 'mathematical' notation changes accordingly.

Piaget writes (1978b, p. 56):

It is therefore clear that until the usually tardy access to sufficiently precise models is achieved, we witness a series of states showing progressive equilibrium, with initial stages reaching only unstable forms of equilibrium because of their gaps, disturbances and above all, because of actual or virtual contradiction . . . Thus, the general model should take the following form:

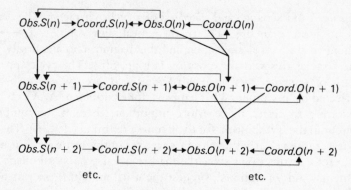

etc.   etc.

Each *obs.S* of a given row is thus a function (thick, oblique lines) of the
Obs.S and *Coord.S* of the preceding row, and each *Obs.O* is likewise a
function of the *Obs.O* and *Coord.O* of the previous level. Thus in like
manner the *Obs.* of the initial row is a function of the more elementary
levels.

To remind the reader, Obs.S represents 'observables relative to the
subject's actions', Obs.O represents 'observables relative to the objects',
Coord.S denotes 'the subject's inferential co-ordinations of actions (or
operations)' and Coord.O denotes 'inferential co-ordinations between the
objects' (see Piaget, 1978b, p. 52).

This diagram (p. 56) is called by Piaget 'the general *model*' (our
emphasis) and its 'generality' rests on the use of the '*n*th' stage of development of equilibration. This is not a co-domain model nor a mathematical
structure exhibiting conditional restraints on a quantitative attribute. It is
pure 'Deeds'; its says no more than a verbal description would, although it
does perform the function of visual condensation. There is a familiar
unclarity between interpreting 'Obs.S' as '*observables relative* to the *subject's
actions*' (that is, Actuality, phenomena) and understanding it as a *predicate-
statement,* that is, '*there are observables* which are relative to the subject's
actions' (that is, primarily dependent on the subject on one hand, and on
the other primarily independent of the subject). The latter is a *logical*
formulation and is already conflated with the Actuality it is supposed to be
distinguished from. But, worse still, the insertion of '*n*', '*n* + 1', etc.,
implies that 'Obs.' (and Coord.) is, or can be treated as a (general)
mathematical manifestation. We have here a prime example of 'wandering', conflation and 'collapse', all embodied in the notation itself.

Further, 'Obs.S', 'Coord.S', and so on, are abbreviated statements
about *qualitative conditions of the subject*. This is true even of 'Obs.O', and so
on, since this contains a reference back to the subject via the word 'observables' (see above). On the other hand, the notation adopted within the
brackets conveys, almost surreptitiously, the idea of an *algebraic series*. In

fact, if we compare this 'general model' with the particular case of it on p. 87 (see above, page 15), these '*n*' 'numbers' refer to nothing else than the designation of particular 'levels', or 'layers'. The 'Deeds' mathematics here subtly relies on a sort of *arousal of 'mathematical expectation'*! The danger in such diagrams is the attribution of necessity and, therefore, the *proof* implicit in standard mathematics, to notions embodied in what is no more than a picture. Finally, the diagram fails on the most important issue of all for the Piagetian system. Beyond the thick, oblique arrows, which are entirely 'silent' from an explicative viewpoint, there is no indication whatsoever as to how the transition from 'layer' to 'layer' takes place.

The same criticisms apply equally to the conceptual apparatus expressed through terms like assimilation, accommodation, schemata, action, and so on. Neither this nor the later terminology (for example, disturbance, virtual compensation) constitute a co-domain (or a model within such a co-domain) distinguishable from a domain. Nor is this terminology meaningful in terms of logical or mathematical structuration. There is no axiomatic or conditional significance such as is required by both logical and mathematical analysis (general inference), nor is there any evidence of theory or law, the application of which involves the exploration of the limits of such a theory or law and which is the very essence of science. The domain itself is entirely blurred in relation to the general field of experience. In short, the methods involve a complete confusion between the realms of models, theory, scientific fact, subject experience and extant phenomena, logic and mathematics.

To summarise, we are compelled to conclude that the Piagetian system fails the indispensable conditions for a science which were indicated at the beginning of this chapter, not because it lacks observation and experiment but because of its overall conflationary character. Nevertheless, the Piagetian system (shorn of its logico-mathematical claims and entanglements) has performed some service by *describing* the actual functioning of Western (and Soviet-type) cultures. This not only applies in the learning process imposed on children and young adults, but also in the categorical, pigeon-holed character of sophisticated, technologically controlled existence in general. The great fault of Genetic Epistemology is the identification of cognition conceived exclusively in logico-mathematical terms with the whole life process and treating what is a highly socially conditioned procedure as intrinsic to the human condition. But as we have said several times already, Piaget is not unique in his misuse of scientific, logical and mathematical tools. His system has a great deal in common with many comparable activities especially in the behavioural and social fields.

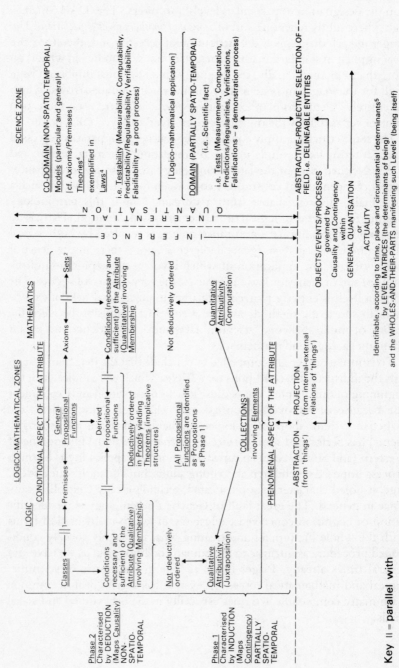

Key ‖ = parallel with

Figure 9.2 Summary schema of logico–mathematics, science and Actuality and their internal and external relations as discussed in the text.

[1] This sign indicates co-existing alternatives. Thus there is a 'parallelism' between sets and classes and a parallelism between both of these and propositional functions (it will be recalled that Russell had some difficulty in deciding whether classes or propositional functions were more basic and opted finally for the former). It is suggested here that the link between these three can be found in the relations between premiss(es) and class and between axiom(s) and set; that is, 'x is a colour' may be an expression of a class or be regarded as a premiss; 'x is a natural number' may be an expression of a set or a definition (axiom). Hence the form 'x is a . . . ' is reserved for propositional functions and although the same predicative form can be used to express this in a conditional way, the latter is more distinctively expressed as '. . . ness', for example, 'colour-ness' is the overall condition in the cited case identifying the class. The actual difference between classes and sets on the one hand and propositional functions (general and derived) on the other is between being non-deductively ordered in the first case and deductively ordered in the second. It should also be stressed that classes and sets are not symmetrically interchangeable because of the difference between qualitative and quantitative attributivity in the first instance The propositional functions paralleling sets may be given a logical form; but propositional functions paralleling classes may not be given a truly mathematical form. Symbolic logic is abbreviative not computational.

[2] See text for a discussion of the group as a special type of set, with particular reference to the fact that it reflects the conditions of stability and symmetry of Quanta.

[3] The following alignment can usefully be made:

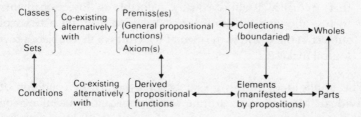

[4] The relations between models, theories and laws should be clarified. The model refers back to the original selection of the field and the delineation of entities in that field. It is, therefore, the quintessential expression of the co-domain–domain interaction. It embodies the often unspoken basic assumptions of the complete science. Thus, the Aristotelean-Linnaean classificatory model and the Darwinian model differ mainly in how they interpret the implications of the structural variations of species not in the structures themselves (that is, ordered in an inclusive logical manner or ordered in a time-change manner).

Theories must not be confused with models since they are specific general statements about behaviour *within* the universes which models set up. The distinction is between, for example, the time-change *model* and the *Theory* of Evolution, or the *model* of an evacuated cosmos containing rigid impenetrable particles and the *Theory* of gravitation. Again, laws should be distinguished from either models or theories since these express the different *periodicities* (see diagram) detectable provided the theory and its model are (for the moment) consistent with each other.

[5] This term has been carefully considered and the paradoxical combination of the idea of accident in the first word and the notion of fixity and constraint in the second was thought to be the best manner of conveying, in a brief phrase, the level–whole, etc., relationship. It suffers, of course, from the usual inadequacies attaching to verbalising experience in any form.

10 Epilogue

Throughout the previous chapters we have attempted to analyse the foundations on which Piaget has erected a complete philosophy intended to cover the human individual in himself, the individual in society and the human phenomenon as a whole in relation to evolution.[102] These foundations rest on two 'self-evident truths':

(a) that the human condition is reducible to a logico-mathematical form and this form is the Actuality of human psychology;

(b) that Actuality itself is equally reducible to logico-mathematical forms, allowing the unmediated transition from the activity of the subject in the world to the mental structures of that subject's psychological make-up.

The implications of this go far beyond the private condition of the individual. Most obvious are the social implications including logico-mathematical ordering of society parallel with the logico-mathematical character of individual mentality. But this is a whole new field in itself and needs much wider coverage than is possible in a book of this sort. Here we have been mainly concerned with the nature of individual knowledge and Piaget's treatment of it; but this cannot be left without some attention to these wider implications even though a full consideration of them must be reserved for another time and place.

Piaget himself has written at considerable length on these issues. *Play, Dreams and Imitation* (1962 edn), for example, relating the system of Genetic Epistemology to certain non-cognitive aspects of early childhood, has a distinct social stance in treating play as 'inferior' (socially speaking) to imitation to be overcome and replaced by the ordered (rule-governed) process of imitation.[103] In *Six Psychological Studies* (1968) this view is succinctly put. Play ('symbolic') is pure egocentricity and despite a suggestion of reciprocity betwen play and cognition, it is made quite clear that the former is antecedent *and* inferior to the latter. The phrase 'a *deforming* assimilation of reality to the self' (our emphasis) describing play says it all (see pp. 23–4). This portrayal of play as inferior is to be contrasted, according to Piaget, with the other (more serious) aspects of early 'egocentric assimilation' which 'characterises the beginnings of thought just as it characterises the process of socialisation' (p. 22).

In *The Moral Judgement of the Child* (1932), one of Piaget's earliest books, the social implications of the cognitive theory, even at this early stage, are stressed. The overall process is conceived as a progress from an (individual) egocentricity to a 'decentered' condition whereby the individual ultimately achieves the capacity to 'see the other viewpoint' or 'place himself in the other person's position'. The process is said to go from unconditional acceptance of adult authority linked with incapacity to form coherent reasons for action and inability to follow rules, to a reasoned rule-governed recognition of authority. It is closely related by Piaget to the development of language as the exclusive rational mode of communication (see also *Six Psychological Studies*, 1968, pp. 18ff). One is impressed not only by the clear hierarchical sequence of 'inferior-to-better' but also by its purely temporal linearity so that the 'better' always *succeeds* the 'inferior' and supplants it.

The process is intimately related to Piaget's concepts of justice and punishment. Flavell has an excellent summary of this (pp. 293ff.) and in essence Piaget's view, which is again descriptive and not analytical, entirely logico-mathematicises justice. As elsewhere in Genetic Epistemology, relationships are exclusively *external*, which necessarily leads to an unqualified acceptance of the notion of punishment as right and inevitable. This is so whatever stage Piaget is referring to. One must remember that the descriptive character of his views means that the different stages are not necessarily inherent in the development of the individual but are reflective of whatever social training he/she has experienced. Thus, 'immanent' justice together with 'expiatory' punishment in early childhood and 'distributive' justice together with 'reciprocity' of punishment in later childhood are too much like the Actuality lying behind the social order not to be at least partially induced.

The theory is intended to be a rationalist one. But as with the basic cognitive theory, for this to be so the consistency of the system cannot be unlimited and it must be possible to challenge its premises (that is, falsify it) from within. Piaget's system of socialised morality, however, does not allow for this. It consequently does not acknowledge the possibility of the paradoxical co-existence of different social-moral positions in which people at all levels of social intercourse and organisation and at all times find themselves. As with the cognitive theory there is no recognition of a transformational 'jump' in assumptions that social relations, even more than the cognitive interactions of subject and milieu, involves. Both in *The Moral Judgement of the Child* and later in *The Growth of Logical Thinking* the 'correct' pathway of socialisation is presented as a progress towards a total identification of the individual with his or her social role(s) and function. The significant link between this treatment of the individual as a social unit and the basic logico-mathematical theory of human personality which we have been criticising all along, is that it requires the obvious conflation of the unique features of the individual and these social roles to the point of total identification. The distinction between the self and the relations existing between the self and others is obliterated and the individual tends towards becoming equivalent to these relations. Perhaps more serious than this is the implied disappearance of any distinction between the reality of the social fabric and the social constructs (institutions, organisations, customary behaviour) which are claimed to embody this fabric. A total acceptance of political authority, however 'democratically' this may be presented, is not far off from this and does not need any more than a tacit, uncritical acceptance of whatever premises are publicly advanced. In short, if the social premises are accepted in the first instance, anything may be justifiably argued – and there is no possible way out of this without violating the exclusive and superior role Piaget assigns to logico-mathematics in the individual–social nexus. One is tempted to see in this viewpoint an explanation of Piaget's outlook at the beginning of the Second World War that 'all we could do was to fold our arms and continue our work' (Boring, *Autobiography*).

Perhaps more than any other Piagetian commentary, *The Growth of Logical Thinking*, particularly its final chapter, spells out the social implications of the system for the young adult arriving at maturity and facing his or her future life. On the one hand (it is argued) the achievement of an integrated cognitive structural form, characterised by the INRC group, signalling the formal operational stage and maturity, is initially manifested in a largeness of view associated with great reforming and creative thoughts. On the other hand, this stage is said to be associated with a renewed 'egocentricity' and the authors (Piaget and Inhelder) make no bones about their contempt for this. Nevertheless, it is emphasised that this 'largeness of view', once it is tempered and disciplined by entry into regular employment, confirms the 'maturity' of the formal operational stage and ensures the slotting-in of the individual's logico-mathematical structuration with his or her social role.

The identity of the individual and the social function of the individual is complete and undisguised. And though the basis of this identity is not overtly authoritarian, the same result is arrived at by the universal apotheosis of 'objective' logico-mathematics as the ultimate determinant of the social 'slotting-in'. There is no room for any discrepant challenge to the system in such a picture – no room for alternative views or styles of life – and again, no possibility of innovatory change. If such overall and universal 'evolution', culminating in perfect equilibrium, is accepted, then the creative leaps into the unknown which characterise the specific story of mankind must be replaced by a narrowing funnel of 'equilibration', juddering to a final, quiescent halt in silence and immobility. The reduction of the 'large thoughts' of adolescence to the four-square restrictions of the office or factory, the three-bedroomed house and an uncomprehending retirement (death?) forty years later is the microcosmic step in the direction of this final 'equilibrium'. It goes almost without saying that this social perspective presupposes a hierarchically structured and bureaucratic social milieu within which the individual, having lost the fresh flexibility of childhood, retains a stale echo of it in the form of dependence and submission well described as 'infantilism'.[104] This is, indeed, a *description* of the contemporary social scene as authority would wish it to exist, and as it is officially presented. But to treat it as if it were a discovery of the inner rational working of Man, society and the universe, as Piaget and Inhelder imply, is to reinforce such authority by bringing reason in on the side of slavish obedience. The description is very accurate and exposes the modern social conditioning process in contemporary, bureaucratised industrial societies particularly well. But by eliminating the individual's power to resist his or her stereotyping, Genetic Epistemology, despite any 'liberal' mask it may wear, spells death to non-conformity, originality, creativity.

Should Piaget have remained aloof from these excursions into social structure? Although Piaget is, as he claims, primarily an epistemologist, it is because he was concerned with the 'genetic' or developmental aspect of knowledge that he was drawn first into its psychological conditions and from there into the social scene underlying this. But it is noteworthy that he entered this arena through *individual* psychology and not through a social model. In Chapters 6 and 7, dealing with the apparatus of cognition and the stage theory, it became clear that this was inevitable and not a matter of choice.

'The mechanisms by which the individual is wholly identified as a social unit are intricate and rest on the interdependence of the social and affective aspects of human personality and also on the assessment by Piaget of the relation between cognitive and affective life. First, the intimate connection between the social and affective aspects of the individual is stressed – a feature brought out by Flavell in a hyphenated link-up between them (1963, p. 81). *The Moral Judgement of the Child* identifies the emergence of affective life with the 'social' relationships which are said to vary at first and ultimately become stabilised between individuals especially in rule-governed games. The quotation marks here indicate a particular and important ambiguity in Piaget's thought on this issue. 'Social' is interpreted, on the one hand, as 'interpersonal'. Yet on the other, especially in the treatment of the adolescent transition to adulthood in *The Growth of Logical Thinking,* socialisation is presented as an increasing conformity to *institutionalised norms*. (In actual experience there is a constant confrontation between the two, one of the best known examples being marriage.) In this way the implication is not just a direct but a necessary link between

individual affectivity and social (institutional) conformity. The exact relationship is never spelled out, however, beyond the unestablished hypothesis of a transference from acceptance of rule-governed games to the
acceptance of social order.

In an important summary section of *Six Psychological Studies* (1964, pp.
54ff.) in effect bringing together the main points elaborated in *The Moral
Judgement of the Child* and *The Growth of Logical Thinking,* Piaget emphasises the transition from the acceptance of adult authority without
question by the 'concrete operational' child (7–11 years) to what he
describes as 'mutual respect' based on acceptance of the 'objective' validity
of rules (this affective-social process is supposed to parallel the emergence
of the 'formal operational' cognitive stage). However, there is no consideration of the *conditions* of rule acceptance. Attention is concentrated on
the *fact* of acceptance as a measure of maturation. Thus, the identification
of the individual with social roles excludes any concern with the *conditionality* of social modes and rules. The 'grandiosity' of adolescence,
associated with the questioning of such rules, is to be identified with
disruptive 'immaturity'. The presentation implies that maturity, social
obedience and (superior) rationality all go together. What is not even
discussed is the overwhelmingly more mature rejection of rules in terms of
more comprehensive moral demands even if these are unclearly or 'ir-
rationally' formulated. Concentration on acceptance as a measure of
'maturity' leads directly to the requirement of 'obedience to orders' irrespective of consequences.

Another equally important key to this social–individual conflation lies
in the relation Piaget sees between affectivity and cognition. Flavell
describes Piaget's view of the affective (and motivational) aspect of human
life as '[providing] the *energétique* of behavior while the cognitive aspect
provides the structure (affect cannot of itself create structures, although it
does influence the selection of the reality content upon which the structures operate)' (1963, p. 81). Affective organisation grows parallel to
intellectual structures, bearing primarily on persons rather than objects
(loc. cit.). Yet, in Piaget's writing in this area the apparatus of cognition is
applied directly. Affective life is described as a 'continual adaptation'; this
is said to imply 'continual assimilation' producing 'affective schemas' and
'continual accommodation of these schemas'. Very specifically, he writes
at one point, 'thus, when speaking of "affective schemas" it must be
understood that what is meant is *merely* [our emphasis] the affective aspect
of the schemas which are also intellectual' (Piaget, 1962a, p. 207). Hence it
is made clear that the categories of thought, and the thinking process, are
worked out exclusively in terms of cognition and then applied to affectivity. Notwithstanding, therefore, that Inhelder and Piaget affirm that
'affectivity is [not] determined by intellect or the contrary, but that both
are indissociably united in the functioning of the personality' (Inhelder and

Piaget, 1958, p. 348), it emerges from the *one-way* application of cognitive categories to affectivity that the latter is effectively subordinated to the former.

The significance of this subordination lies in the fact that it makes possible the dominance of the cognitive over the affective aspect of mentality while at the same time these are clearly held separate in accordance with their differing behavioural manifestations. Because of the affective-social interlock, the individual automatically becomes manipulable through an alternating appeal to the rational (sooner than the 'merely emotional') on the one hand and the emotional (sooner than the 'coldly rational') on the other. The necessary condition for this is a strict separation of these aspects, yet with a necessary and hierarchical order between them giving dominance to the cognitive-rational, traditionally associated with age and the male sex, and a subjection of the affective-emotional, again, traditionally associated with youth and the female sex.

To sustain the structure another problem needs resolution. What pertains to the individual (cognition) and what pertains to the social (system) and relies on the affective but is cognitively controlled may easily become indistinguishable and wholly subsumed under purely logico-mathematical categories. This is not altogether unwelcome and, in fact, reflects the original premises of the Piagetian thesis. But individual and social zones must nevertheless appear to remain separate in order that the socially determined order may be maintained as a 'natural' state and the individual may go through a 'learning' process which is actually an *adjustment* to this order (via logical groupings – see the reference to Flavell below). Two distinct concepts are used to resolve this problem, each fulfilling a different role.

First, the 'epistemic subject' (see Rotman) is a notion which affirms not directly but by implication that the basic process of cognition is common (inborn?) to all individuals but that this commonality (actually indistinguishable from Piaget's concept of the a priori) must not be confused with particular manifestations of it in the individual. The generality and inherence of the 'epistemic subject', together with its abstracted, almost Platonic character, approximates to a form of social determinism since it is a universally shared aspect of the individual unconsciously working within him.[105] But the artificiality of the notion points more in the direction of an abstract link between a totally logico-mathematical individual and an equally logico-mathematical society. Such a link must lie within the terms of reference of Genetic Epistemology and hence must itself be logico-mathematical. There is actually no evidence of the 'epistemic subject' and it appears to fulfil the role of an ad hoc hypothesis, accounting for occurrences which may challenge the current model, but not sufficiently to count as a falsification of it. Any basis for the existence of an 'epistemic subject' derives from (claimed) common phases of growth and behaviour which themselves depend upon the theoretical model in the first place. While the 'epistemic subject' does no more than assert (with strong echoes of 'Deeds') the logico-mathematical basis to the individual–social nexus in a pseudo-theoretical form, it strongly reinforces the *dependence* of the former on the latter. Hence, it confronts the real person as an intangible but seemingly powerful force with the backing of social necessity and order behind it. The only 'novelty' here is an increased stress on the role of language in relation to a succession of stages. In this sense, there is in some of Piaget's latest work an implicitly greater emphasis on the social as distinct from the individual aspects of the system.[106]

An obverse solution to the problem of keeping separate while relating the individual and society in a dependent manner is provided by that concept already referred to – 'interpersonal relations' – which can open-endedly interconnect to society as a whole, while at the same time firmly tying this to individual (personal) relationships. The provision of this interpersonal condition as a sort of 'buffer' between the individual and society and the treatment of the individual's social roles *as if* these were reducible to the inter-*personal*, is quite conflationary but its advantage is that through it the individual may be treated through his/her (affective) relations as a purely social unit. This notion of 'interpersonal personal' relations is also helpful, in holding the cognitive and affective somewhat apart from each other. It allows Piaget to treat the development of the affective side of the individual subject's mentality as a mirror-image of cognition itself and yet distinct from it. For, while Piaget clearly does not wish to identify affectivity completely with the social roles of the in-dividual, by using the idea of the interpersonal he can seemingly open-endedly relate the individual to the social while at the same time tying this aspect of the individual's psychology firmly into cognition.

The fact that he does this is amply demonstrated in writings referred to in Flavell's text (see pp. 200–1).Commenting on Piaget's understandng of 'interpersonal relations', Flavell writes: 'although Piaget has not been nearly so specific regarding these, cognitive operations concerning things like *values* (e.g. Piaget, 1941, p. 258) and *interpersonal relations* (e.g. Piaget, 1950a, Ch. 6) are also said to have grouping properties' (Flavell, 1963, p. 171). The nature of this identification is very specific. Later on Flavell has this to say, and it speaks for itself with very little extra comment:

> It is extremely difficult to render anything very specific on the structure of such behaviours because Piaget's own treatment of them, although at times interesting and provocative, has been anything but specific (e.g. 1950a, Ch. 6; 1953–1954a, 1954c, 1955–56b). The essential position, however, seems to be this. As the child enters the concrete-operational years, the grouping structure comes to describe not only the organi-zation of his logical and infralogical actions but also that of his inter-

personal interactions, his values, etc. That is, the systematic and organized character which the grouping structure lends to intellectual activities in the narrow sense also pervades the remaining miscellany of adaptive acts in which he emerges. For instance, as the child grows older his goals and values, initially unstable and momentary, begin to become organized into more or less stable and enduring hierarchies, e.g. goal A is a means to the attainment of goal B which in turn is a means to C, and so forth. Such asymmetric series, Piaget asserts, are isomorphic to Grouping V (1953–54a). Similarly, with the growth of moral values, norms of moral conduct and the notion of moral obligation enter the child's thought in parallel with logical norms and the notion of logical necessity; the 'ought' of duty begins to seem to him as *a priori* and compelling as the necessity of $A < C$ from $A < B$ and $B < C$ – compelling in principle if not in his everyday moral behaviour (1953–54a, p. 535).[107]

There are also claimed liaisons between logical groupings structure and interpersonal interactions (Flavell refers to Piaget 1950a, ch. 6; 1955–56b). First of all Piaget claims that interpersonal interaction – and most of all bilateral and reciprocal interaction among peers – is an indispensable condition for the very formation of logical grouping structures in middle childhood (for example, Flavell, reference to Piaget, 1951d). By and large, Piaget is not prone to isolate specific antecedent conditions for cognitive change, but he clearly does here. Through repeated and often frustrating interchanges with his peers, the child is supposed to come to cognitive grips with other viewpoints and perspectives which differ from his own. And from such encounters he is said to move, gradually, from a static and centrated egocentrism to the multi-perspective reversibility which is the hallmark of the grouping structure.

But the reverse is also supposed to be true; and here is the intended isomorphism between interactional and grouping structure. Coherent and organised interchanges between people already require, in turn, something like grouping structure in the individuals concerned because these interchanges themselves form a grouping-like system of operations (Flavell references: Piaget, 1950a, pp. 163–5; Piaget, 1950b, Vol. 3, pp. 236–72). A general statement of his position here is found in the following:

> (without) interchange of thought and co-operation with others the individual would never come to group his operations into a coherent whole: in this sense, therefore, operational grouping presupposes social life. But, on the other hand, actual exchanges of thought obey a law of equilibrium which again could only be an operational grouping, since to co-operate is also to co-ordinate operations. The grouping is therefore a form of equilibrium in inter-individual actions as well as of

individual actions, and it thus regains its autonomy at the very core of
social life. (Piaget, 1950a, pp. 163–4); quoted Flavell, 1963, pp. 200–1).

It is quite clear from this that 'interpersonal' (alternatively inter-
individual) relates to the operational structure of cognition but also that
the connection with 'the very core of social life' is equivalently significant.
The ultimate objective of (social)-affective development is to arrive at a
reciprocal or co-operative situation in which interpersonal relations are
mediated by the highly cognitive process of decentring. Social relationships in any group, however large, resolve themselves into this ideal
condition of reciprocity. But when one cuts through the tangle of Piaget's
words it can easily be seen that this objective is achieved through 'slipping'
back and forth between public and private aspects of the individual by
using the device of a common attribution of logico-mathematical structuration to both and to the interpersonal-affective link between them. By
subsuming the latter under cognitive categories, the impression is
conveyed that the social has been subsumed in this way also.

Figure 10.1 might help to clarify the position. Complicated though this
may seem, it can be seen very quickly (see the dotted arrows) that individual logico-mathematical structuration determines everything else.
After what has been said in earlier chapters, this works out to be a recipe
for stasis not dynamism, conformity not creativity.

This was the situation until relatively recently when, with the publication of *Success and Understanding* (1975) and *The Grasp of Consciousness*
(1977), Piaget extended his experimental work on cognition to include a
consideration of the relation between 'knowing how' and the conscious
awareness of this. The term he applies to this awareness is 'cognizance'. In
the course of considering several new experiments he concludes that the
learning process is not only unconscious in the first instance but its
expression through words ('cognizance') involves a delay in accurately
reflecting the action. This may even be cognitively inhibiting when the
subject's action itself is perfectly clear. Here, the emphasis is upon the
subject's growing self-awareness which it is claimed is reflected in the
increasing accuracy with which he can describe his actions from very
young to maturity.[108] Piaget is, of course, emphasising the role of verbalisation in reinforcing cognition itself. This may seem a somewhat different
approach to the one we are used to in the conventional Piagetian system.
There is also some conflict between the idea of (conscious) cognizance and
that of the 'epistemic subject' which implies some sort of unconscious
control/influence. Despite this, the basic Piagetian system is reinforced by
the increased weighting given to language in the achievement of equilibrium. Piaget seems to have tended to redress the balance in regard to his
later excursions into System Theory and returned again to the individual
foundation of his cognitive system, although the experiments in both

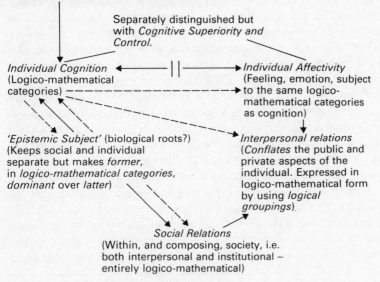

Produced by the universal
trend towards 'equilibrium'
(logico-mathematical) expressed
especially through the biological
manifestation of this (i.e. what is
inborn in the individual to start with)

Separately distinguished but
with *Cognitive Superiority and
Control.*

Individual Cognition
(Logico-mathematical
categories)

Individual Affectivity
(Feeling, emotion, subject
to the same logico-
mathematical categories
as cognition)

'Epistemic Subject' (biological roots?)
(Keeps social and individual
separate but makes *former,*
in *logico-mathematical categories,*
dominant over *latter*)

Interpersonal relations
(*Conflates* the public and
private aspects of the
individual. Expressed in
logico-mathematical form
by using *logical
groupings*).

Social Relations
(Within, and composing, society, i.e.
both interpersonal and institutional –
entirely logico-mathematical)

Key: ⟶ indicates origin and derivation
    ‖ indicates parallel existence
    ---► indicates direction and predominance of influence

Note
'Growth' and 'learning' can arise only as a progressive *adjustment* of the individual to the
biological-social norm which is predetermined anyway because of a common logico-
mathematical basis.

Figure 10.1 Abstract of the relations between social and individual categories.

Success and Understanding and *The Grasp of Consciousness* exemplify clear
social influence both in the nature of the actions and the verbalisation of
them.[109]

As we said previously, the implications and significance of the
'collapsed' and conflationary character of Piaget's logico–mathematical
model for personal psychology and social order needs much more space
than can be given to it here to do it full justice. We have tried to do no more
than indicate the inevitable direction that application of his system must,
and does, take. And, indeed, this direction has very sinister implications of
which Piaget, himself, must have been unconscious. For most of his life
Piaget was somewhat of a 'loner', attracting a following mainly after the
Second World War and mainly in the fields of education and child psychology. His influence has spread far beyond any direct acknowledgement

extensive though this is. His 'loner' position as well as his attraction for these fields is no accident. In the days when Piaget began his studies and writing, the bureaucratic and technocratic character of sophisticated society (Eastern as well as Western) was still in relative infancy. Fifty to sixty years later this society is burgeoning and there is an increasing emphasis on the quantification of all aspects of human existence, from science to sex, from aesthetics to eating. Parallel with this is a rapidly expanding tendency for responsibility at all levels to disappear into manifold committees and for human action and decision to be supported or 'corrected' by the computer. The Piagetian mode of thought is certainly not isolated from this. Rather it is a theoretical substrate, whether acknowledged or not, an 'adaptive/adjustment' philosophy in a situation in which what is required is general 'equilibrium' under an unquestioned authority which can never actually be identified but which appears, never-theless, as a universal, undeniable law of existence.

We have said that Piaget describes what *is* and this is not surprising since every society has produced its philosophers whose teaching aims to demonstrate the identity of that society's structure and rules with uni-versal and unchanging law. What is distinct about contemporary society is its need to create an authority which is as far as possible unseen, and demand submission to that authority without apparent reference to an 'outside' source. This is where the roles of logic and mathematics, dis-torted and misapplied beyond their normal, positive and healthy func-tion, become supremely important. The extraordinary creative surge of thought and activity, associated with what we called the self-referential features of the European cultural tradition, has itself required 'disciplining' if it was to be harnessed to an establishment in the time-honoured way. This 'disciplining' has been the undercurrent of all our discussions of Piaget, because his thought is one of the most succinct expressions of this and, because its target is inevitably the young, one of the most influential forces in the modern world.

The central issues have been the collapse and/or conflation of Actuality and thought spelled out as between subject and object, cognition and feeling (affectivity), the public and private aspects of the individual, in-cluding notions of justice and morality. The ambiguity inevitably involved in this conflation, if the self-referential theme is to be maintained side by side with authority, enables the individual to be rendered helpless before social and other abstractions which are presented as unchallenge-able 'Actuality'. Such ambiguity has made it possible to manipulate the individual without clearly revealing the manipulators and to confuse 'flesh and blood' love and loyalty with commitment to abstractions laid down elsewhere. If there is any hope for the future it lies in the rejection of this ambiguity and a re-established quest for Actuality where thought and action are clearly distinguished in order that they may be related as logic, mathematics and feeling, altogether, in a holistic interaction with the world.

Notes

Chapter 1

1   Piaget's production, at about 11 years old, of a one-page article on an albino sparrow for a local natural history journal brought him into contact with Paul Godet, the director of the Neuchâtel Musée d'histoire naturelle and a specialist on molluscs. His classificatory experience as assistant to Godet for four years undoubtedly had a deep influence on him. His interest in molluscs seems to have remained with him for a large part of his life. He wrote his doctoral thesis in this field in 1918 and continued research in 1919–20. At various stages in his subsequent writings, especially on the subject of adaptation, the molluscs reappear. One can speculate as to whether the enormous stability of molluscs has any connection with Piaget's conviction that transformation and logical order are reconcilable. See Piaget's autobiography in E. G. Boring, H. S. Langsfield, H. Werner and R. M. Yerkes (eds), *A History of Psychology in Autobiography* (New York: Russell, 1969; repr, of 1952 edn), Vol. IV, pp. 237–56.

2   C. D. Darlington, *The Facts of Life* (London: Allen & Unwin, 1953), pp. 219–21. Quoted by A. Koestler, *The Case of the Midwife Toad* (London: Hutchinson, 1971), p. 37.

3   His father's personality emerges in Piaget's remark about a book he wrote at the age of 10 – 'a book on "our birds", which, after my father's ironic remarks, I had to recognise, regretfully, as a mere compilation' (see Boring *et al.,* op. cit., p. 322).

4   Heidegger is probably the most outstanding in this respect as compared with Sartre. In fact, his notion of 'Dasein' as the especial feature of man in comparison with all other beings, animate or inanimate, is a pure distillation of relation conceived of as total 'openness'. Seen by Heidegger, man is nothing if not primarily open to relations with the whole cosmos, whereas all other things possess this characteristic only limitedly. See W. Biemel, *Martin Heidegger: An Illustrated Study,* trans. J. L. Melita (London: Routledge & Kegan Paul, 1977), *passim.*

5   Some confusion could arise between the use of the words 'being' and 'ontology'. However, for the purposes of this discussion anyway (and possibly in general), there is a viable distinction in so far as 'ontology' is a traditional science of the existence of things and involves no idea of *inherent* dynamism, whereas 'being', even when considered on its own, carries with it a *connection* with 'becoming' in the absence of which it ceases to have any meaning whatever. It is Hegel's genius to have grasped, so untypically of his time, this necessary 'indeterminate' aspect of determinacy.

6   The developments within social anthropology and linguistics associated with Chomsky and Levi-Strauss in particular, and involving the emergence of modern Structuralism, are not fundamentally different from the other schools as regards the relation of being to becoming.

7   A different and noteworthy response to this common crisis is to be found in Bridgeman's 'operationism' (current in the later 1930s and 1940s especially) and directed at resolving the conceptual inconsistencies existing between micro- and macro-physics. 'Operationism' proposes that such concepts shall be defined by the operations carried out in order to measure them, thus obviating the contradictions demonstrated in the Heisenberg Indeterminacy Principle. Knowledge thus becomes essentially dependent on 'activity' rather than the objects acted upon – a position very close to Piaget's. In a sense this constitutes another mode of excluding considerations of becoming in relation to being.

8   See M. Čapek, 'The significance of Piaget's researches on the psychogenesis of atomism', in R. C. Buckard and R. S. Cohen (eds), *Boston Studies in the Philosophy of Science,* Vol. VIII (Dordrecht, Holland: Reidel, 1970), pp. 446–55. All references in the remainder of this paragraph are to this article.

9 George Melhuish provides an interesting discussion of his suggested 'paradoxical philosophy' in *Vicious Circles and Infinity* (Hughes and Brecht, 1976, pp. 84–9). In this, contradiction and non-identity are incorporated together with non-contradiction and identity, in order to express actual change. This is fully dealt with in Melhuish's *The Paradoxical Nature of Reality* (Bristol: St Vincent's Press, 1973).

   Such 'change' as would follow from such an axiomatic system would still be a form of logical 'unpacking' involving no contingent relationships – the source of the truly novel in that it lies outside the axiomatically prescribed system. Melhuish's device, in other words, cannot dispose of the essential 'lack of surprise' which is a necessary built-in feature of the 'either–or-ness' of any n-valued logical system.

10 This is common to philosophical schools deriving either from the analytical tradition or from the phenomenological or existential tradition.

11 There is a possible hint of more influence from Brunschvicg here than we allowed for, in relation especially to the priority of the spirit in stimulating activity.

12 A. Koestler, *The Case of the Midwife Toad* (London: Hutchinson, 1971). This book, in fact, should be read by all concerned with this problem. It reveals quite startlingly how a scientific 'establishment' can come into being on grounds scarcely more respectable than those of a rival and unsuccessful 'establishment' which it has defeated.

13 See Rosemary Dinnage, 'The Piaget way', *New York Review of Books,* 21 December 1978, pp. 18–23.

14 Developed especially in *Structuralism,* Paris, 1967 (Fr. edn).

15 *L'Equilibration des structures cognitives* (Paris: Presses Universitaires de France, 1975); Eng. trans.: *The Development of Thought,* trans. A. Rosin (Oxford: Blackwell, 1978). This book has been said by Piaget to be a definitive latest statement of the theory of Genetic Epistemology.

16 Piaget himself is not justified in his attempt to identify his system with the ideas of Bertalanffy. The latter, on the other hand, is also unacceptable in that he draws an artifical distinction here. The only way to distinguish between the state of being 'open' and being 'closed' is by the possibility or not of contingent relationships between the system and the milieu. A 'closed' system is barred from such relationships but an 'open' system, intimately connected as it is with its milieu, will, of necessity, interact contingently with that milieu.

17 Note in this respect David Bohm's latest book, *Wholeness and the Implicate Order* (London, Routledge & Kegan Paul, 1980).

18 A particularly jarring example of such transformation may be found in the following proposition: 'A concentration camp is a transformation of/on a holiday camp.' The example has very specific facets. One should not forget the concentration camp 'orchestras' and the soap and towel issues to gas chamber victims, officially scheduled for a 'shower', all done in the name of 'humaneness'. Seen in such a context transformation can easily be demonstrated as a process of reducing reality, truth, or whatever one likes to call it, to the transformations themselves. The doctrine of whatever is, is.

19 See, for example, R. Macksey and E. Donato (eds), *The Structuralist Controversy* (Baltimore, Md, and London: Johns Hopkins, University Press 1970).

20 A great deal of the Piagetian corpus appears in J. Piaget *et al.*, *Etudes d'épistemologie génétique* (Paris: Presses Universitaires de France, 1957–). Piaget directed these studies and, together with his collaborators, has produced many well-known, recent and detailed statements of the Piagetian viewpoint. The studies as such are almost impossible to obtain in the UK, but an (almost?) complete set is to be found in the Donaldson library of University College, London.

21 See J. Piaget, *The Grasp of Consciousness* (London: Routledge & Kegan Paul, 1977), pp. 21ff. The analysis given in the text of these pages should be looked at but it is, in fact, unconvincing. Recognition of the tangential relation of direction of the missile to the circle of 'swing' is central to this maturation, according to Piaget. It is the case, however, that, in practice, control of this directon is *not* dependent on a tangential relation but on a slightly 'off' tangent one, for example

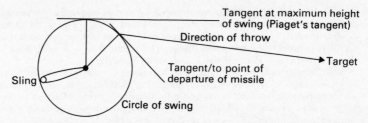

It is the degree of this 'offness' which determines the accuracy of the throw. Thus the whole question of controlled aim is an integral combination of geometrised analysis and 'feel'. It most certainly cannot be *reduced* to the former. The self-regulation–compensation approach of *The Development of Thought* does not alter this; for this, itself, constitutes a (new?) reductionist process to exclusively logico–mathematical categories.

22 See J. Piaget, *Le Structuralisme* (Paris: Presses Universitaires de France,1968); Eng. trans. by Chaninah Maschler (London; Routledge & Kegan Paul, 1971, repr. 1973). The translation is a very 'free' one and sometimes involves slight ambiguities but not sufficient to obscure the meaning of the original text.

23 Notice that novelty is accounted for in terms of 'completing the incomplete' which has the (desired) effect of subsuming it under structuration. This is, indeed, in line with Piaget's general view regarding increasing universal equilibrium – the underlying theme of *The Development of Thought*.

24 The 'Bourbaki' have changed the nature of their 'parent structures' in recent years.

25 Quoted by Dinnage, op. cit.

Chapter 2

26 J. Piaget, 'Le développement intellectual [sic] chez les jeunes enfants', *Mind*, vol. 40 (1941), p. 149 (quoted in A. M. Battro, *Piaget: Dictionary of Terms,* trans. and ed. E. Rütschi-Herrmann and S. F. Campbell, Oxford: Pergamon, 1973, p. 168).

27 E. W. Beth and J. Piaget, *Mathematical Epistemology and Psychology,* trans. W. Mays (Dordrecht, Holland: Reidel, 1966).

28 J. Piaget, *Les Relations entre l'affectivité et l'intelligence dans le développement mental de l'enfant* (Paris: CDU, 1962), p. 10. Quoted in Battro, *Dictionary of Terms.*

29 J. F. Bruner, 'Inhelder and Piaget's *The Growth of Logical Thinking,* I. A psychologist's viewpoint', *British Journal of Psychology,* vol. 50, no. 4 (1959), pp. 363–70.

Chapter 3

30 Actually, TL and LO refer to eight groupings. Flavell, however, refers (Flavell, 1963, p. 187) to a *ninth* grouping for which he provides a reference from *Classes, relations et nombres* (1942), pp. 33–4. This is said to be a very simple grouping involving the addition of a symmetrical relation:

> Its *compositions* are of the form $(A = B) + (B = C) = (A = C)$; such compositions are clearly *associative*; the *inverse* of an operation $(A = B)$ is, analogous to Grouping VI, $(B = A)$; the *general identity* is $(A = A)$; and each equality plays the role of *special identity* with itself and every other equality, e.g.
> $$(A = B) + (A = B) = (A = B) \text{ and}$$
> $$(A = B) + (C = D) = (C = D).$$

31 See Robert R. Stoll, *Sets, Logic and Axiomatic Theories* (San Francisco and London: Freeman, 1961) for an elementary account. The nearest idea to addition is 'union' of relations, also intersection (p. 30). More appropriate is the account of logical relations

in D. D. Runes (ed.), *Dictionary of Philosophy* (London: Peter Owen, 1960).

Chapter 4

32 This is one of the occasions when Piaget brings logical structures so close to actual extant entities within the brain-mind as virtually to identify them.

Chapter 5

33 Piaget seems to solve this problem via isomorphism expressed initially in the relation between 'specific heredity' and 'general heredity' (see Flavell, 1963, pp. 42ff.; also, *Origins of Intelligence in Children,* New York: International University Press, 1952, pp. 1–3, quoted by Flavell). It is also noteworthy that the quotation from Piaget given by Flavell on p. 44, and which is from pp. 2–3 of the work just referred to, presents an *opposite* viewpoint by Piaget on the question of the a priori from what is later put forward by him in *Six Psychological Studies* (p. 157 especially). The earlier reference here is an entirely conventional concept of the a priori as opposed to the later one.

34 There is a very large number of sources for Piaget's theory of perception (see, for example, Flavell, 1963, p. 225). Flavell presents a concise account (ibid., pp. 226ff.). In essence, the (mechanical) perceptive process involves a progressive approximation to the actuality of that which is perceived. Flavell gives us a very clear example:

> The statement of the model begins with a theoretical account of what happens when the visual system fixates or centers on a simple visual stimulus, e.g., a straight line.[7] Piaget assumes that the perception of the line is a developing process which takes place over a very brief period of time. One could think of this period of time between no percept and a completed, relatively stable one as divided into arbitrarily small micro-intervals, the construction of the fully formed percept gradually taking place across these intervals . . . The perceptual act which occurs during this interval is assumed to involve a set of *encounters (rencontres)* between some of the elements of the visual system and some of the elements of the stimulus. The nature of the elements and the nature of their mutual encounters are left wholly undefined by the model. Piaget thinks that an encounter might be something like a tiny eye movement which crosses (hence encounters) a point on the stimulus line. Thus the totality of encounters in a given micro-interval would be the totality of such crossings . . . The important thing for the model is the abstract concept of encounter, not its concrete specification in reality.
>
> The model assumes that not all the encounterable elements of the line will in fact be encountered during the initial micro-interval, but only some fixed fraction of them. It is as though the perceptual apparatus took a random sample of the total number of encounterable elements during this brief time period. So much for the first interval; what of the second?
>
> The model asserts that a second sampling occurs here, not a sampling of the total number but of the total remaining number of elements. That is, the elements sampled in the first interval are assumed to have been 'used up' in some sense – no longer part of the available, to-be-encountered pool. Moreover, the further assumption is made that the percentage of the remaining pool sampled is the same as it was the first time. This sampling procedure continues through the whole succession of micro-intervals: a fixed proportion of the pool is sampled, then the same proportion of the remaining pool (that is, the original pool minus the elements just sampled), and so forth . . . The relevance of the encounter model for visual perception is easy to state. Encounters are taken to be the stuff and substance of percepts. In the case of our line stimulus, *its perceived length at*

[7] Piaget does not see the model as limited to visual phenomena alone, despite the fact that most of the supporting research data concerns visual effects and also despite the fact that his description of the model is couched in visual terms.

any moment of time is believed to be a direct function of the number of encounters accumulated up to that time.

There are numerous cases of perception which do not justify this view. Any optical illusion raises immediate queries (see note 73 below, for example). Also the notion of the sum of the parts being equal to the whole is quite at variance with Piaget's favourable acknowledgement of Gestalt theory elsewhere (namely, in *Structuralism*).

35   B. L. Whorf, 'An American Indian model of the universe', *International Journal of American Linguistics,* Vol. 16 (1950); reprinted from Whorf, *Language, Thought and Reality* (Cambridge, Mass.: MIT) in R. M. Gale (ed.), *The Philosophy of Time,* 1968 (Hassocks, Sussex: Harvester Press repr., 1978), pp. 378–86.

36   The distinction between homeostasis and homeorhesis is subtle. The former refers to any mechanism preserving a *constant* situation; the latter a mechanism monitoring *constancy of change.*

Chapter 6

37   In a footnote on p. 23 of *Genetic Epistemology* Piaget has a bad example of inconclusiveness in relation to the actual existence of such structures and, by implication, the elements of such structures.

> The reader may ask here whether 'structures' have real, objective existence or are only tools used by us to analyze reality. This problem is only a special case of a more general question: do relations have objective independent existence? Our answer will be that it is nearly impossible to understand and justify the validity of our knowledge without presupposing the existence of relations. But this answer implies that the word existence has to be taken to have a multiplicity of meanings.

38   Contradicted later in *Structuralism* in a characteristic manner where he affirms that 'while the second structure (emerging from a previous one) is explained in terms of this transition, the transition itself can only be understood in transformational terms if both of *its termini are known*' (our emphasis) (pp. 127–8).

39   Strictly Piaget is wrong here. $1 + 1 = 2$ may well be defined in terms of limits if 2 were equated with (the limit of) $1 \cdot 9$. Thus the point he is asserting regarding additivity only applies when dealing with integers and is thus very conditional. Moreover, if the whole number is treated strictly as a limit then it conforms to the Gestalt concept of the whole not being equal to the parts and additivity is achieved only by ignoring this. Note the Zeno paradoxes especially in this connection.

40   One more passage serves to confirm this inconsistency and demonstrates that it is not simply a slip on Piaget's part.

> (The) operations which make possible the combination or the dissociation of classes or relations are actions prior to their becoming operations of thought. Before he can combine or dissociate relatively universal and abstract classes, such as the classes of birds or of animals, the child can already classify collections of objects in the same perceptual field; he can combine or dissociate them manually before he can do so linguistically. (Piaget, *Six Psychological Studies,* 1968, p. 93)

Notice how the physical, perceptual processes, clearly functional, are carried over into the cognitive and operational zones without any reference to the fundamental difference between the two zones nor any clue as to how this happens.

41   Note the differences between this diagram and the infant diagram as far as the *arrows* are concerned. Also note the 'sign[s?] mark an overall durable or momentary equilibrium' (p. 52). These points might well be kept in mind when reading the latter part of Chapter 9 below which discusses the employment of pseudo–mathematical techniques by Piaget.

42   Note the similarity to the view of the a priori and necessity already referred to several times in *Six Psychological Studies*, p. 157, and also to the notion of 'distortion' which is attributed to the initial 'primitive' interaction at the sensory phase of the subject's relationship with the milieu.

43   It should be recalled that in a mathematical-type transformation the element *as such* is unaffected by the operation. The same applies in logic.

44   Although the notion of intrusion still does not carry with it the necessary 'element'-concept the absence of which has been noteworthy in all the internal Piagetian cognitive notions.

45   He accurately identifies the central question at issue in the early part of the sentence. 'The problem, then, is to find a notion which expresses what is common to structure as an entity and structure as a process' (loc. cit.).

46   There is a rather tricky translation point here. The quotation given appears in the *Dictionary of Terms* (p. 15 under 'Mental Assimilation') and is supposed to be from the Piercey and Berlyne translation. A check with the Routledge & Kegan Paul edition of the latter yields a different wording where for 'schema', 'pattern' is used and for 'capture of the actions', 'the whole gamut of actions' is used. The *Dictionary of Terms* uses an American (reprint?) of RKP. The issue would be unimportant except that in the quotation given the concept and role of 'schema' is much more *linear* than in the original translation. Schema 'is equated with pattern' which gives it no status as a 'phenomenon' at all, only as an *arrangement*. This tallies, of course, with the non-terminality in general of Piaget's thought. Similarly 'gamut of actions' is quite a different notion from 'capture of actions'. The latter greatly stresses the 'out–in' aspect of Piaget's views and eliminates the aspect of 'in parallel' which is a definite distortion. Nevertheless, we must not forget that the *Dictionary of Terms* gets Piaget's full endorsement.

47   Four of these references occur in publications between 1959 and 1962. Two others occur much earlier in 1948, just before publication of TL. It is almost as if Piaget moved from a general use of the notion to a restricted use of it, latterly, to non-structural situations.

48   Flavell offers three features of schemata: repetition, generalisation and differentiation recognition. Piaget really regards these as one (see Flavell, 1963, p. 57; Piaget, 1963, pp. 37–8) and in any case the latter two features are subject to the problem of non-terminality whereas at least repetition repeats (see Flavell, pp. 56–7). Note that differentiation always means for Piaget a process of specialised breakdown of an originally global activity.

49   With L. Apostell, B. Mandelbrot and A. Morf, *Etudes d'épistémologie génétique*, *Vol.* III (Paris: Presses Universitaires de France, 1957). See Battro, *Dictionary of Terms*, p. 14.

50   Although this view is expressed relatively early in the 'later' phase of Piaget's thought, there is no evidence that he has rejected this equivalence of directionality notion since. In fact, the simultaneous 'two-way-ness' of assimilation and accommodation is an indispensable adjunct to the fundamental idea of (mobile) equilibrium itself. In *The Development of Thought* this is specifically spelt out: see pp. 6–8, but especially:

> If the reciprocal assimilations are not accompanied by accommodations that are also reciprocal, there will be a distorted merger and no coordination between the systems to be linked . . . Any scheme of assimilation tends to feed itself, that is, to incorporate outside elements compatible with its nature into itself . . . The entire scheme of assimilation must alter as it accommodates to the elements it assimilates. (Piaget, 1978b, p. 7)

51   In fact, the idea of directionality possessing a quantitativity in its own right independent of any separate point of reference runs very deep in Genetic Epistemology. The concept of 'improving' equilibrium exemplifies this itself. But Piaget is also quite inclined to the notion of directional significance embodied in vectors. Note his attraction to the term 'vectional' change, as he calls it, instead of evolution (see Rotman, 1977, pp. 60 and 70). Also the association of the (inferior) condition of non-conservation as a 'scalar' matter and (superior) conservationism as 'vector' awareness is looked on with some favour (see *Genetic Epistemology*, p. 49).

52 Here, as elsewhere, the presentation by Piaget of assimilation/accommodation in their reciprocal dependence implies a symmetry in this relationship. However, as in the mathematics of functional dependence, changing the independent into the dependent variable (as in $y = x^2$ into $x = \pm \sqrt{y}$) by no means involves a symmetry in the two situations. Moreover, although he defines each in terms of the other in the quoted passage, it must be noted that in *Play, Dreams and Imitation* (1962) play is *absolutely* relatable to assimilation and imitation *absolutely* to accommodation. Such absoluteness implies a terminality in the definition of the concepts which the mutually dependent function idea rules out.

53   But it is clear that if the accommodation is constantly subordinated to the assimilation (for it is always the accommodation of a scheme of assimilation), this accommodation is smaller and above all more forseeable in the case of these reciprocal accommodations than when new 'observables' and adaptations must be made to the outside objects $A'\ B'\ C'$. (Piaget, 1978b, p. 7)

It is true that this occurs in a discussion of the relation of the cognitive sub-systems to each other. Nevertheless, in the context of *The Development of Thought's* concentration on equilibration, it would not be surprising if the assimilation tended to outweigh the accommodation (always keeping in mind, of course, the 'source' of each).

54 See also *Six Psychological Studies,* pp. 6–7, which seeks to relate need, disequilibrium, action and the re-establishment of equilibrium.

55 The issue emerges in any consideration of the basic quantised nature of the world. In passing, it also raises a tentative solution to the astronomical problem known as Olber's Paradox which concerns the fact that the night sky is mostly 'dark' not 'light'. At first sight this seems strange in view of the number of 'light bodies' in the universe. At second sight, however, the extremely attenuated condition of matter in interstellar space might explain the limited transmission of light and hence a dark sky full of pinpointed stars and planetary bodies, not an overall light sky resulting from the massed build up of light emitting bodies throughout the universe.

56 That is, the Law of Identity ($A = A$); the Law of Non-Contradiction (A and not-A cannot be simultaneously true); the Law of the Excluded Middle (either A or not-A must be true).

Chapter 7

57 Piaget is very keen that the notion of egocentricity shall not be thought of in the derogatory sense of 'egotistical'. He is at pains to stress that, by using this term, far from implying the Freudian concept of narcissism, he wishes to indicate the opposite – absence of self-awareness (ibid., p. 21). However, this is not sustained.

58 It is not surprising that co-ordination should be assuming a more important role in this book. *Genetic Epistemology*, published in French in 1970, after all, belongs to the period of reassessment leading to the 'restatement' (in 1978b) by Piaget of the whole basic theory of Genetic Epistemology. The role of co-ordination is supreme in this restatement.

59 This discrepancy is given very full treatment in a relatively recent work, *The Grasp of Consciousness* (1977).

60 Actually it is a moot point whether introducing any *level* notion together with isomorphism is acceptable. The mathematical meaning of isomorphism is essentially 'one-level', or, more accurately, 'no-level'. The idea of increasing complexity brings in, inevitably, another dimension of structural measurement not accountable for within the isomorphic parameter.

61 See below, Chapter 9 on Piaget's methodology in general and also the Appendices to Chapter 4. Margaret Donaldson's book, *Children's Minds* (1978), is particularly relevant on this question. The theme of her book is particularly important to note as it stresses the crucial difference between the adult's concept of the question that is asked of the child and the child's actual understanding of what is said. The problem is a special case of the general problem of communication via language anyway and underscores

the point in the text that repeated experimental critiques of Piaget cannot, in fact, approach a serious exposure of the errors of assumption in his methodology.

62 Speech when receiving the Erasmus Prize for contribution to European culture, *Le Monde,* 21 December 1976, p. 18, quoted by Rotman, 1977, p. 8.

63 In Flavell's classic commentary there is no separate item in the Index, for example, for genesis.

64 The unresolved situation regarding the genesis of the new is embodied within this very passage. Only a few lines earlier Piaget writes: 'It is thus within the organism and not [or not only?] through external experience that the subject's structures are related to those of physical reality.' Contrast this with the notion in the passage given in the text which talks of physical activities such as eating, breathing, looking, and so on, as 'gaining access' to the non-temporal (mental) world and 'transcending' the physical world. Which direction are we supposed to take as decisive?

65 There is a curious error to be found in *Six Psychological Studies* on p. 155. Piaget writes, in connection with the experiment with the clay ball turned into a sausage, in order to show that the 'strategy' he describes for each phase has highest probability at that phase:

> To take a quantified example, let us say arbitrarily that length equals a probability of · 7, assuming that in seven out of ten cases length is mentioned, while breadth is mentioned in three cases, and hence has a probability of · 3. From the moment the child reasons about one dimension and not about the other and judges them to be independent, the probability of both at the same time will be · 21 and in all intermediate cases it will be between · 21 and · 3 or · 21 and · 7. Two at a time is more difficult than one alone. The most probable reaction at the point of departure is thus centration on a single dimension.

It is not the independence of length and breadth that is necessary in order for the probability 'of both at the same time' to be the product of each separately. The events that have to be independent are 'the child's view of the length' and 'the child's view of the breadth'. These events are clearly *not* independent and so the probability *cannot be calculated* as a product of *separate* probabilities.

66 Notions of 'overtaking' and 'over-determination', and so on, are not entirely new (as is usually the case for Piaget). But the former tends to be seen as primarily a matter of ordering (logical) and not of development and the latter primarily as a primitive manifestation of over-('deforming') assimilations. In neither of these cases is the genesis of novelty really involved. See J. Piaget, *The Child's Conception of Movement and Speed* (Fr. edn. 1946) (New York: Basic Books, 1970), pp. 163, 177, 184, 293. See also *Judgement and Reasoning in the Child* (original translation from French 1926) (Paterson, NJ: Littlefield, Adams, 1964), pp. 158, 159, 176. Quoted in Battro, *Dictionary of Terms,* p. 125.

67 The only other attempt by Piaget to resolve the problem of genesis is to be found in a marginal flirtation with dialectical materialism briefly referred to in *Structuralism* (pp. 120ff.). His knowledge of Marxism in general seems largely to have been influenced by the rarefied (and structuralist in the French case) French and German schools of Althusser and the Frankfurt school (Marcuse *et al.*). Even this appears very superficial. Certainly his discussion, in the reference given, to the supposed reflection of the notion of the 'negation of the negation' in the emergence of non-Euclidean geometries out of the denial of Euclid's parallel postulate is naive in the extreme and betrays a lack of understanding of what Marx and Engels and, for that matter, Hegel were about.

Chapter 8

68 The term 'logic' as used in the present chapter (and also by Piaget himself) applies to what is normally called 'formal logic'. The analysis in the text, based upon the concept of Phases 1 and 2, applies most obviously to this. There are, however, a number of applied logics, such as the logic of preference or belief, and their 'algebras', and such alternative logics as mereology, to which the same structural analysis applies. In short,

the same conflationary dangers exist and in some cases the use of the concept 'logic' is really inapplicable due to the unclear incorporation of what we have called holistic features of subject–object relationships. These are not susceptible to the basic requirement of all logic, that is, non-quantitative 'either–or-ness'. Generally, the ramifications of applied logics suggest attempts to solve the same problems revealed in the present chapter.

The pressing need for a solution such as we propose in this chapter to the problems and dilemmas revealed in Chapters 1–7 is demonstrated from another quarter. The work of Dean, Chaband and Bridges (1981 pp. 84–112), following that of Markham (1976 and 1979) on children's strategies in solving the Piagetian class inclusion problem, is based on a distinction between what they term 'collections' (enumerable) and 'classes' (holistic). The ambiguities they discuss in their conclusion may possibly be related to lack of clarity in basic definition of collection and class.

69   The notion has an extensive literature dating back at least as far as the origins of Taoism, Buddhism and Hinduism (*c.* 500–200 BC?) in the Far Eastern tradition and much farther in the Middle Eastern tradition. There is also a considerable modern Western body of literature with its own historical roots (for example, Meister Eckhart in the thirteenth to fourteenth centuries). To mention only a few examples of such literature, Martin Buber's *I and Thou* (1970) is outstanding, many of the books of Alan Watts (for example, *This is IT*, New York, Rider, 1978) handle the same theme most effectively, and among many other names, Pierre Teilhard de Chardin and Aldous Huxley are noteworthy. Querying previous translations and interpretations of Freud's 'ego' and 'libido', a modern view is to translate them as 'I' and 'It', claiming this as closer to Freud's own intentions. The concept, of course, recurs constantly in metaphysical and epistemological writings in general. A more recent expansion of interest in relation to self-identity is to be found in the experimental work carried out with dolphins and apes (for example, see K. Laidler, *The Talking Ape,* 1980). Some of this is rather dominated by a mix up between recognition of the *physical* being of the animal (use of mirrors, and so on) and the recognition of 'I' as opposed to 'It'. The latter involves 'why' questions, not simply 'what' questions. It is not possible yet clearly to identify any of the latter with regard to animals. This does not mean, of course, that they are not there.

70   As usual, Piaget produces an essentially *descriptive* picture of this together with a pseudo-explanation. His notions of 'differentiation' and 'decentring', both related to infantile 'ego-centricity', are intended to *explain*, respectively, a growing awareness of the differences between things in the subject's milieu and the distinctions to be drawn between the self and others in personal (social?) relations. The pseudo character of the explanation lies in the assumption of ultimately purely logico-mathematical objectives in both processes and a 'backward control', as it were, of these objectives over the processes themselves.

71   The plurality of holisms has another aspect. The intention is also to convey that the relations between the subject (or any Quantum) with the milieu are separately identifiable yet there is no absolute barrier to their translation or merger. An analogy may be found in the role of surface tension which separately identifies droplets of water up to a point but under the right degree of proximity encourages rather than opposes their flow together.

72   This is the essence of T. Kuhn's paradigmatic treatment of scientific development in *The Structure of Scientific Revolutions*.

73   The notion is closely related to that of 'probing'. A large number of visual (and aural – see, for example, D. Deutsch, 'Musical illusions' *Scientific American,* October 1975, pp. 92–104) experiments on this issue have been conducted under widely different conditions. Some of the best-known involve optical illusions such as the Muller-Lyer example:

and the invertible cube:

There are a large number of recorded examples and the experience is a common one in everyday living (see, for example, F. Ratcliff, 'Contour and contrast', *Scientific American*, June 1972, pp. 90ff. Which indicates a quite extensive special field in neurophysiology devoted to the physical probe mechanism involved in all vision). Relevant also is the extensive link-up now taking place between linguistics and language studies on the one hand and neurophysiology of the brain on the other. What is called the 'cross-modal' character of language (that is, involving different forms of neural response like sight and touch) is notably relevant to considering selective probing particularly as the social connotation of language is especially important. Piaget has been at loggerheads especially with Vygotsky and Chomsky on this issue (see note 109 below). (For comprehensive surveys of recent developments in brain studies, particularly useful from this viewpoint, see S. Rose, *The Conscious Brain*, 1976, and K. R. Ropper and J. Eccles, *The Self and its Brain*, 1977. Even though these are recent, however, the speed of brain research is such that new information has accumulated since the latter date, but not such that unstabilises the groundwork indicated in these books.)

74 'Complex' has been used by analogy with mathematics to indicate a change into a different dimension which is similar to the dimensional relation between the real and imaginary parts of a complex number. The 'presence but unseen-ness' of one dimension of existence relative to another which is complex to it, has echoes in mechanics in which a force has no component in a direction perpendicular to itself, but the force nevertheless is there. The perpendicularity of the real and imaginary parts in an Argand diagram is a mapping of the *incomparability* of the real and imaginary parts, that is, neither is representable in the 'space' of the other.

75 Predicative statements take the form 'x is . . . ', for example, 'the triangle is red'. Conventionally they are distinguished from relational statements of the form 'x is related to y', for example, 'John is in love with Kate'. The latter may be described as a predicative statement with two arguments.

76 It is sometimes suggested that in modern abstract algebra the elements have no numerical reference and hence in these spheres mathematics is 'non-quantitative'. It is, in short, pure relationship and involves the disappearance of the distinction between quality and quantity. It would follow that logic and mathematics would become indistinguishable. If this were so then the case against Piaget for conflating them would no longer stand up. It is the view here that however 'abstracted' the elements become in abstract algebra, their roots are still quantitative and they are *operated on computatively*. They retain all the standard features of number. All forms of symbolic logic, on the other hand, operate in an *abbreviated* manner and not computatively.

77 One (non-rigorous) definition of a limit involves the notion of a sequence of values (numbers, functions, and so on) approaching 'as close as we please' to a fixed value. This maps the approach to a frontier of any phenomenon in Actuality in which there is the paradoxicality of 'if the frontier is achieved it shouldn't be' and on the other

hand, 'if the frontier is not achieved it should be'. Alternatively, the paradox may be expressed as 'the frontier is discernible only if we have not arrived at it'; on the other hand, 'if we arrive at the frontier it disappears'. This is so irrespective of whether the frontier is approached from within or without.

78 There is a case for rejecting the use of 'class' and 'set' as viable logico–mathematical terms for Phase 2, since they suffer in practice from conflationary implications. However, provided the phenomenal and conditional aspects of the attribute are strictly adhered to, continuing use of the terms is acceptable.

79 The idea of propositional function should not be confused with the idea of a proposition as the common *meaning* of a collection of sentences. Meaning, involving as it does contingency, has no place in logic as such.

80 The distinction between collection and set may be further clarified. For, if set and collection could be identified, then (for example) the rationals would be a subset/ subcollection of the reals. In fact, the rationals form a collection isomorphic to a subcollection of the reals. The calculable numbers must be strictly disinguished from the attributes defining hem.

81 The terms have been assigned in this manner by the authors using current terminology. Normally 'membership' and 'element' are used interchangeably.

82 It follows that the theory and manipulation of classes and mathematical sets, apart from the fundamental problems posed by Russell, remain unchanged, provided this is understood to refer to collections (or aggregates or ensembles).

83 We are looking here at something very like cardinality and ordinality in sets (that is, collections) of numbers. The logical mapping of causality reveals on the one hand, the 'linkages' of the system laid out in a deductive sequence (suggesting cardinality) and, on the other hand, the order itself in which each stage occurs (ordinality).

84 It may appear that the distinction drawn later in the text in the discussion of the Russell contradiction between the interchangeability of propositional functions and non-interchangeability of set conditions (or 'axioms') is contradicted by the present discussion of the mapping of the 'level leap' in logico–mathematics by discontinuous change of premises/axioms. It might seem that logic cannot map the 'level leap' referred to, but mathematics can. However, such interchange of premises in the case of the logical class is not to be identified with the discontinuous change of premises necessary to map novelty, which always calls for such premises to be replaced by new ones. It should be stressed that the 'freedom' with regard to premises in logic (which it is argued later in the text is the basis of the solution offered to the Russell 'paradox') does not alter the fact that a substitution of premises involves a *different deductive sequence*.

85 The Piagetian seriation experiments referred to earlier illustrate the point in the text. The subject can operate the process of ordering the sticks or blocks according to length in different ways, for example, by prior (visual) assessment of the lengths and an uninterrupted sequence of (correct?) movements; by a random ordering followed by a rearrangement *within* the sequence established (there are other ways of approaching the task). The point is that there is no 'right' way of doing this. All sequences constitute alternative routes within the system. The system in this case is the basic requirement of ordering by length. This is the deductive map of the event. The directional connections of the system's causality are mapped by the 'unfolding' of its deductive 'links'. The *choice* of pathways points directly towards contingency and the 'enfolding' here involves being able to sort out the pathway taken as the subject goes along. The error in the Piagetian approach to this case is, as usual, to reduce the whole event to an exclusively logico–mathematical one. Whatever the subject's approach, it is clear that the Actuality event is *holistic* – to the extent even of abandoning the original task because other patterns of lengths 'look nicer' (an attribute possibly accounting for the very young child's so-called inability to perform the required task).

86 See, for example, the discussion in ch. II by J. N. Findlay, *Plato, the Written and Unwritten Doctrines* (1974). Here Professor Findlay regards the 'second world' view of Plato's 'Eide' (ideas) as 'the most total *ignorationes elenchi* in the whole of philosophical history' (p. 33) to be laid originally at Aristotle's door. According to Findlay the notion of 'eidos' is as a mode of being of things, not a separate world derived from them. 'Eidos' appears something like the 'unit-ness' of things which is therefore a feature held

in common by all discernible Quanta. Some of Descartes' views on 'unit' and 'unity' expressed in the *Regulae* come close to this but at the same time go beyond it.

87 'Thingness' is a notion closer to 'quantum' in that it points to the whole-and-its-parts. The derivation of 'one-ness', on the other hand, is, in precisely the Cartesian sense, an extraction of *all* characteristics/properties of the 'thing' leaving only *quantity*. This, in fact, can only refer to what the 'thing' is *not*, not what it is, and quantitatively one is thus left with only *separateness*, that is, discreteness.

88 Russell himself always refers to 'contradiction' not 'paradox'.

89 The most modern manifestation of this relation between science and philosophy on the one hand and socio-political authority on the other is the subordination of the former absolutely to the latter. Outstanding examples are to be seen in explicitly authoritarian states and systems (left or right wing makes no odds). But we commit a grave error if we suppose that other systems are immune. The guise of the benevolent or liberal 'front' is, if anything, a more potent and subtle instrument of this subordination. Piaget's own system partly exemplifies just this feature although it is certain that he believed himself to be a genuine liberal humanist.

Chapter 9

90 The term 'symbol' used here is not identical with its use in the discussion below of symbolism, but there is some similarity in that symbol as used here does involve a *distinct* ideogram from that which it symbolises and, in the context of myth, is in some degree 'manipulable' – although, of course, not (normally) in a quantitative sense.

91 It is worth noting that in general the nearer one approaches, historically, proto-societies (there are virtually none left uninfluenced) the less evident are symbols and myths *separate* from direct experience itself. Contemporary and archaeological evidence demonstrates that the sophisticated god is a long way away from its natural ancestor, which is a direct incorporation of a feature(s) of the natural environment, for example, the animal which is a clan totem; the rock or stream that 'lives'. Parallel (but not identical) phases are well known in very early childhood. Among other sources, Piaget's *Play, Dreams and Imitation* handles this latter, but again from the viewpoint of the growth of logico-mathematical cognitive structures as the touchstone of progress from the 'inferior' to the 'superior'.

92 The intensity of isolation associated with subject–object separation is brilliantly portrayed right at the beginning of this 300–year period by the seventeenth century philosopher and mathematician Blaise Pascal. The following is only one example of his many acknowledgements of this:

> When I consider the short extent of my life, swallowed up in the eternity before and after, the small space that I fill or even use, engulfed in the infinite immensity of spaces unknown to me and which know me not, I am terrified and astonished to find myself here, not there. For there is no reason why it should be here, not there, why now rather than at another time. Who put me here? By whose order and design have this place and time been allotted to me? . . . The eternal silence of those infinite spaces strikes me with terror! (B. Pascal, *Pensées*, trans. J. M. Cohen, Harmondsworth: Penguin, 1961).

93 One of the most complete survivals of such a 'dream time' culture is to be found among Australian Aboriginals.

94 This term should not be interpreted naively. The physical form of this extension constitutes only one manifestation of it. Logical extension can be identified as all things possessing a given attribute and mathematical extension as, for example, a space of number-pairs or the non-physical extension of an axiomatic geometry.

95 This view is central to Feyerabend's argument for the freedom of construction of model and theory in science and an abandonment of all paradigmatic constraints (see *passim* in *Against Method,* 1978).

96 In effect, verifiability is a co-domain mapping of the exactitude of scientific fact in the domain and ultimately of the causal integrity of phenomena themselves. Similarly,

falsifiability is a co-domain mapping of the approximative aspect of scientific fact and ultimately the causal–contingent interactions of phenomena.

97   It is important to underline that the *scientific fact,* because of its precision and measurability, cannot be wholly spatio-temporal. This is so despite appearances and assumptions to the contrary. A geological stratum is not just a strip of rock in the ground, but is a calculated and precisely described geological phenomenon extracted from the strip in the ground. The point is very obviously made by all geological and biological theories of evolution. This whole issue serves to underline the reciprocal interaction (alternation?) between model/theory and scientific fact, that is, between co-domain and domain, which parallels an equivalent interaction between Phases 1 and 2 in logic and mathematics.

98   Much 'statistical criticism' of Piaget is on such grounds.

99   Margaret Donaldson's recounting of the well-known story of Laurie Lee as a new boy at achool who was told by the teacher to 'wait here for the present' and refused to go back the next day because he didn't get one, is a case in point (see Donaldson, 1978).

100   The practice is adopted here of using 'sign' to describe abbreviations and reserving 'symbol' strictly for *mathematical objects.* This includes particular and general number and all operational script. It is argued that the degree of 'abstraction' of the mathematics itself does not alter the nature of mathematical objects. It is the case that some conventional mathematical script does not strictly observe the computation–abbreviation distinction.

101   That is, measurable distance, position (in reference to some fixed point(s)) and direction (in reference to some grid). A fully qualitative attribute cannot be so reduced; for example, in '*x* is a teacher', the predicate is absolutely not reducible to a quantitative expression except in a trivial or (logically) nonsensical way (that is, taking ' . . . is a teacher' to signify 'one (1) teacher'!).

Chapter 10

102   The best overall statement of these positions by Piaget are to be found in his 'Autobiography' (1950) (in Boring *et al.,* 1969) and in *Insights and Illusions* (1966) plus an addition to this in S. F. Campbell, *Piaget Sampler* (1976).

103   A view confirmed in the following passage from *Six Psychological Studies,* pp. 18–19: 'interpersonal relations germinate as of the second half of the first year, thanks to *imitation* since imitation is closely linked to sensorimotor development . . . through imitation thought becomes conscious to the degree to which the child is able to communicate it' (our emphasis). For Piaget 'interpersonal' is identified as 'social' and is closely aligned with language development.

104   There is a particularly disturbing 'analysis' by Piaget of the growing concept of nationality in the individual which identifies maturation in this respect with conventional jingoism seemingly mitigated by an 'equivalent point of view' rationalisation (that is, all nations – undifferentiated from the state – have a right to their viewpoint). There is a distinctly Swiss neutralist element here. On the basis of such a view no one would have had the right to interfere in the internal process of Nazi Germany – or even criticise it. On the other hand, the complacent endorsement of 'one's country' as the political *summum bonum* on the grounds of the formal operational 'maturity' of this view leaves the way open for absolute obedience (see J. Piaget, 'The development in children of the idea of the homeland and the [*sic*] relations with the other countries', repr. Campbell, *Piaget Sampler,* 1976, pp. 37–58.

105   The notion of the 'epistemic subject' runs counter to another notion of Piaget's that the social (historical) development of mankind is measurable in terms of an 'advancing' degree of maturation in the individual. In support of the latter, Piaget offers the view that Greek mathematics and Greek children, at equivalent ages, were inferior to their modern counterparts. The notion clearly derives something from the 'repetition of the history of the race' thesis supposedly demonstrated by the foetal replication of earlier biological stages. What is ignored in this view, and also in Piaget's view of sociocultural development, is that whatever previous evolutionary phases may partially reflect themselves in development, they are, all relative to their eras, *fully formed* which

their foetal reflections are not. Archimedes is thus, relative to his era and society, no less mature than Einstein is to his. Any other proposition than this is pure socio-cultural chauvinism.

106 Actually the 'epistemic subject' is curiously kept clear of any biological inheritance implications – apart from indirect ones, that is. Presumably to be over-explicit about this would expose the deepest unresolved problem of Piaget's thought too crudely by demanding a reconciliation between inheritance, logico-mathematical exclusiveness regarding both individual and society, and finally the individual learning process itself.

107 All references in parentheses as in Flavell refer to specific Piaget sources.

108 The 'sling experiment', described above in note 21, exemplifies this.

There is considerable support for the holistic view in recent investigation into the neurophysiology of skills acquisitions. Eccles (Popper and Eccles, 1977) discusses at length the relation between the 'lower brain' (cerebellum), to which he attributes actual skill performance, and the neocortical association areas (surface laminae of the neo-cortex) (see pp. 288–93). Citing Mountcastle's work in this field, Eccles points to the 'command' role of these areas which are now most closely linked with the 'thinking' process as opposed to conditional response. So, while there is (it is argued) a 'feedback loop' process mirroring a *correction* procedure (cf. the process of compensation in Piaget's later writings), which is characteristic of cerebellum processes in particular, the *orders* are issued from the neocortical zones. We must not, in short, muddle up the 'gears of the car' (cerebellum feed-back) with the 'driver who changes them' (neocortex). As Eccles writes: 'trained movements are largely pre-programmed, whereas exploratory movements, which constitute an important fraction of our movement repertoire, are imperfectly pre-programmed, being provisional and subject to constant revision' (1977, p. 292). With Piaget's latest excursions into experiment and the consequent rider to Genetic Epistemology in the notion of 'cognizance', it can be seen that conflation has taken on a new form, that is, between trained response, which is a neurological parallel to the 'either–or' of logic, and the fluid, holistic exploration of the milieu by the subject which is the source of creativity. This is evidenced as much in a simple movement like throwing a projectile at a target as in the highly involved construction of a work of art or equivalent objective. In passing, Piaget's frequent reference to the work of W. S. McCulloch and W. Pitt as the (sole?) representatives of brain neurology underlines the points just made. McCulloch and Pitt attempted to mathematicise the activity of neurons in the late 1950s (they were, in fact, mathematicians not brain physiologists). The following is a comment by Steven Rose in *The Conscious Brain* (1976, pp. 357–8): '[they were succeeded by the] much more complex mathematics . . . attempted by Jack Cowan in Chicago . . . This mathematics [Cowan's] does enable a prediction to be made, for a simple neuron, of its response to particular patterns of input. But even when such predictions are perfected – and I have no doubt that in due course they will be – the neurons of the brain are still not behaving like the units of the computer. They are far more subtle and complex.'

109 There has been no attempt in this book to embark on an extensive discussion of Piaget's views on language. The main reasons for this are that the subject itself, both Piaget's writings on it and the criticisms of his viewpoint, are so large as to warrant a separate study, and secondly, the authors have specifically committed themselves to the logico-mathematical structuration of Piaget's system, considering this to be most fundamental to his thought. But some comments on the language issue might be useful if only from the viewpoint that Piaget's approach to language shows the same characteristics as other areas of his thought.

Piaget has entered into confrontations with such eminent linguistic specialists as Noam Chomsky, Vygotsky and others. His principal line in all cases is to advocate a process of development which goes from autistic (incomprehensible) speech to egocentric speech (spoken aloud) and thence to reasoned logical speech (increasingly with an 'internalised', or silent speech aspect) based on reflection and manifested in structural forms. His confrontation with Chomsky has centred largely on the latter's 'innatist' views (although Piaget's own views regarding the 'epistemic subject' are essentially innatist and presumably do not exclude language). His opposition to Vygotsky has centred on the latter's stress on socialisation (in accordance with Marxist orthodoxy) as the source of language development. Piaget, for his part, has ambivalently related individual development of structured speech to interpersonal exchange and vice versa. The difference between them (Piaget and Vygotsky) resolves itself into arguing which position is to be taken up by the 'general of the army' – in front of the troops or behind them. Nobody denies, however, the absolute authority of the general – in this case society and social forms.

The following extracts from *Six Psychological Studies* and *Structuralism* are a very good summary of Piaget's viewpoint on the subject. As usual there are many signs of conflation in different directions. But in particular it is the absolute role of social norms and their alignment with the superiority of logico–mathematics which is most obvious. Needless to say, Piaget, again, *describes the facts* of contemporary forms of social imposition. But, also again, he endorses them by giving them the status of inevitable natural occurrences.

> What are the elementary functions of language? . . . First, there is the subordination and psychological constraint imposed by the adult on the child . . . the child derives an 'ego ideal' from his superiors, whom he seeks to emulate . . . respect makes the child accept the orders and commands of the adult and makes him consider them obligatory . . . the child develops an unconscious intellectual and affective submission as a result of the psychological constraint imposed by the adult. (Piaget, 1968, pp. 19–20).

> Language is a group institution. Its rules are imposed on individuals. One generation coercively transmits it to the next, and this has been true for a long as there have been men. Any given form of it, any particular spoken language, derives from some still more primitive form, and so on, indefinitely, without a break, all the way back to the one or more ancestral languages . . . Language, in short, is independent of the decision of individuals; it is the bearer of multi-millennial traditions; and it is every man's indispensable instrument of thought. (Piaget, 1971, pp. 74–5)

> He [the child] now becomes able, thanks to language, to reconstitute his past actions in the form of recapitulation and to anticipate his future actions through verbal representation. This has three consequences essential to mental development: (1) the possibility of verbal exchange with other persons, which heralds the onset of the socialization of actions; (2) the internalization of words, i.e., the appearance of thought itself, supported by internal language and a system of signs; (3) last and most important, the internalization of action as such which from now on, rather than being purely perceptual and motor as it has been heretofore, can represent itself intuitively by means of pictures and 'mental experiments'. (Piaget, 1968, p. 17)

> There are all the exchanges with the adult himself or with other children; these interconnections also play a decisive role in determining the course of action. To the extent that they lead to the formulation of action itself and to the recall of past actions, they transform material behaviour into thought. (Piaget, 1968, p. 20)

Select Bibliography

Aristotle, *Metaphysics* (London: Heinemann, 1980).

Asch, S. E., *Social Psychology* (Englewood Cliffs, NJ: Prentice-Hall, 1952).

Battro, A. M., *Piaget: Dictionary of Terms,* ed. and trans. E. Rütschi-Herrmann and S. F. Campbell (Oxford and New York: Pergamon, 1973).

Beck, L. W., *Six Secular Philosophers* (New York: The Free Press, 1966).

Bell, R. T., *Sociolinguistics – Goals, Approaches and Problems* (London: Batsford, 1976).

Bertalanffy, L. von, *General System Theory: Foundations Development Applications* (Harmondsworth: Penguin, 1971).

Berth, E. W., and Piaget, J., *Mathematical Epistemology and Psychology,* trans. W. Mays (Dordrecht, Holland: Reidel, 1966).

Bohm, D., *Causality and Chance in Modern Physics* (London: Routledge & Kegan Paul, 1957).

Bohm, D., 'On the relationship between methodology in scientific research and the content of scientific knowledge', *British Journal for the Philosophy of Science,* vol. XII, no. 46 (August 1961), pp. 103–16.

Bohm, D., *Wholeness and the Implicate Order* (London: Routledge & Kegan Paul, 1980).

Boring, E. G., Langfeld, H. S., Werner, H., and Yerkes, R. M. (eds), *A History of Psychology in Autobiography,* Vol. IV (New York: Russell, 1969; repr. of 1952 edn).

Boyer, C. B., *The History of the Calculus and its Conceptual Development* (New York: Dover, 1959).

Boyer, C. B., *A History of Mathematics* (New York: Wiley, 1968).

Brown, G., and Desforges, C., *Piaget's Theory: A Psychological Critique* (London: Routledge & Kegan Paul, 1979).

Buber, M., *I and Thou,* trans. W. Kaufman (Edinburgh: Clark, 1970).

Bunge, M., 'Levels: a semantical preliminary', *Review of Metaphysics,* vol. 13 (1960), pp. 396–406.

Campbell, S. F., *Piaget Sampler: An Introduction to Jean Piaget through his Own Words* (New York: Wiley, 1976).

Cantor, G., *Contributions to the Founding of the Theory of Transfinite Numbers* (Chicago: Open Court, 1915).

Čapek, M., 'The significance of Piaget's researches on the psychogenesis of atomism', in R. C. Buckard and R. S. Cohen (eds), *Boston Studies in the Philosophy of Science* (Dordrecht, Holland: Reidel, 1970), pp. 446–55.

Capra, F., *The Tao of Physics* (Glasgow: Fontana/Collins, 1975).

Crossley, J. N., *et al., What Is Mathematical Logic?* (London: OUP, 1972).

Dean, A., Chaband, S., and Bridges, E., 'Classes, collections and distinctive features: alternative strategies for solving inclusion problems', *Cognitive Psychology,* vol. 13 (1981), pp. 84–112.

De Bono, E., *Children Solve Problems* (Harmondsworth: Penguin, 1972).

Dinnage, R., 'The Piaget way': A review of *The Essential Piaget,* ed. H. E. Gruber and J. J. Vonèche, *New York Review of Books,* 21 December 1978, pp. 18–23.

Donaldson, M., *Children's Minds* (Glasgow: Fontana/Collins, 1978).

Donnellan, T., *Lattice Theory* (Oxford: Pergamon, 1968).

Drever, J., *Dictionary of Psychology* (Harmondsworth: Penguin, 1952).

Feyerabend, P., *Against Method: Outline of an Anarchist Theory of Knowledge* (London: Verso, 1978).

Findlay, J. N., *Plato, the Written and Unwritten Doctrines* (London: Routledge & Kegan Paul, 1974).

Flavell, J. H., *The Developmental Psychology of Jean Piaget* (Princeton, NJ: Van Nostrand, 1963).

Furth, H., *Piaget and Knowledge: Theoretical Foundations* (Englewood Cliffs, NJ: Prentice-Hall, 1969).

Gardner, M., *The Ambidextrous Universe* (Harmondsworth: Penguin, 1977).

Glae, R. M. (ed.), *The Philosophy of Time, a Collection of Essays* (Hassocks, Sussex: Harvester, 1968).

Gibbs, J. C. 'Evaluating Piaget', *Harvard Educational Review*, vol. 49, no. 2 (May 1979), pp. 248–54.

Goodstein, R. L., *Mathematical Logic* (Leicester: Leicester University Press, 1965).

Grattan-Guinness, I., *Dear Russell – Dear Jourdain: A Commentary on Russell's Logic, Based on his Correspondence with Philip Jourdain* (London: Duckworth, 1977).

Halliday, M. A. K., *Explanations in the Functions of Language* (London: Edward Arnold, 1973).

Hamilton, P., *Knowledge and Social Structure, an Introduction to the Classical Argument in the Sociology of Knowledge* (London: Routledge & Kegan Paul, 1974).

Hamlyn, D. W., *Experience and the Growth of Understanding* (London: Routledge & Kegan Paul, 1978).

Heidegger, M., *Being and Time* (Oxford: Blackwell, 1978).

Hughes, P., and Brecht, G., *Vicious Circles and Infinity: A Panoply of Paradoxes* (London: Cape, 1976).

Hofstadter, D., *Gödel, Escher, Bach: An Eternal Golden Braid* (Hassocks, Sussex: Harvester, 1979).

Inhelder, B., and Piaget, J., *The Growth of Logical Thinking from Childhood to Adolescence*, trans. A. Parsons and S. Milgram (London: Routledge & Kegan Paul, 1958).

Isaacs, S., 'Review of Jean Piaget's *Language and Thought of the Child, Judgment and Reasoning in the Child, The Child's Conception of the World*', *The Pedagogical Seminary and Journal of Genetic Psychology*, no. 26 (1929), pp. 597–609.

Kleene, S. C., *Mathematical Logic* (New York: Wiley, 1967).

Klein, J., *Greek Mathematical Thought and the Origins of Algebra* (Cambridge, Mass.: MIT Press, 1972).

Kneebone, G. T., *Mathematical Logic and the Foundations of Mathematics* (Princeton, NJ: Van Nostrand, 1963).

Körner, S., *The Philosophy of Mathematics* (London: Hutchinson 1960).

Koestler, A. *The Case of the Midwife Toad* (London: Hutchinson, 1971).

Kuhn, D., 'The application of Piaget's theory of cognitive development to education', *Harvard Educational Review*, vol. 49, no. 3 (August 1979), pp. 340–60.

Kuhn, T. S., *The Structure of Scientific Revolutions* (Chicago: Chicago University Press, 1970).

Lakatos, I., and Musgrave, A. (eds), *Criticism and the Growth of Knowledge* (Cambridge: CUP, 1970).

Lakatos, I., Worrall, J., and Currie, G. (eds), *Mathematics, Science and Epistemology* (Cambridge: CUP, 1980).

Lane, M., *Structuralism: A Reader* (London: Cape, 1970).

Laver, J., and Hutcheson, S. (eds), *Communication in Face to Face Interaction* (Harmondsworth: Penguin, 1972).

Lenin, V. I., *Materialism and Empirio-Criticism* (Moscow: Foreign Languages Publishing House, 1947).

Lenin, V. I., *Philosophical Notebooks* (Moscow: Foreign Languages Publishing House, 1961).

Macksey, R., and Donato, E. (eds), *The Structuralist Controversy: The Languages of Criticism and the Sciences of Man* (Baltimore, Md, and London: Johns Hopkins University Press, 1972).

Marshak, A., *The Roots of Civilisation: the Cognitive Beginnings of Man's First Art, Symbol and Notation* (London: Weidenfeld & Nicolson, 1972).

Moscovici, S. (ed.), *The Psychosociology of Language* (Chicago: Markham, 1972).

Nagel, E., and Newman, J. R., 'Goedel's proof', in *The World of Mathematics*, presented by J. R. Newman (London: Allen & Unwin, 1960).

Nagel, E., and Newman, J., 'Putnam's review of Gödel's proof', *Philosophy of Science*, vol. 28, no. 2 (April 1961), pp. 209–11.

Parsons, G., 'Inhelder and Piaget's *The Growth of Logical Thinking*, II. A logician's viewpoint', *British Journal of Psychology*, vol. 51, no. 1 (1960), pp. 75–84.

Piaget, J., *The Child's Conception of the World* (London: Routledge & Kegan Paul, 1929).

Piaget, J., *The Moral Judgement of the Child* (Harmondsworth: Penguin, 1932),

Piaget, J., *Classes, relations et nombres* (Paris: Librairie Philosophique, Vrin, 1942).

Piaget, J., *Traité de logique: Essai de logistique opératoire* (Paris: Librairie Armand Colin, 1949).

Piaget, J., *The Psychology of Intelligence,* trans. M. Piercey and D. E. Berlyne (London: Routledge & Kegan Paul, 1950).

Piaget, J., *Essai sur les transformations des opérations logiques: Les 256 opérations ternaires de la logique bivalente des propositions* (Paris: Presses Universitaires de France, 1952a).

Piaget, J., *The Child's Conception of Number,* trans. C. Gattegno and F. M. Hodgson (London: Routledge & Kegan Paul, 1952b).

Piaget, J., *Logic and Psychology* (Manchester: Manchester University Press, 1953).

Piaget, J., *Play, Dreams and Imitation of Childhood,* trans. C. Gattegno and F. M. Hodgson (London: Routledge & Kegan Paul, 1962a).

Piaget, J., *Comments on Vigotsky* (Cambridge, Mass.: MIT, 1962b).

Piaget, J., *The Origins of Intelligence in Children* (New York: Norton, 2nd edn., 1963).

Piaget, J., *Judgment and Reasoning in the Child* (Paterson, NJ: Littlefield, Adams, 1964).

Piaget, J., *Six Psychological Studies* (London: University of London Press, 1968).

Piaget, J., *The Mechanisms of Perception,* trans. C. N. Seagrim (London: Routledge & Kegan Paul, 1969).

Piaget, J., *Genetic Epistemology* (New York: Columbia University Press, 1970).

Piaget, J., *Structuralism,* trans. C. Maschler (London: Routledge & Kegan Paul, 1971).

Piaget, J., *Essai de logique opératoire,* 2nd edn of the *Traité de logique,* established by (établie par) Jean-Blaise Grize (Paris: Dunod, 1972a).

Piaget, J., *The Principles of Genetic Epistemology* (London: Routledge & Kegan Paul, 1972b).

Piaget, J., *Insights and Illusions of Philosopny,* trans. W. Mays (London: Routledge & Kegan Paul, 1972c).

Piaget, J., *Psychology and Epistemology: Towards a Theory of Knowledge,* trans. P. A. Wells (Harmondsworth: Penguin University Books, 1972d).

Piaget, J., *Main Trends in Psychology* (London: Allen & Unwin, 1973).

Piaget, J., *The Child and Reality* (New York: Viking, 1974).

Piaget, J., *The Grasp of Consciousness: Action and Concept in the Young Child* (London: Routledge & Kegan Paul, 1977).

Piaget, J. *et al, Success and Understanding*, trans. A. J. Pomerans (London:Routledge & Kegan Paul, 1978a).

Piaget, J., *The Development of Thought: Equilibration of Cognitive Structures*, trans. A. Rosin (Oxford: Blackwell, 1978b).

Piaget, J., *Behaviour and Evolution* (London: Routledge & Kegan Paul, 1979).

Piaget, J., and Beth, E., *Mathematical Epistemology and Psychology* (Dordrecht, Holland: Reidel, 1965).

Piaget, J., and Inhelder, B., *The Child's Conception of Space* (London: Routledge & Kegan Paul, 1956).

Piaget, J., Inhelder, B., and Szeminska, A., *The Child's Conception of Geometry* (London: Routledge & Kegan Paul, 1960).

Piattelli-Palmarini, M. (ed.), *Language and Learning, the Debate between Jean Piaget and Noam Chomsky* (London: Routledge & Kegan Paul, 1980).

Plato, *Gorgias, Theaetetus, Parmenides, Timaeus* (Princeton, NJ: Princeton University Press, 1964).

Popper, K. R., *The Logic of Scientific Discovery*, trans. from *Logik der Forschung*, 1934 (London: Hutchinson, 1959).

Popper, K. R., *Objective Knowledge: An Evolutionary Approach* (Oxford: Clarendon, 1973).

Popper, K. R., *Conjectures and Refutations* (London: Routledge & Kegan PauL, 1974).

Popper, K. R., and Eccles, J., *The Self and its Brain* (Heidelberg: Springer International, 1977).

Presseisen, B. Z., Goldstein, D., and Appel, M. H. (eds), *Topics in Cognitive Development Vol. 2 Language and Operational Thought* (New York: Plenum Press, 1978).

Putnam, H., Review of E. Nagel and J. Newman, *Gödel's Proof*, in *Philosophy of Science*, vol. 27, no. 2 (April 1960), pp. 205–8.

Robey, D. (ed.), *Structuralism: An Introduction* (London: OUP, 1973).

Rose, S., *The Conscious Brain* (Harmondsworth: Penguin, 1976).

Rotman, B., *Jean Piaget: Psychologist of the Real* (Hassocks, Sussex: Harvester, 1977).

Runes, D. D. (ed.), *Dictionary of Philosophy* (London: Peter Owen, 1960).

Russell, B., *The Principles of Mathematics* (London: Allen & Unwin, 1937).

Ryle, G., *The Concept of Mind* (Harmondsworth: Penguin, 1949).

Sartre, J.-P., *Being and Nothingness,* trans. H. E. Barnes, intro. M. Warnock (London: Methuen, 1969).

Siegel, L. S., and Brainerd, C. J. (eds), *Alternatives to Piaget: Critical Essays on the Theory* (New York: Academic Press, 1978).

Singleton, W. T., Spurgeon, P., and Stammers, R. B. (eds), *The Analysis of Social Skill* (New York and London: Plenum Press, 1979).

Stace, W. T., *The Philosophy of Hegel* (New York: Dover Publications, 1955).

Stewart, I., and Hall, D., *The Foundations of Mathematics* (London: OUP, 1977).

Stoll, R. R., *Sets, Logic and Axiomatic Theories* (San Francisco and London: Freeman, 1961).

Van Heijenoort, J., *From Frege to Gödel: A Source Book in Mathematical Logic, 1879–1931* (Cambridge, Mass.: Harvard University Press, 1967).

Varma, V. P., and Williams, P. (eds), *Piaget, Psychology and Education*) London: Hodder & Stoughton, 1976).

Vygotsky, L. S., *Thought and Language,* ed. and trans. E. Haufmann and G. Vakar (Cambridge, Mass.: MIT, 1962).

Whitehead, A. N., and Russell, B., *Principia Mathematica* (Cambridge: CUP, 1927).

Whitehead, A. N., and Russell, B., *Principia Mathematica,* to *56 (Cambridge: CUP, 1962).

Whitrow, G. J., *The Nature of Time* (Harmondsworth: Penguin, 1975).

Wittgenstein, L., *Philosophical Investigations,* trans. G. E. M. Anscombe (Oxford: Blackwell, 1978a).

Wittgenstein, L., *Remarks on the Foundations of Mathematics,* ed. G. H. Anscombe (Oxford: Blackwell, 1978b).

Wittgenstein, L., *Tractatus Logico-Philosophicus,* trans. D. F. Pears and B. F. McGuinness, intro, B. Russell (London: Routledge & Kegan Paul, 1961).

Zukav, G., *The Dancing Wu Li Masters: An Overview of the New Physics* (London: Rider/Hutchinson, 1979).

Name index

Subject index